CHILDREN OF THE WHALES

Story and Art by Abi Umeda

Volume

8

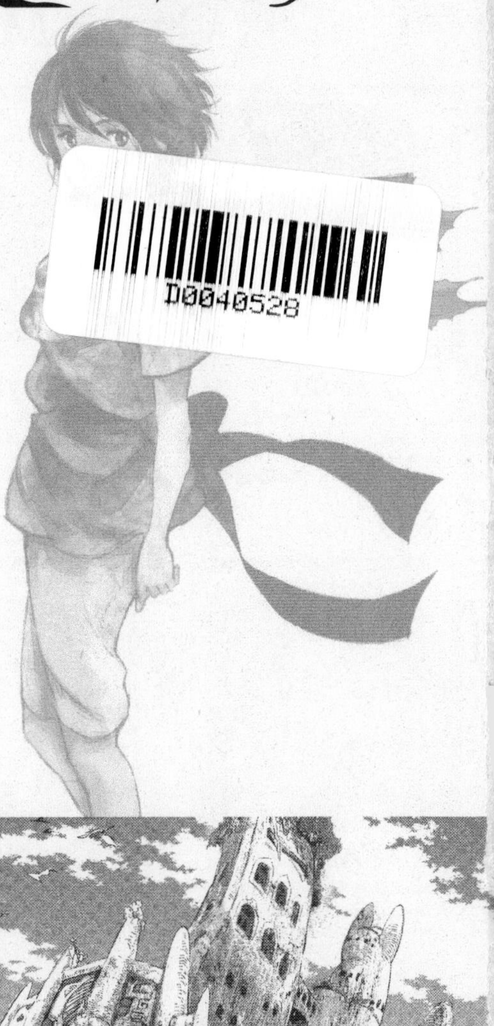

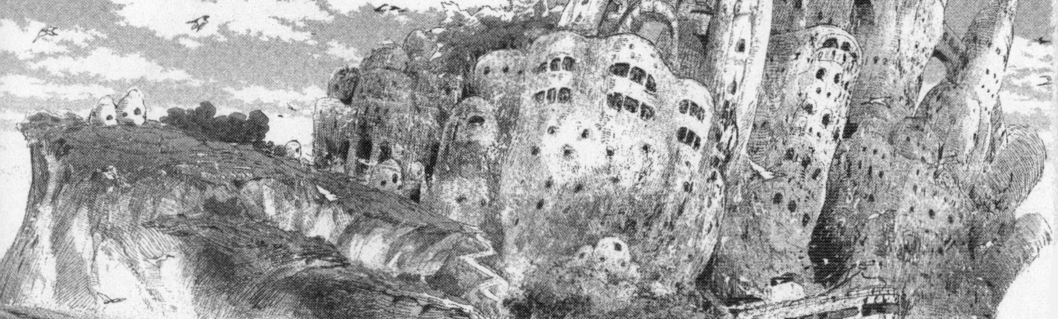

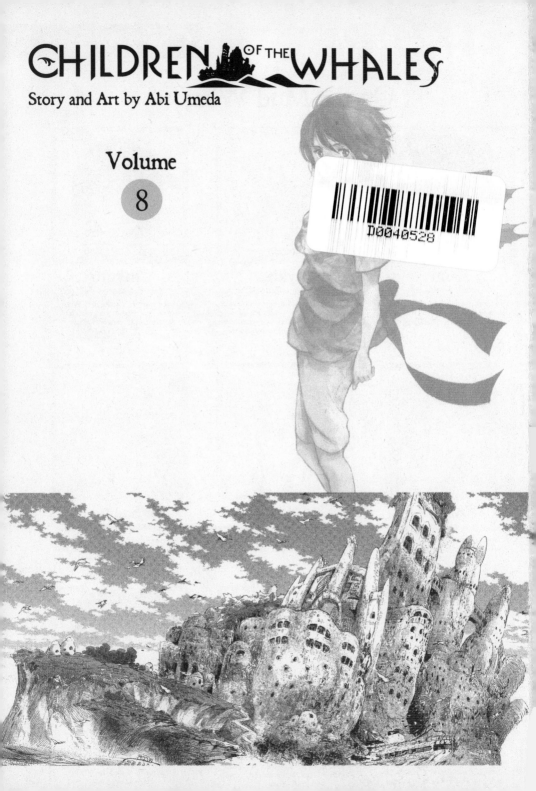

On the Mud Whale

Ouni
(Marked, 16 years old)

A very powerful thymia user. He has the power to destroy Nouses and is called the daímonas by the Allied Empire.

Lykos
(Marked, 14 years old)

A girl from the Allied Empire who comes aboard the Mud Whale. She has a connection with Chakuro and others on the Mud Whale and decides to stay with them.

Chakuro
(Marked, 14 years old)

The young archivist of the Mud Whale. He has hypergraphia, a disorder that compels him to record everything.

Aíma
(???)

She appears to Chakuro after Neri disappears. She gives Chakuro the Mud Whale's rudder.

Neri
(???)

A girl with superhuman powers who disappears when Aíma appears.

Suou
(Unmarked, 17 years old)

The new mayor of the Mud Whale. He has decided to find a way to escape the Mud Whale in order to save the Marked.

Amonlogia

Rochalízo
(???, 17 years old)

He is the son of the duke of Amonlogia, of the United Kingdom of Suidelasia. He is leading the Mud Whale to his country.

Allied Empire

Orca

A high-ranking official from the Allied Empire and Lykos's brother. His battleship Skyros was sunk when he attacked the Mud Whale, but he managed to evade punishment.

Mud Whale
of the Past

Midén
(???)

The daímonas born to Dyo, first mayor of the Mud Whale. He looks like Ouni.

Glossary of the Sea of Sand

The Mud Whale	A huge, drifting island-ship. Those in the empire who resisted giving up their emotions were exiled here, along with all their descendants.
Thymia	Telekinetic power derived from emotions.
The Marked	The 90 percent of the Mud Whale population who are thymia users. They are all short-lived.
The Unmarked	The members of the Mud Whale population who cannot use thymia. Unlike the Marked, they are long-lived.
Nous	A unique organism that obtains energy from peoples' emotions and gives people the power of thymia in return.
Nous Fálaina	A Nous that dwells deep within the Belly of the Mud Whale. Unlike other Nouses, it consumes the life force of humans rather than their emotions.
The Allied Empire	A large nation on the Sea of Sand that controls its citizenry through the Nouses and their absorption of emotions.
Daímonas	A legend from the empire. A being said to be able to destroy a Nous.

A Record of the Mud Whale and the Sea of Sand

Year 93 of the Sand Exile.

The Mud Whale drifts endlessly through the Sea of Sand, home to about 500 people who know nothing of the outside world.

Then the empire suddenly attacks the Mud Whale, and its normally peaceful people are only just able to win the battle. Chakuro, Lykos and the rest of the survivors soon have another encounter—with Sir Rochalízo and his crew. To avoid coming under further attack from the empire, the Mud Whale makes for Amonlogia, Rochalízo's homeland.

As the Mud Whale travels though the Sea of Sand, a vision of the past prompts Chakuro and his friends to discover Midĕn's Room, a chamber hidden deep inside the island.

There, Chakuro finds records of a boy named Midĕn, who was born on the Mud Whale. Even though others called him daímonas, he dreamed of freedom...

"The Mud Whale was our entire world."

Table of Contents

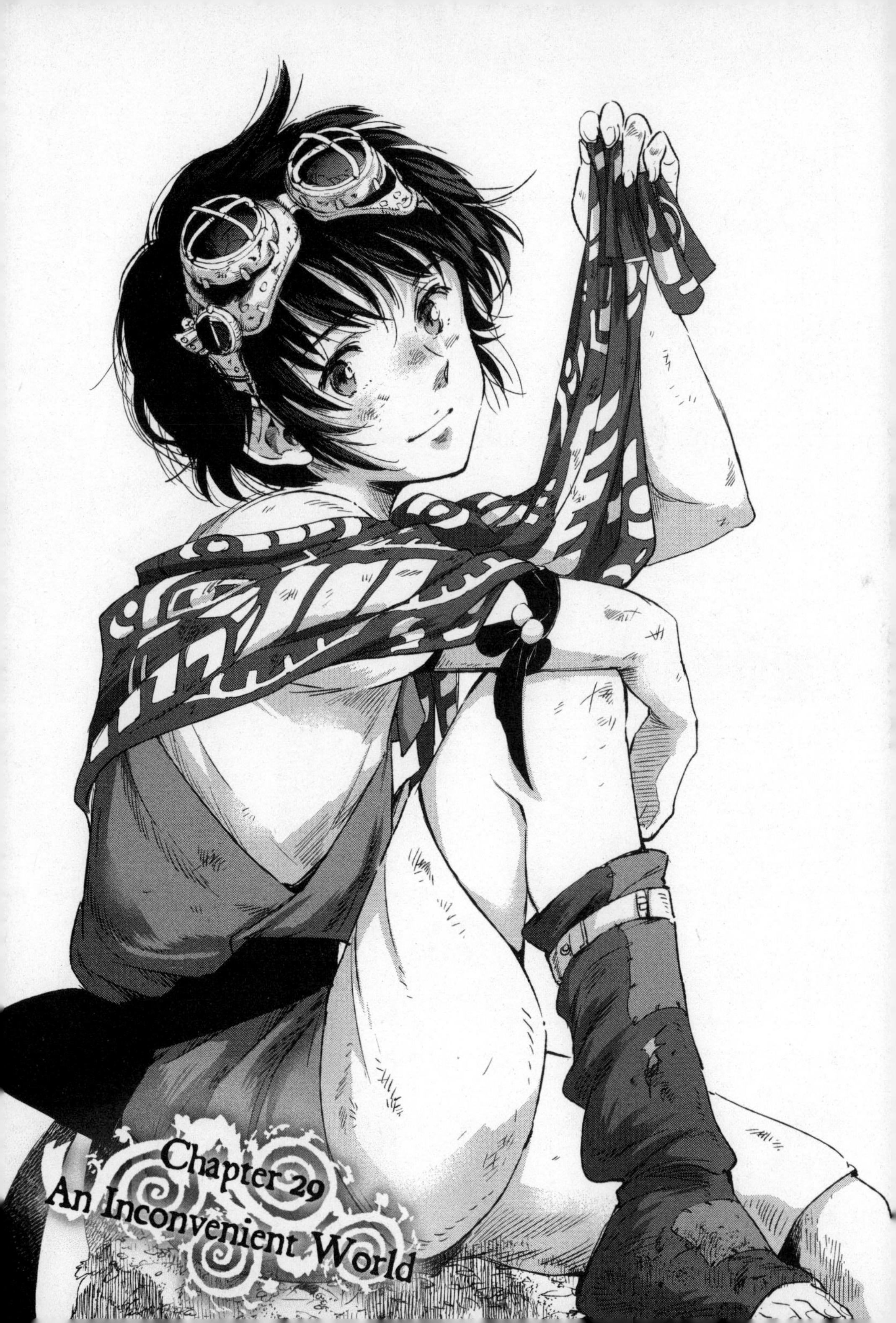
Chapter 29
An Inconvenient World

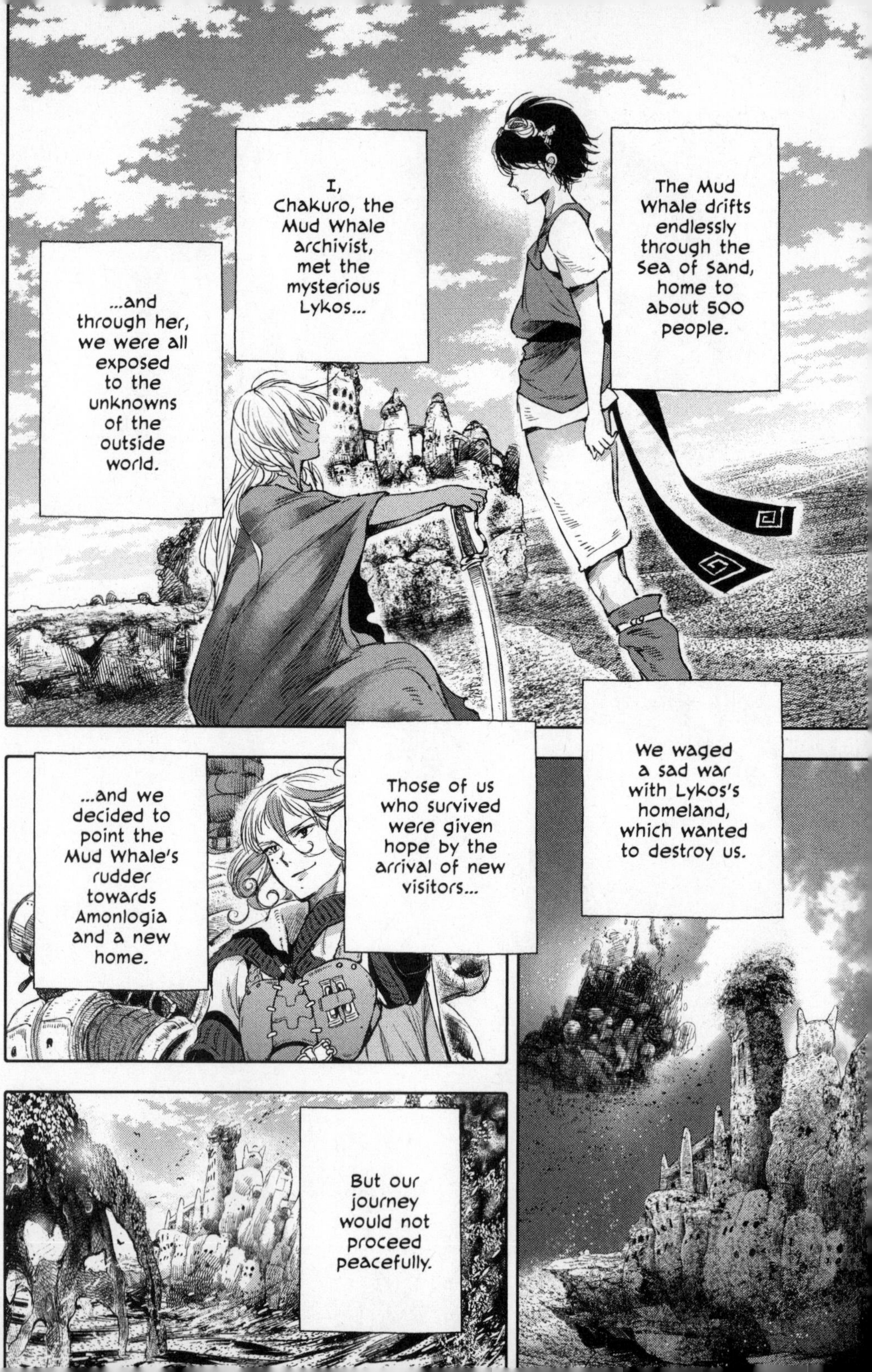
The Mud Whale drifts endlessly through the Sea of Sand, home to about 500 people.
I, Chakuro, the Mud Whale archivist, met the mysterious Lykos...
...and through her, we were all exposed to the unknowns of the outside world.
We waged a sad war with Lykos's homeland, which wanted to destroy us.
Those of us who survived were given hope by the arrival of new visitors...
...and we decided to point the Mud Whale's rudder towards Amonlogia and a new home.
But our journey would not proceed peacefully.

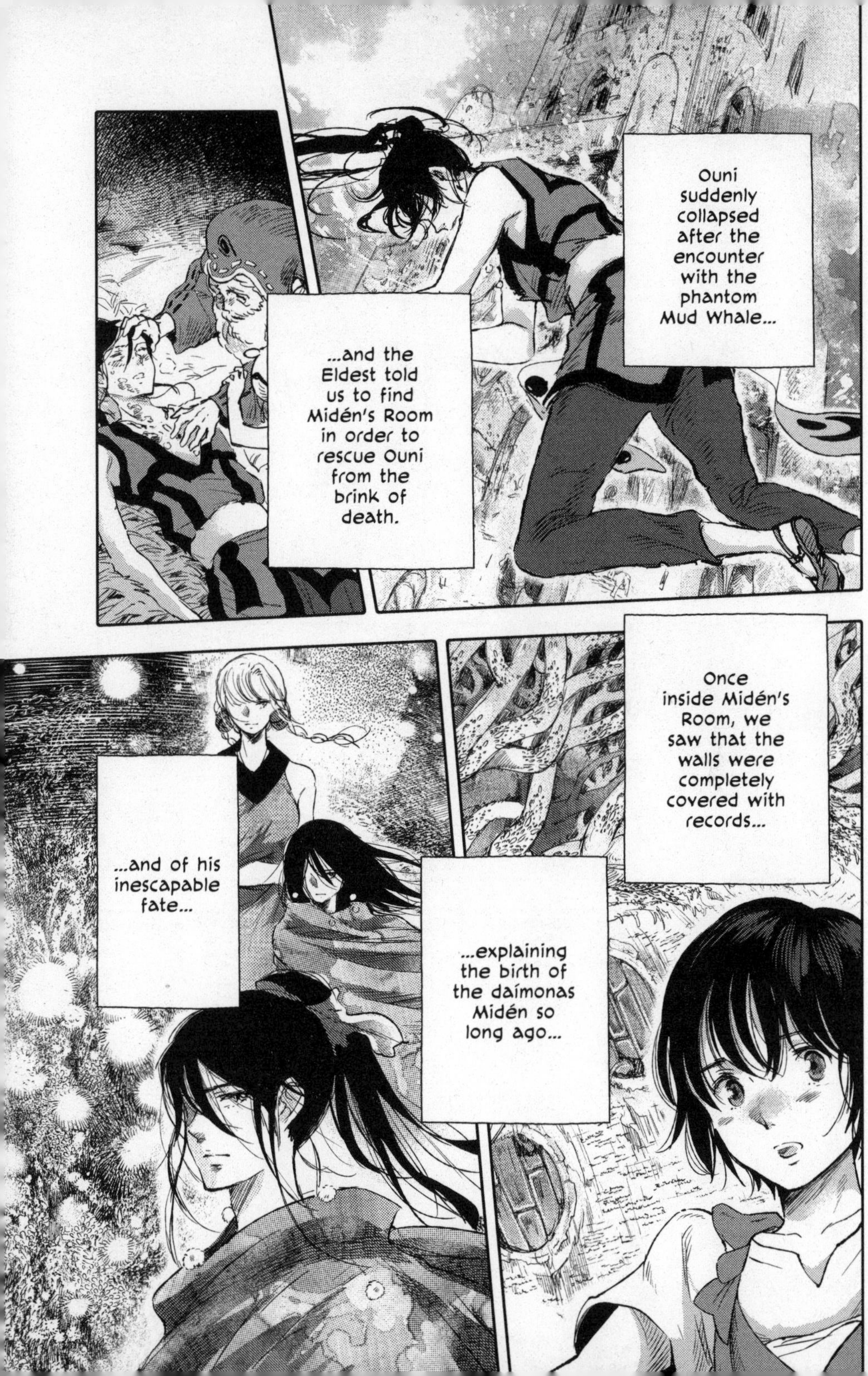
Ouni suddenly collapsed after the encounter with the phantom Mud Whale...
...and the Eldest told us to find Midén's Room in order to rescue Ouni from the brink of death.
Once inside Midén's Room, we saw that the walls were completely covered with records...
...explaining the birth of the daímonas Midén so long ago...
...and of his inescapable fate...

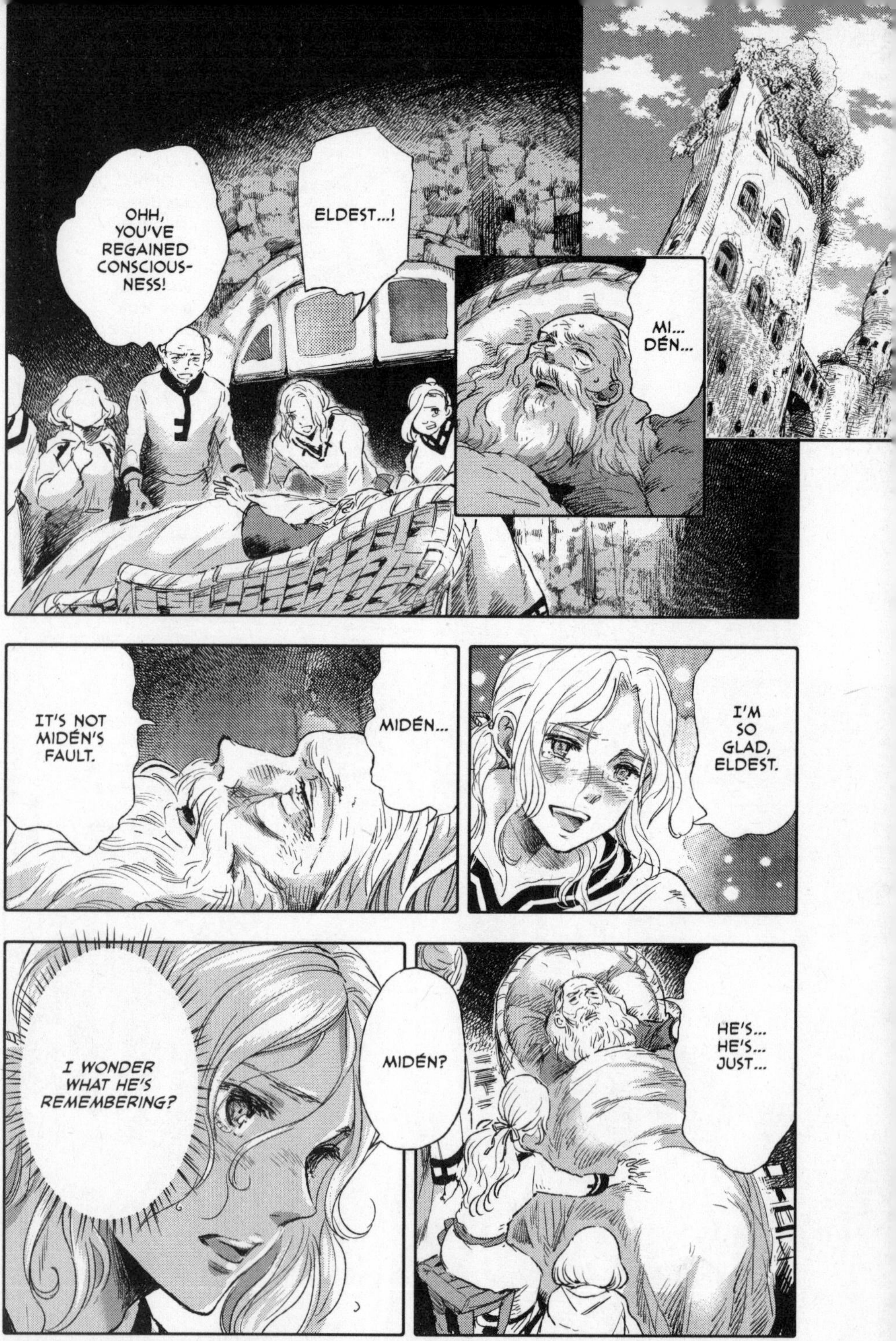
ELDEST...!
OHH, YOU'VE REGAINED CONSCIOUS-NESS!
MI... DÉN...
I'M SO GLAD, ELDEST.
MIDÉN...
IT'S NOT MIDÉN'S FAULT.
HE'S... HE'S... JUST...
MIDÉN?
I WONDER WHAT HE'S REMEMBERING?

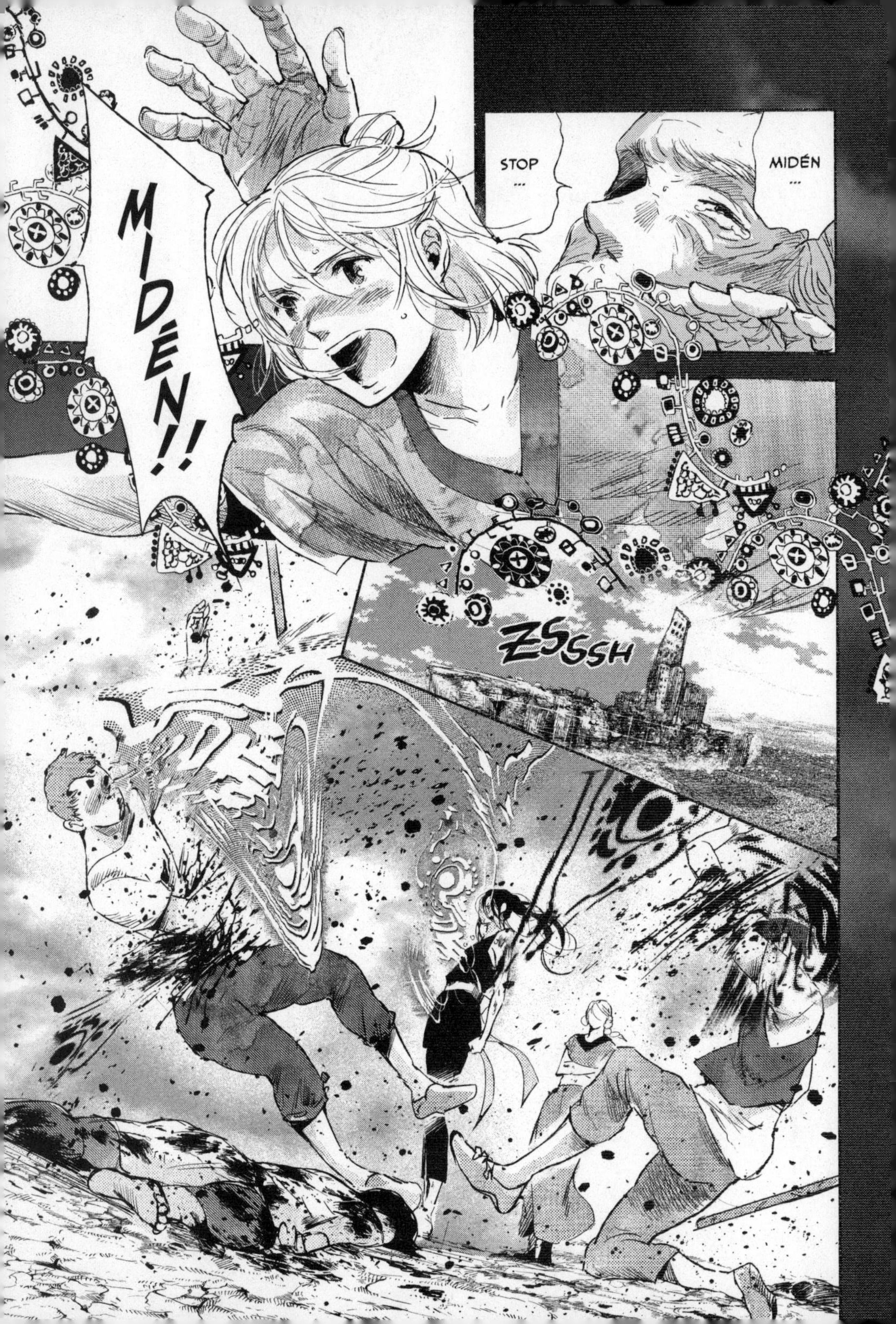
MIDÉN ...
STOP ...
MIDÉN!!
ZSSSH

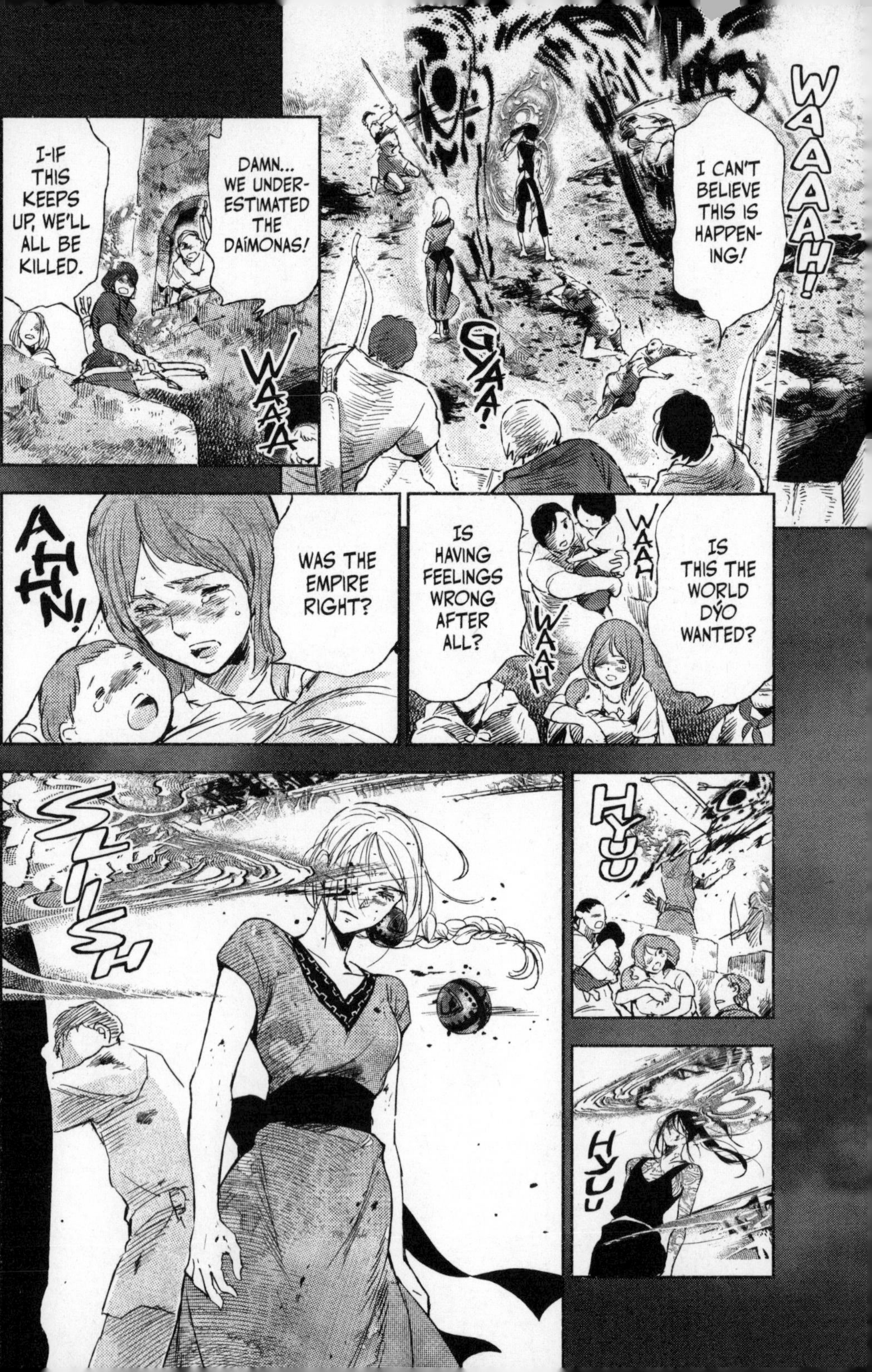
WAAAAAH!
I CAN'T BELIEVE THIS IS HAPPEN-ING!
GYAA!
DAMN... WE UNDER-ESTIMATED THE DAÍMONAS!
I-IF THIS KEEPS UP, WE'LL ALL BE KILLED.
WAAA
IS THIS THE WORLD DÝO WANTED?
WAAH
WAAH
IS HAVING FEELINGS WRONG AFTER ALL?
WAS THE EMPIRE RIGHT?
AHHN!
HYUU
HYUU
SLIIISH

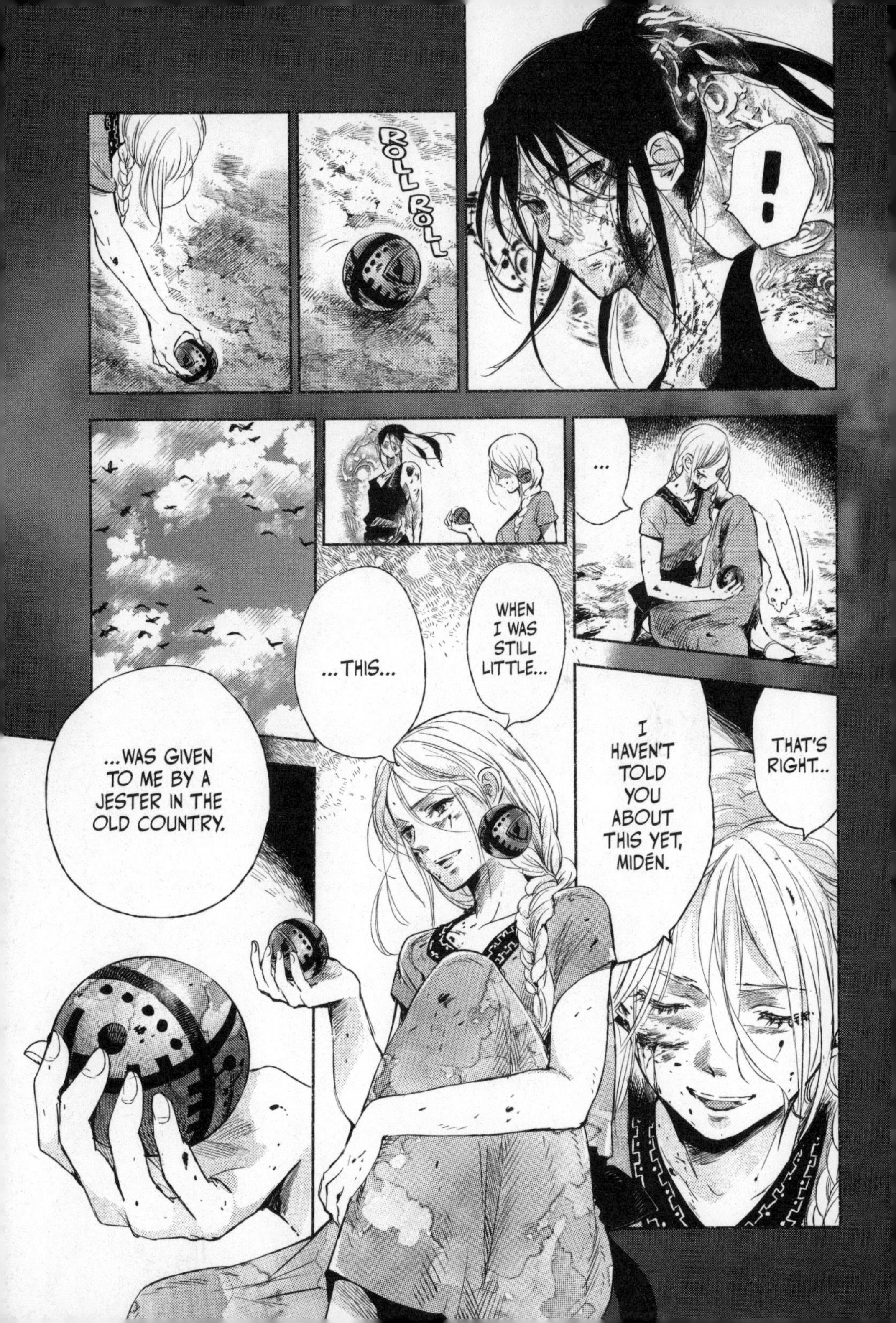
!
ROLL ROLL
...
THAT'S RIGHT...
I HAVEN'T TOLD YOU ABOUT THIS YET, MIDÉN.
WHEN I WAS STILL LITTLE...
...THIS...
...WAS GIVEN TO ME BY A JESTER IN THE OLD COUNTRY.

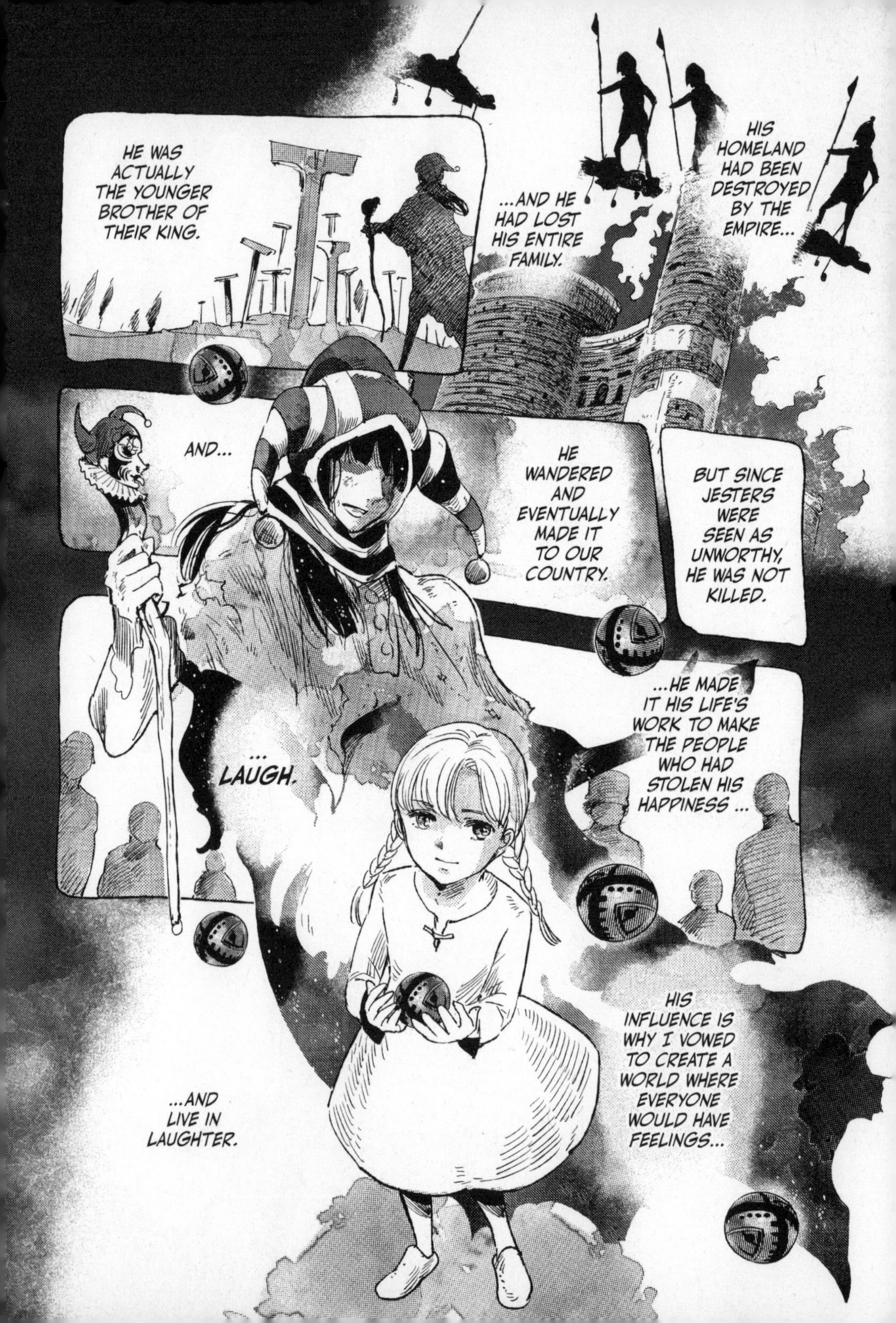
HIS HOMELAND HAD BEEN DESTROYED BY THE EMPIRE...
...AND HE HAD LOST HIS ENTIRE FAMILY.
HE WAS ACTUALLY THE YOUNGER BROTHER OF THEIR KING.
BUT SINCE JESTERS WERE SEEN AS UNWORTHY, HE WAS NOT KILLED.
HE WANDERED AND EVENTUALLY MADE IT TO OUR COUNTRY.
AND...
...HE MADE IT HIS LIFE'S WORK TO MAKE THE PEOPLE WHO HAD STOLEN HIS HAPPINESS ...
... LAUGH.
HIS INFLUENCE IS WHY I VOWED TO CREATE A WORLD WHERE EVERYONE WOULD HAVE FEELINGS...
...AND LIVE IN LAUGHTER.

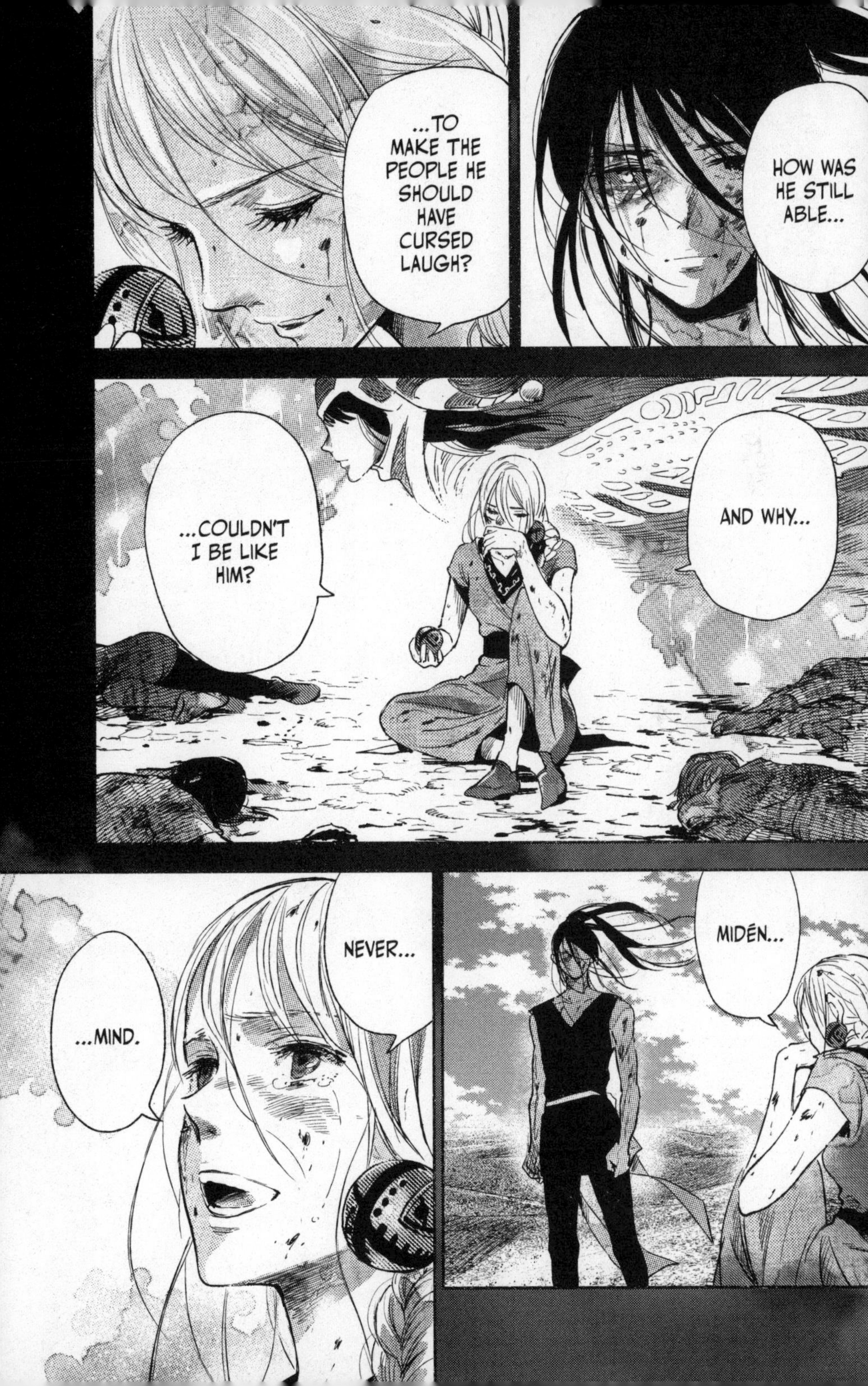
HOW WAS HE STILL ABLE...
...TO MAKE THE PEOPLE HE SHOULD HAVE CURSED LAUGH?
AND WHY...
...COULDN'T I BE LIKE HIM?
MIDEN...
NEVER...
...MIND.

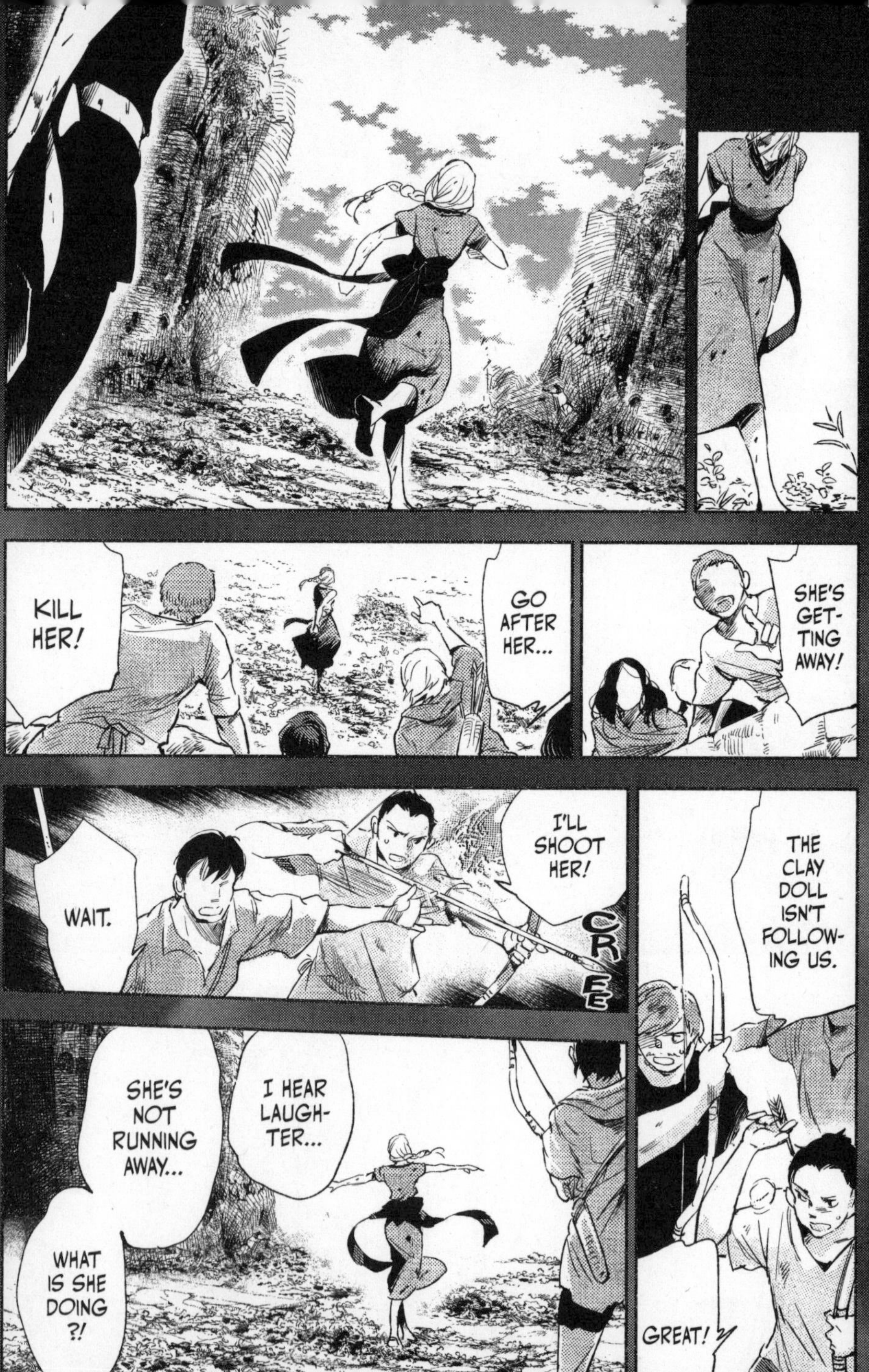
SHE'S GET-TING AWAY!
GO AFTER HER...
KILL HER!
THE CLAY DOLL ISN'T FOLLOW-ING US.
GREAT!
I'LL SHOOT HER!
CREE
WAIT.
I HEAR LAUGH-TER...
SHE'S NOT RUNNING AWAY...
WHAT IS SHE DOING?!

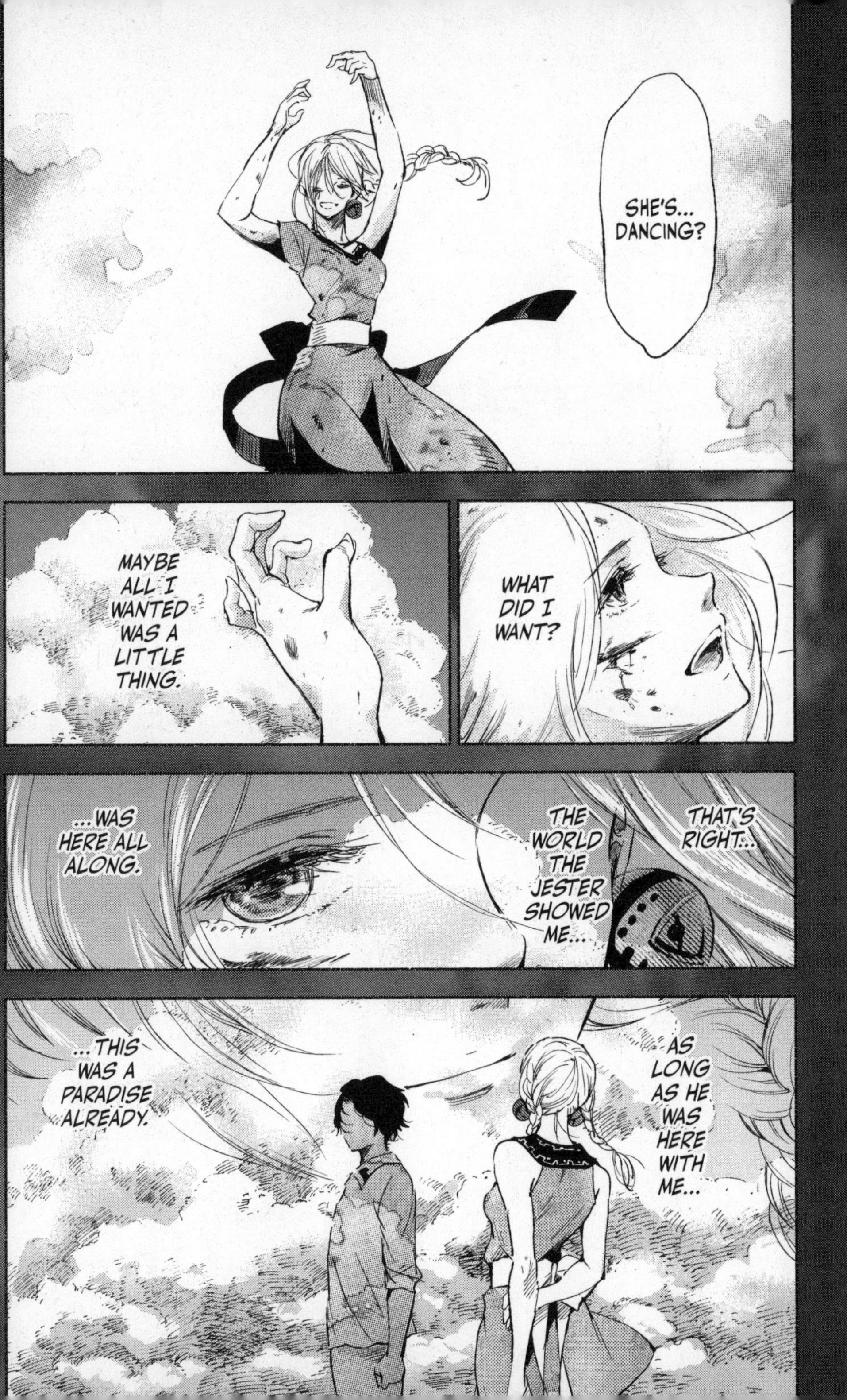
SHE'S... DANCING?
WHAT DID I WANT?
MAYBE ALL I WANTED WAS A LITTLE THING.
THAT'S RIGHT...
THE WORLD THE JESTER SHOWED ME...
...WAS HERE ALL ALONG.
AS LONG AS HE WAS HERE WITH ME...
...THIS WAS A PARADISE ALREADY.

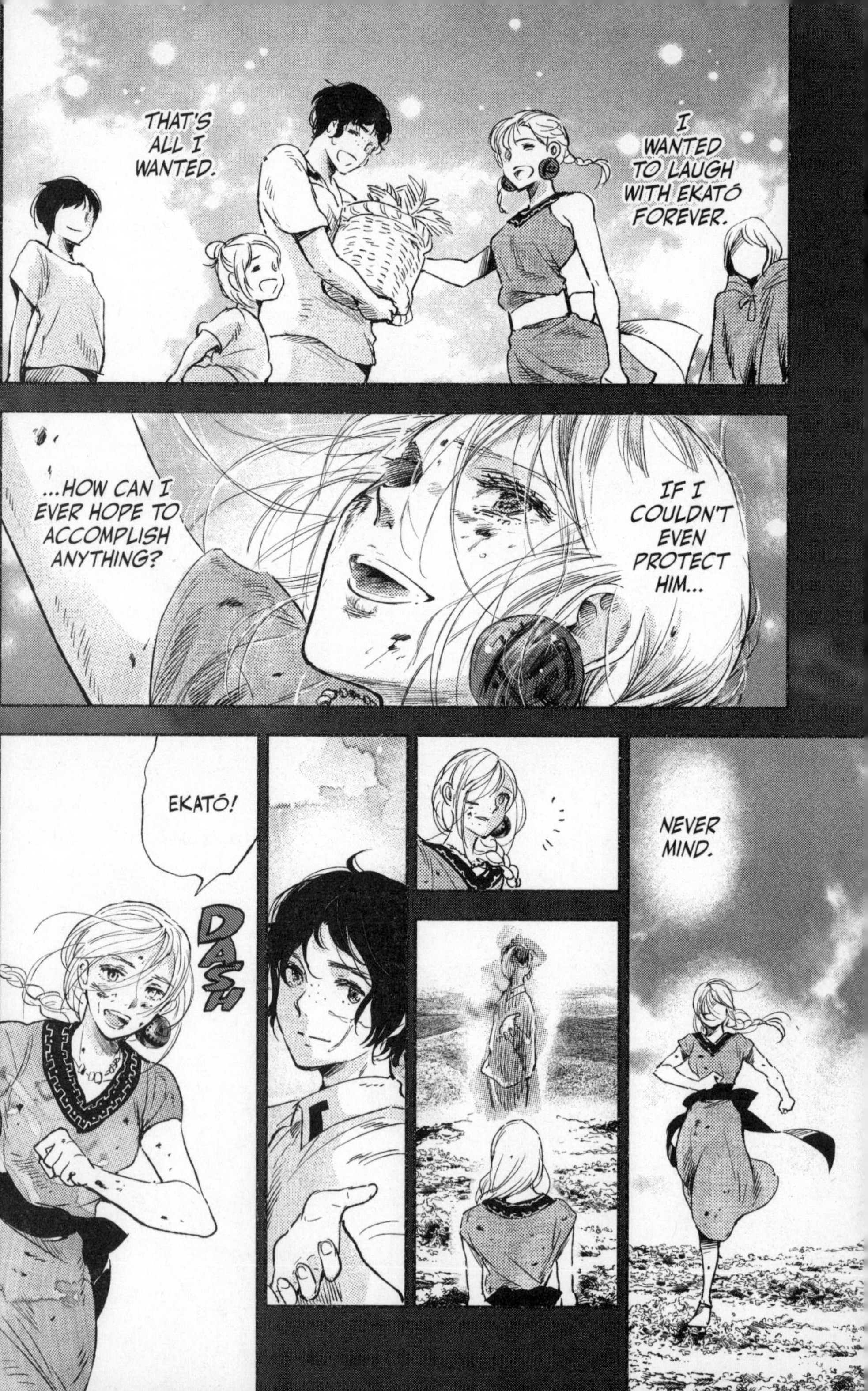
I WANTED TO LAUGH WITH EKATÓ FOREVER.
THAT'S ALL I WANTED.
IF I COULDN'T EVEN PROTECT HIM...
...HOW CAN I EVER HOPE TO ACCOMPLISH ANYTHING?
NEVER MIND.
EKATÓ!
DASH

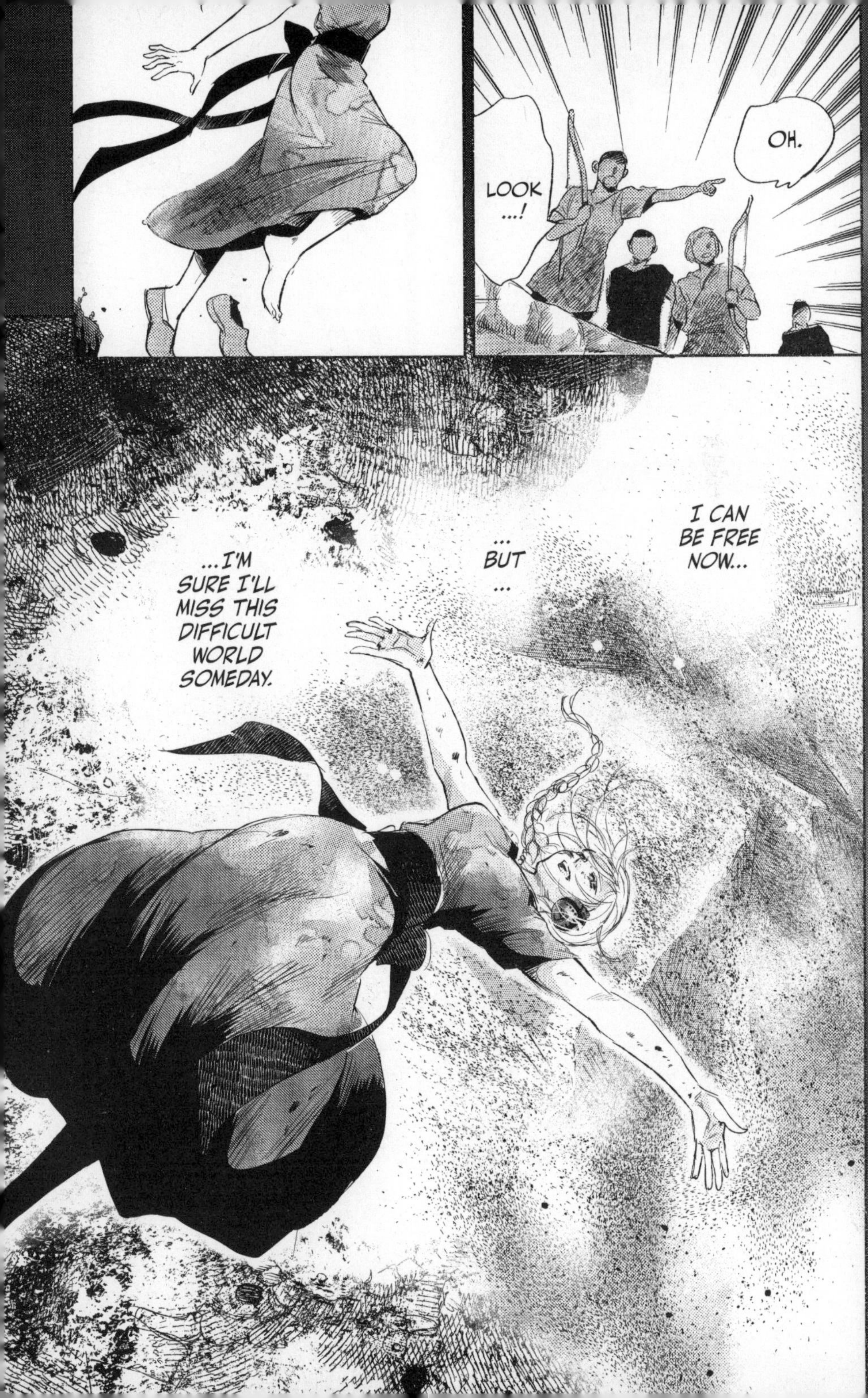
OH.
LOOK ...!
I CAN BE FREE NOW...
... BUT ...
...I'M SURE I'LL MISS THIS DIFFICULT WORLD SOMEDAY.

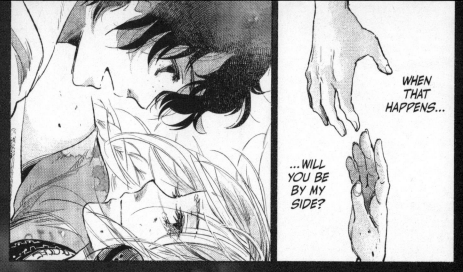

WHEN
THAT
HAPPENS...

...WILL
YOU BE
BY MY
SIDE?

I'M
SORRY...

...
MIDÉN.

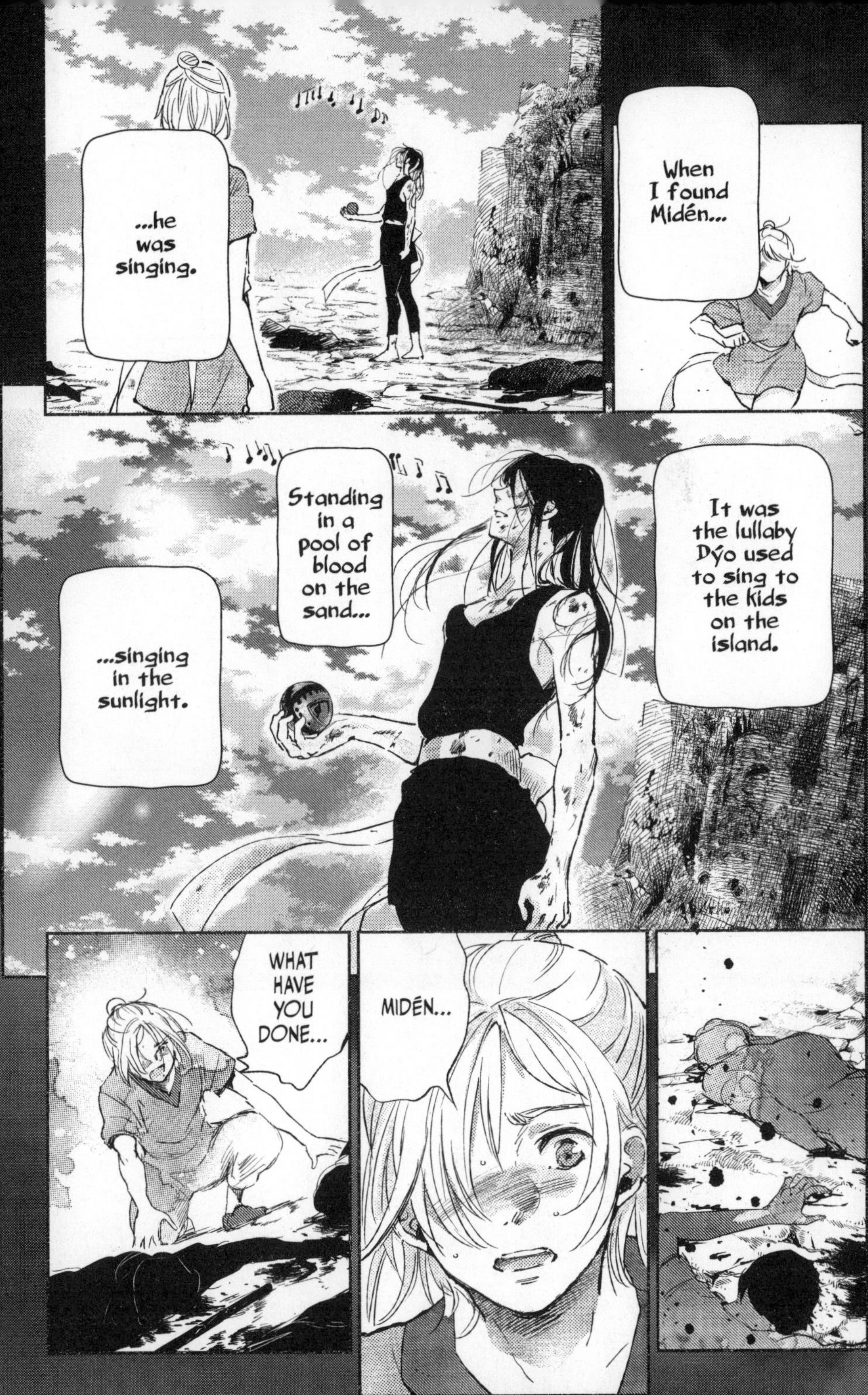
When I found Midén...
...he was singing.
It was the lullaby Dýo used to sing to the kids on the island.
Standing in a pool of blood on the sand...
...singing in the sunlight.
MIDÉN...
WHAT HAVE YOU DONE...

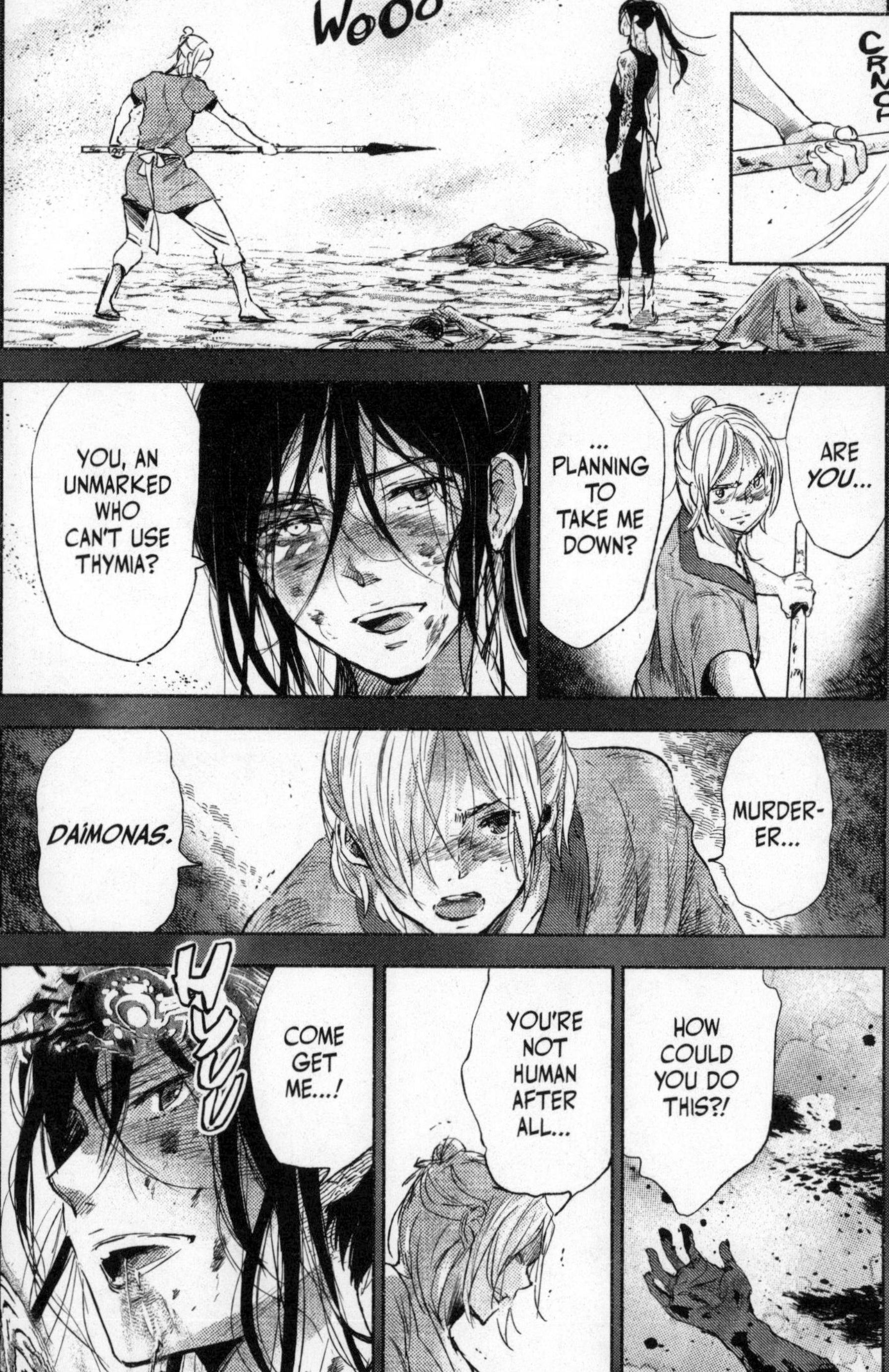
CRNCH
WOOO
ARE YOU...
...PLANNING TO TAKE ME DOWN?
YOU, AN UNMARKED WHO CAN'T USE THYMIA?
MURDER-ER...
DAIMONAS.
HOW COULD YOU DO THIS?!
YOU'RE NOT HUMAN AFTER ALL...
COME GET ME...!
HYUUU

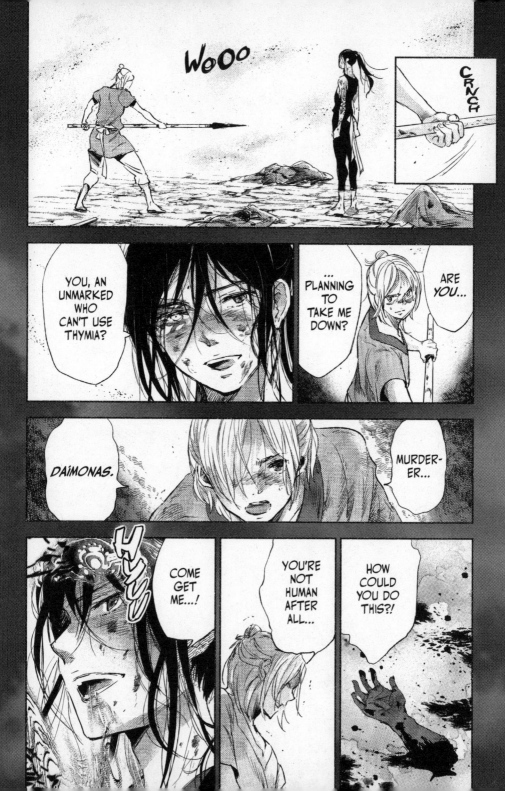

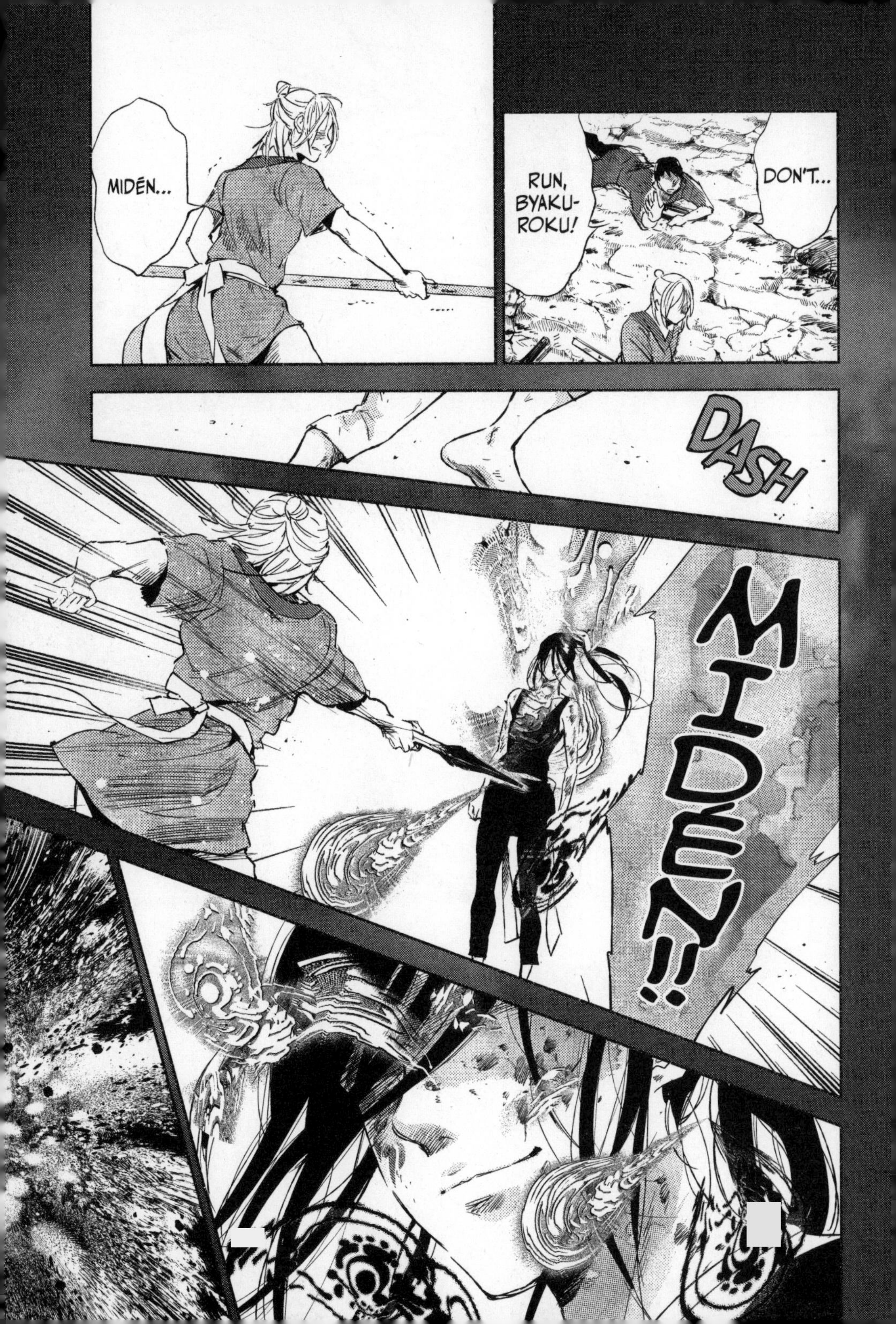
DON'T...
RUN, BYAKU-ROKU!
MIDÉN...
DASH
MIDÉN!!

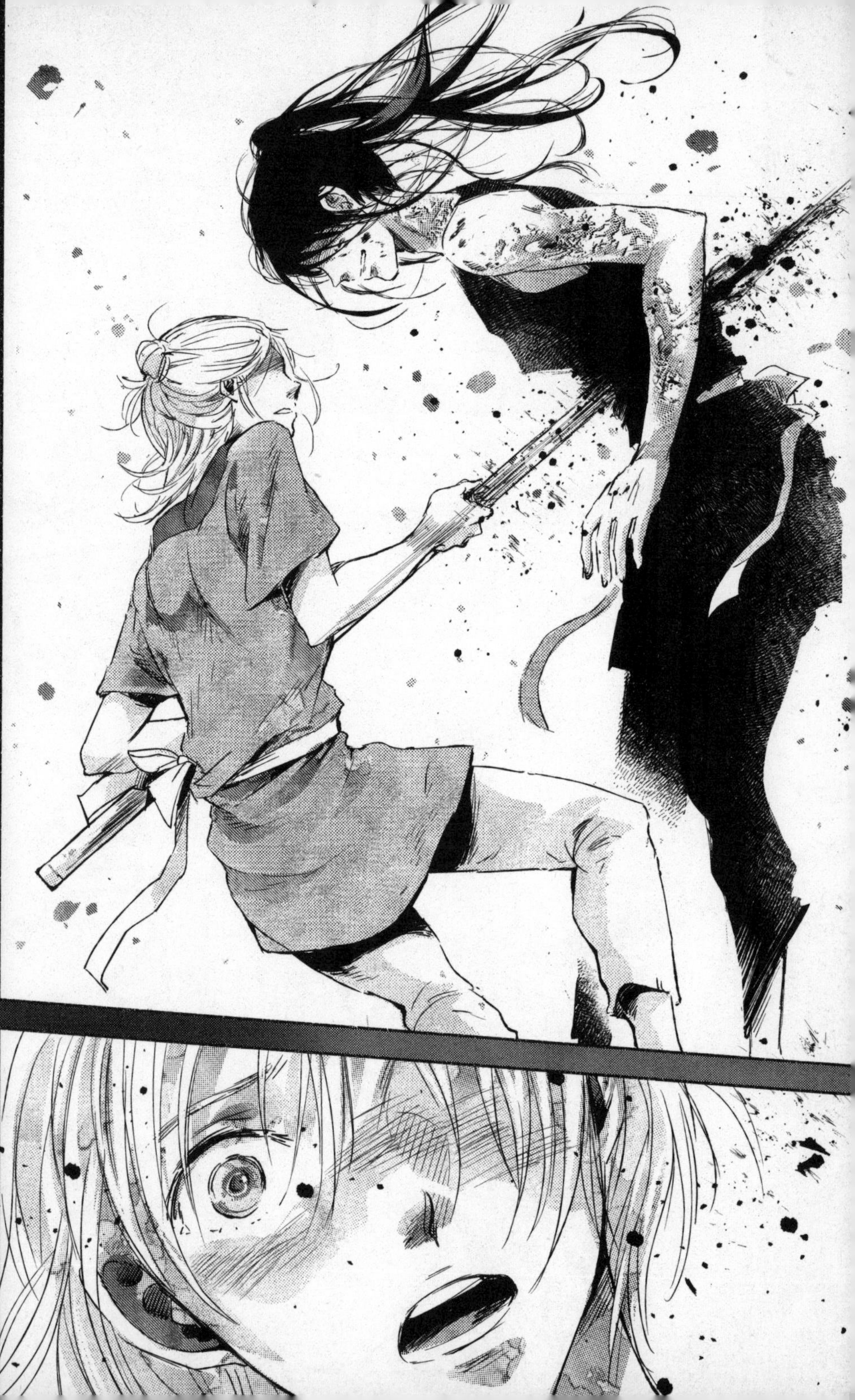

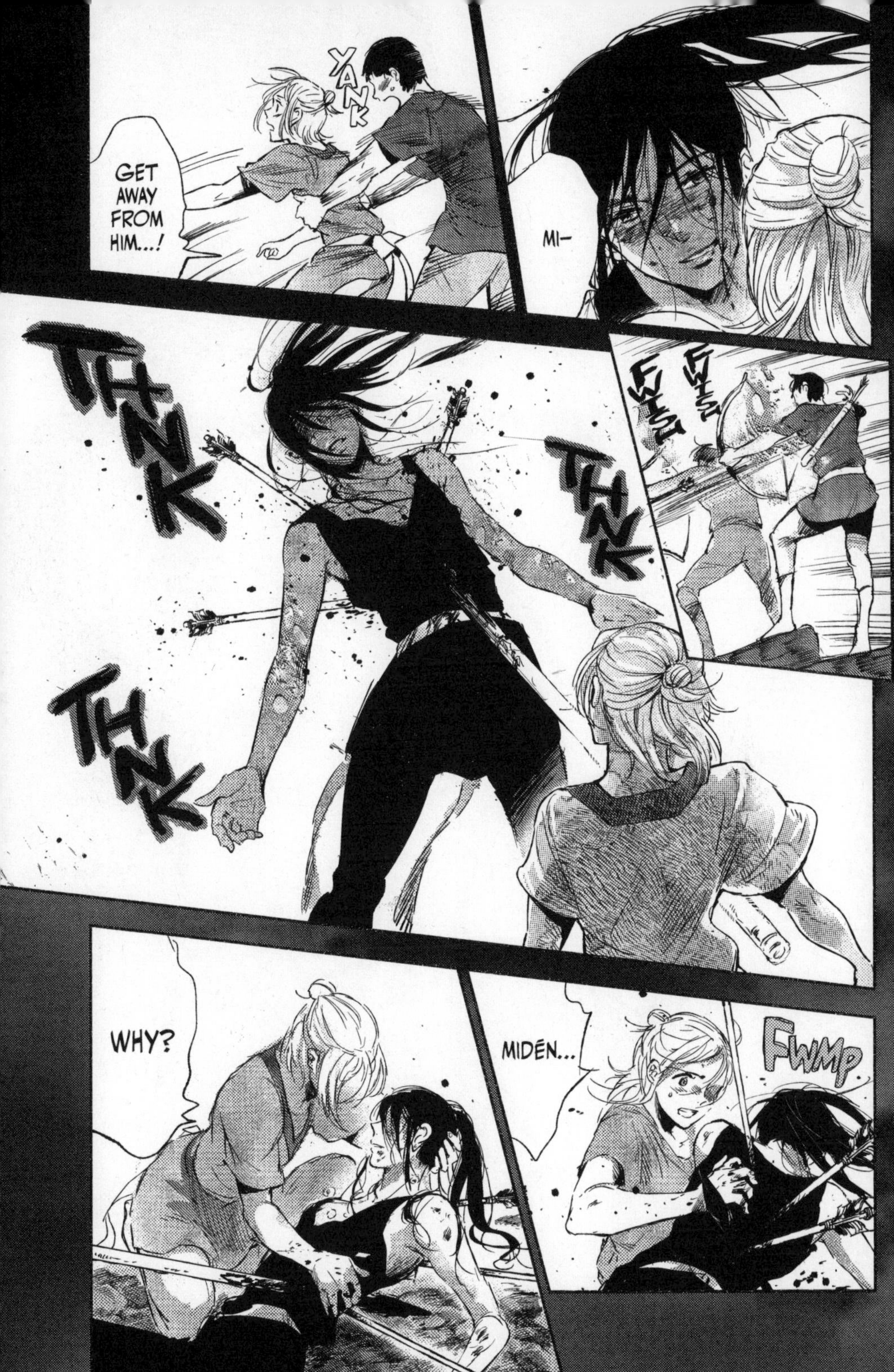
MI–
YANK
GET AWAY FROM HIM...!
FWISH
FWISH
THNK
THNK
THNK
FWMP
MIDÉN...
WHY?

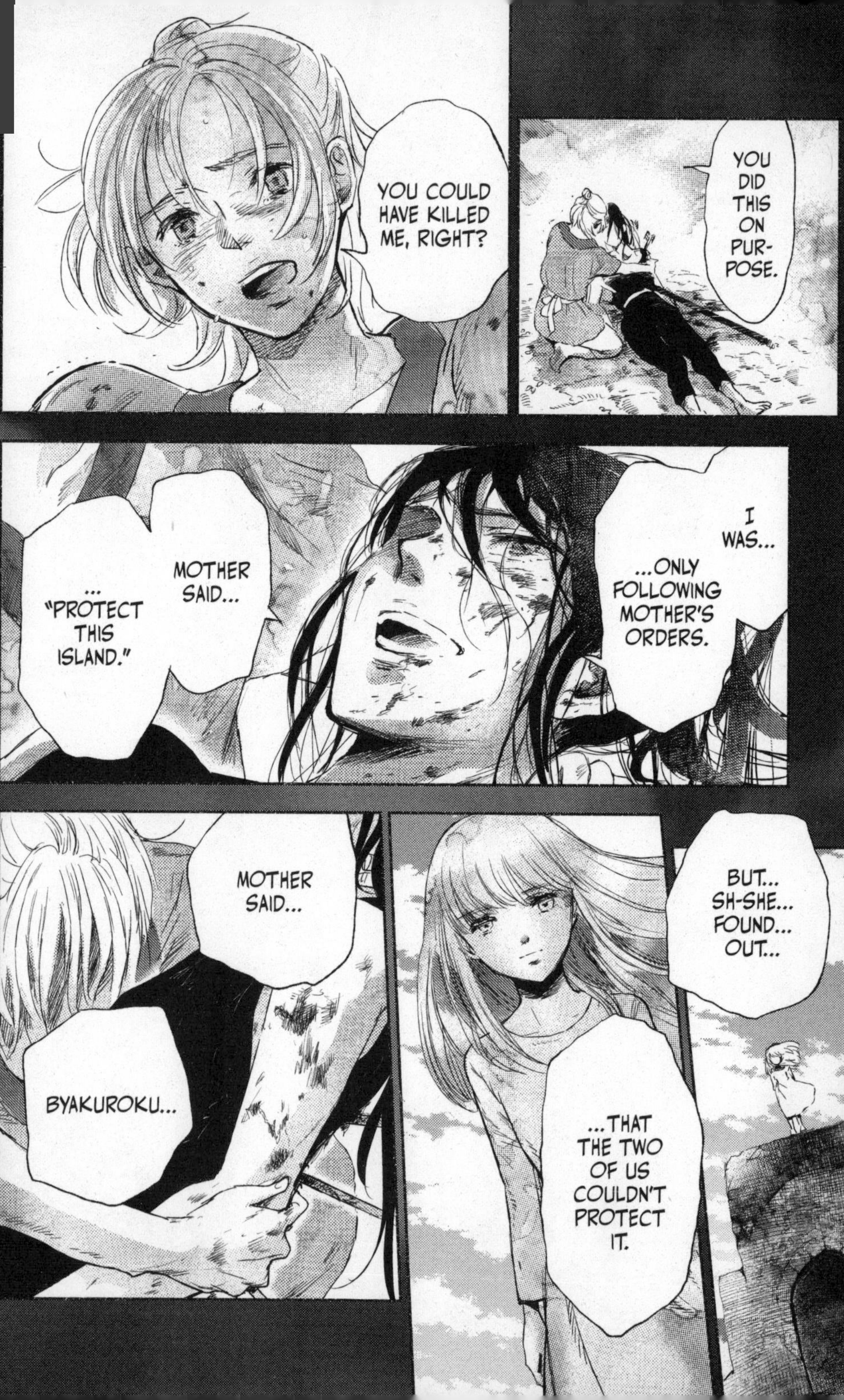
YOU DID THIS ON PUR-POSE.
YOU COULD HAVE KILLED ME, RIGHT?
I WAS...
...ONLY FOLLOWING MOTHER'S ORDERS.
MOTHER SAID...
... "PROTECT THIS ISLAND."
BUT... SH-SHE... FOUND... OUT...
...THAT THE TWO OF US COULDN'T PROTECT IT.
MOTHER SAID...
BYAKUROKU...

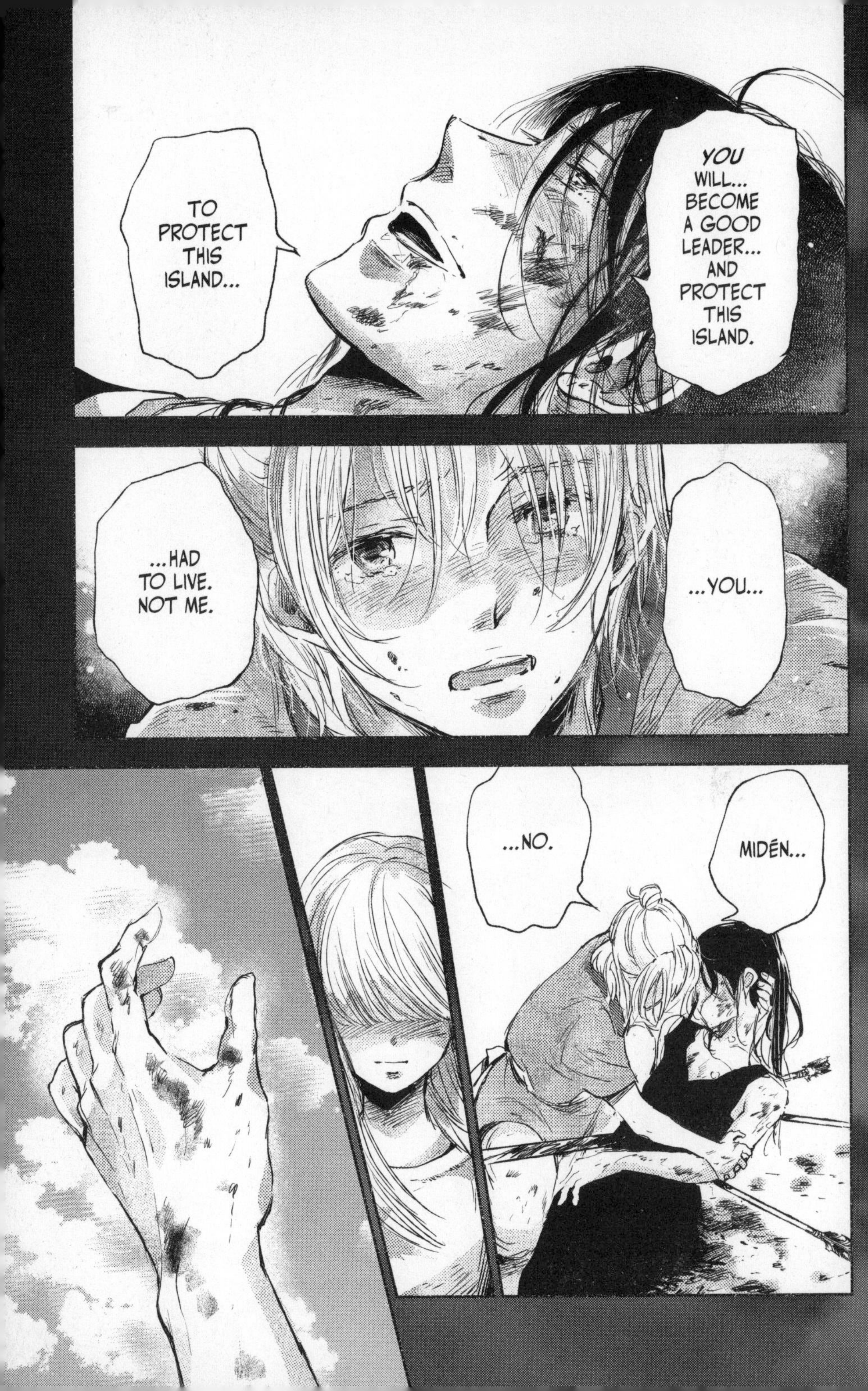

YOU WILL... BECOME A GOOD LEADER... AND PROTECT THIS ISLAND.
TO PROTECT THIS ISLAND...
...YOU...
...HAD TO LIVE. NOT ME.
MIDÉN...
...NO.

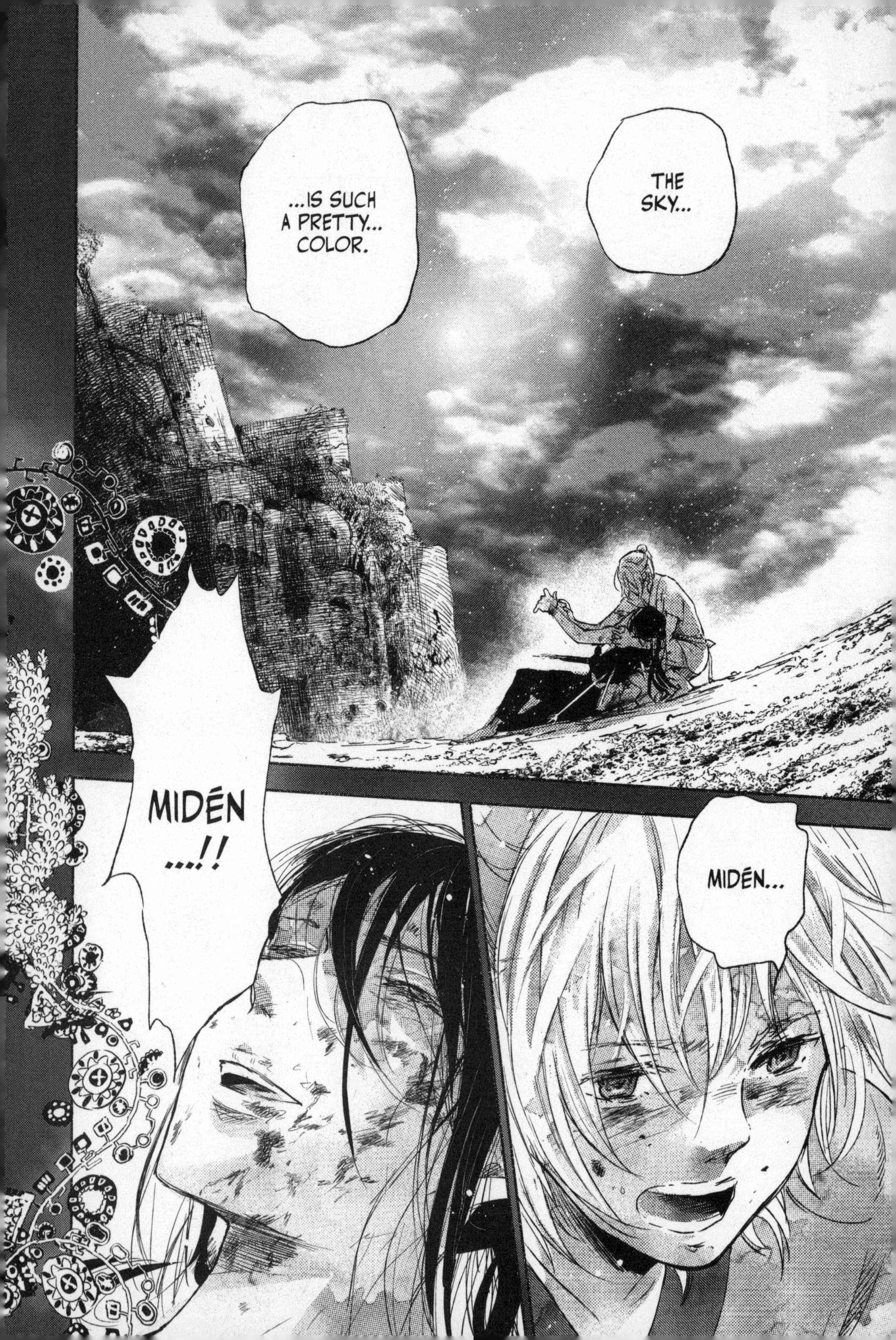
THE SKY...
...IS SUCH A PRETTY... COLOR.
MIDÉN...
MIDÉN ...!!

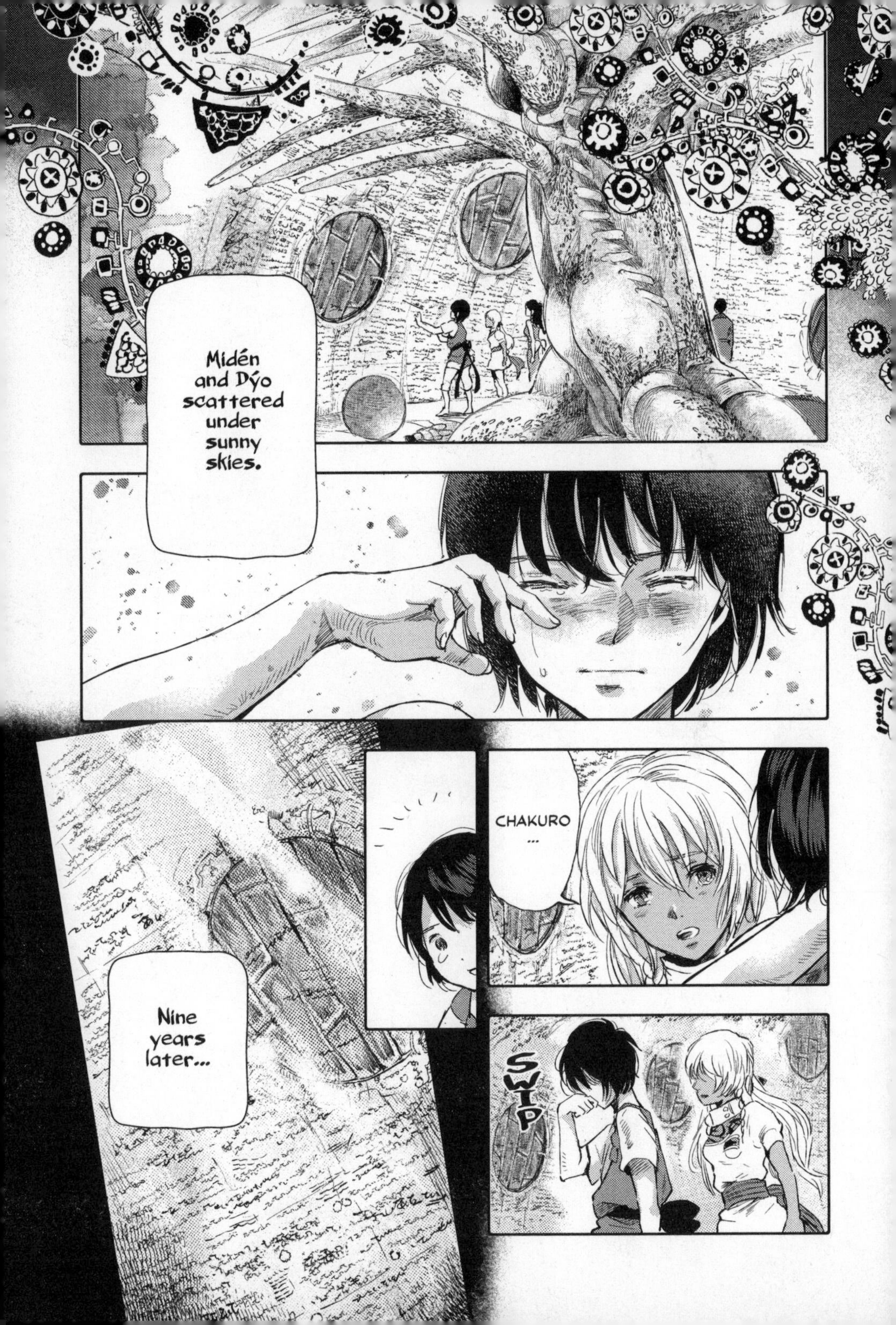
Midén and Dýo scattered under sunny skies.
CHAKURO ...
SWIP
Nine years later...

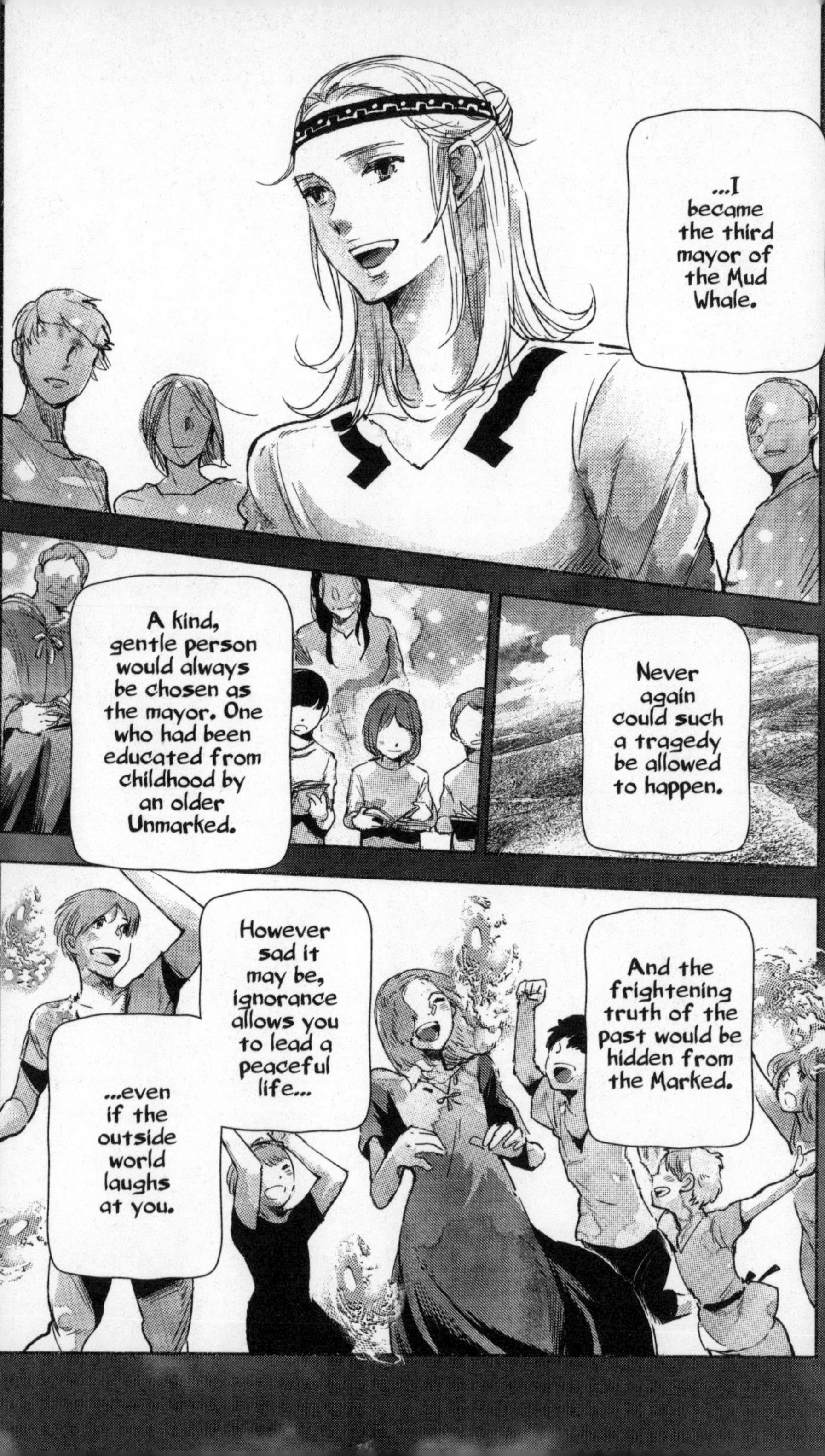
...I became the third mayor of the Mud Whale.
Never again could such a tragedy be allowed to happen.
A kind, gentle person would always be chosen as the mayor. One who had been educated from childhood by an older Unmarked.
And the frightening truth of the past would be hidden from the Marked.
However sad it may be, ignorance allows you to lead a peaceful life...
...even if the outside world laughs at you.

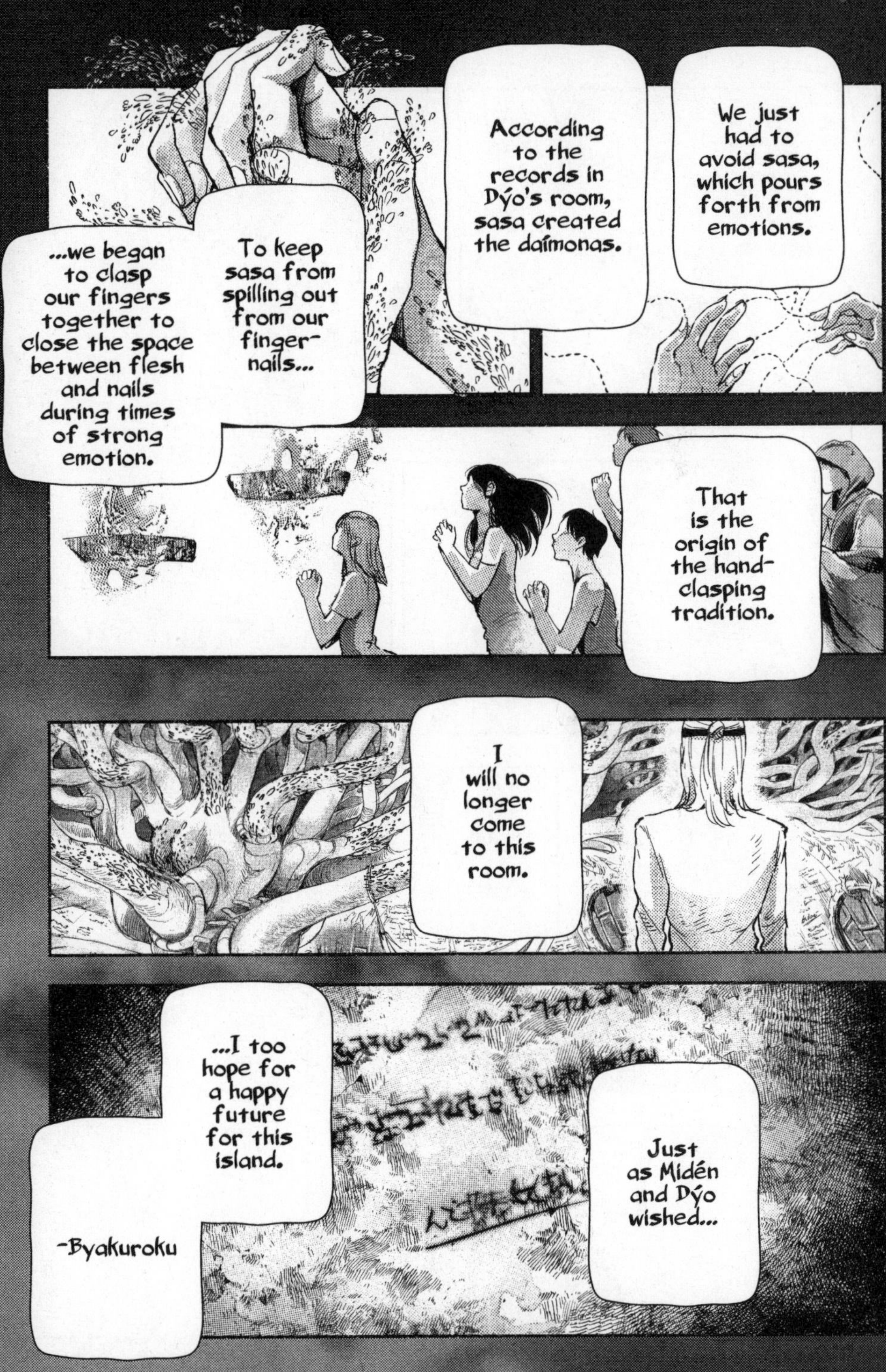
According to the records in Dýo's room, sasa created the daímonas.
We just had to avoid sasa, which pours forth from emotions.
To keep sasa from spilling out from our finger-nails...
...we began to clasp our fingers together to close the space between flesh and nails during times of strong emotion.
That is the origin of the hand-clasping tradition.
I will no longer come to this room.
Just as Midén and Dýo wished...
...I too hope for a happy future for this island.
-Byakuroku

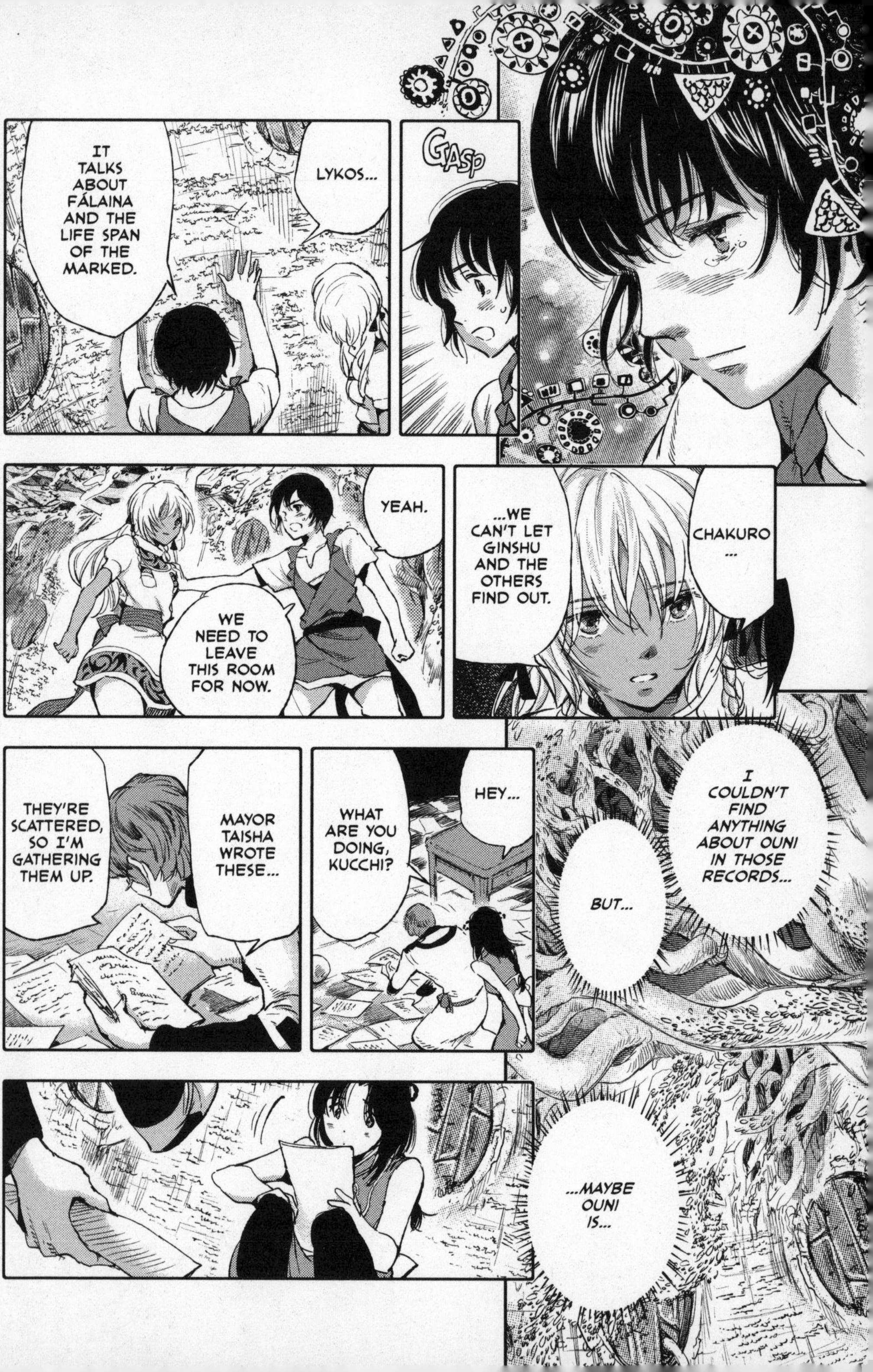
GASP
LYKOS...
IT TALKS ABOUT FÁLAINA AND THE LIFE SPAN OF THE MARKED.
CHAKURO...
...WE CAN'T LET GINSHU AND THE OTHERS FIND OUT.
YEAH.
WE NEED TO LEAVE THIS ROOM FOR NOW.
I COULDN'T FIND ANYTHING ABOUT OUNI IN THOSE RECORDS...
BUT...
...MAYBE OUNI IS...
HEY...
WHAT ARE YOU DOING, KUCCHI?
MAYOR TAISHA WROTE THESE...
THEY'RE SCATTERED, SO I'M GATHERING THEM UP.

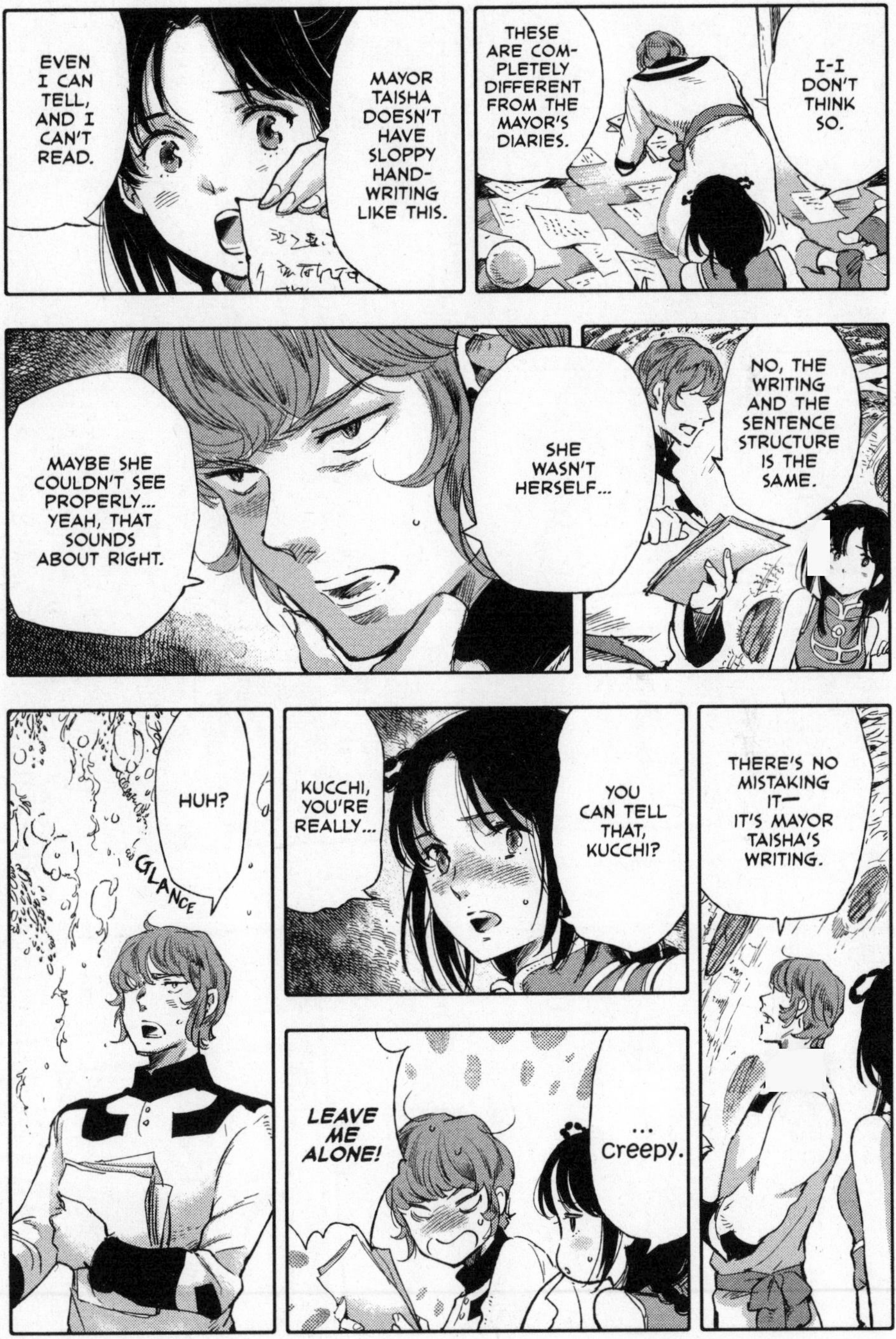
I-I DON'T THINK SO.
THESE ARE COMPLETELY DIFFERENT FROM THE MAYOR'S DIARIES.
MAYOR TAISHA DOESN'T HAVE SLOPPY HANDWRITING LIKE THIS.
EVEN I CAN TELL, AND I CAN'T READ.
NO, THE WRITING AND THE SENTENCE STRUCTURE IS THE SAME.
SHE WASN'T HERSELF...
MAYBE SHE COULDN'T SEE PROPERLY... YEAH, THAT SOUNDS ABOUT RIGHT.
THERE'S NO MISTAKING IT— IT'S MAYOR TAISHA'S WRITING.
YOU CAN TELL THAT, KUCCHI?
KUCCHI, YOU'RE REALLY...
... Creepy.
LEAVE ME ALONE!
HUH?
GLANCE

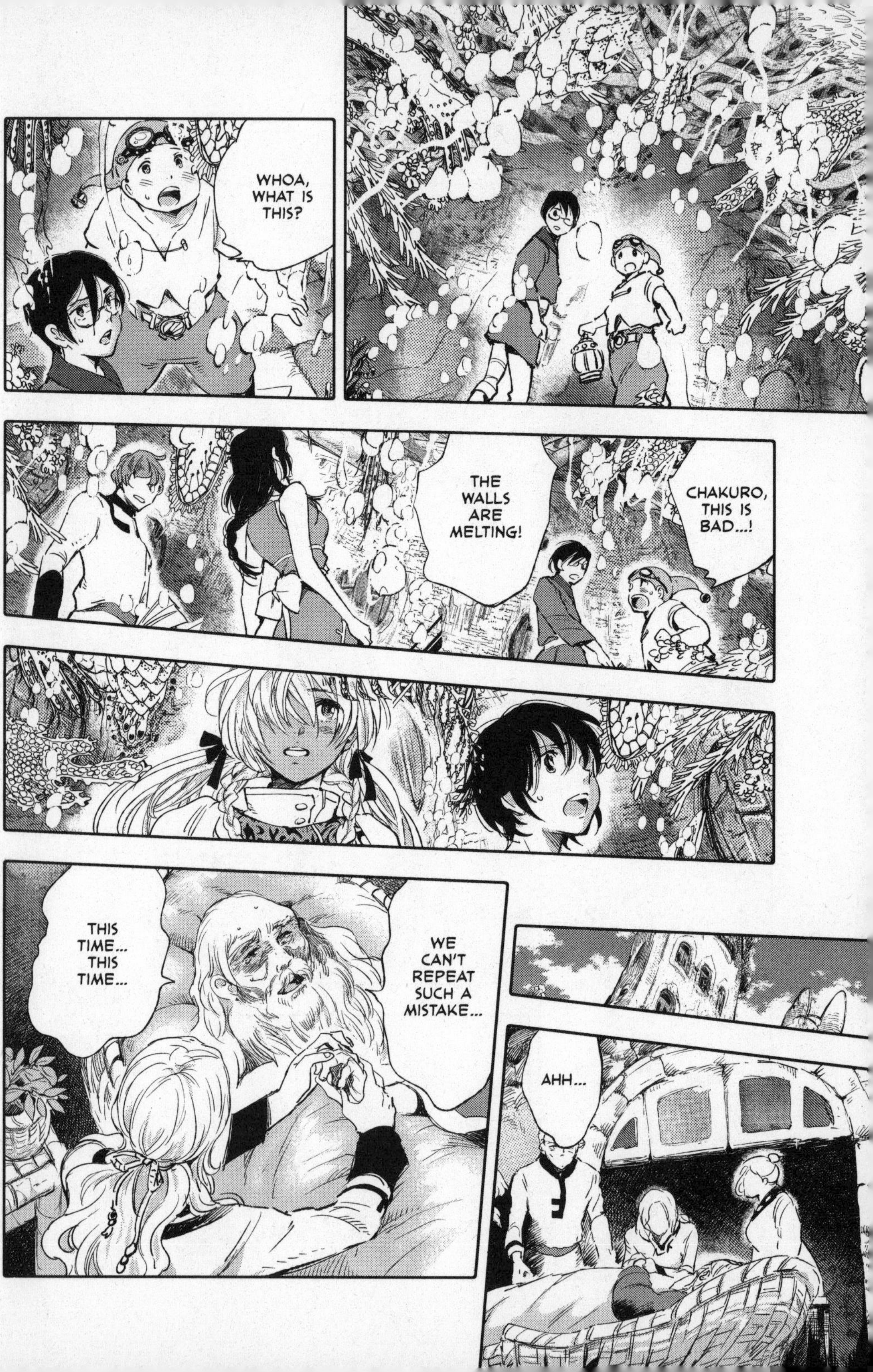
WHOA, WHAT IS THIS?
CHAKURO, THIS IS BAD...!
THE WALLS ARE MELTING!
AHH...
WE CAN'T REPEAT SUCH A MISTAKE...
THIS TIME... THIS TIME...

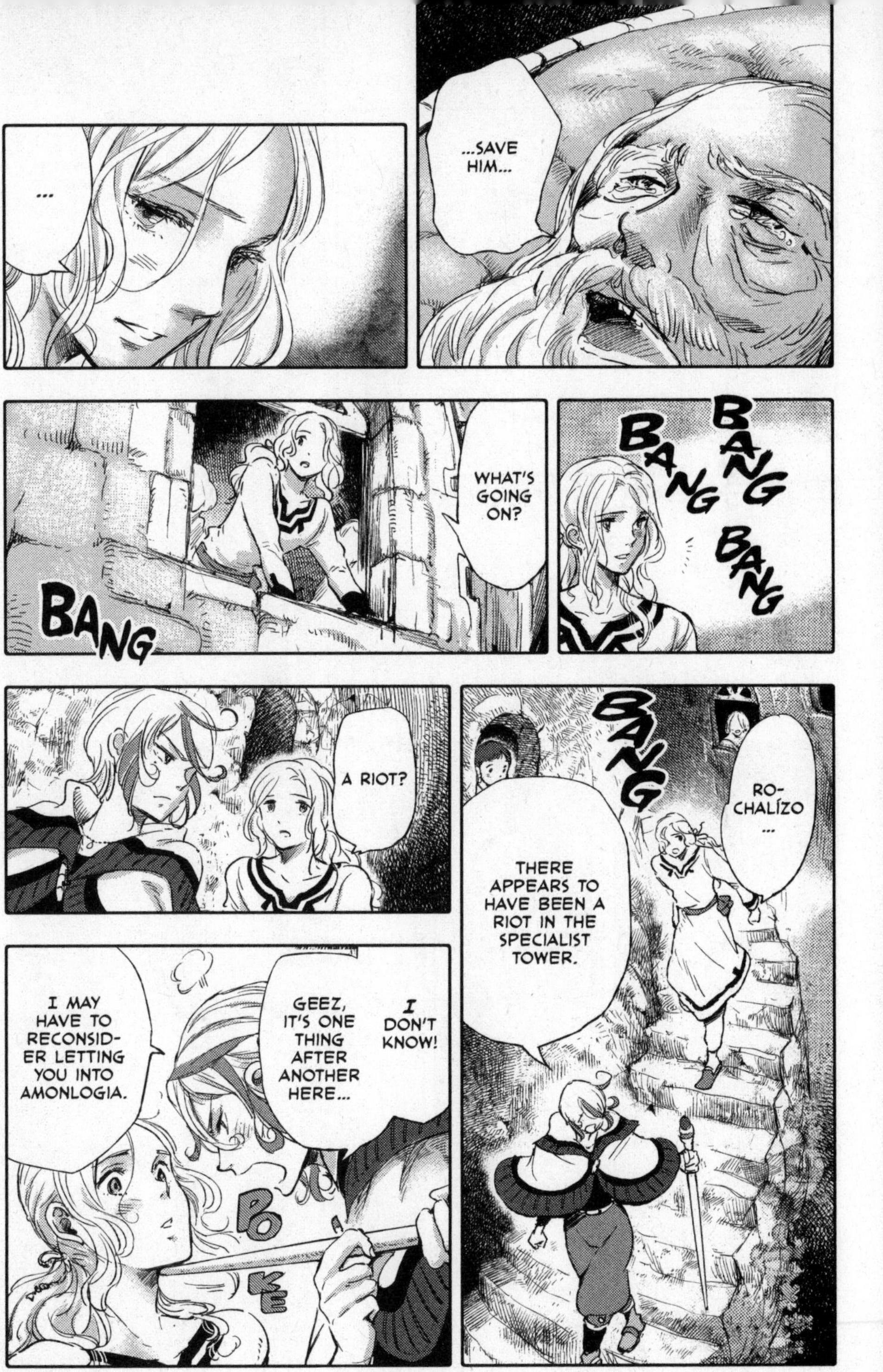
...SAVE HIM...
...
BANG
BANG
BANG
WHAT'S GOING ON?
BANG
BANG
RO-CHALÍZO ...
THERE APPEARS TO HAVE BEEN A RIOT IN THE SPECIALIST TOWER.
A RIOT?
I DON'T KNOW!
GEEZ, IT'S ONE THING AFTER ANOTHER HERE...
I MAY HAVE TO RECONSIDER LETTING YOU INTO AMONLOGIA.
POKE

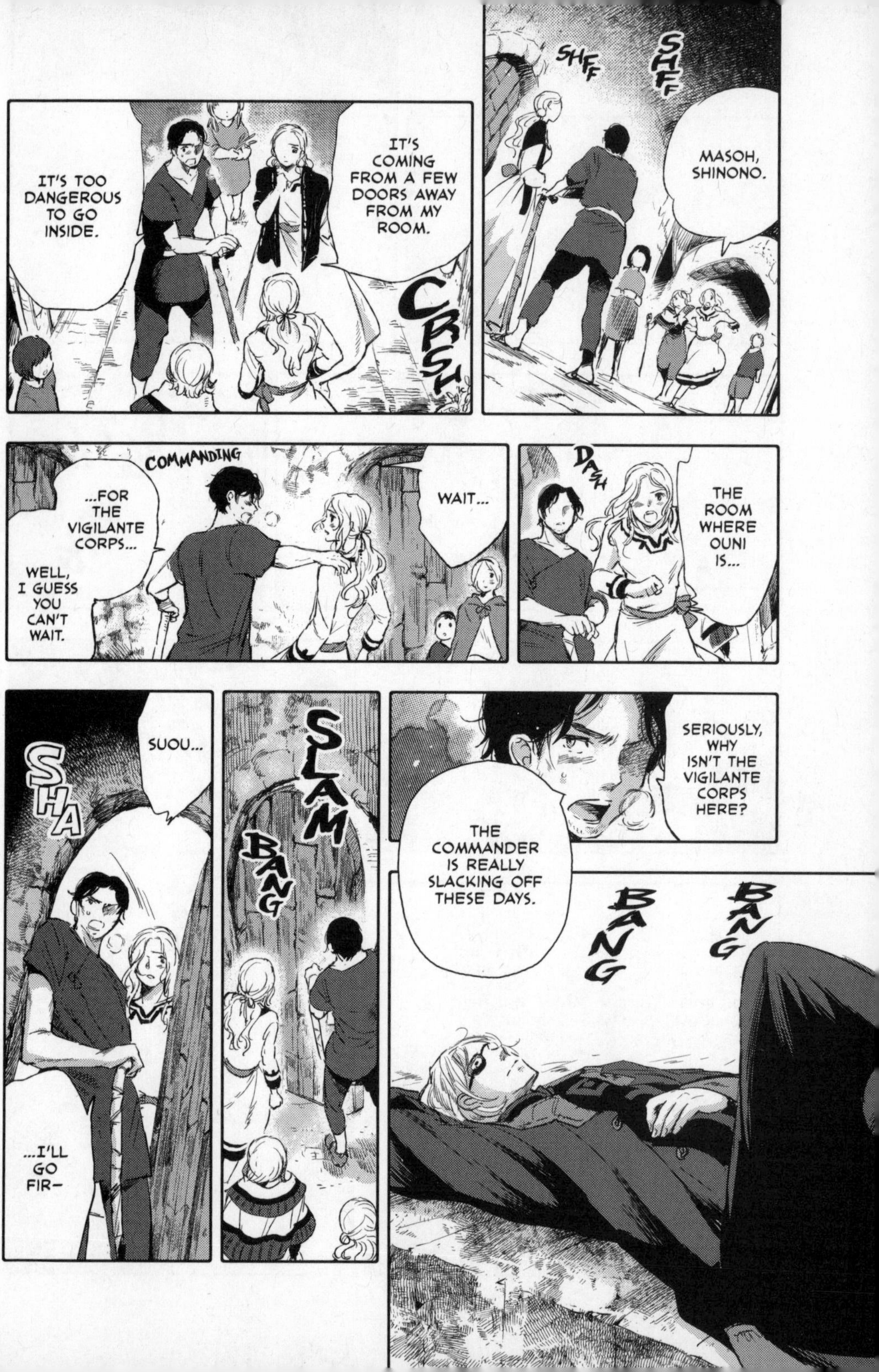
SHFF
SHFF
MASOH, SHINONO.
IT'S COMING FROM A FEW DOORS AWAY FROM MY ROOM.
IT'S TOO DANGEROUS TO GO INSIDE.
CRSH
DASH
THE ROOM WHERE OUNI IS...
WAIT...
COMMANDING
...FOR THE VIGILANTE CORPS...
WELL, I GUESS YOU CAN'T WAIT.
SERIOUSLY, WHY ISN'T THE VIGILANTE CORPS HERE?
THE COMMANDER IS REALLY SLACKING OFF THESE DAYS.
BANG
BANG
BANG
BANG
SLAM
BANG
SUOU...
SHA
...I'LL GO FIR–

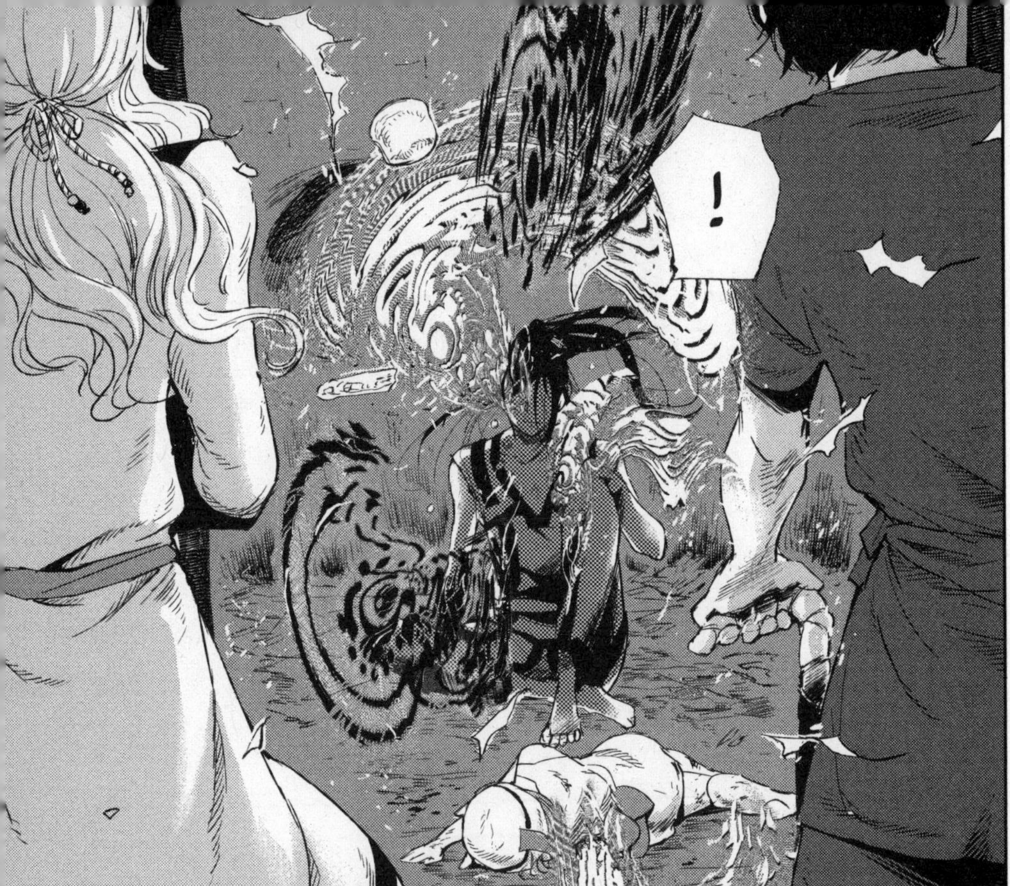
!

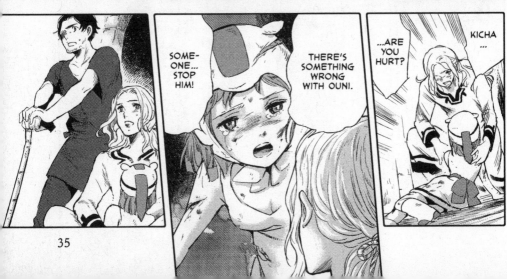

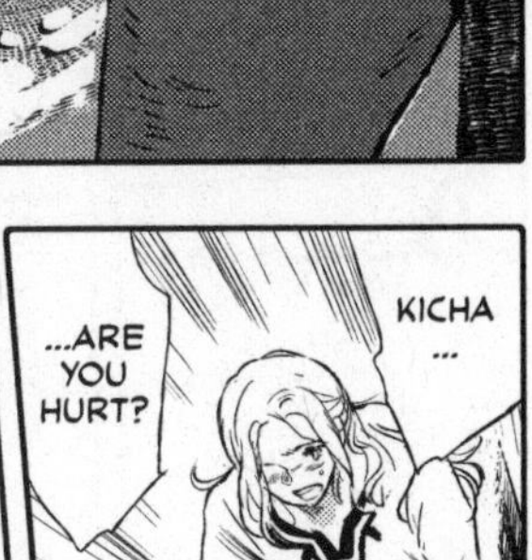
KICHA ...
...ARE YOU HURT?

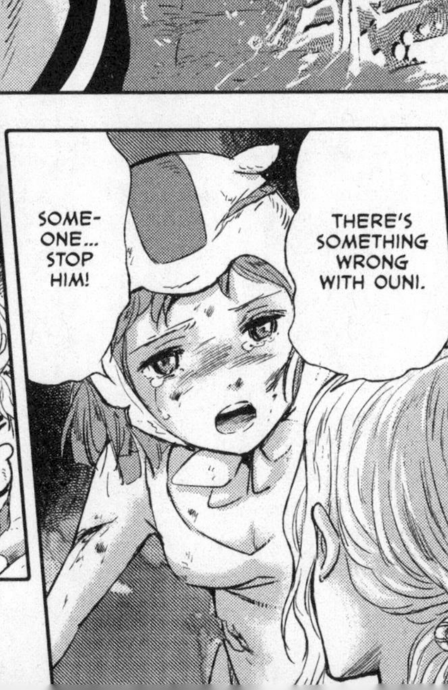
THERE'S SOMETHING WRONG WITH OUNI.
SOME-ONE... STOP HIM!

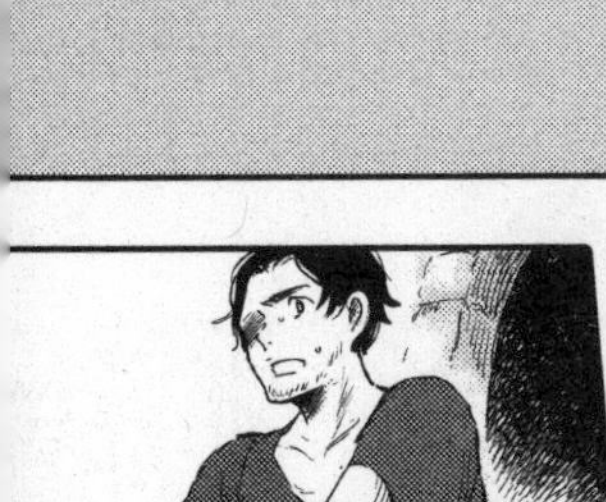

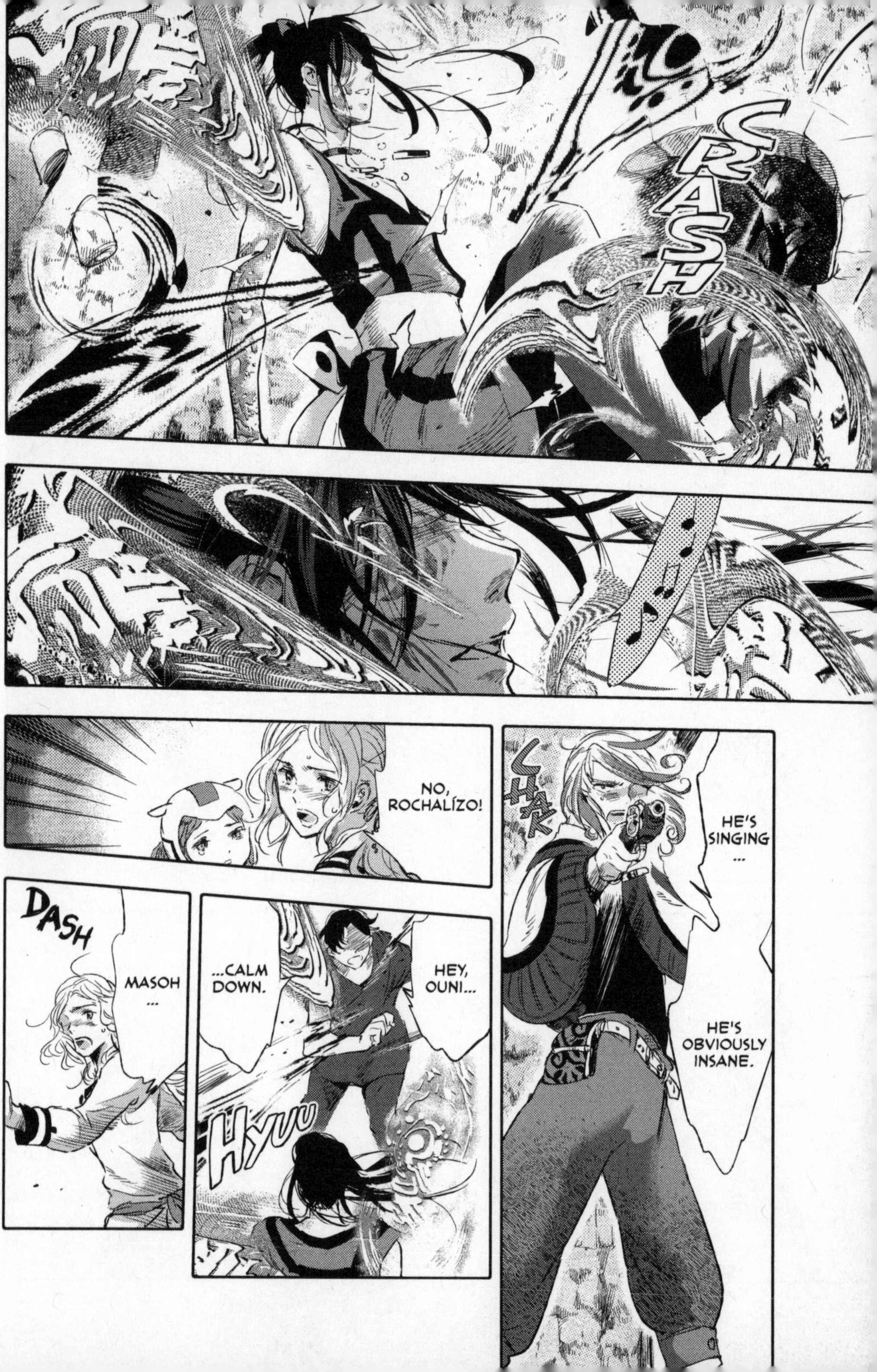
CRASH
SHAK
HE'S SINGING...
HE'S OBVIOUSLY INSANE.
NO, ROCHALÍZO!
HEY, OUNI...
...CALM DOWN.
HYUU
DASH
MASOH...

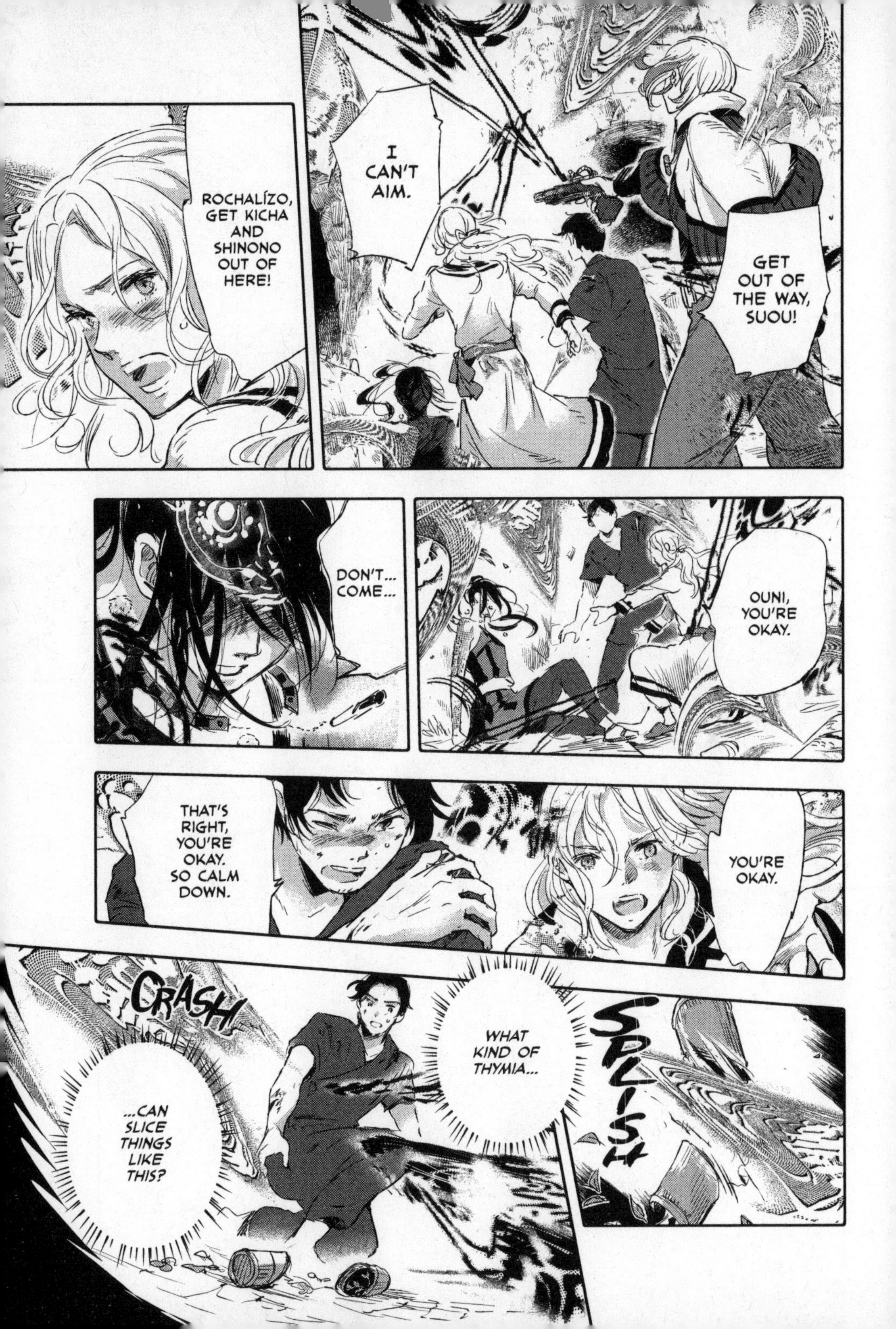
I CAN'T AIM.
GET OUT OF THE WAY, SUOU!
ROCHALÍZO, GET KICHA AND SHINONO OUT OF HERE!
OUNI, YOU'RE OKAY.
DON'T... COME...
YOU'RE OKAY.
THAT'S RIGHT, YOU'RE OKAY. SO CALM DOWN.
SPLISH
CRASH
WHAT KIND OF THYMIA...
...CAN SLICE THINGS LIKE THIS?

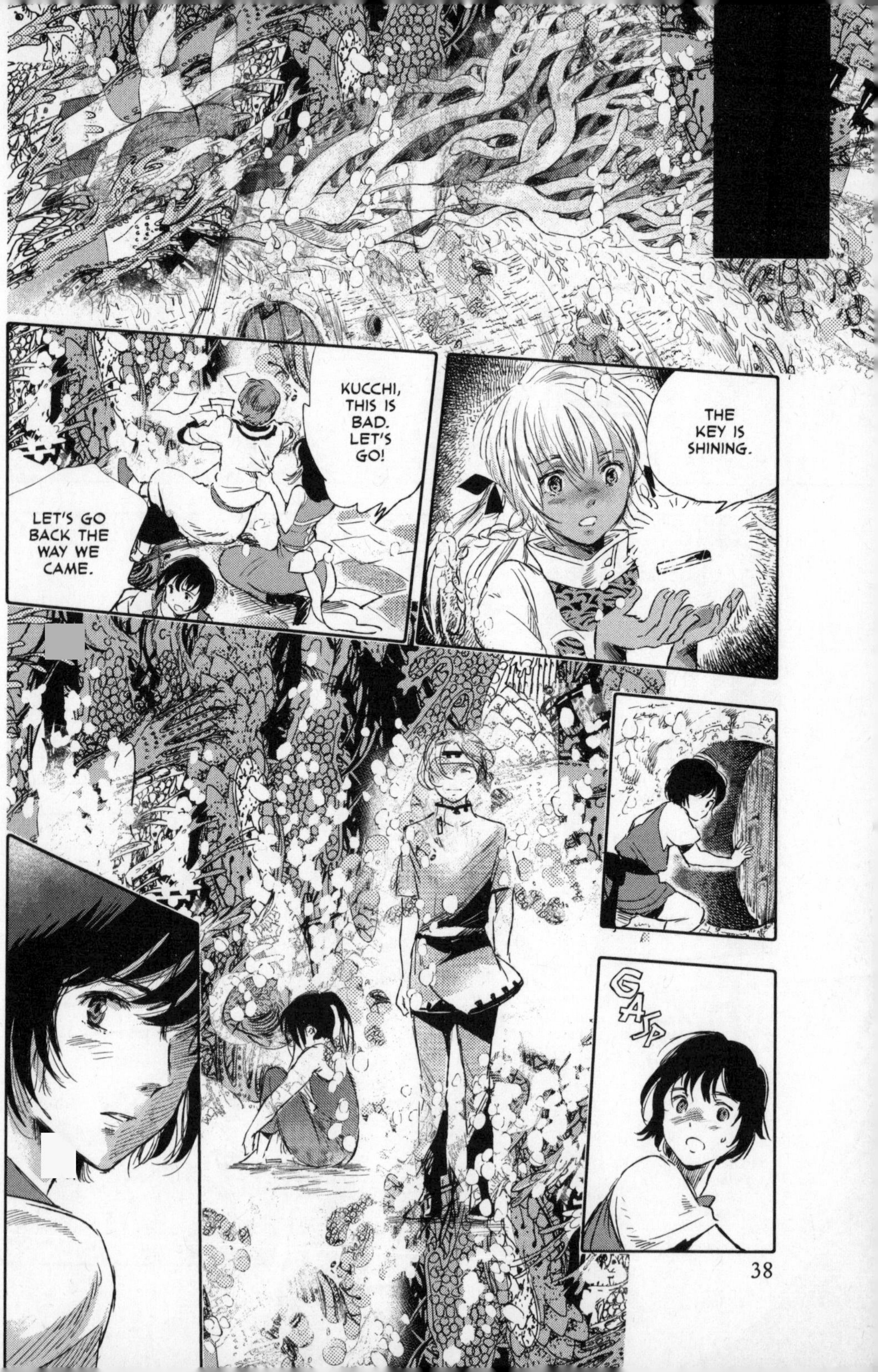
[redacted]
THE KEY IS SHINING.
KUCCHI, THIS IS BAD. LET'S GO!
LET'S GO BACK THE WAY WE CAME.
GASP

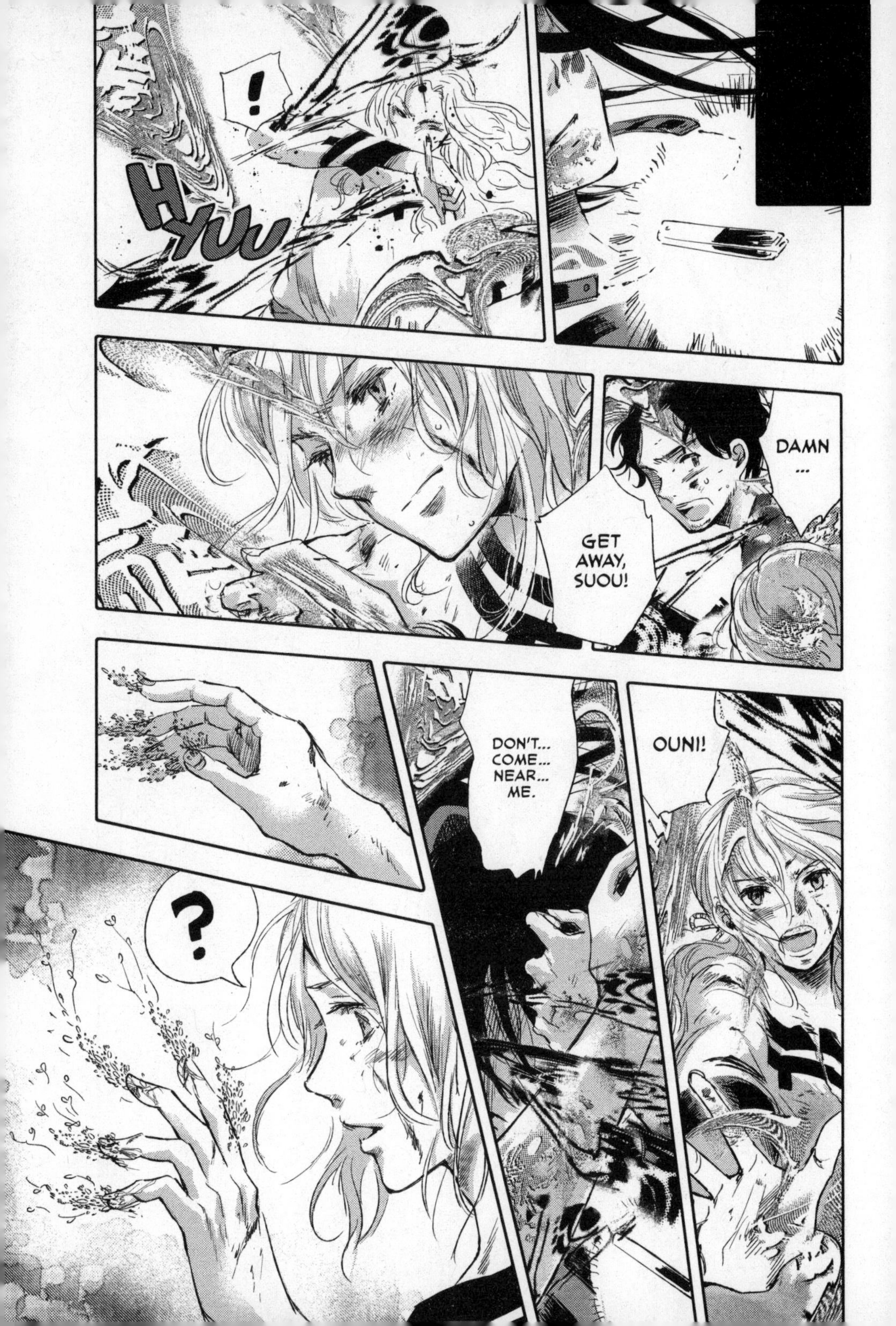
!
HYUU
DAMN...
GET AWAY, SUOU!
OUNI!
DON'T... COME... NEAR... ME.
?

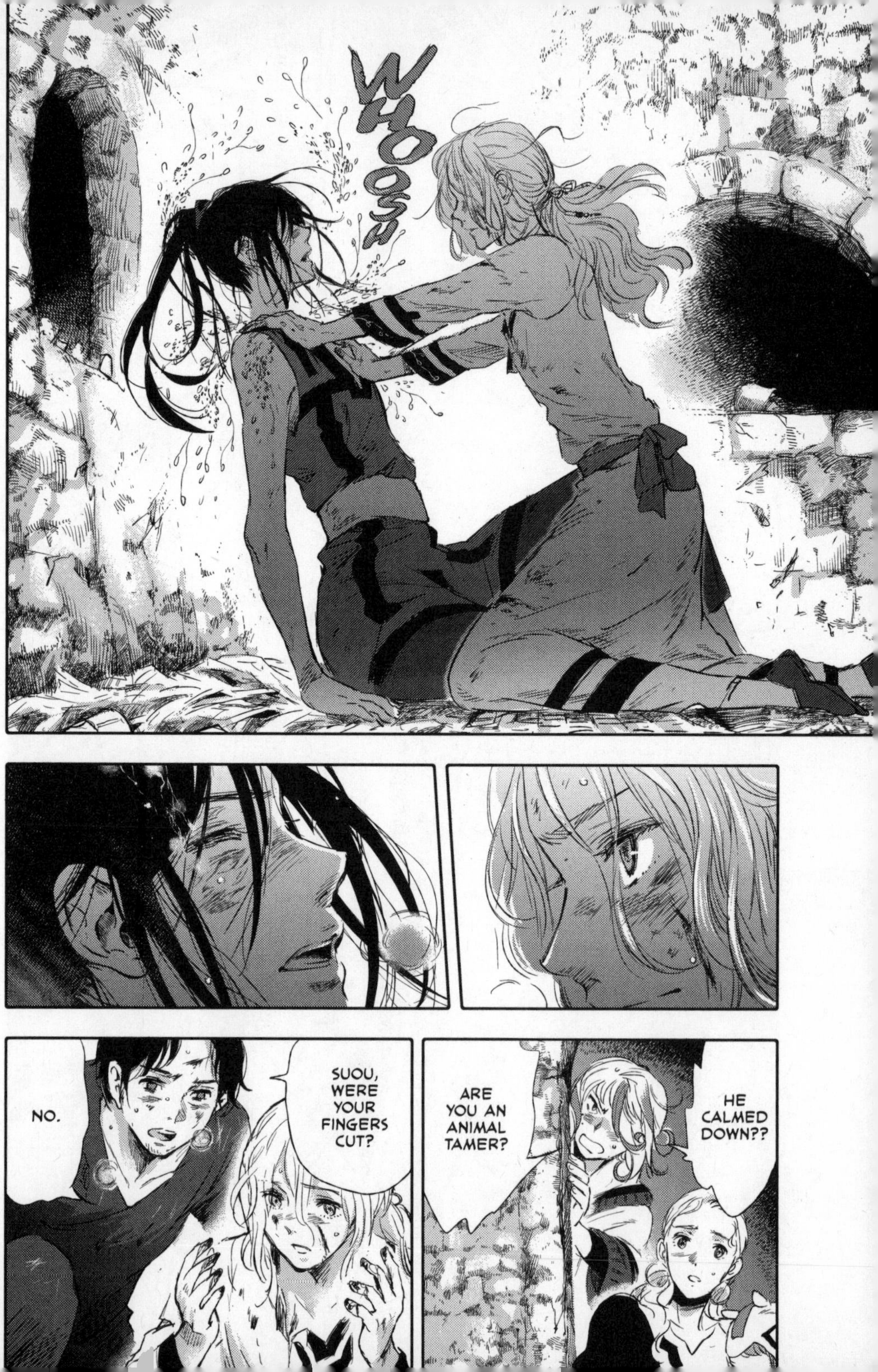
WHOOSH
HE CALMED DOWN??
ARE YOU AN ANIMAL TAMER?
SUOU, WERE YOUR FINGERS CUT?
NO.

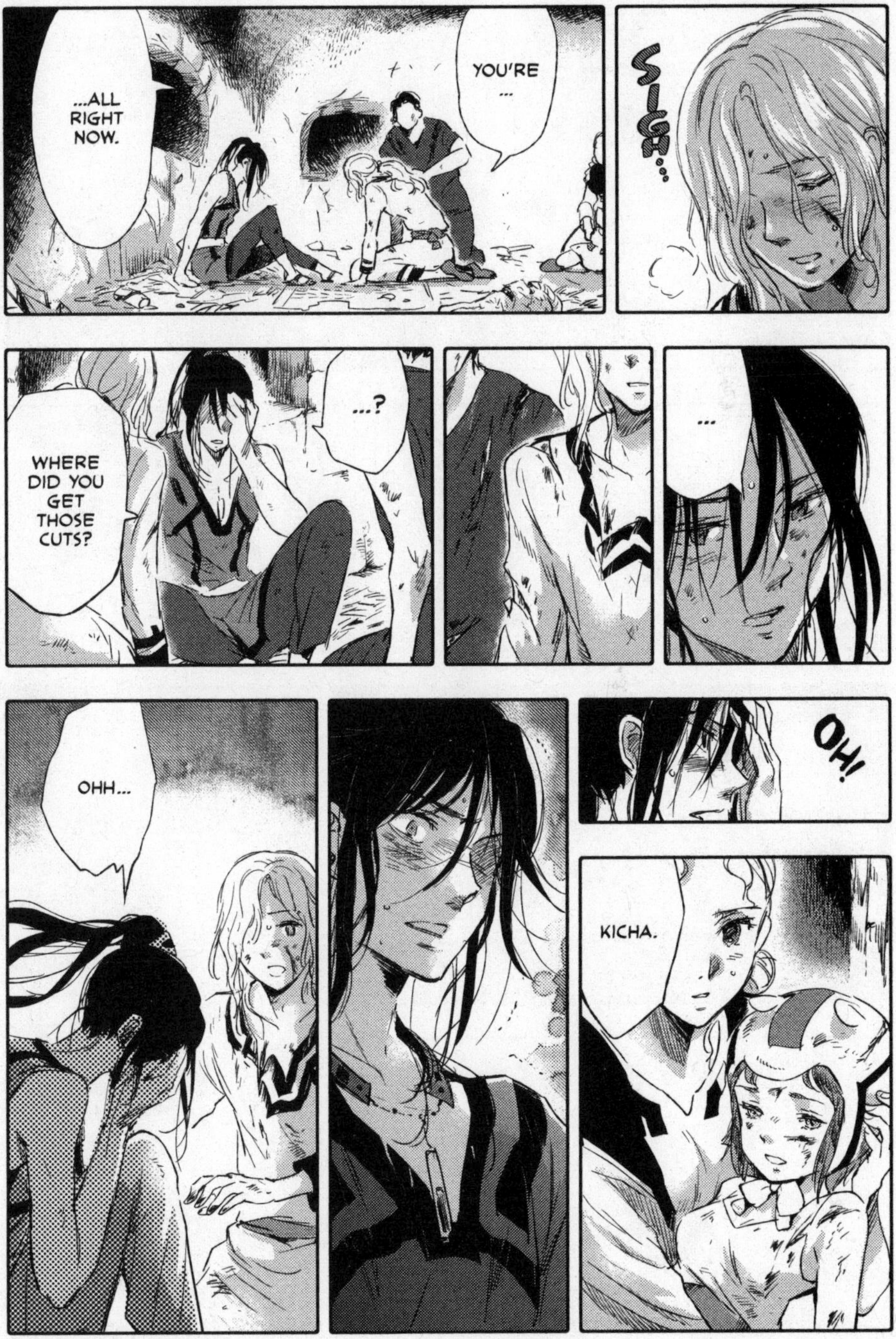
SIGH...
YOU'RE ...
...ALL RIGHT NOW.
...
...?
WHERE DID YOU GET THOSE CUTS?
OH!
KICHA.
OHH...

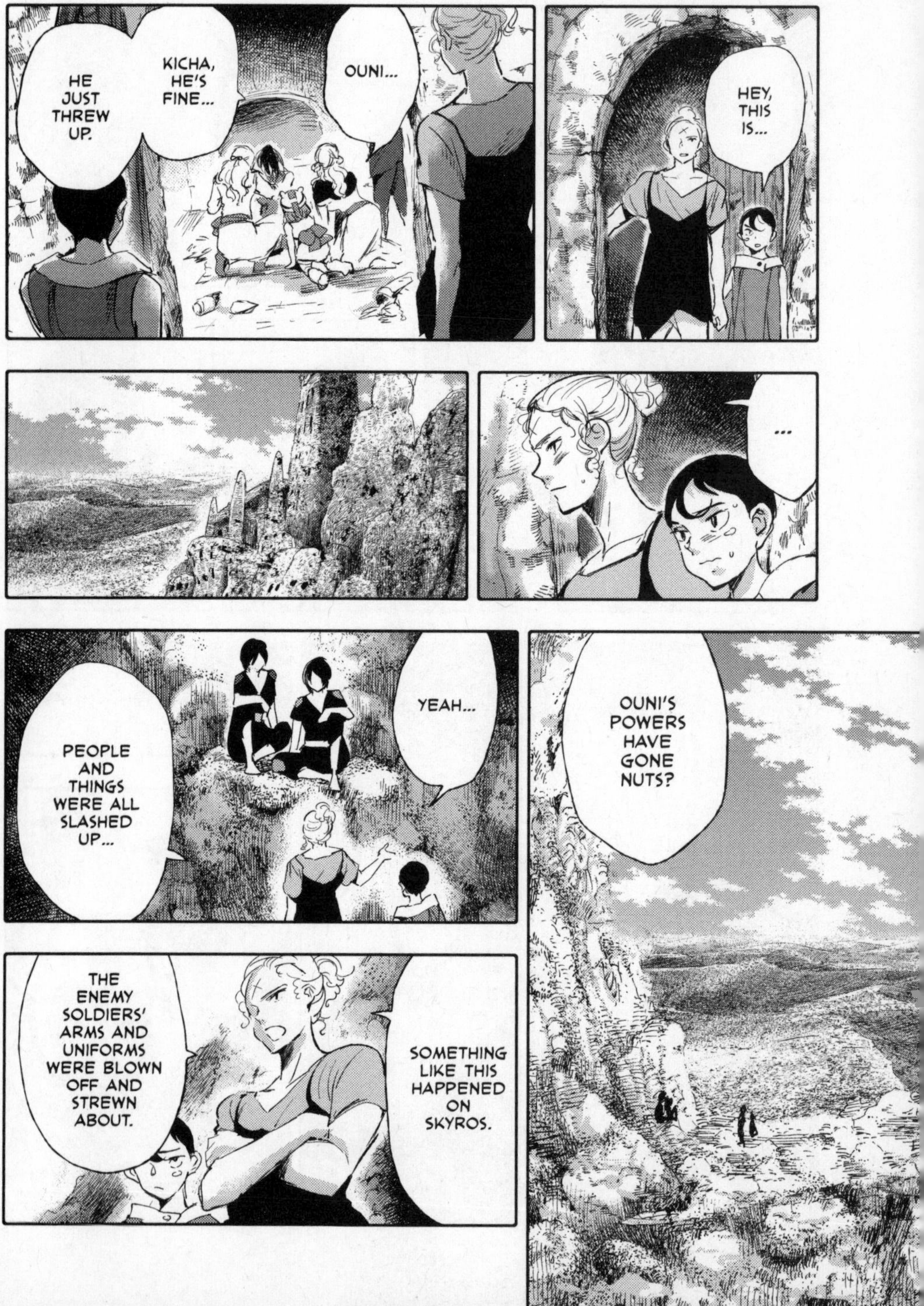
HEY, THIS IS...
OUNI...
KICHA, HE'S FINE...
HE JUST THREW UP.
...
OUNI'S POWERS HAVE GONE NUTS?
YEAH...
PEOPLE AND THINGS WERE ALL SLASHED UP...
SOMETHING LIKE THIS HAPPENED ON SKYROS.
THE ENEMY SOLDIERS' ARMS AND UNIFORMS WERE BLOWN OFF AND STREWN ABOUT.

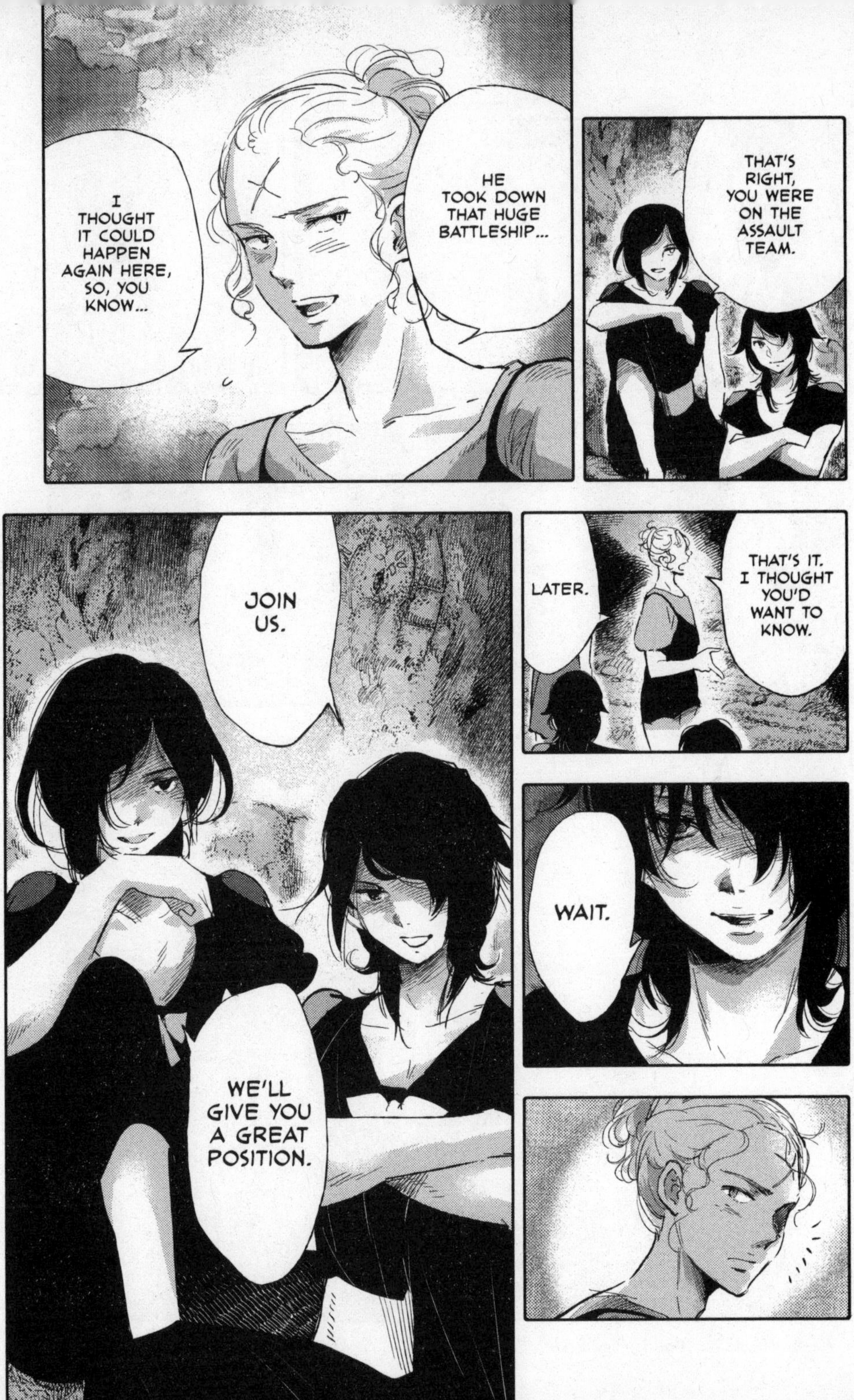
THAT'S RIGHT, YOU WERE ON THE ASSAULT TEAM.
HE TOOK DOWN THAT HUGE BATTLESHIP...
I THOUGHT IT COULD HAPPEN AGAIN HERE, SO, YOU KNOW...
THAT'S IT. I THOUGHT YOU'D WANT TO KNOW.
LATER.
WAIT.
JOIN US.
WE'LL GIVE YOU A GREAT POSITION.

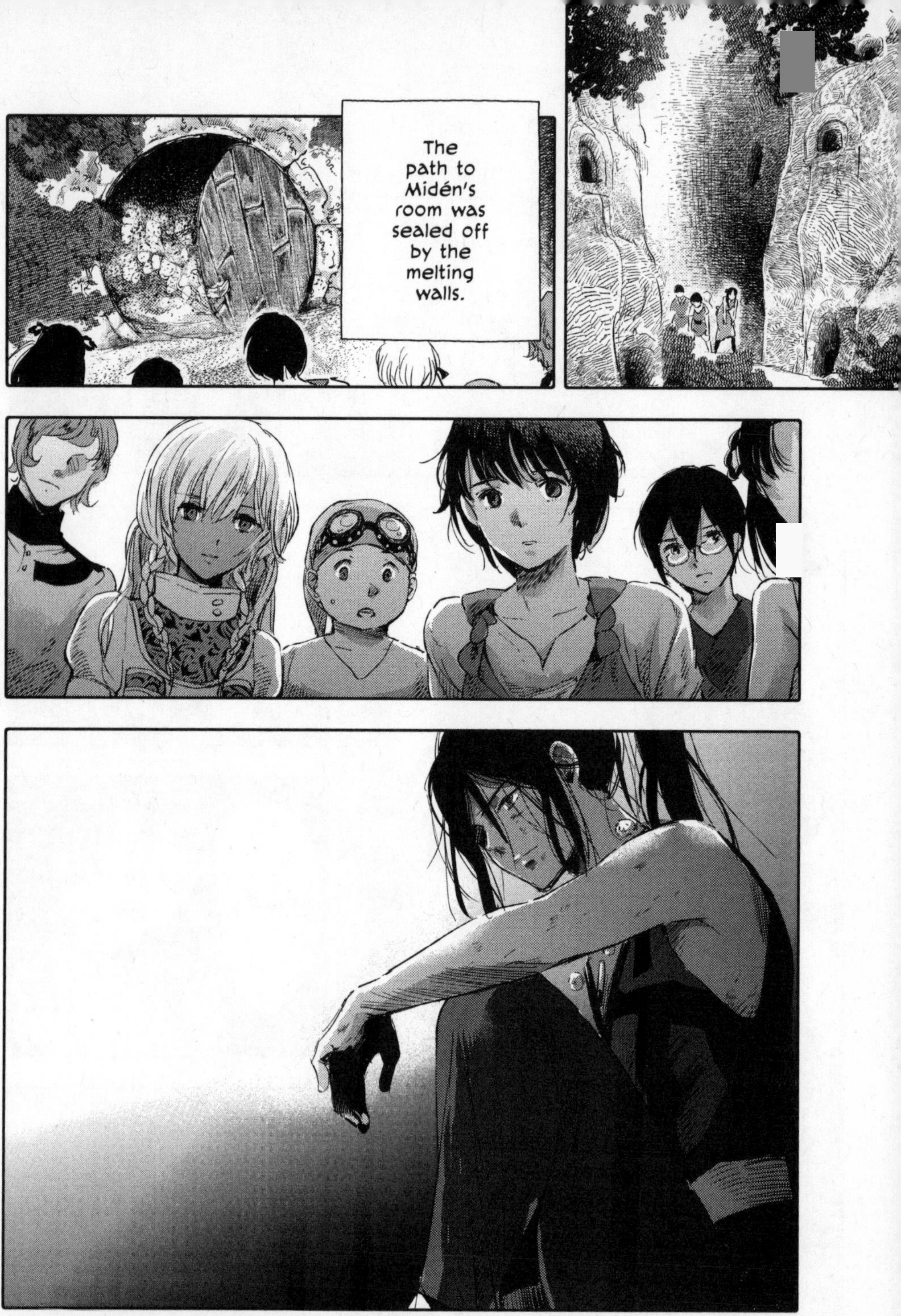
The path to Midén's room was sealed off by the melting walls.

An Inconvenient World -The End-

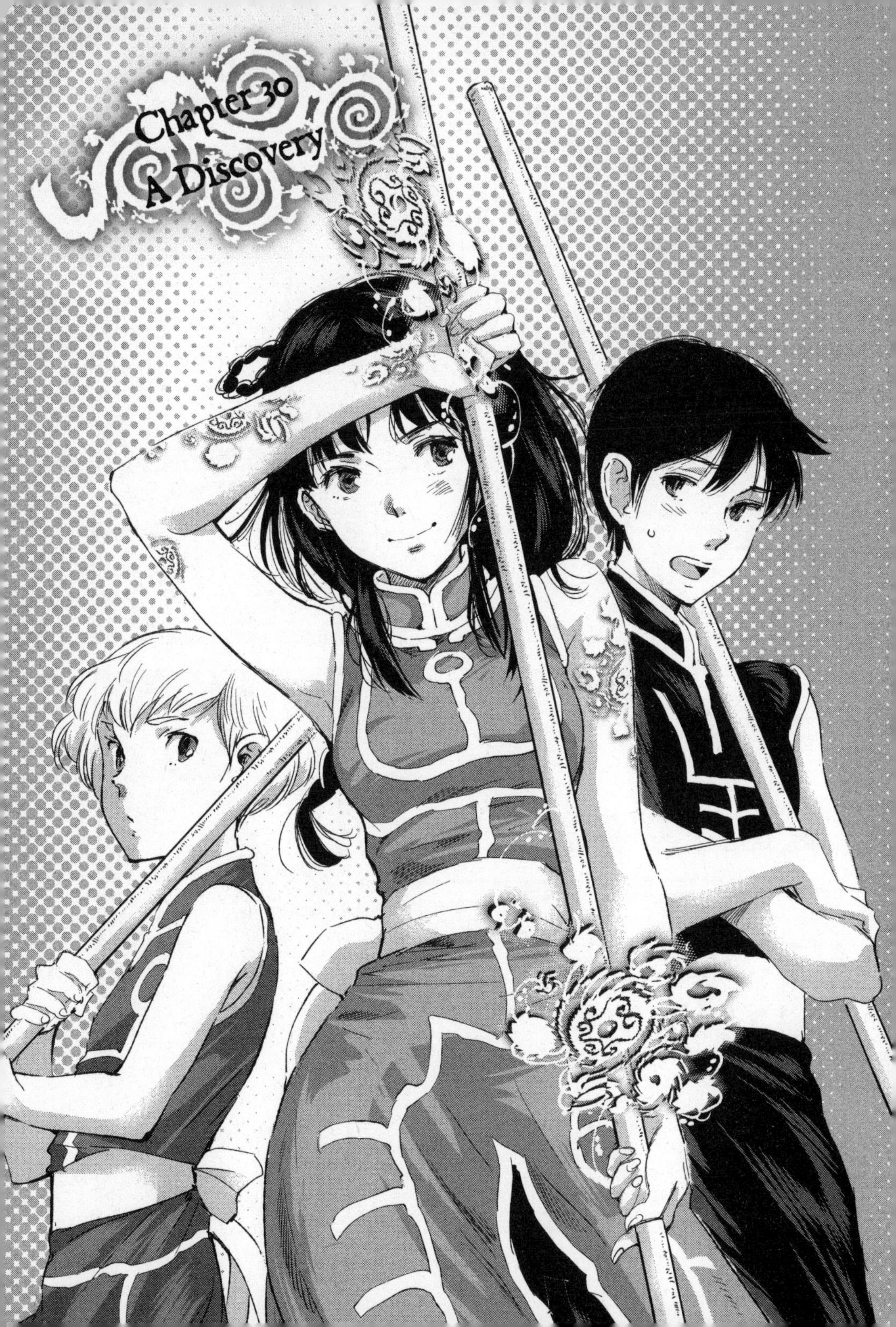
Chapter 30
A Discovery

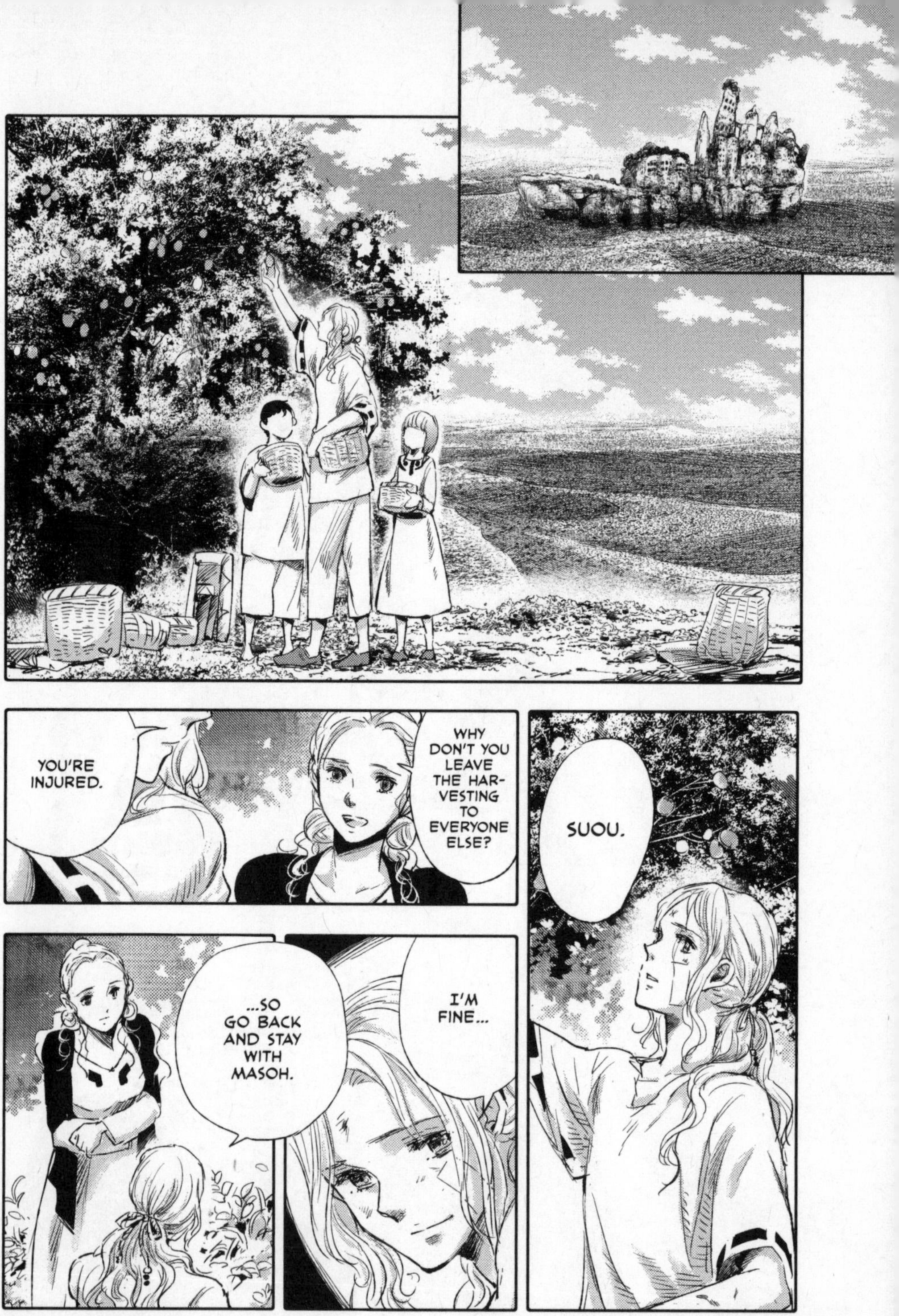
SUOU.
WHY DON'T YOU LEAVE THE HAR-VESTING TO EVERYONE ELSE?
YOU'RE INJURED.
I'M FINE...
...SO GO BACK AND STAY WITH MASOH.

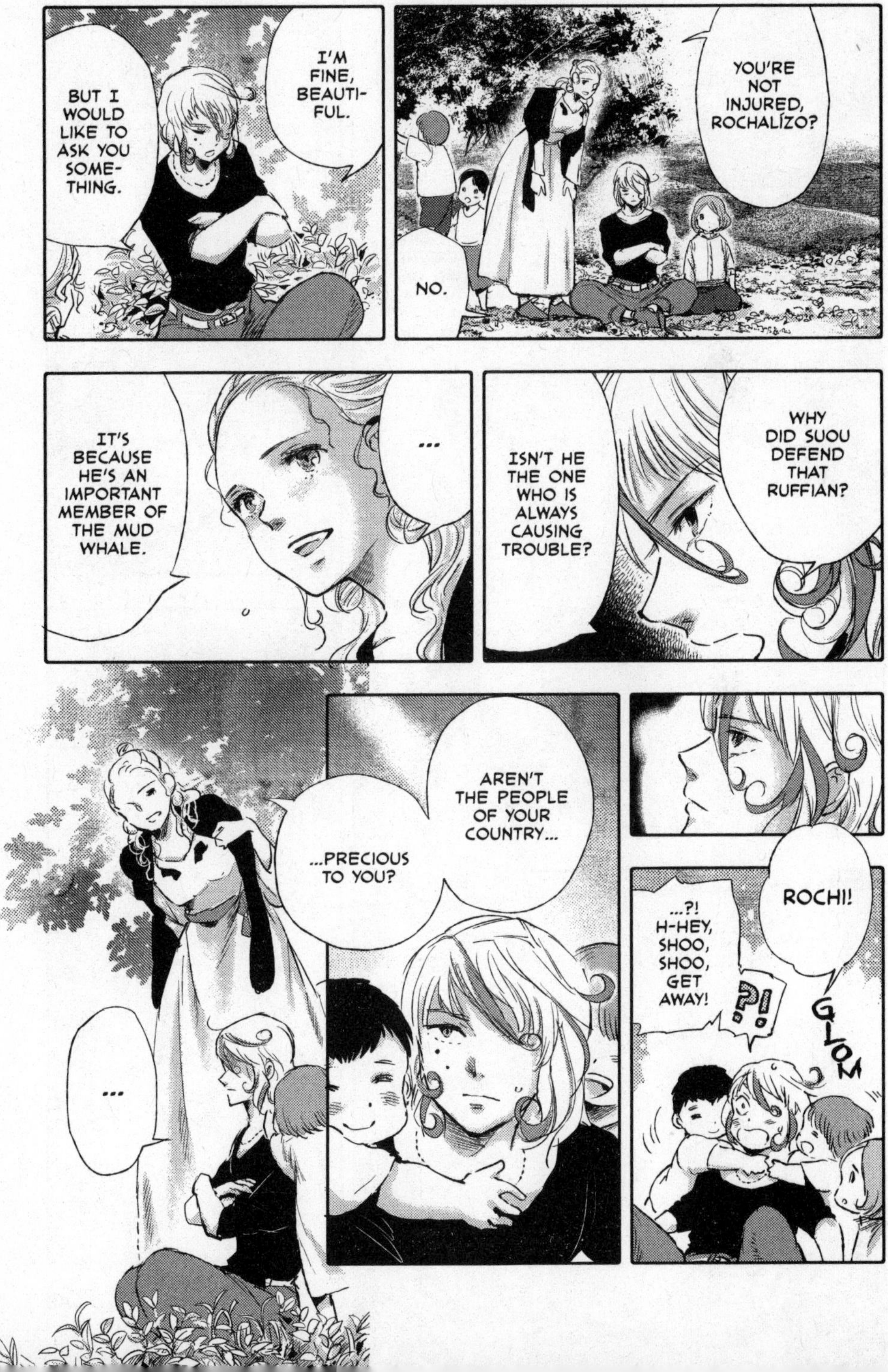
YOU'RE NOT INJURED, ROCHALÍZO?
NO.
I'M FINE, BEAUTIFUL.
BUT I WOULD LIKE TO ASK YOU SOMETHING.
WHY DID SUOU DEFEND THAT RUFFIAN?
ISN'T HE THE ONE WHO IS ALWAYS CAUSING TROUBLE?
...
IT'S BECAUSE HE'S AN IMPORTANT MEMBER OF THE MUD WHALE.
ROCHI!
GLOM
?!
...?! H-HEY, SHOO, SHOO, GET AWAY!
AREN'T THE PEOPLE OF YOUR COUNTRY...
...PRECIOUS TO YOU?
...

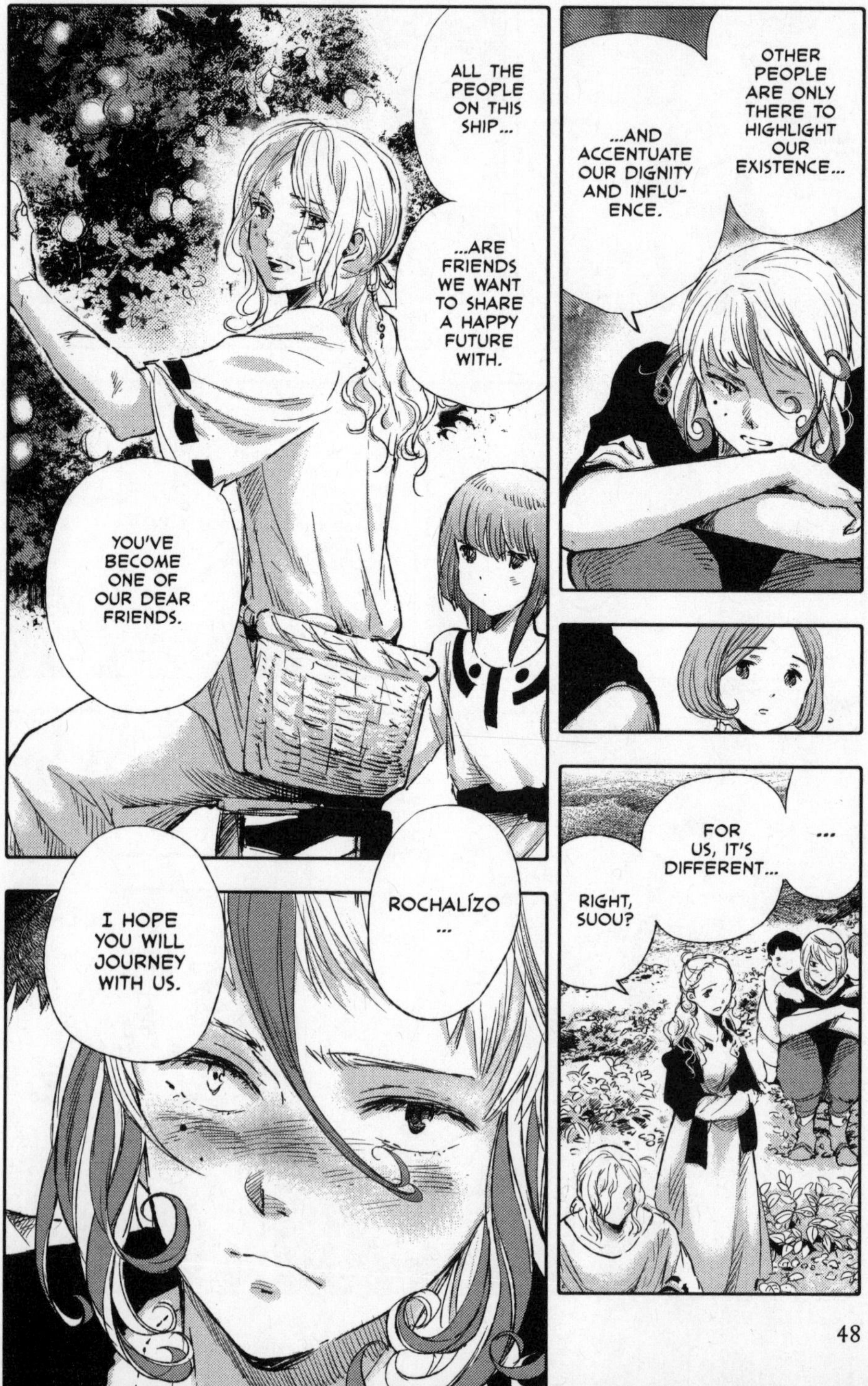
OTHER PEOPLE ARE ONLY THERE TO HIGHLIGHT OUR EXISTENCE...
...AND ACCENTUATE OUR DIGNITY AND INFLU- ENCE.
...
FOR US, IT'S DIFFERENT...
RIGHT, SUOU?
ALL THE PEOPLE ON THIS SHIP...
...ARE FRIENDS WE WANT TO SHARE A HAPPY FUTURE WITH.
YOU'VE BECOME ONE OF OUR DEAR FRIENDS.
ROCHALÍZO ...
I HOPE YOU WILL JOURNEY WITH US.

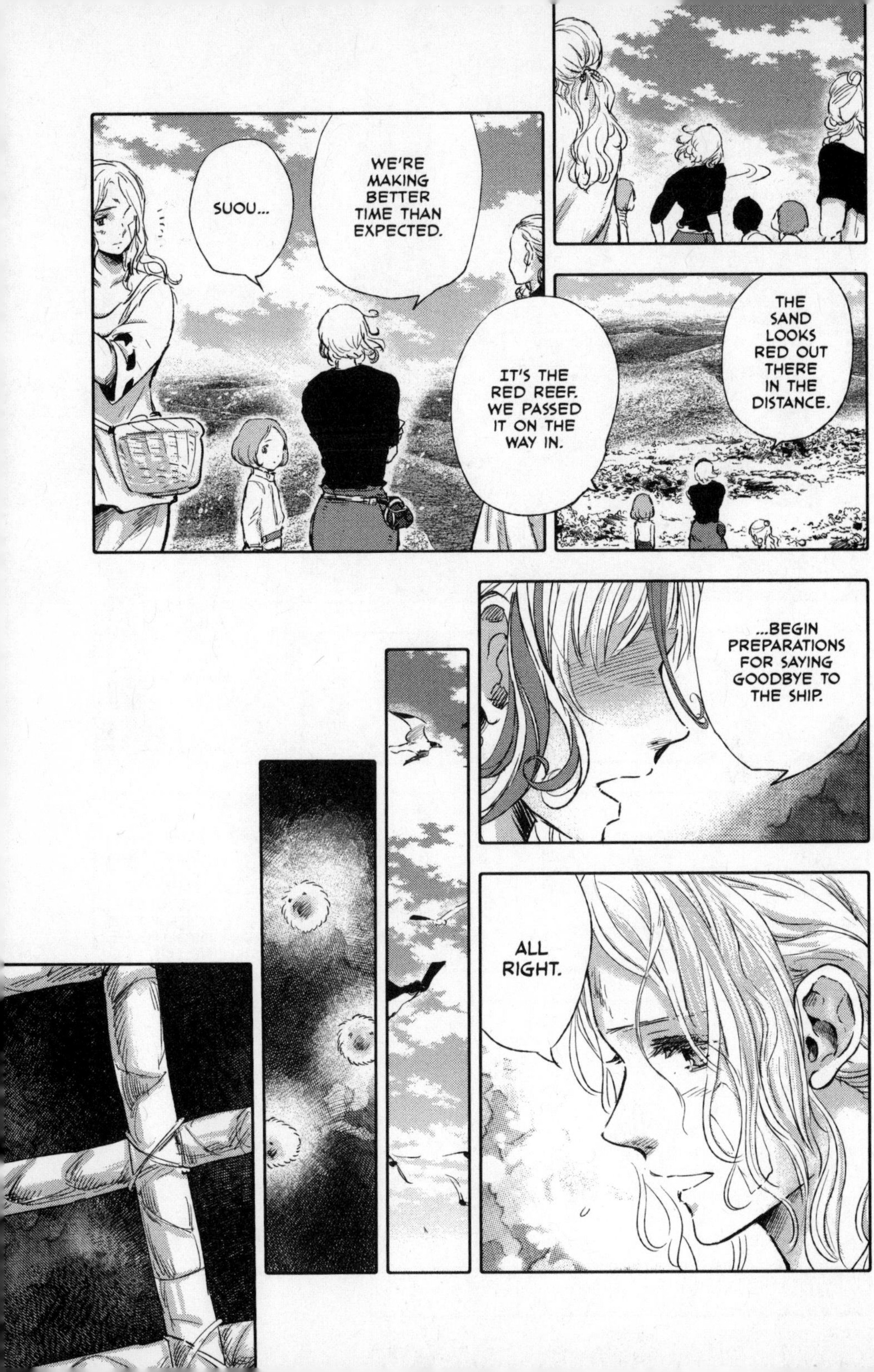
THE SAND LOOKS RED OUT THERE IN THE DISTANCE.
IT'S THE RED REEF. WE PASSED IT ON THE WAY IN.
WE'RE MAKING BETTER TIME THAN EXPECTED.
SUOU...
...BEGIN PREPARATIONS FOR SAYING GOODBYE TO THE SHIP.
ALL RIGHT.

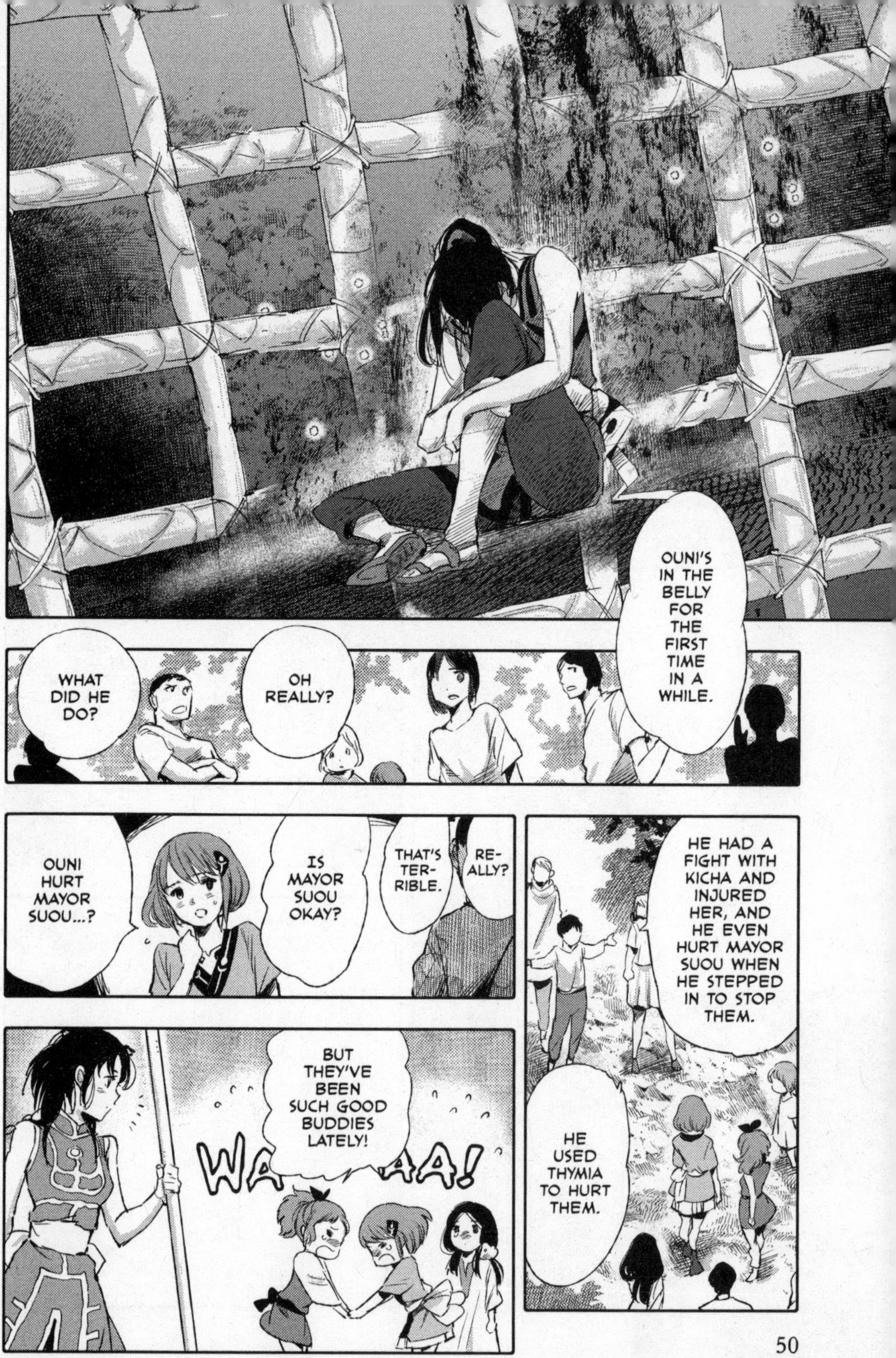

OUNI'S IN THE BELLY FOR THE FIRST TIME IN A WHILE.
OH REALLY?
WHAT DID HE DO?
HE HAD A FIGHT WITH KICHA AND INJURED HER, AND HE EVEN HURT MAYOR SUOU WHEN HE STEPPED IN TO STOP THEM.
HE USED THYMIA TO HURT THEM.
RE-ALLY?
THAT'S TER-RIBLE.
IS MAYOR SUOU OKAY?
OUNI HURT MAYOR SUOU...?
BUT THEY'VE BEEN SUCH GOOD BUDDIES LATELY!
WA AA!

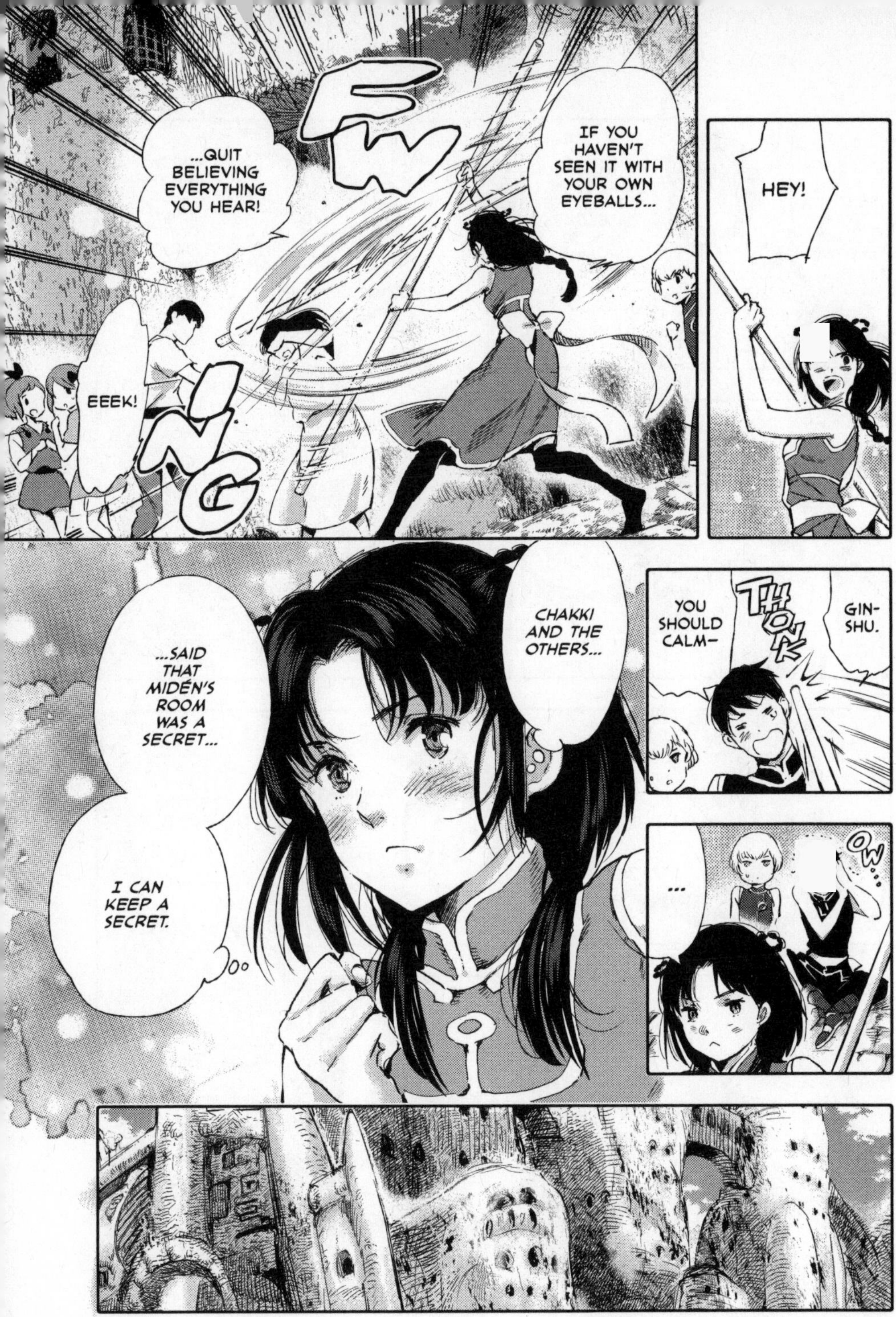
HEY!
IF YOU HAVEN'T SEEN IT WITH YOUR OWN EYEBALLS...
FW
...QUIT BELIEVING EVERYTHING YOU HEAR!
EEEK!
ING
GIN-SHU.
THONK
YOU SHOULD CALM—
OW...
...
CHAKKI AND THE OTHERS...
...SAID THAT MIDÉN'S ROOM WAS A SECRET...
I CAN KEEP A SECRET.

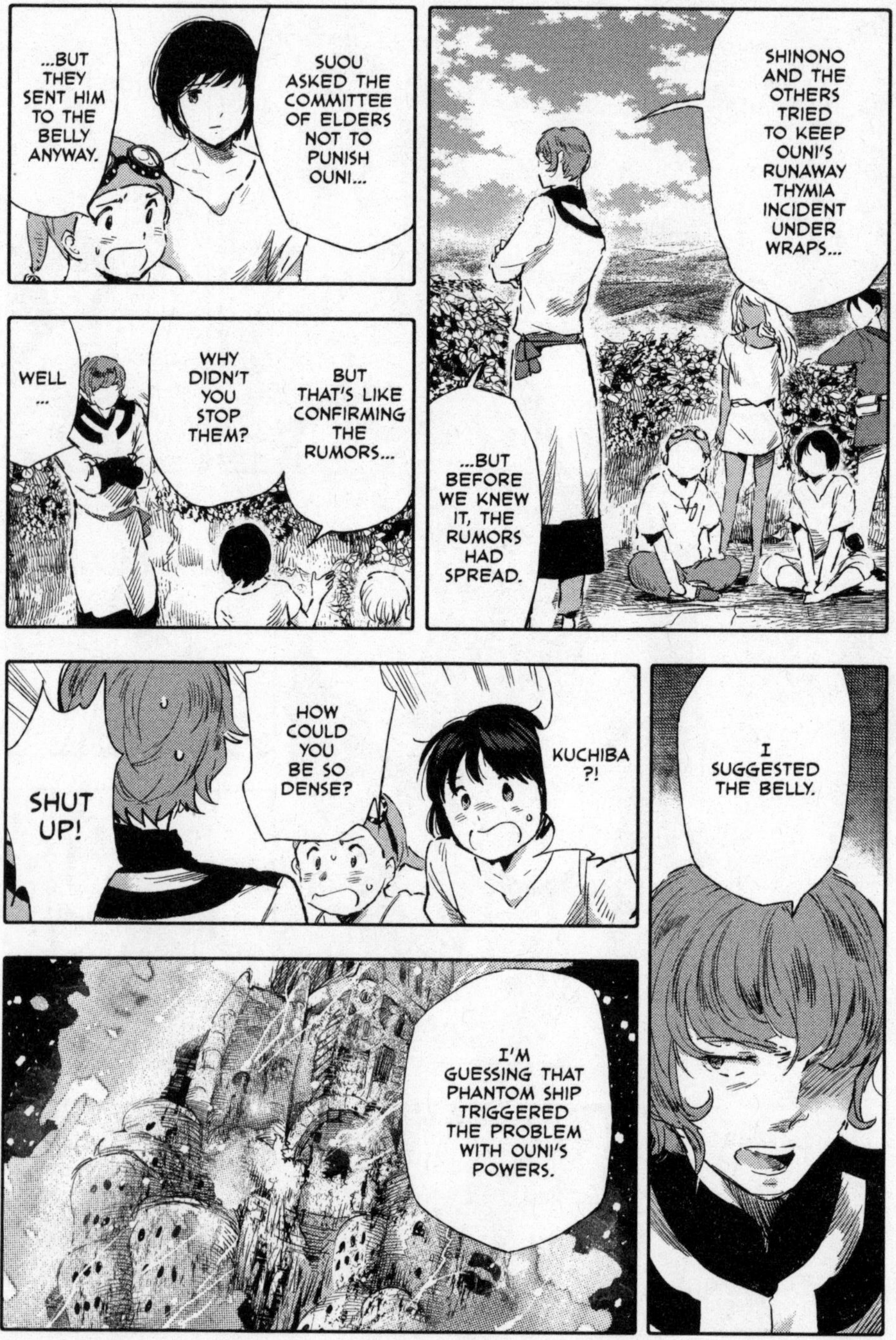
SHINONO AND THE OTHERS TRIED TO KEEP OUNI'S RUNAWAY THYMIA INCIDENT UNDER WRAPS...
...BUT BEFORE WE KNEW IT, THE RUMORS HAD SPREAD.
SUOU ASKED THE COMMITTEE OF ELDERS NOT TO PUNISH OUNI...
...BUT THEY SENT HIM TO THE BELLY ANYWAY.
BUT THAT'S LIKE CONFIRMING THE RUMORS...
WHY DIDN'T YOU STOP THEM?
WELL ...
I SUGGESTED THE BELLY.
KUCHIBA ?!
HOW COULD YOU BE SO DENSE?
SHUT UP!
I'M GUESSING THAT PHANTOM SHIP TRIGGERED THE PROBLEM WITH OUNI'S POWERS.

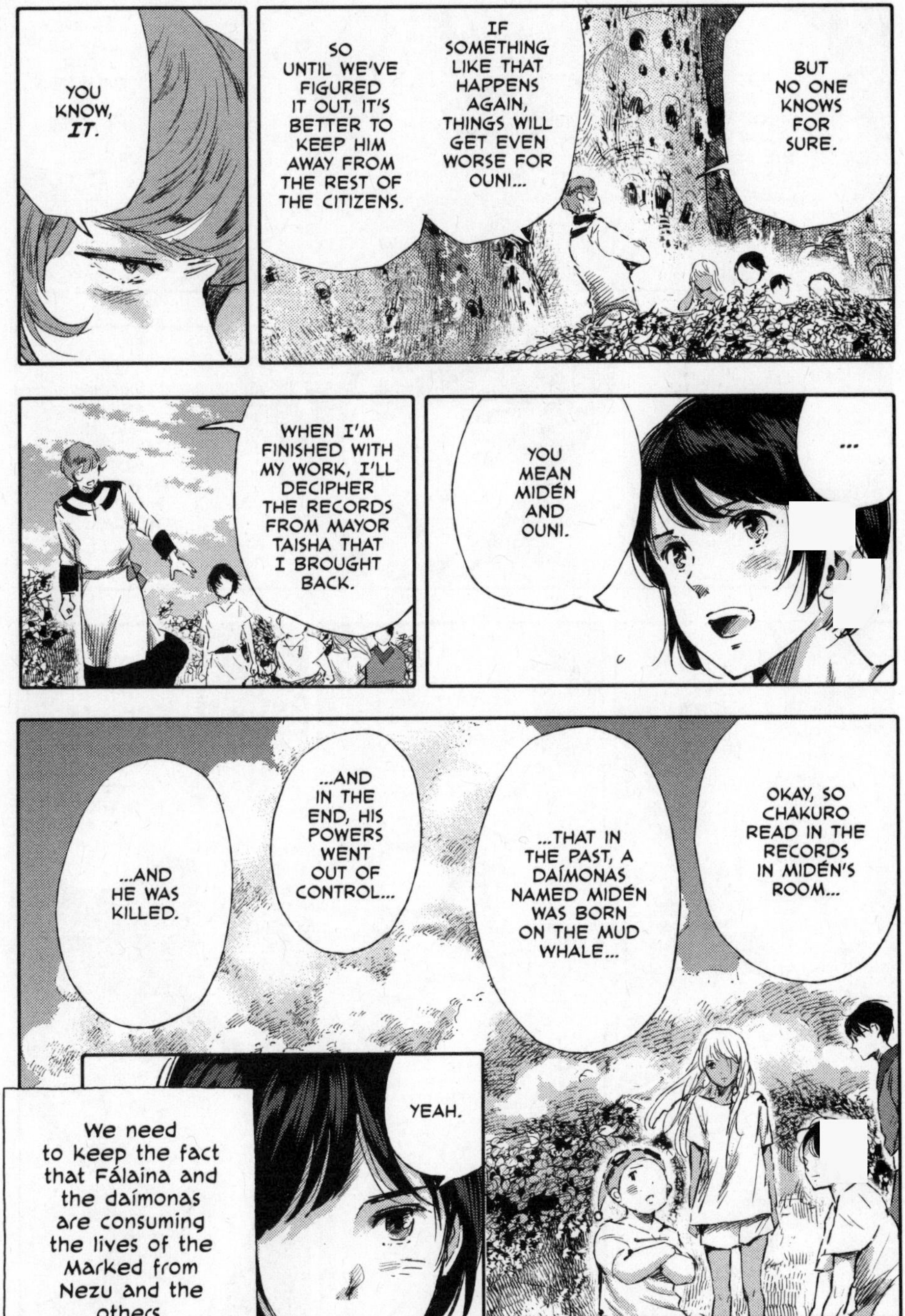
BUT NO ONE KNOWS FOR SURE.
IF SOMETHING LIKE THAT HAPPENS AGAIN, THINGS WILL GET EVEN WORSE FOR OUNI...
SO UNTIL WE'VE FIGURED IT OUT, IT'S BETTER TO KEEP HIM AWAY FROM THE REST OF THE CITIZENS.
YOU KNOW, *IT*.
...
YOU MEAN MIDÉN AND OUNI.
WHEN I'M FINISHED WITH MY WORK, I'LL DECIPHER THE RECORDS FROM MAYOR TAISHA THAT I BROUGHT BACK.
OKAY, SO CHAKURO READ IN THE RECORDS IN MIDÉN'S ROOM...
...THAT IN THE PAST, A DAÍMONAS NAMED MIDÉN WAS BORN ON THE MUD WHALE...
...AND IN THE END, HIS POWERS WENT OUT OF CONTROL...
...AND HE WAS KILLED.
YEAH.
We need to keep the fact that Fálaina and the daímonas are consuming the lives of the Marked from Nezu and the others.

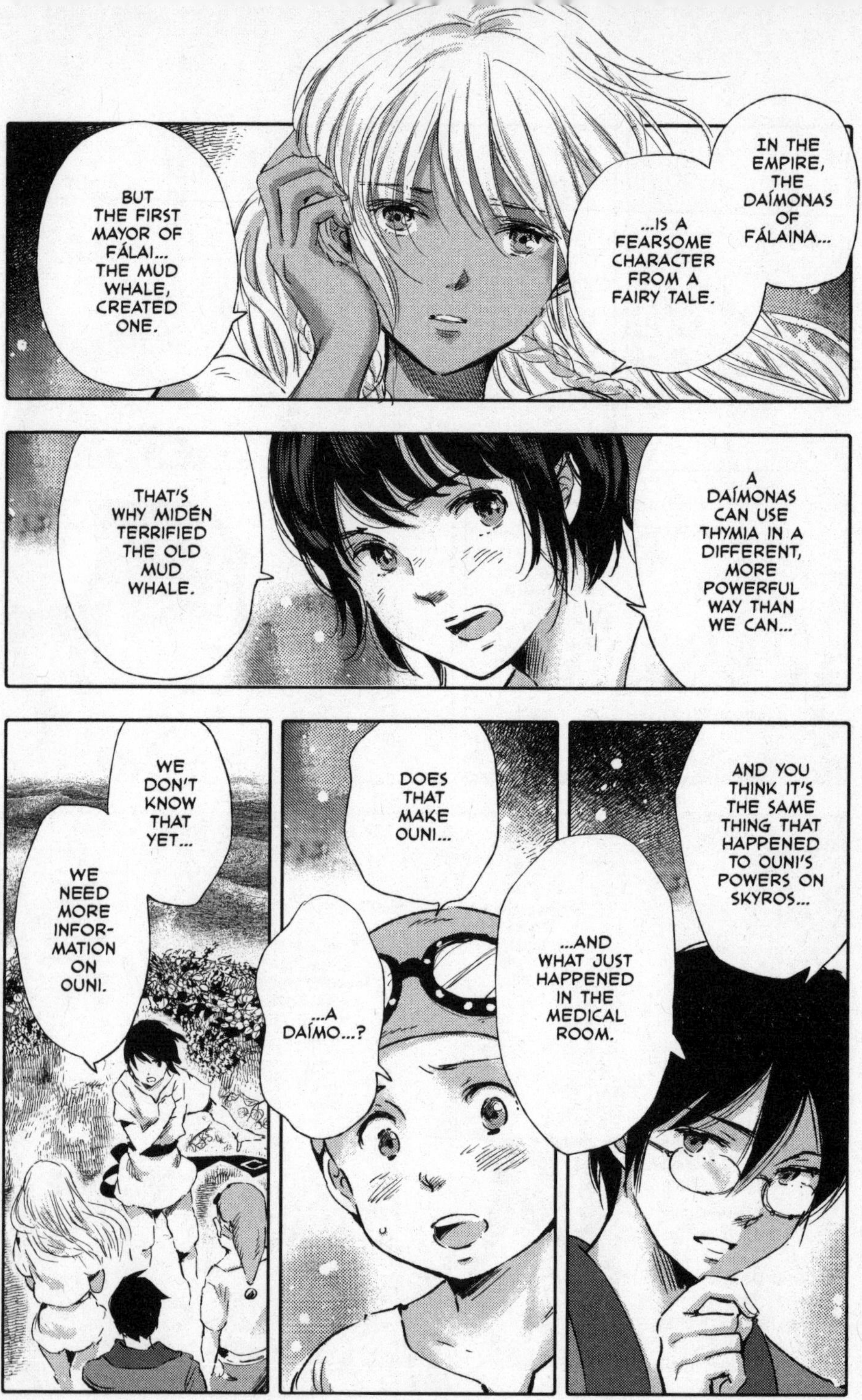
IN THE EMPIRE, THE DAÍMONAS OF FÁLAINA...
...IS A FEARSOME CHARACTER FROM A FAIRY TALE.
BUT THE FIRST MAYOR OF FÁLAI... THE MUD WHALE, CREATED ONE.
A DAÍMONAS CAN USE THYMIA IN A DIFFERENT, MORE POWERFUL WAY THAN WE CAN...
THAT'S WHY MIDÉN TERRIFIED THE OLD MUD WHALE.
AND YOU THINK IT'S THE SAME THING THAT HAPPENED TO OUNI'S POWERS ON SKYROS...
...AND WHAT JUST HAPPENED IN THE MEDICAL ROOM.
DOES THAT MAKE OUNI...
...A DAÍMO...?
WE DON'T KNOW THAT YET...
WE NEED MORE INFOR-MATION ON OUNI.

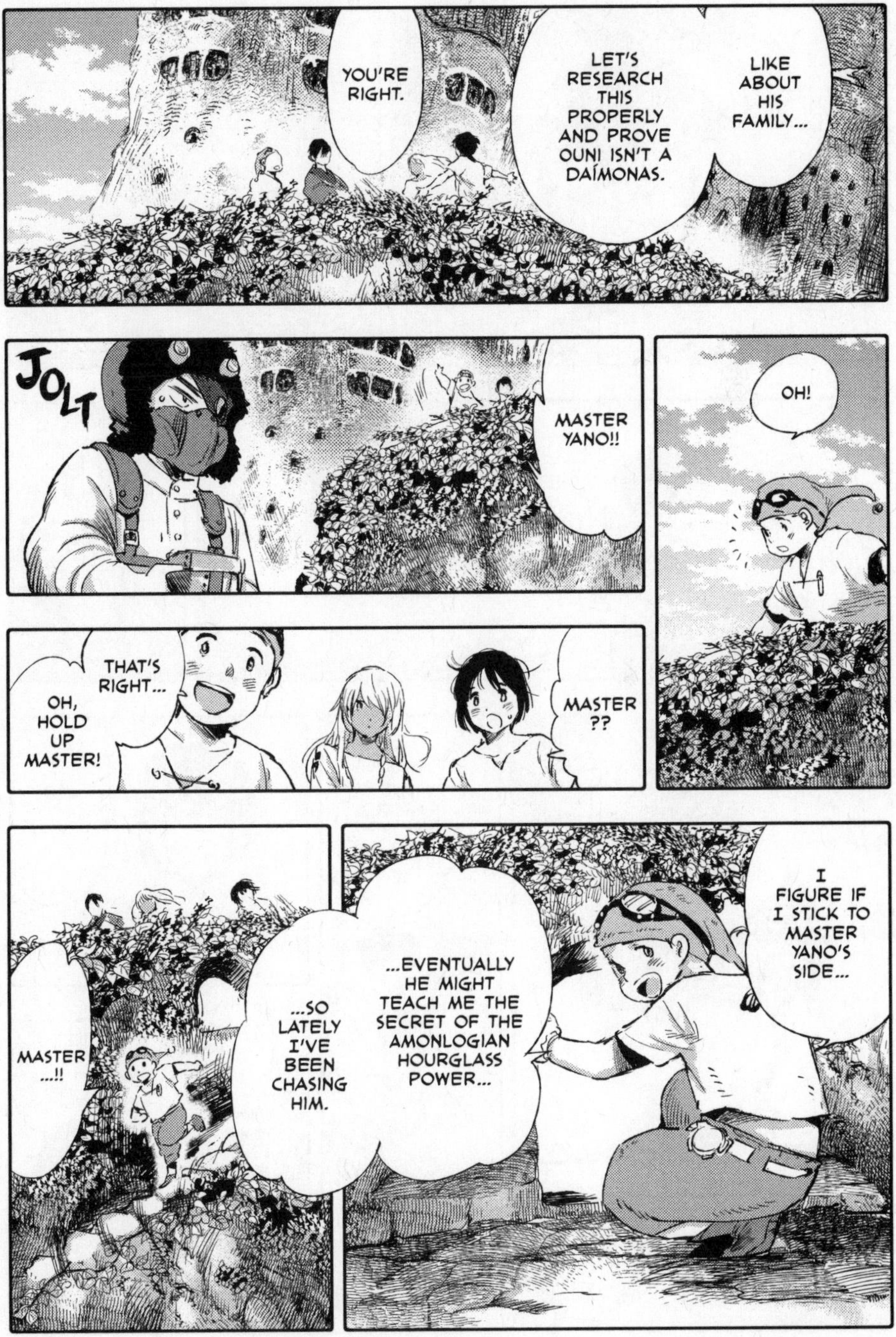

LET'S RESEARCH THIS PROPERLY AND PROVE OUNI ISN'T A DAÍMONAS.
LIKE ABOUT HIS FAMILY...
YOU'RE RIGHT.
OH!
MASTER YANO!!
JOLT
MASTER ??
THAT'S RIGHT...
OH, HOLD UP MASTER!
I FIGURE IF I STICK TO MASTER YANO'S SIDE...
...EVENTUALLY HE MIGHT TEACH ME THE SECRET OF THE AMONLOGIAN HOURGLASS POWER...
...SO LATELY I'VE BEEN CHASING HIM.
MASTER ...!!

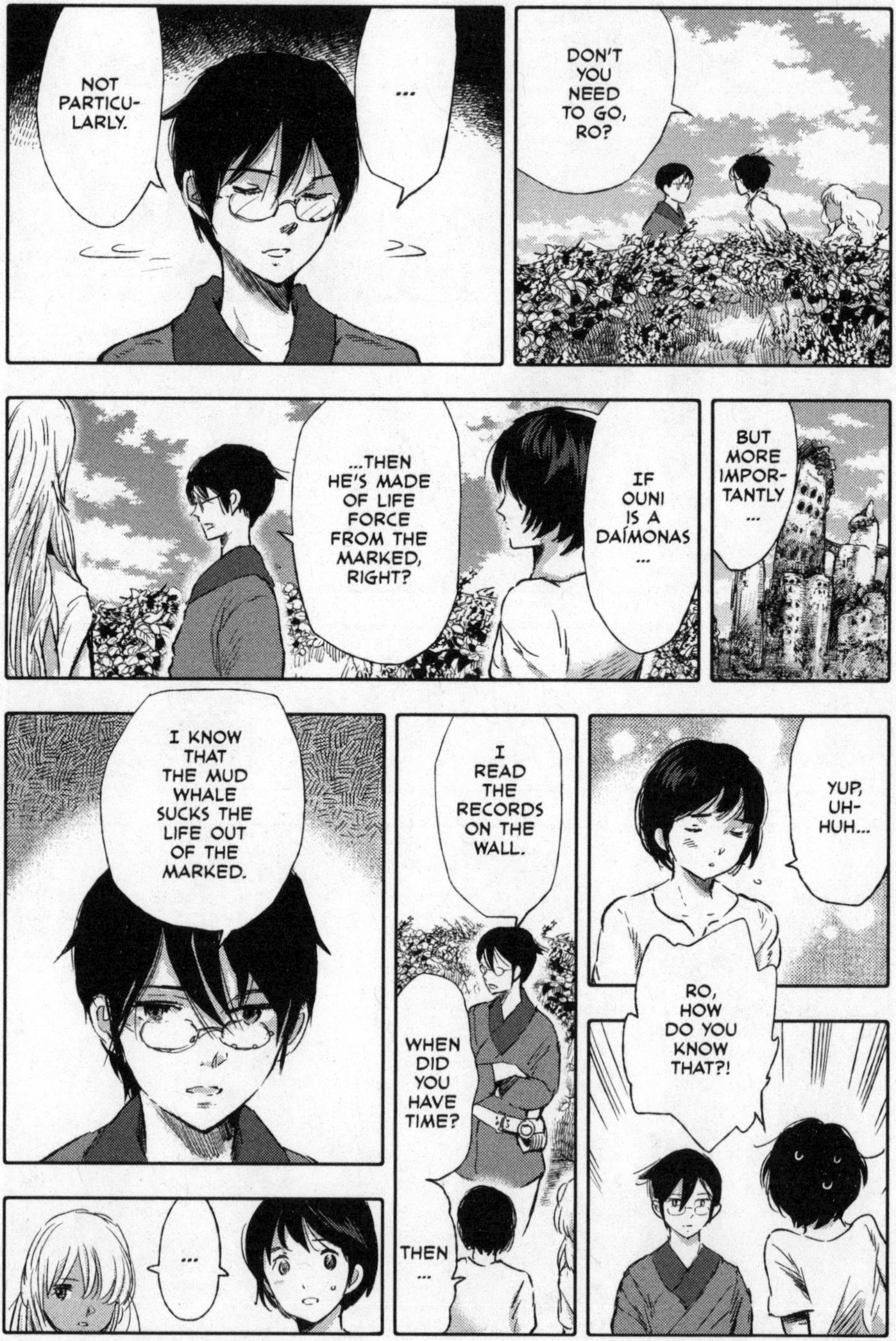
DON'T YOU NEED TO GO, RO?
...
NOT PARTICULARLY.
BUT MORE IMPORTANTLY ...
IF OUNI IS A DAÍMONAS ...
...THEN HE'S MADE OF LIFE FORCE FROM THE MARKED, RIGHT?
YUP, UH-HUH...
RO, HOW DO YOU KNOW THAT?!
I READ THE RECORDS ON THE WALL.
WHEN DID YOU HAVE TIME?
THEN ...
I KNOW THAT THE MUD WHALE SUCKS THE LIFE OUT OF THE MARKED.
...

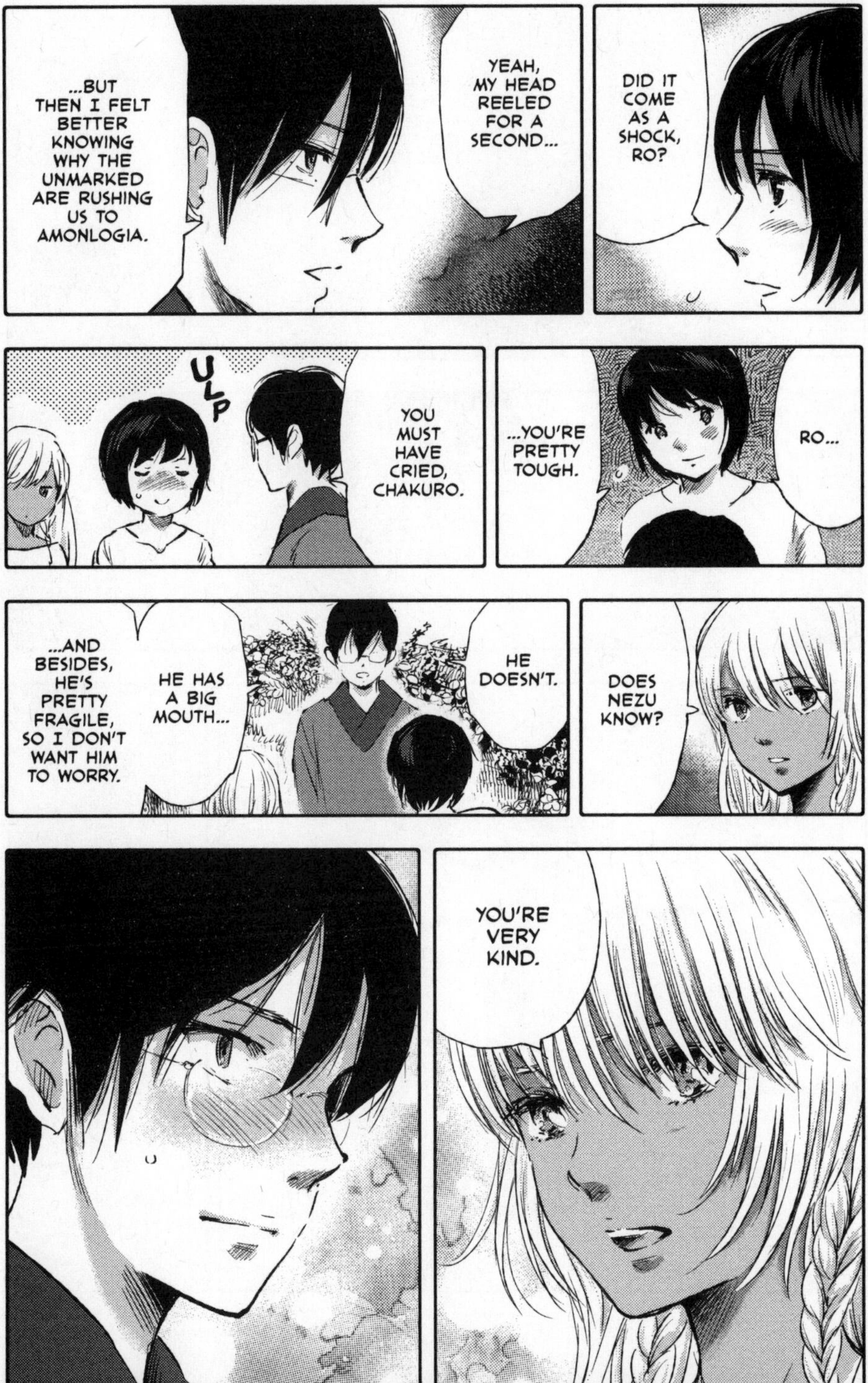
DID IT COME AS A SHOCK, RO?
YEAH, MY HEAD REELED FOR A SECOND...
...BUT THEN I FELT BETTER KNOWING WHY THE UNMARKED ARE RUSHING US TO AMONLOGIA.
RO...
...YOU'RE PRETTY TOUGH.
YOU MUST HAVE CRIED, CHAKURO.
ULP
DOES NEZU KNOW?
HE DOESN'T.
HE HAS A BIG MOUTH...
...AND BESIDES, HE'S PRETTY FRAGILE, SO I DON'T WANT HIM TO WORRY.
YOU'RE VERY KIND.

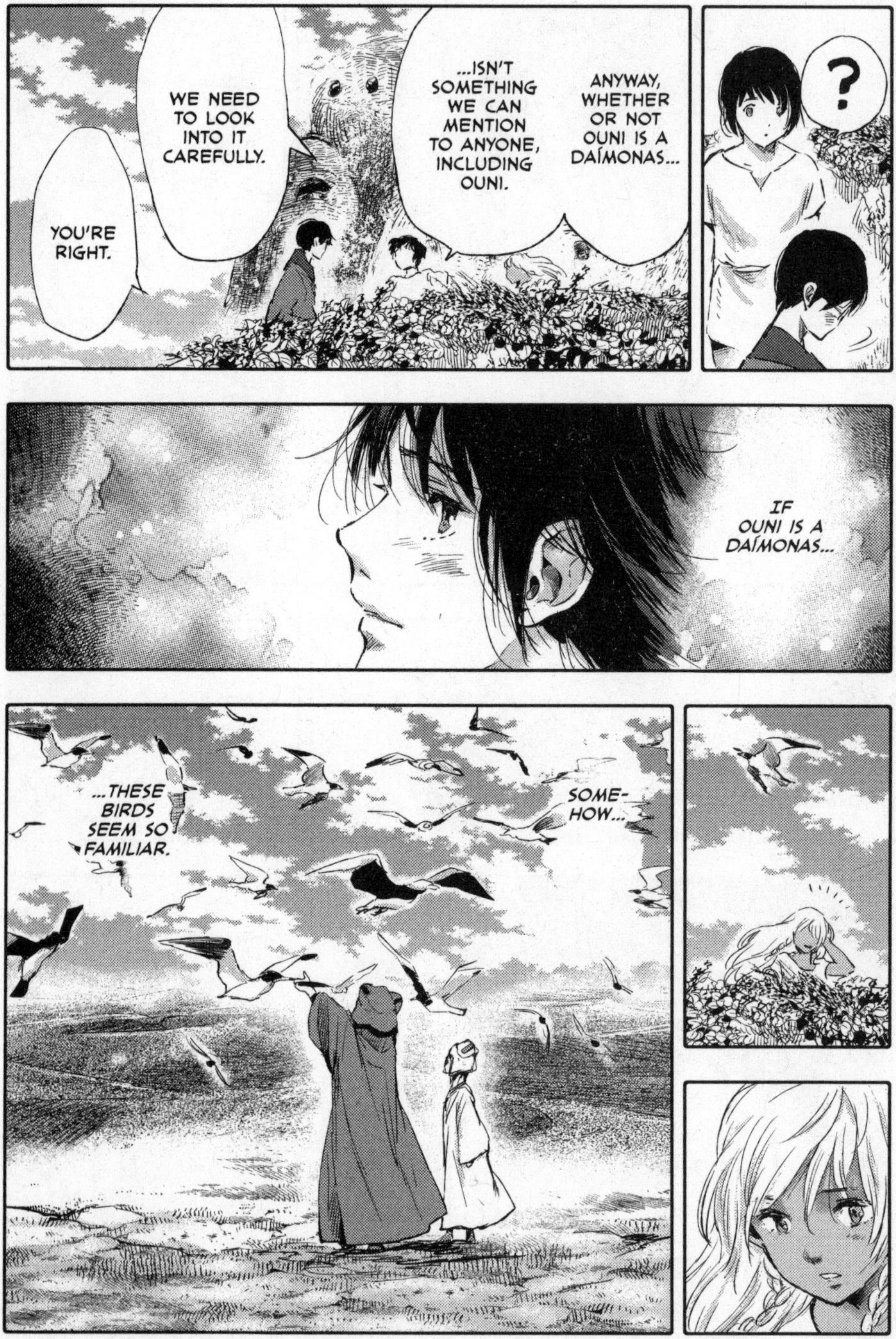
?
ANYWAY, WHETHER OR NOT OUNI IS A DAÍMONAS...
...ISN'T SOMETHING WE CAN MENTION TO ANYONE, INCLUDING OUNI.
WE NEED TO LOOK INTO IT CAREFULLY.
YOU'RE RIGHT.
IF OUNI IS A DAÍMONAS...
SOME-HOW...
...THESE BIRDS SEEM SO FAMILIAR.

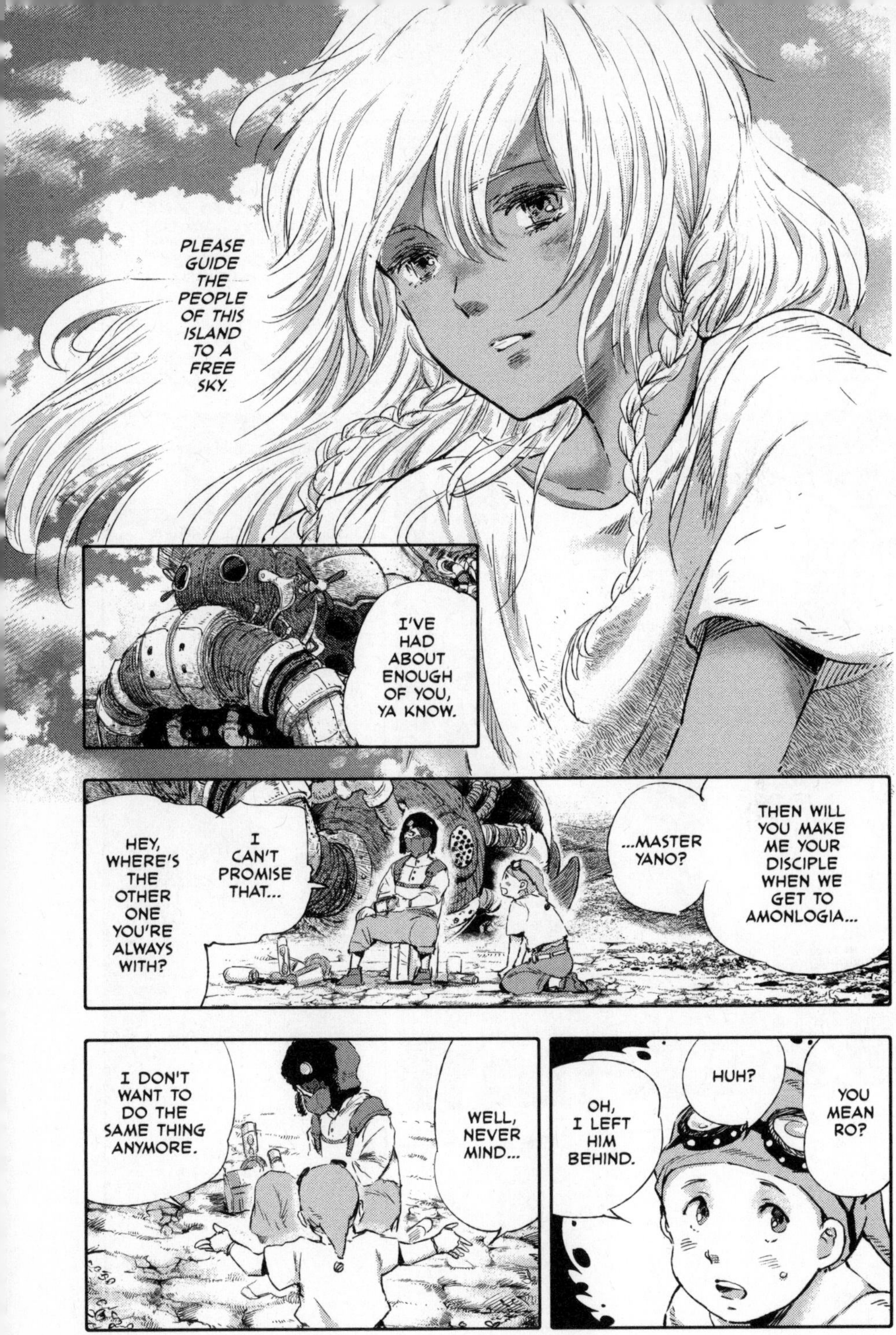
PLEASE GUIDE THE PEOPLE OF THIS ISLAND TO A FREE SKY.
I'VE HAD ABOUT ENOUGH OF YOU, YA KNOW.
THEN WILL YOU MAKE ME YOUR DISCIPLE WHEN WE GET TO AMONLOGIA...
...MASTER YANO?
I CAN'T PROMISE THAT...
HEY, WHERE'S THE OTHER ONE YOU'RE ALWAYS WITH?
HUH?
YOU MEAN RO?
OH, I LEFT HIM BEHIND.
WELL, NEVER MIND...
I DON'T WANT TO DO THE SAME THING ANYMORE.

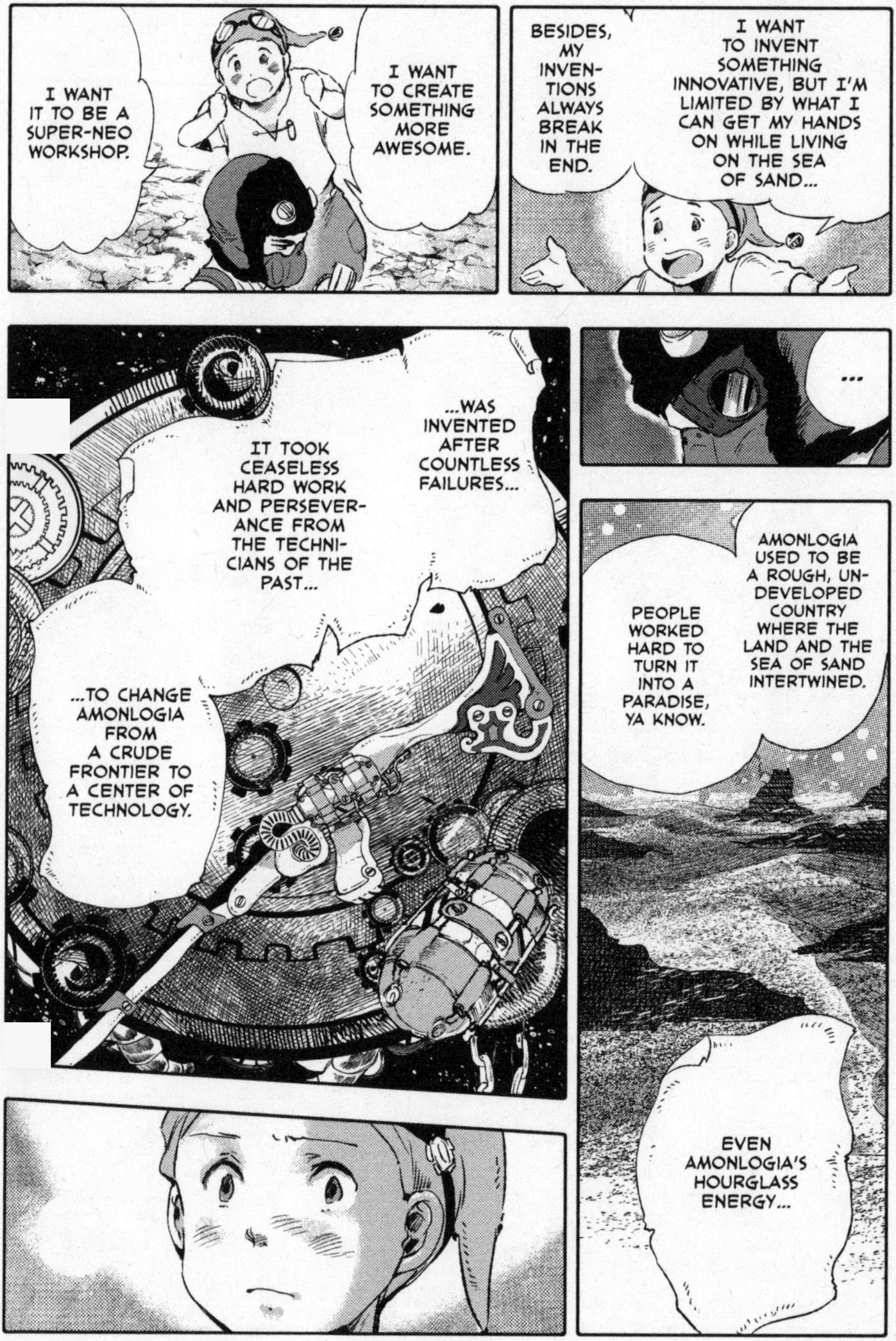
I WANT TO INVENT SOMETHING INNOVATIVE, BUT I'M LIMITED BY WHAT I CAN GET MY HANDS ON WHILE LIVING ON THE SEA OF SAND...
BESIDES, MY INVEN-TIONS ALWAYS BREAK IN THE END.
I WANT TO CREATE SOMETHING MORE AWESOME.
I WANT IT TO BE A SUPER-NEO WORKSHOP.
...
AMONLOGIA USED TO BE A ROUGH, UN-DEVELOPED COUNTRY WHERE THE LAND AND THE SEA OF SAND INTERTWINED.
PEOPLE WORKED HARD TO TURN IT INTO A PARADISE, YA KNOW.
EVEN AMONLOGIA'S HOURGLASS ENERGY...
...WAS INVENTED AFTER COUNTLESS FAILURES...
IT TOOK CEASELESS HARD WORK AND PERSEVER-ANCE FROM THE TECHNI-CIANS OF THE PAST...
...TO CHANGE AMONLOGIA FROM A CRUDE FRONTIER TO A CENTER OF TECHNOLOGY.

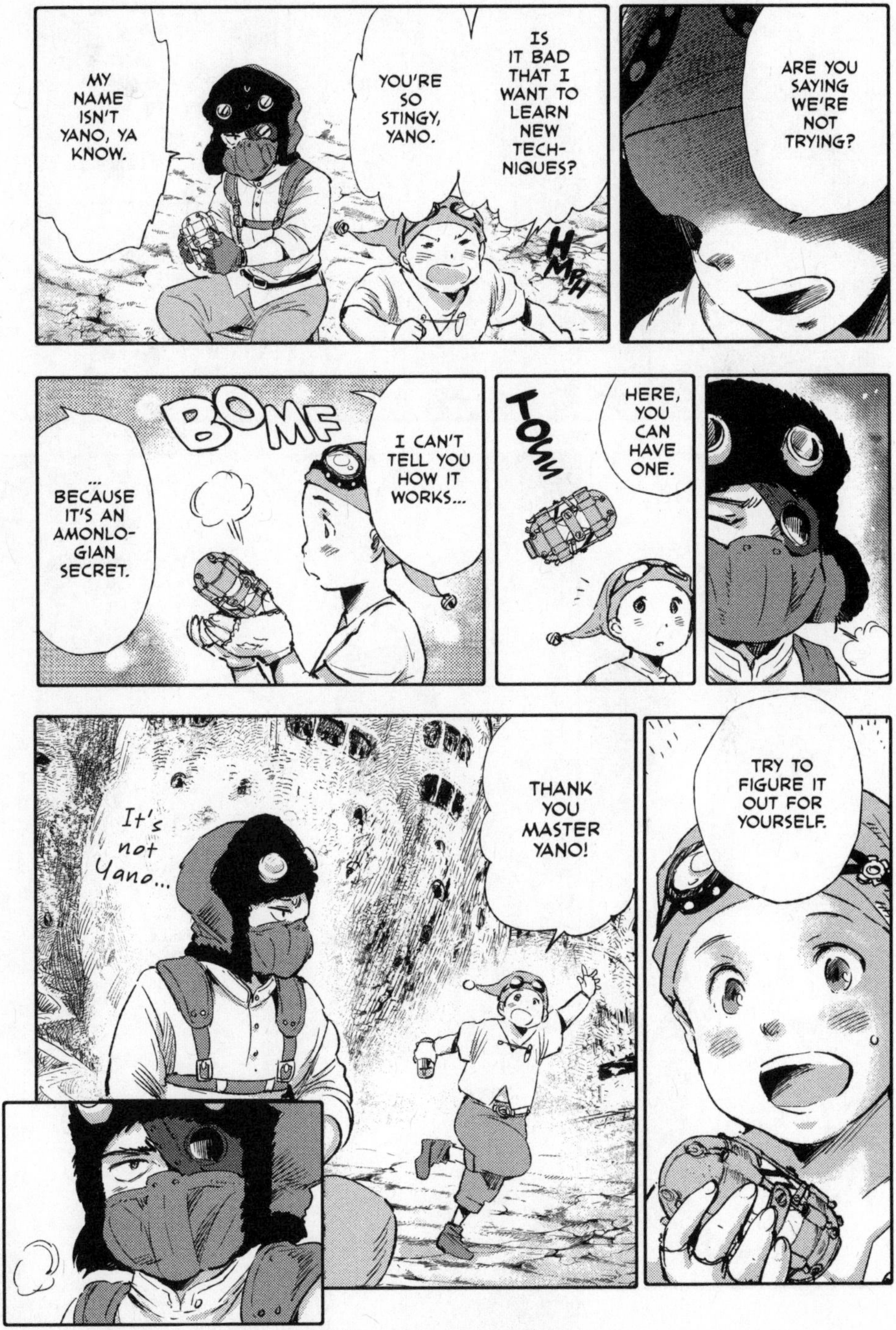
ARE YOU SAYING WE'RE NOT TRYING?
IS IT BAD THAT I WANT TO LEARN NEW TECHNIQUES?
YOU'RE SO STINGY, YANO.
HMPH
MY NAME ISN'T YANO, YA KNOW.
HERE, YOU CAN HAVE ONE.
TOMM
I CAN'T TELL YOU HOW IT WORKS...
BOMF
... BECAUSE IT'S AN AMONLOGIAN SECRET.
TRY TO FIGURE IT OUT FOR YOURSELF.
THANK YOU MASTER YANO!
It's not Yano...

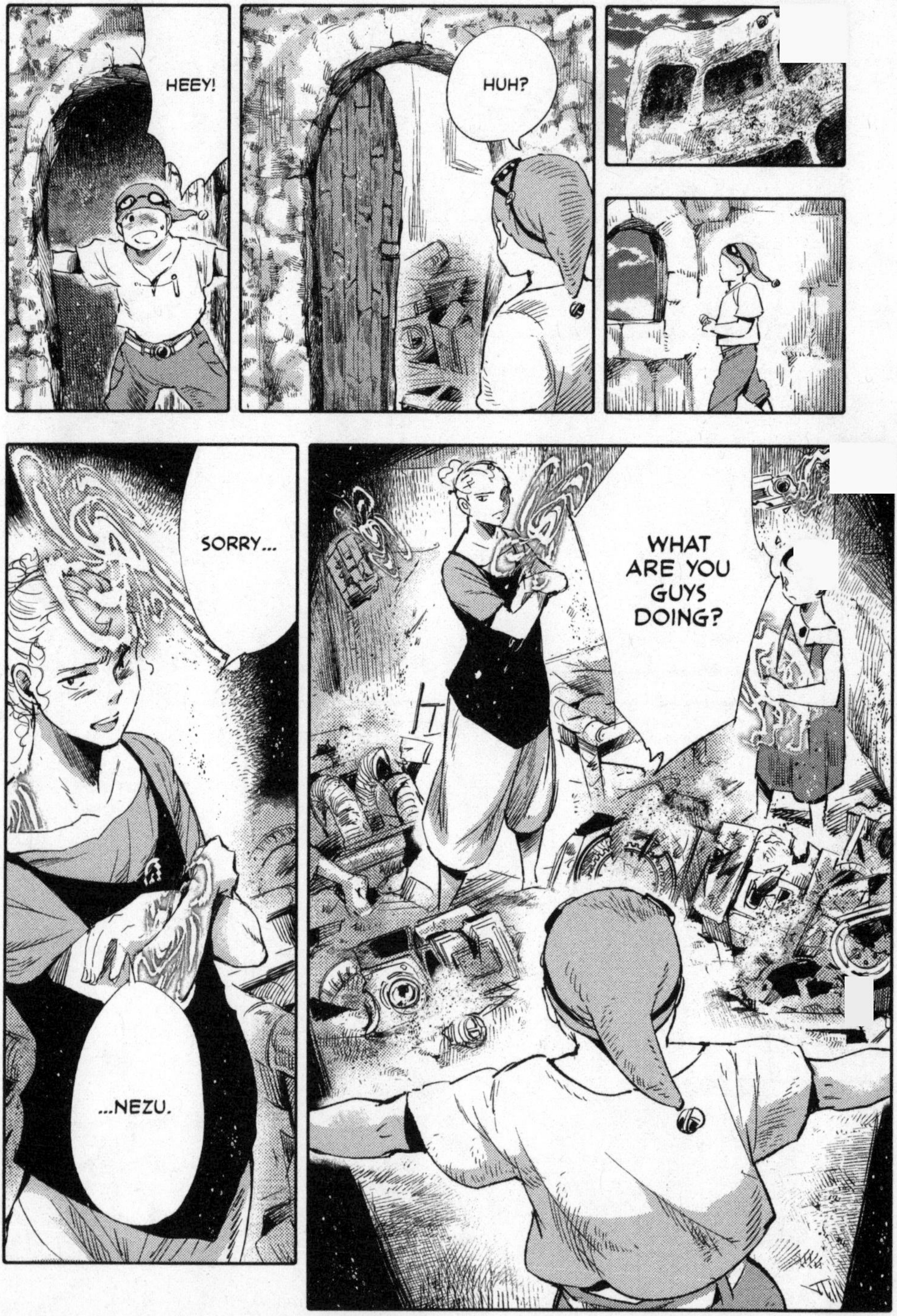
HUH?
HEEY!
WHAT ARE YOU GUYS DOING?
SORRY...
...NEZU.

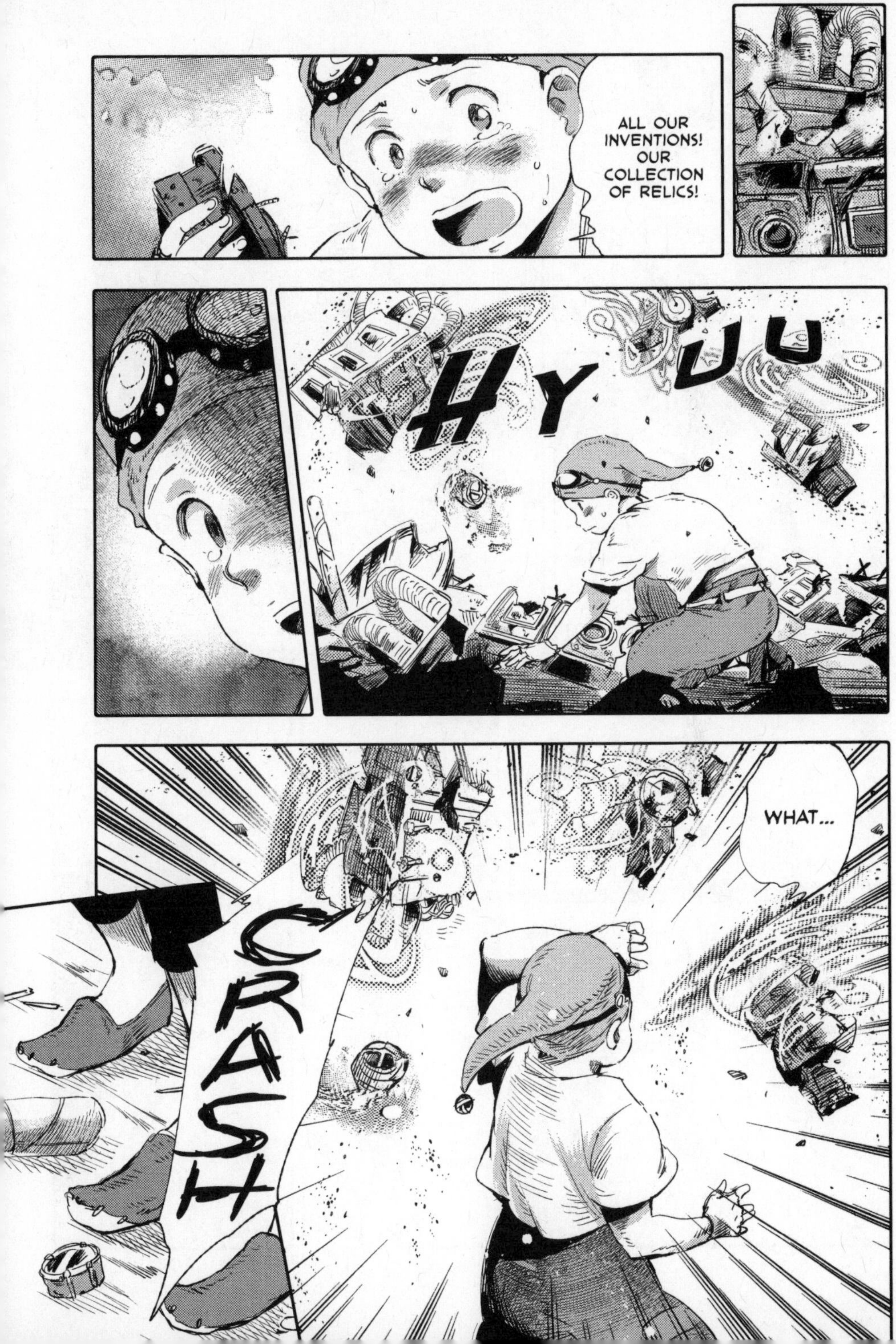
ALL OUR INVENTIONS! OUR COLLECTION OF RELICS!
HYUU
WHAT...
CRASH

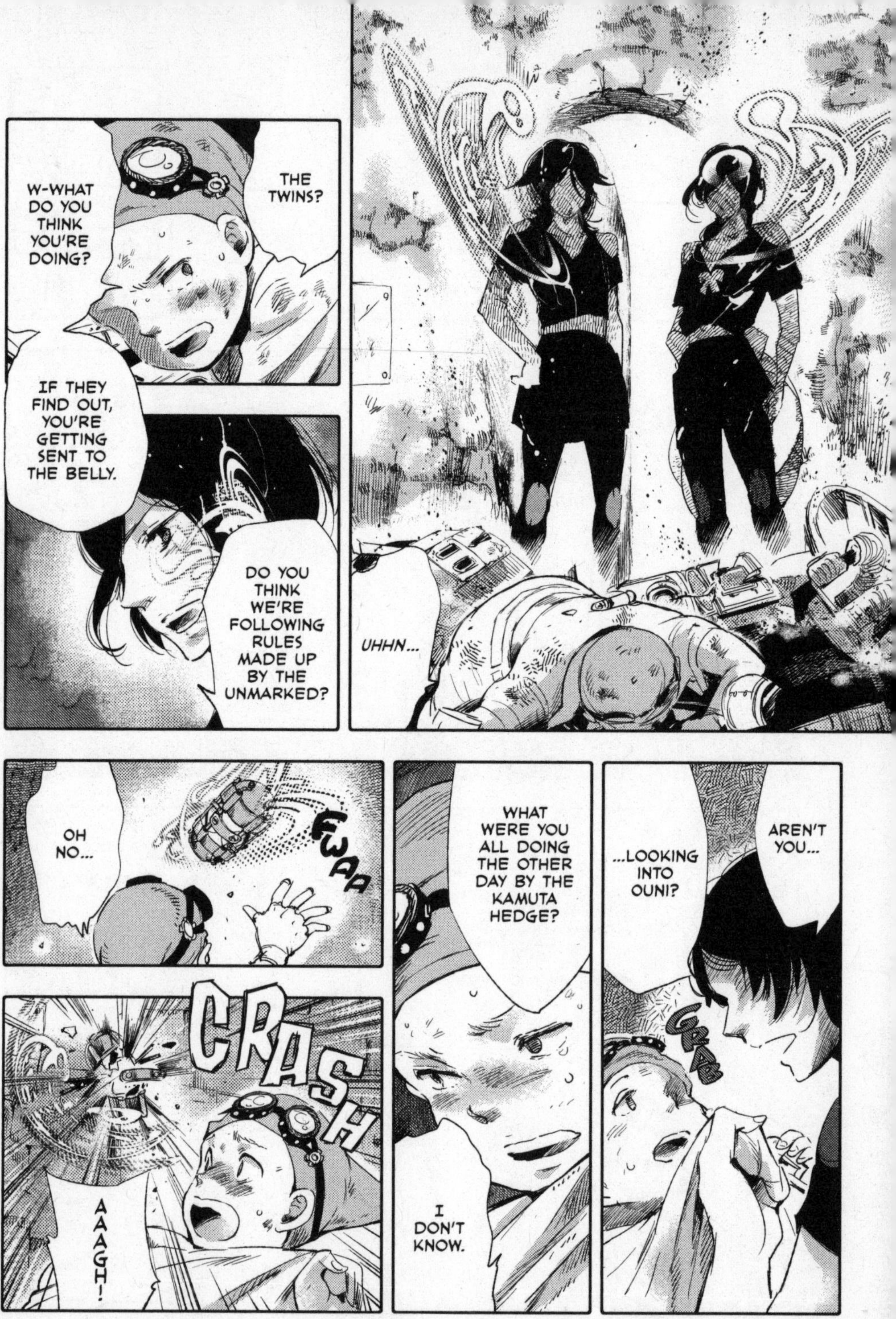
UHHN...
THE TWINS?
W-WHAT DO YOU THINK YOU'RE DOING?
IF THEY FIND OUT, YOU'RE GETTING SENT TO THE BELLY.
DO YOU THINK WE'RE FOLLOWING RULES MADE UP BY THE UNMARKED?
AREN'T YOU...
...LOOKING INTO OUNI?
WHAT WERE YOU ALL DOING THE OTHER DAY BY THE KAMUTA HEDGE?
I DON'T KNOW.
OH NO...
FWAP
CRASH
AAAGH!

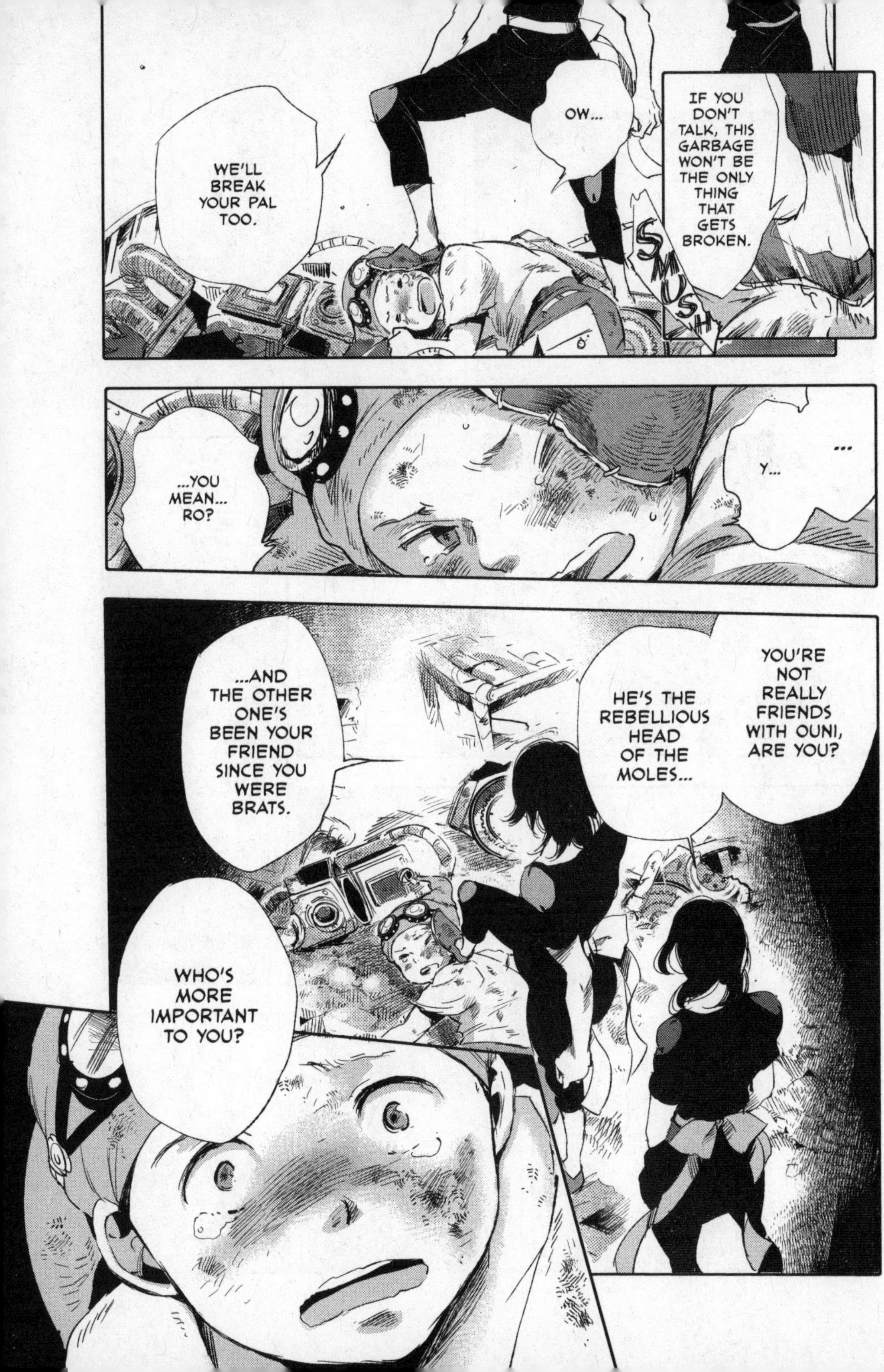
IF YOU DON'T TALK, THIS GARBAGE WON'T BE THE ONLY THING THAT GETS BROKEN.
SMUSH
OW...
WE'LL BREAK YOUR PAL TOO.
...
Y...
...YOU MEAN... RO?
YOU'RE NOT REALLY FRIENDS WITH OUNI, ARE YOU?
HE'S THE REBELLIOUS HEAD OF THE MOLES...
...AND THE OTHER ONE'S BEEN YOUR FRIEND SINCE YOU WERE BRATS.
WHO'S MORE IMPORTANT TO YOU?

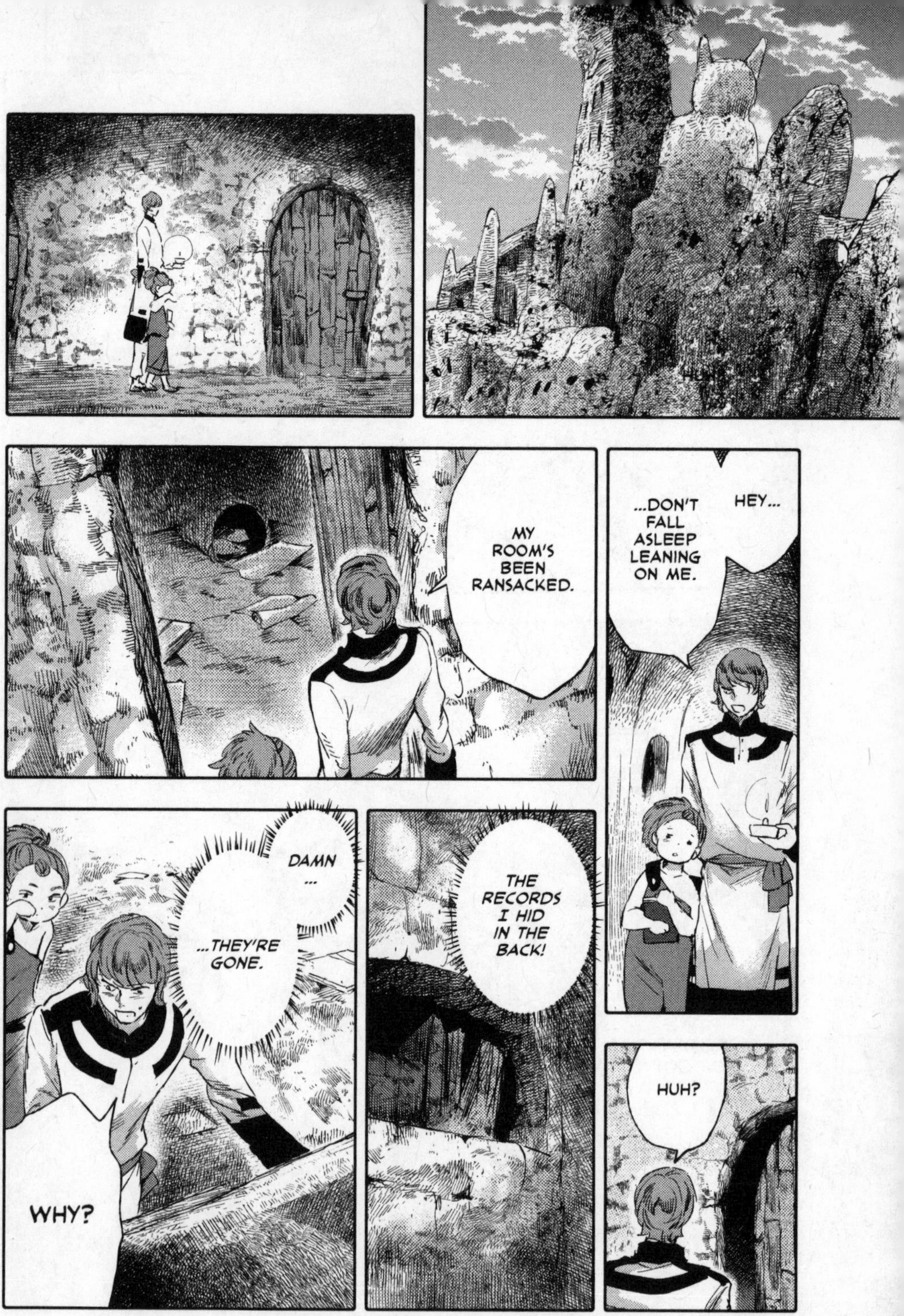
HUH
HEY...
...DON'T FALL ASLEEP LEANING ON ME.
MY ROOM'S BEEN RANSACKED.
HUH?
THE RECORDS I HID IN THE BACK!
DAMN ...
...THEY'RE GONE.
WHY?

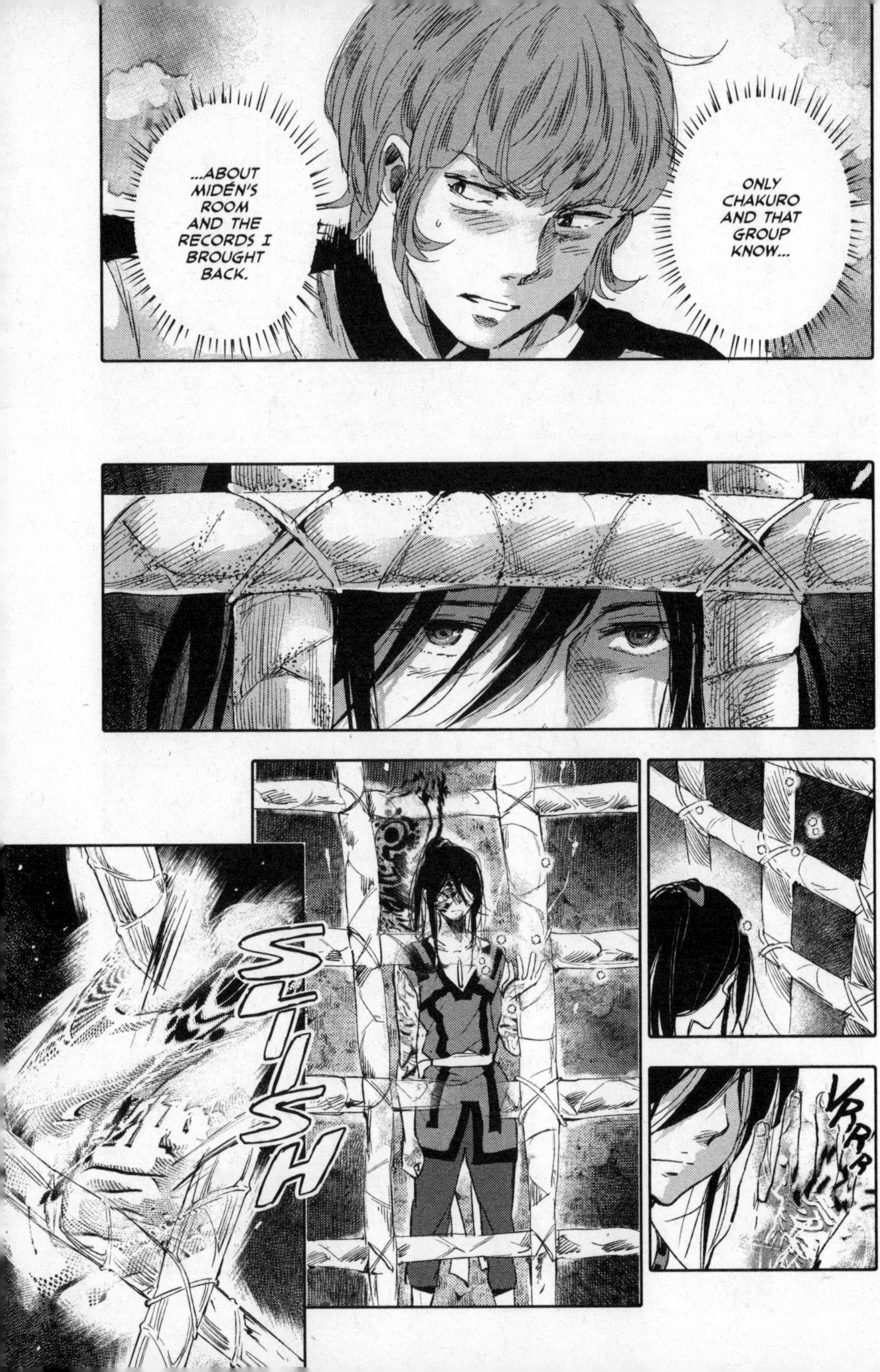
ONLY CHAKURO AND THAT GROUP KNOW...
...ABOUT MIDÉN'S ROOM AND THE RECORDS I BROUGHT BACK.
VRRR
SLIISH

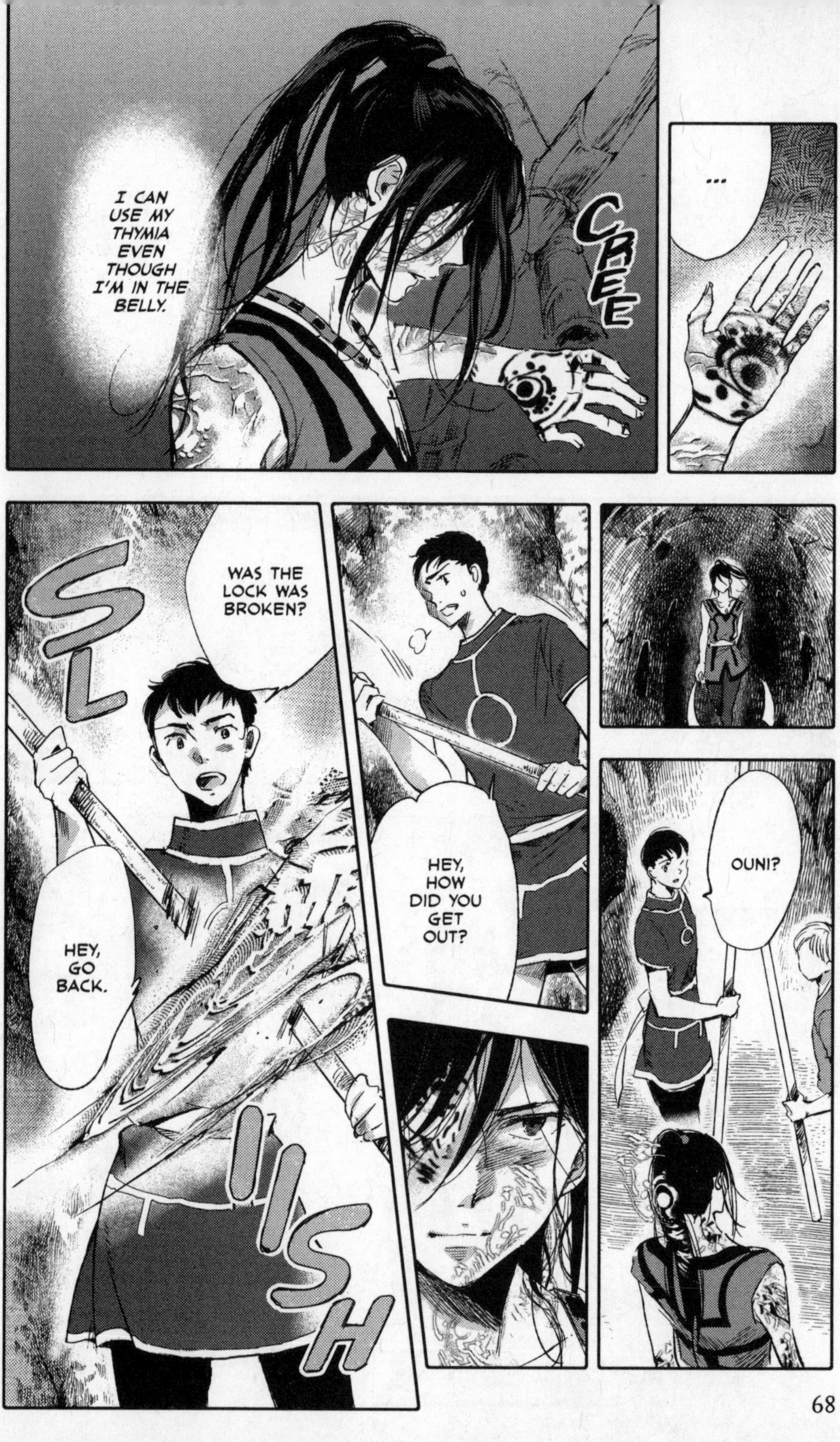
...
I CAN USE MY THYMIA EVEN THOUGH I'M IN THE BELLY.
CREE
OUNI?
HEY, HOW DID YOU GET OUT?
WAS THE LOCK WAS BROKEN?
SL
HEY, GO BACK.
IISH

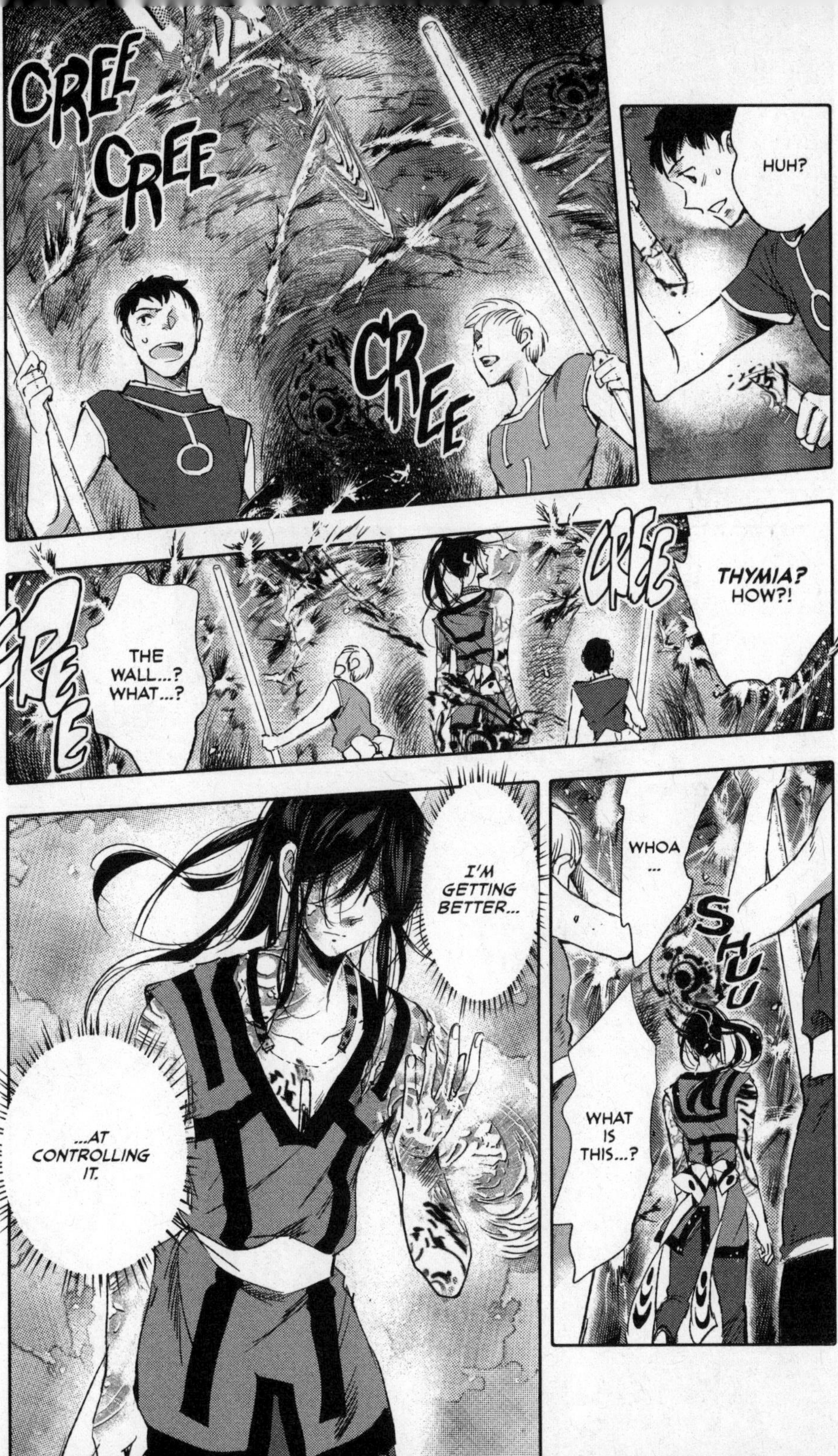
HUH?
CREE CREE
CREE
THYMIA? HOW?!
CREE
THE WALL...? WHAT...?
CREE
WHOA ...
SHUU
WHAT IS THIS...?
I'M GETTING BETTER...
...AT CONTROLLING IT.

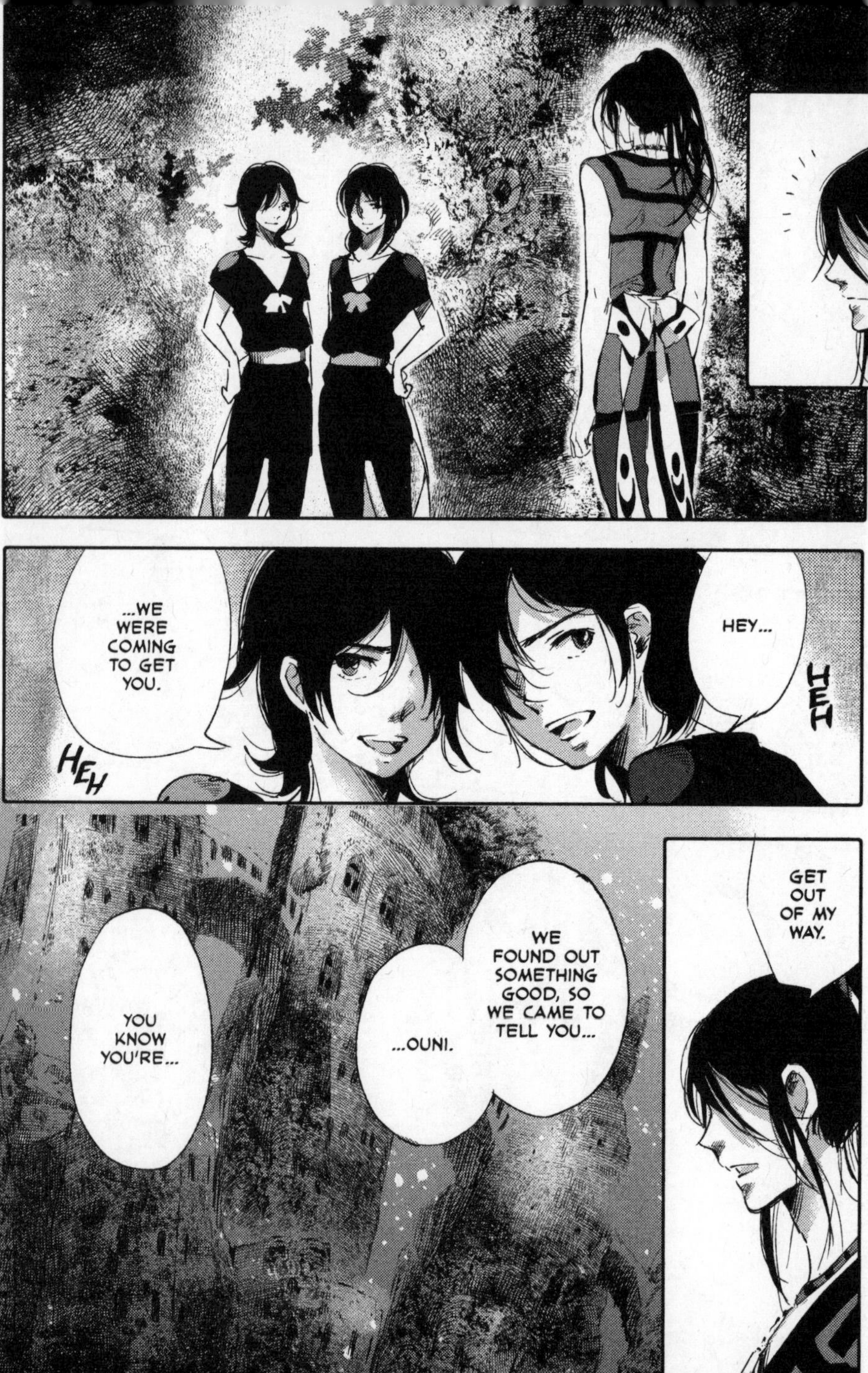
HEY...
HEH
...WE WERE COMING TO GET YOU.
HEH
GET OUT OF MY WAY.
WE FOUND OUT SOMETHING GOOD, SO WE CAME TO TELL YOU...
...OUNI.
YOU KNOW YOU'RE...

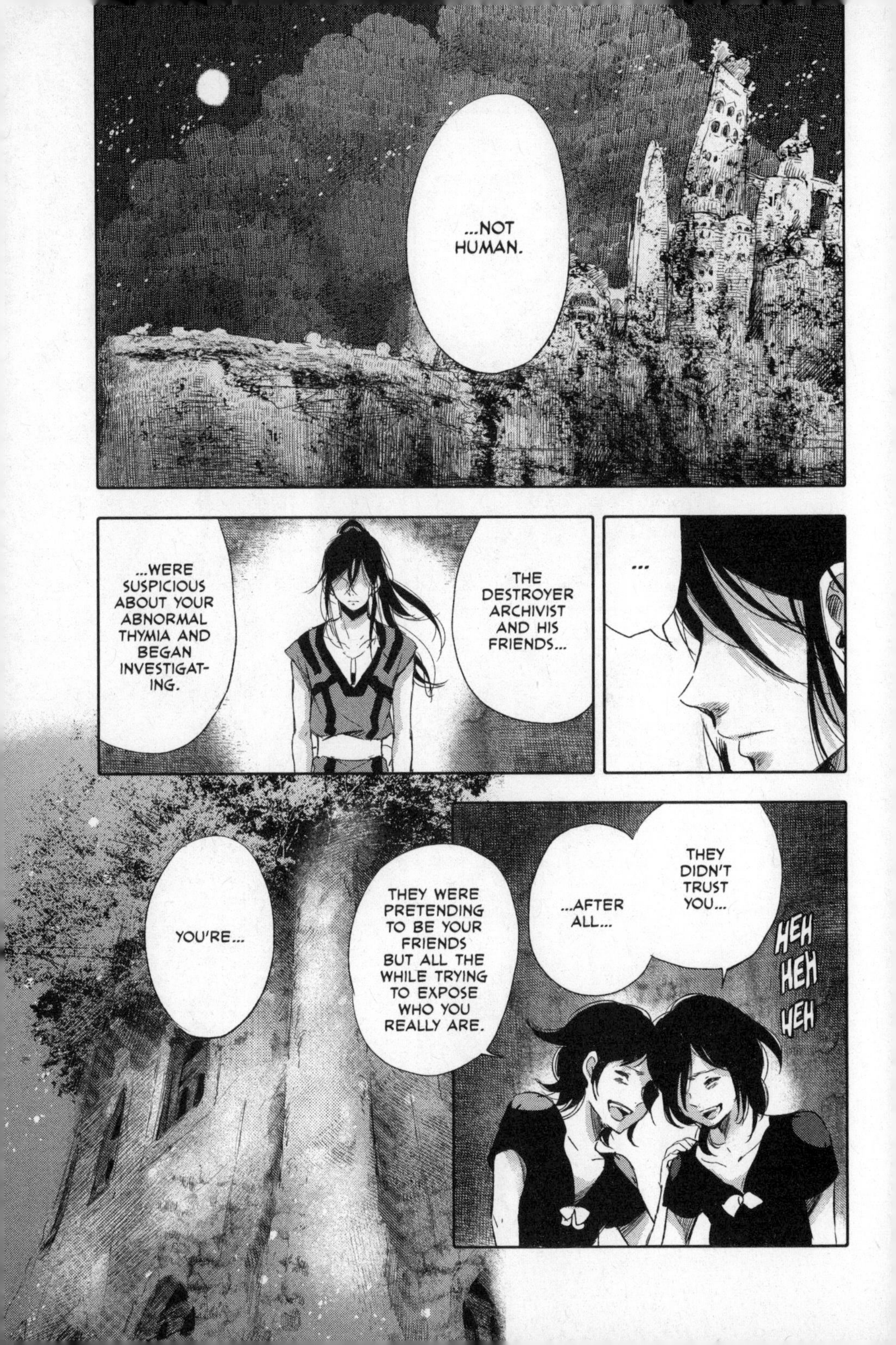
...NOT HUMAN.
...
THE DESTROYER ARCHIVIST AND HIS FRIENDS...
...WERE SUSPICIOUS ABOUT YOUR ABNORMAL THYMIA AND BEGAN INVESTIGAT-ING.
THEY DIDN'T TRUST YOU...
...AFTER ALL...
HEH HEH HEH
THEY WERE PRETENDING TO BE YOUR FRIENDS BUT ALL THE WHILE TRYING TO EXPOSE WHO YOU REALLY ARE.
YOU'RE...

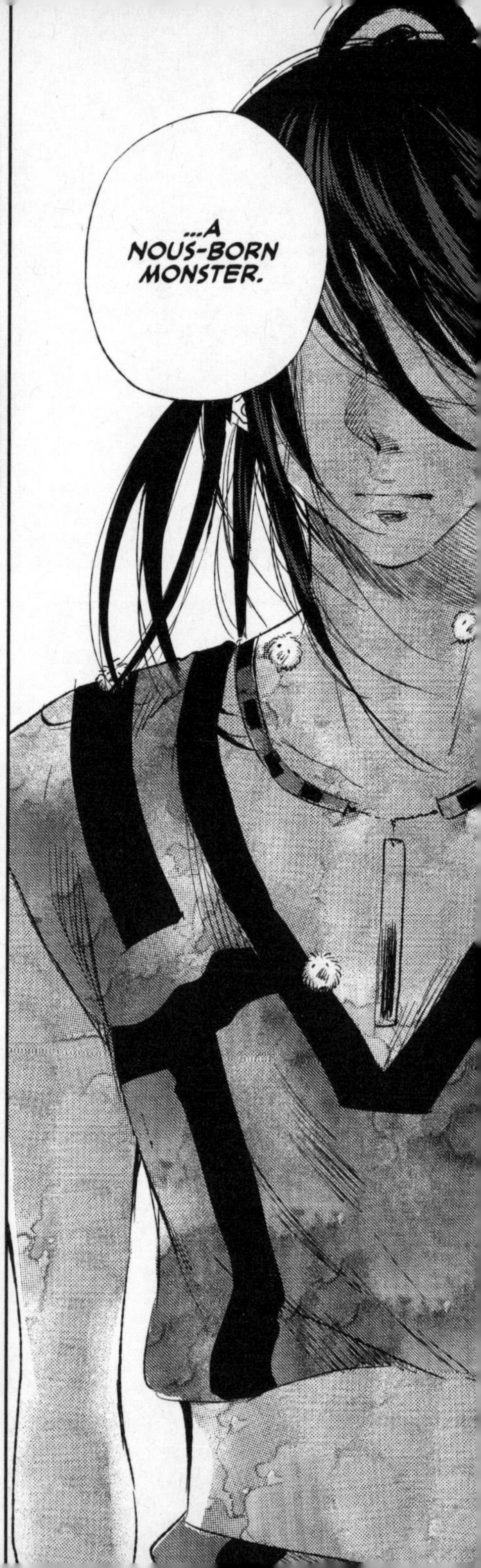
...A NOUS-BORN MONSTER.

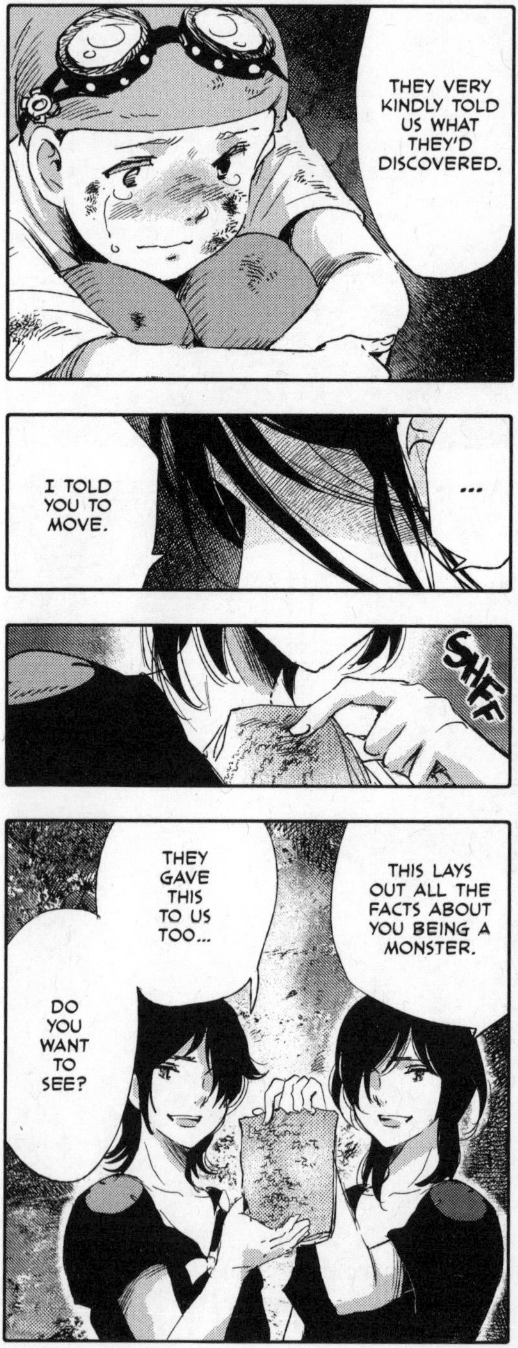
THEY VERY KINDLY TOLD US WHAT THEY'D DISCOVERED.
...
I TOLD YOU TO MOVE.
SHFF
THIS LAYS OUT ALL THE FACTS ABOUT YOU BEING A MONSTER.
THEY GAVE THIS TO US TOO...
DO YOU WANT TO SEE?

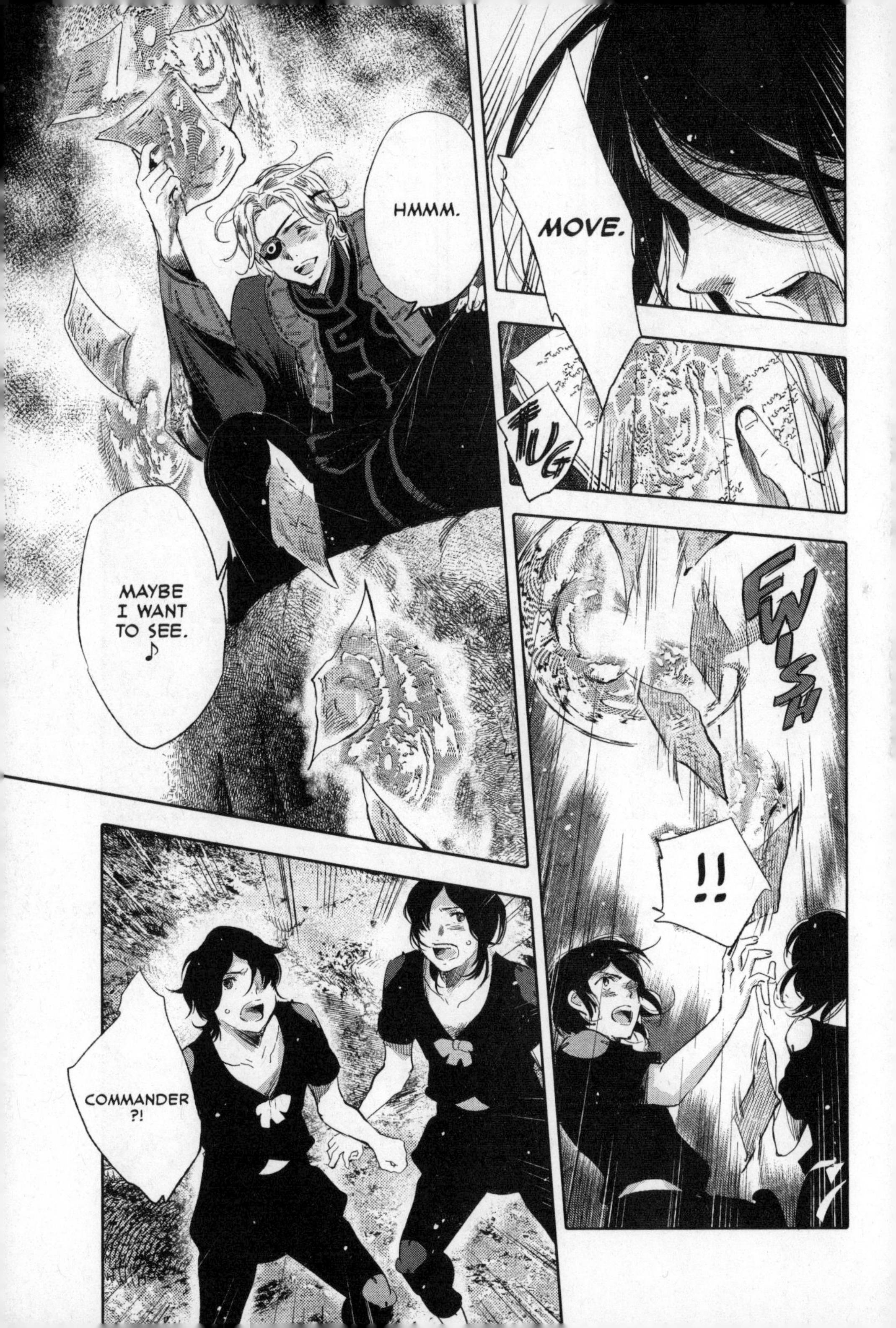
MOVE.
TUG
FWISH
!!
HMMM.
MAYBE I WANT TO SEE. ♪
COMMANDER ?!

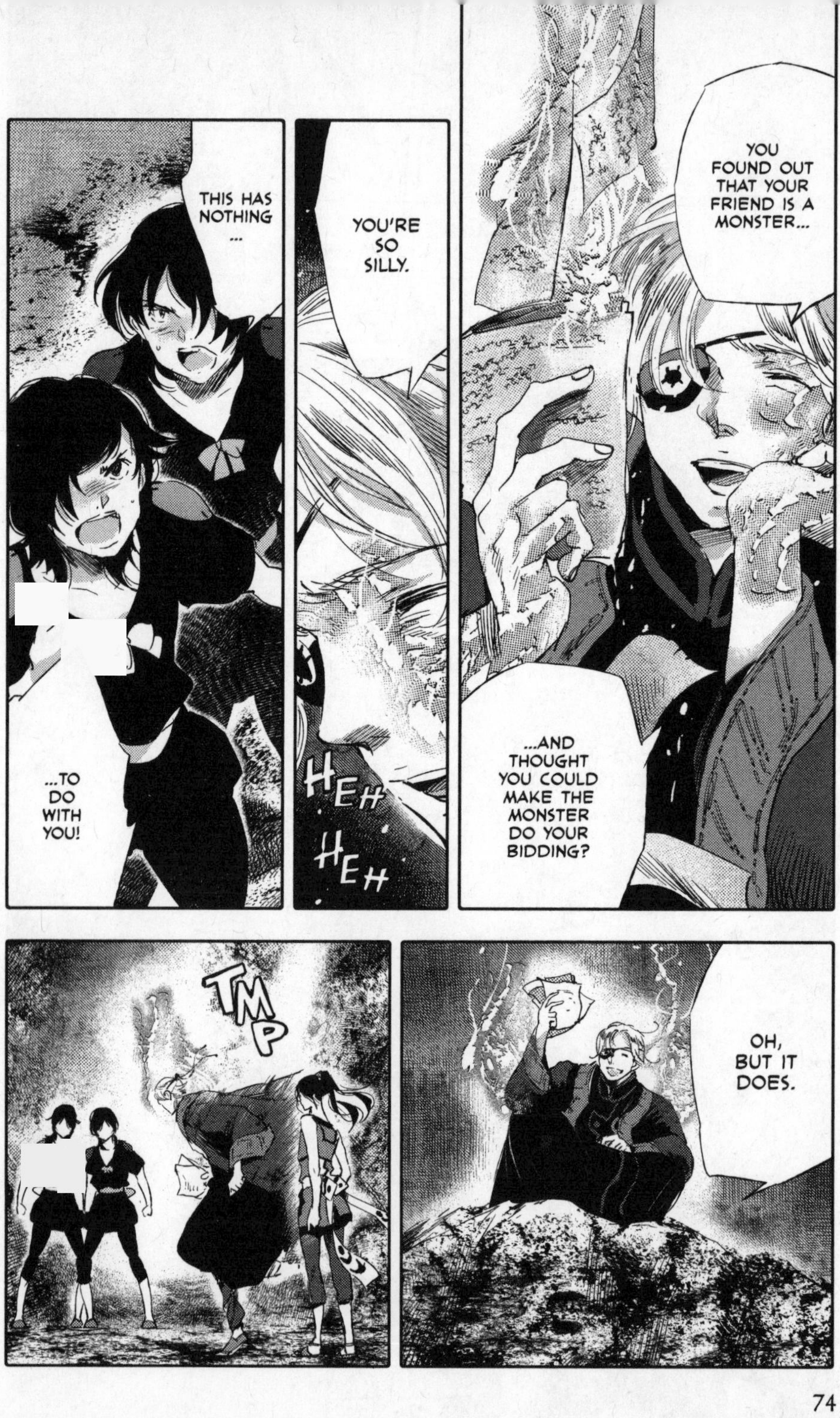
YOU FOUND OUT THAT YOUR FRIEND IS A MONSTER...
...AND THOUGHT YOU COULD MAKE THE MONSTER DO YOUR BIDDING?
YOU'RE SO SILLY.
HEH HEH
THIS HAS NOTHING...
...TO DO WITH YOU!
OH, BUT IT DOES.
TMP

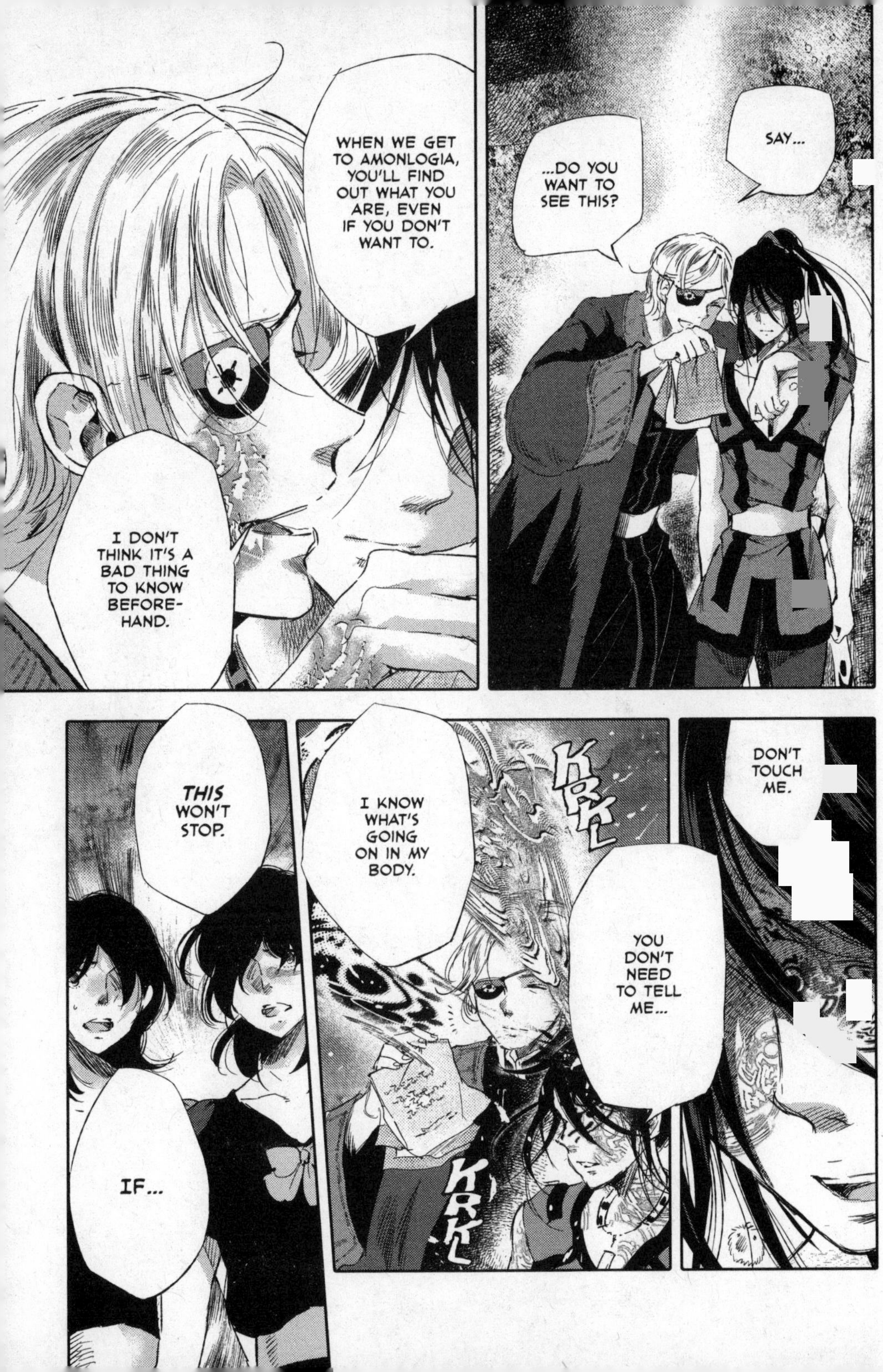
SAY...
...DO YOU WANT TO SEE THIS?
WHEN WE GET TO AMONLOGIA, YOU'LL FIND OUT WHAT YOU ARE, EVEN IF YOU DON'T WANT TO.
I DON'T THINK IT'S A BAD THING TO KNOW BEFORE-HAND.
DON'T TOUCH ME.
YOU DON'T NEED TO TELL ME...
KRKL
I KNOW WHAT'S GOING ON IN MY BODY.
KRKL
THIS WON'T STOP.
IF...

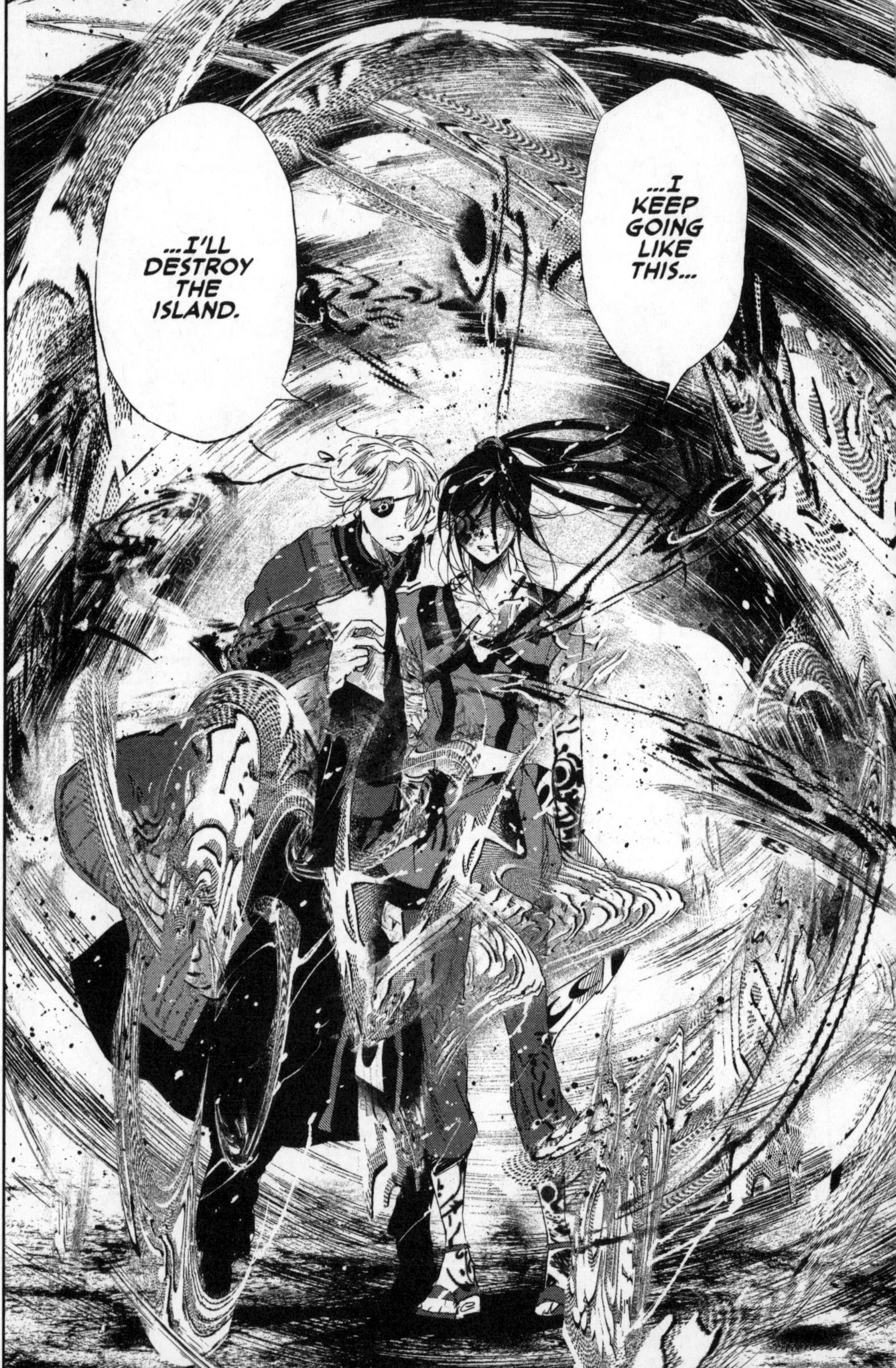
...I KEEP GOING LIKE THIS...
...I'LL DESTROY THE ISLAND.

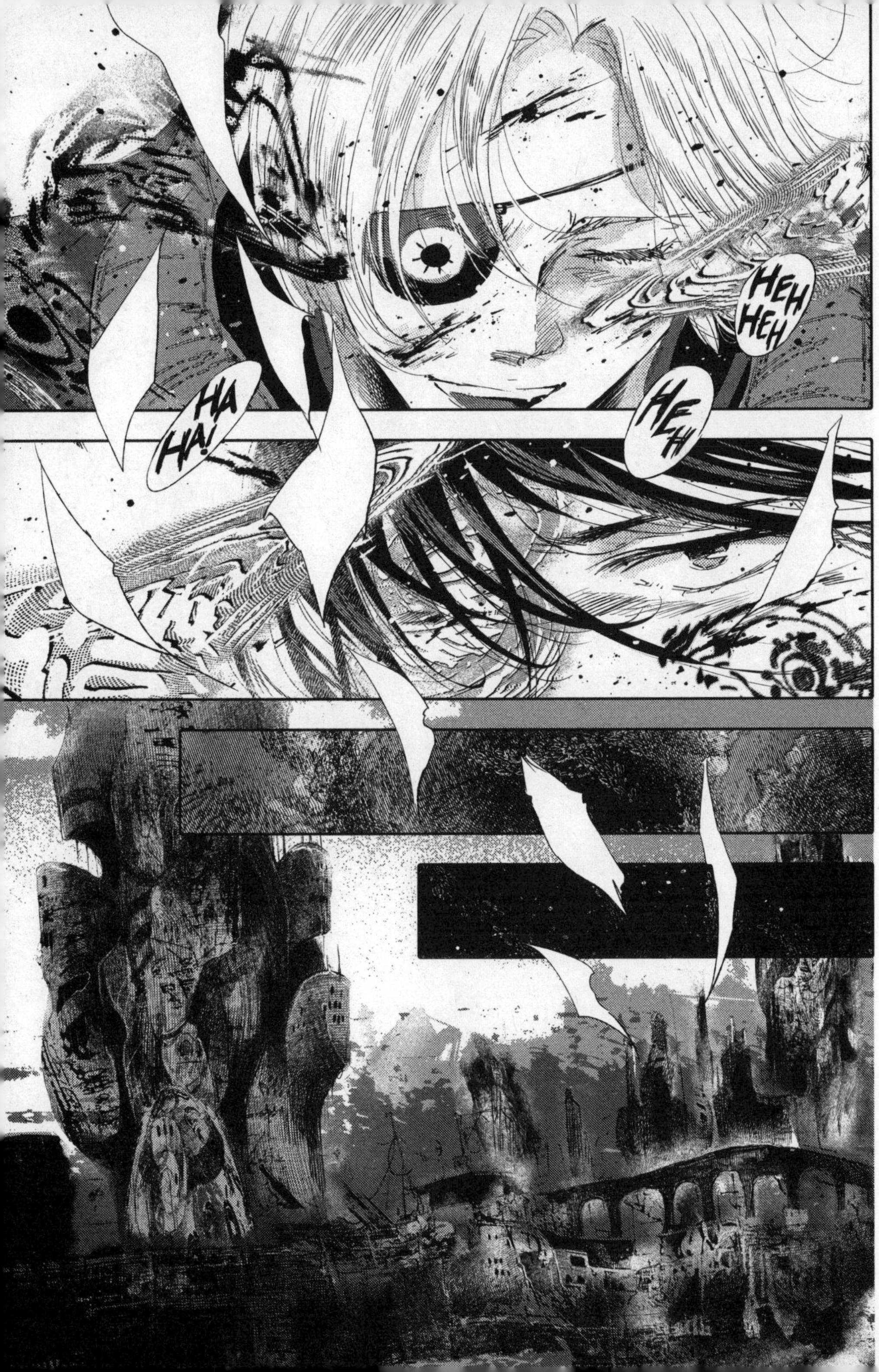
HEH HEH
HEH
HA HA!

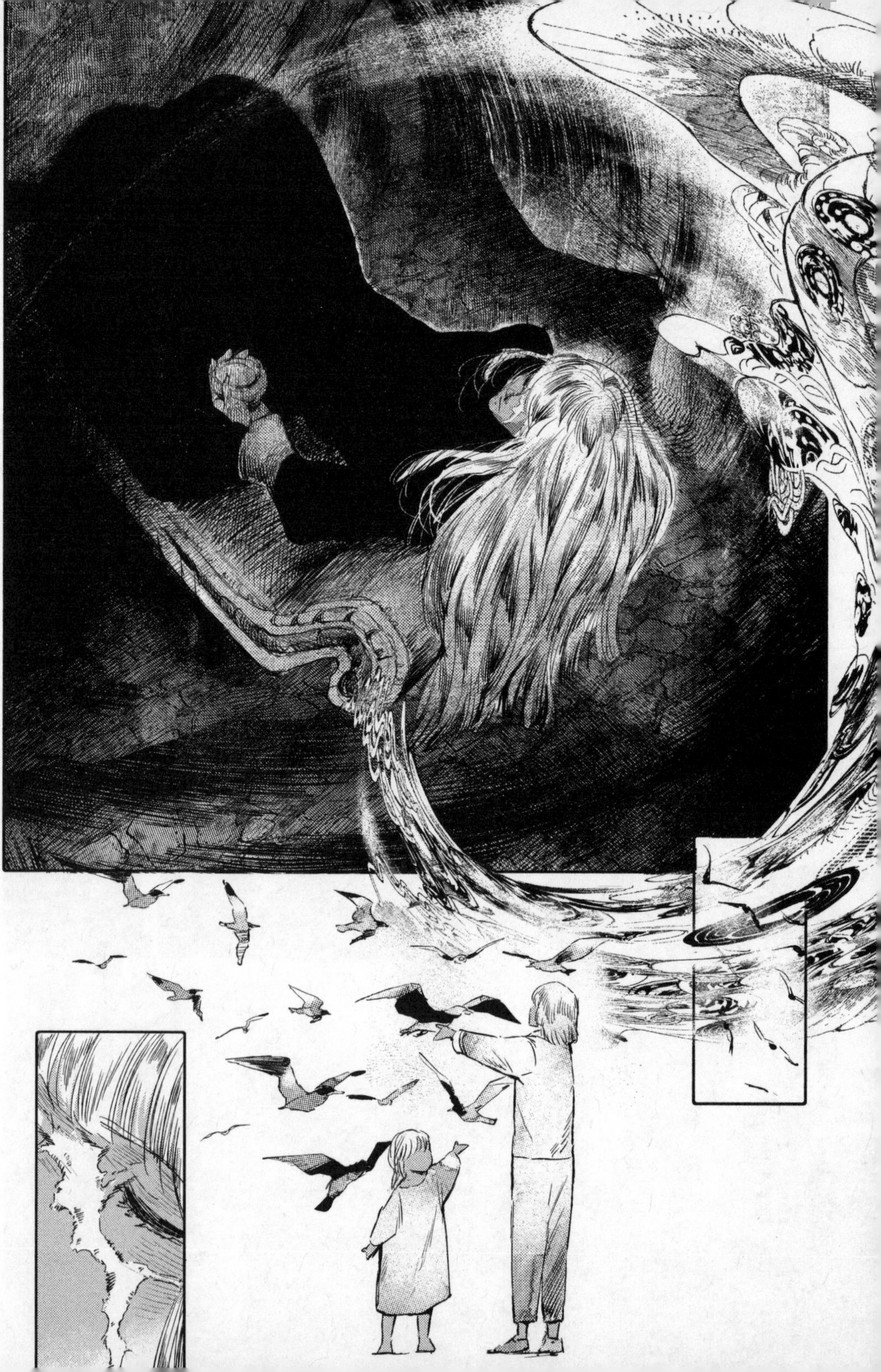

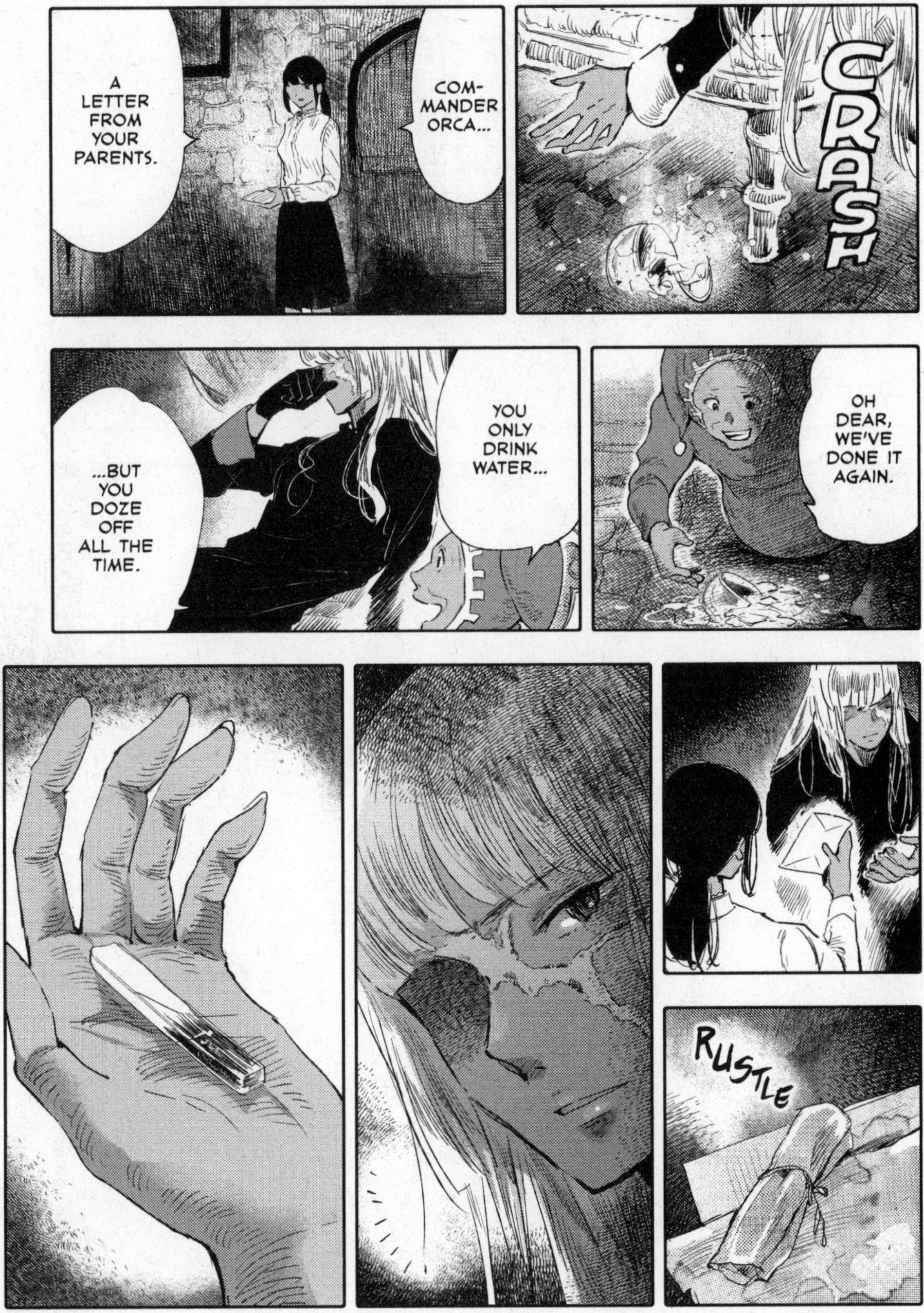
CRASH
COM-MANDER ORCA...
A LETTER FROM YOUR PARENTS.
OH DEAR, WE'VE DONE IT AGAIN.
YOU ONLY DRINK WATER...
...BUT YOU DOZE OFF ALL THE TIME.
RUSTLE

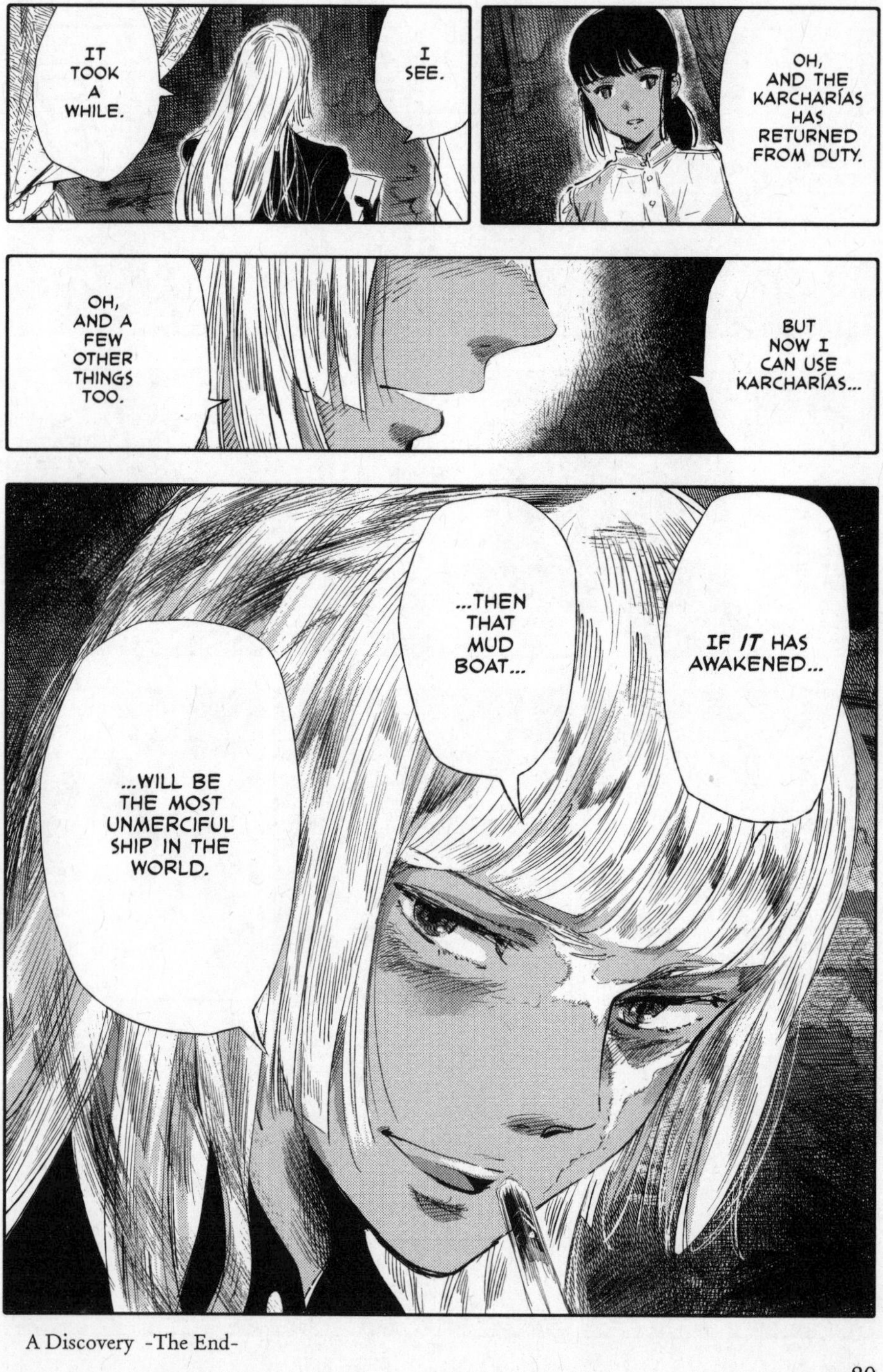
OH, AND THE KARCHARÍAS HAS RETURNED FROM DUTY.
I SEE.
IT TOOK A WHILE.
BUT NOW I CAN USE KARCHARÍAS...
OH, AND A FEW OTHER THINGS TOO.
IF *IT* HAS AWAKENED...
...THEN THAT MUD BOAT...
...WILL BE THE MOST UNMERCIFUL SHIP IN THE WORLD.

A Discovery -The End-

Chapter 31 The Hollow Sound of Bells

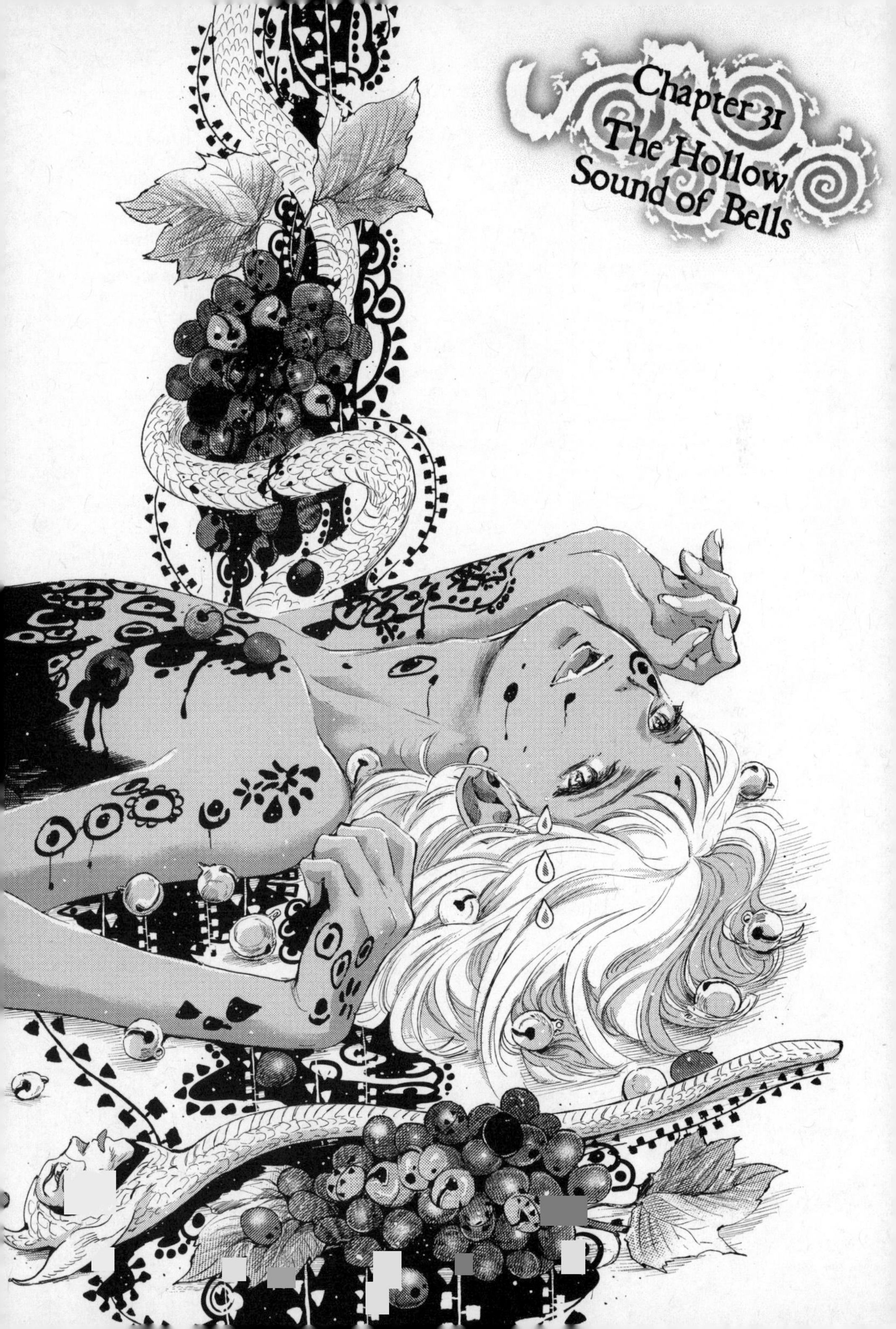

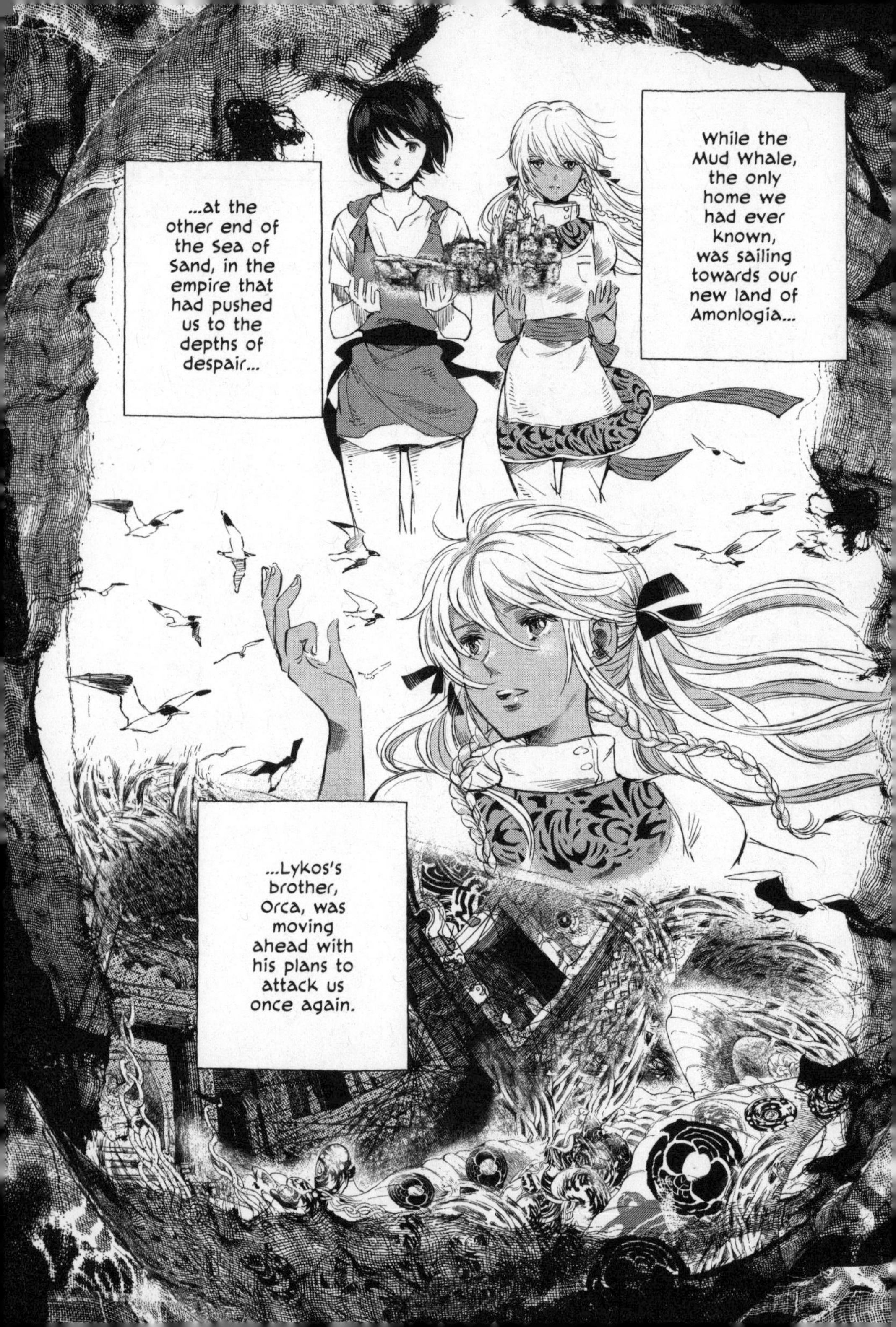
While the Mud Whale, the only home we had ever known, was sailing towards our new land of Amonlogia...
...at the other end of the Sea of Sand, in the empire that had pushed us to the depths of despair...
...Lykos's brother, Orca, was moving ahead with his plans to attack us once again.

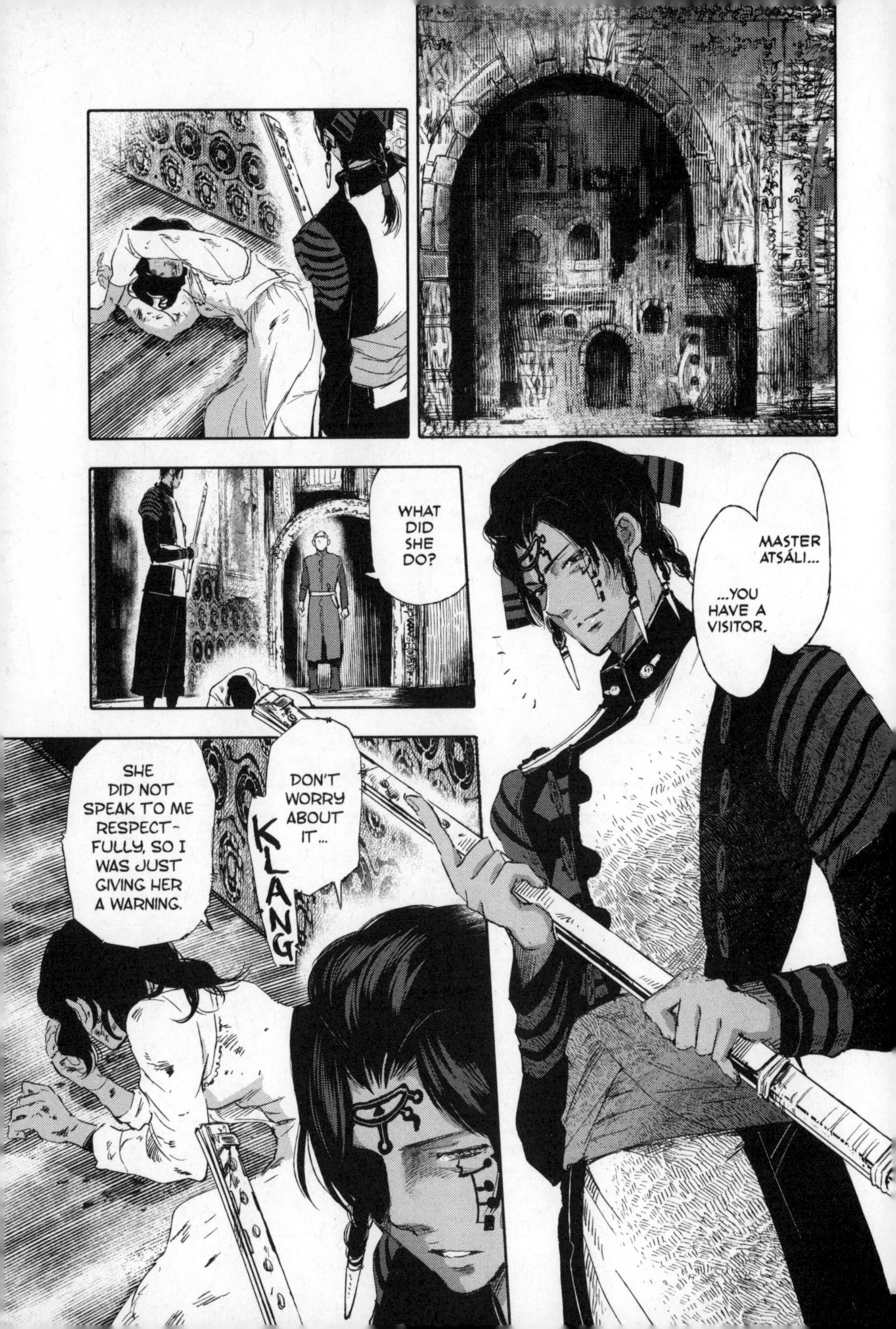
MASTER ATSÁLI...
...YOU HAVE A VISITOR.
WHAT DID SHE DO?
DON'T WORRY ABOUT IT...
KLANG
SHE DID NOT SPEAK TO ME RESPECT-FULLY, SO I WAS JUST GIVING HER A WARNING.

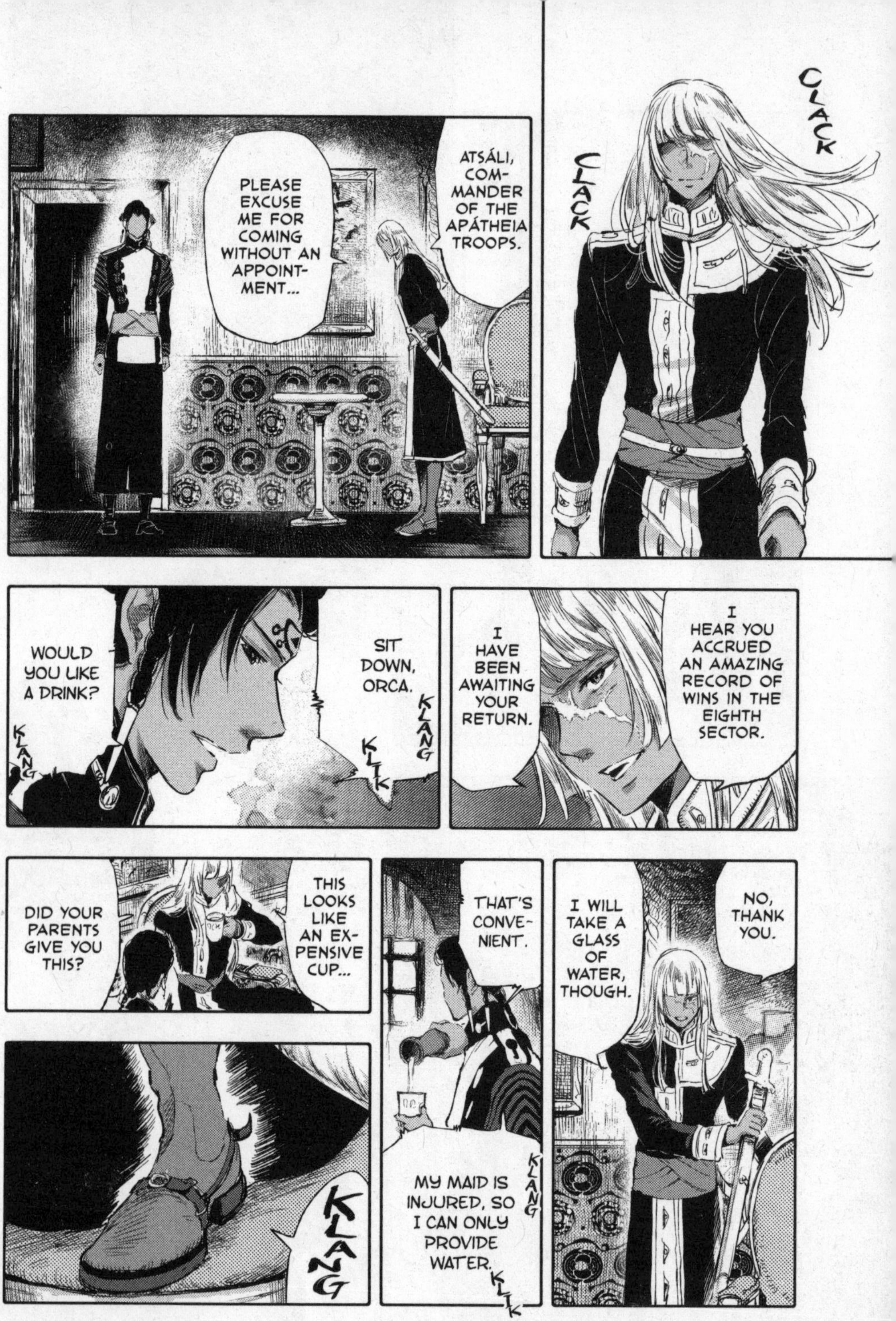

CLACK
CLACK
ATSÁLI, COMMANDER OF THE APÁTHEIA TROOPS.
PLEASE EXCUSE ME FOR COMING WITHOUT AN APPOINTMENT...
I HEAR YOU ACCRUED AN AMAZING RECORD OF WINS IN THE EIGHTH SECTOR.
I HAVE BEEN AWAITING YOUR RETURN.
SIT DOWN, ORCA.
KLANG
KLIK
WOULD YOU LIKE A DRINK?
KLANG
NO, THANK YOU.
I WILL TAKE A GLASS OF WATER, THOUGH.
THAT'S CONVENIENT.
KLANG
MY MAID IS INJURED, SO I CAN ONLY PROVIDE WATER.
KLIK
THIS LOOKS LIKE AN EXPENSIVE CUP...
DID YOUR PARENTS GIVE YOU THIS?
KLANG

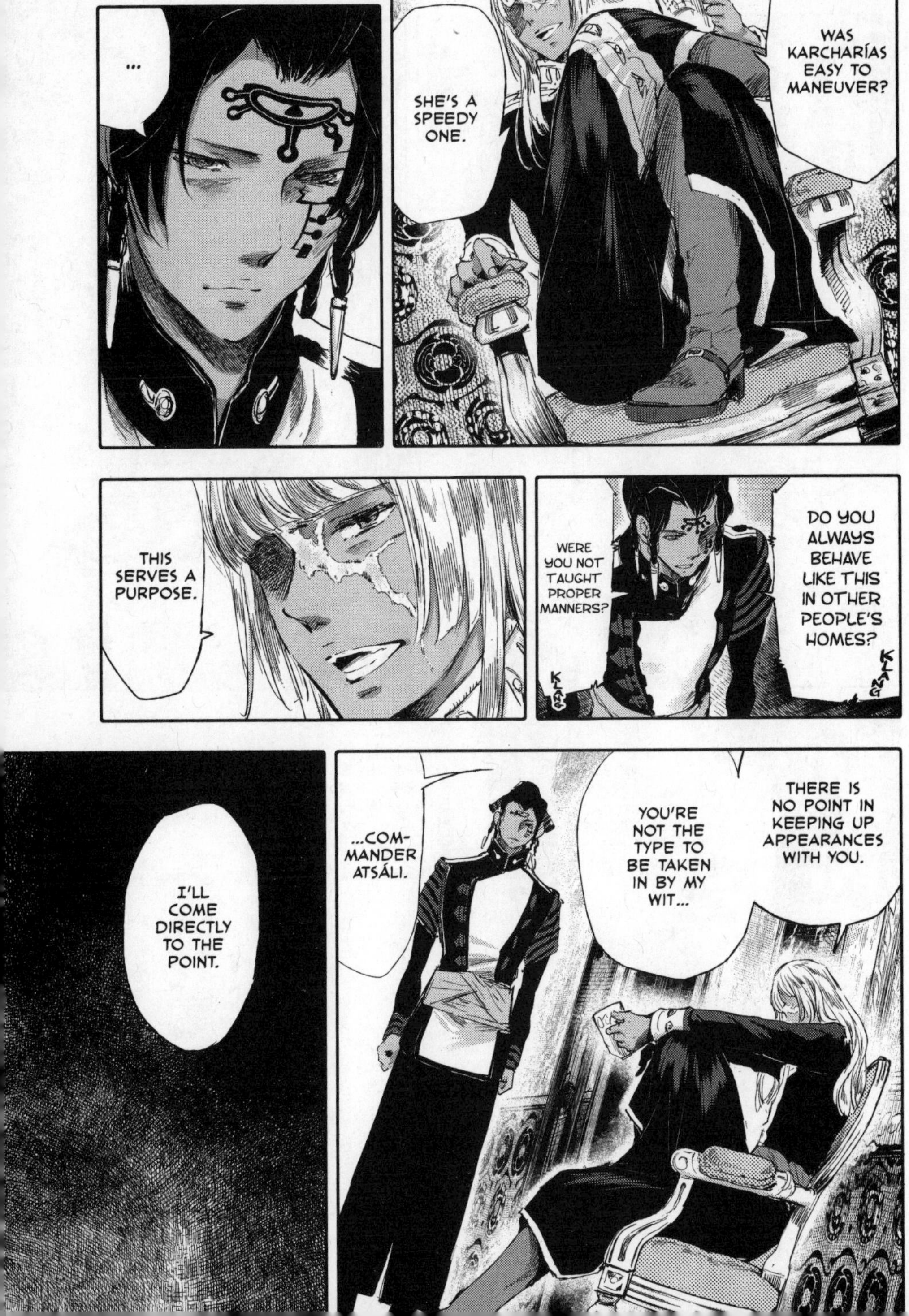
WAS KARCHARÍAS EASY TO MANEUVER?
SHE'S A SPEEDY ONE.
...
DO YOU ALWAYS BEHAVE LIKE THIS IN OTHER PEOPLE'S HOMES?
KLANG
WERE YOU NOT TAUGHT PROPER MANNERS?
KLANG
THIS SERVES A PURPOSE.
THERE IS NO POINT IN KEEPING UP APPEARANCES WITH YOU.
YOU'RE NOT THE TYPE TO BE TAKEN IN BY MY WIT...
...COM-MANDER ATSÁLI.
I'LL COME DIRECTLY TO THE POINT.

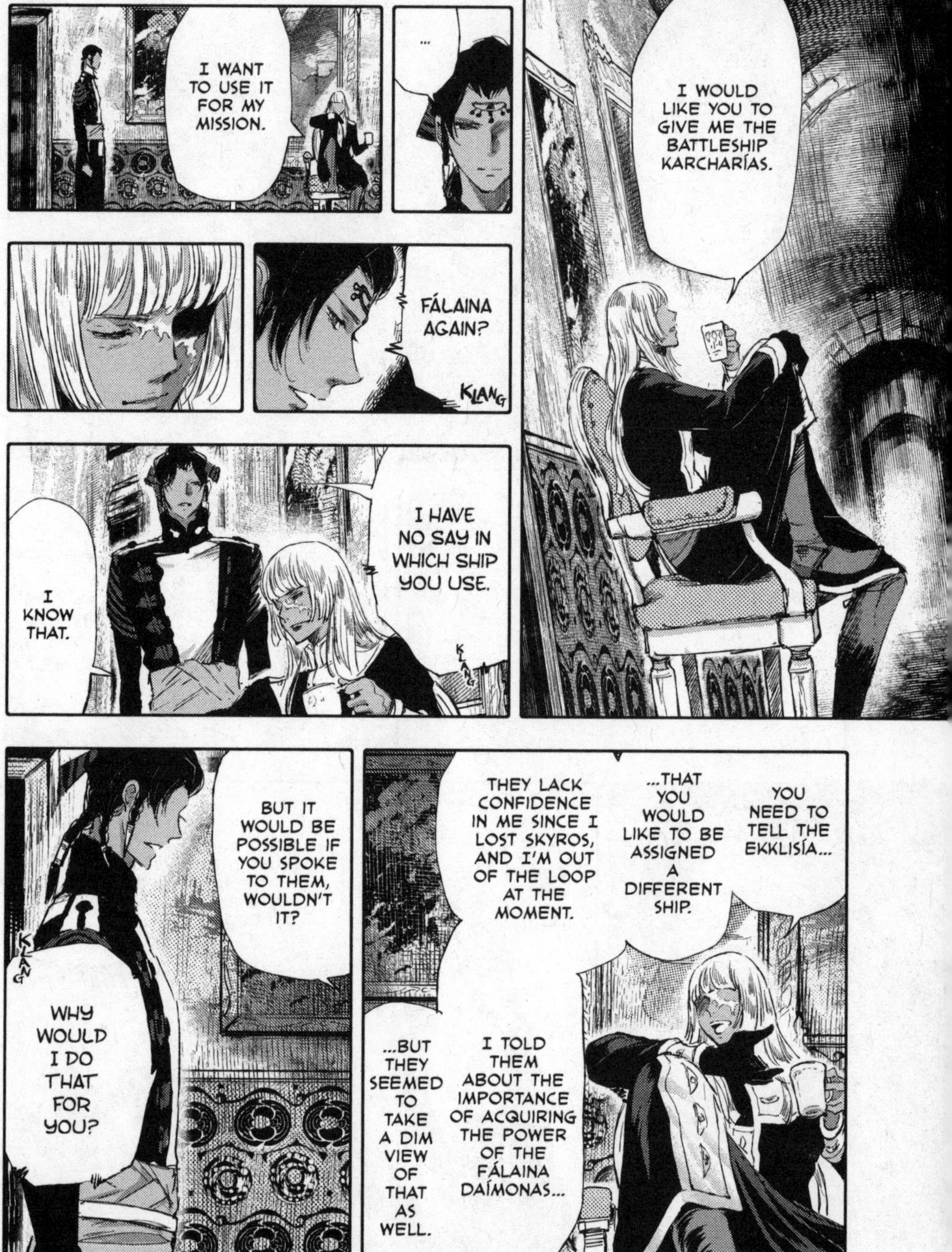
I WOULD LIKE YOU TO GIVE ME THE BATTLESHIP KARCHARÍAS.
...
I WANT TO USE IT FOR MY MISSION.
FÁLAINA AGAIN?
KLANG
I HAVE NO SAY IN WHICH SHIP YOU USE.
KLANG
I KNOW THAT.
YOU NEED TO TELL THE EKKLISÍA...
...THAT YOU WOULD LIKE TO BE ASSIGNED A DIFFERENT SHIP.
THEY LACK CONFIDENCE IN ME SINCE I LOST SKYROS, AND I'M OUT OF THE LOOP AT THE MOMENT.
I TOLD THEM ABOUT THE IMPORTANCE OF ACQUIRING THE POWER OF THE FÁLAINA DAÍMONAS...
...BUT THEY SEEMED TO TAKE A DIM VIEW OF THAT AS WELL.
BUT IT WOULD BE POSSIBLE IF YOU SPOKE TO THEM, WOULDN'T IT?
KLANG
WHY WOULD I DO THAT FOR YOU?

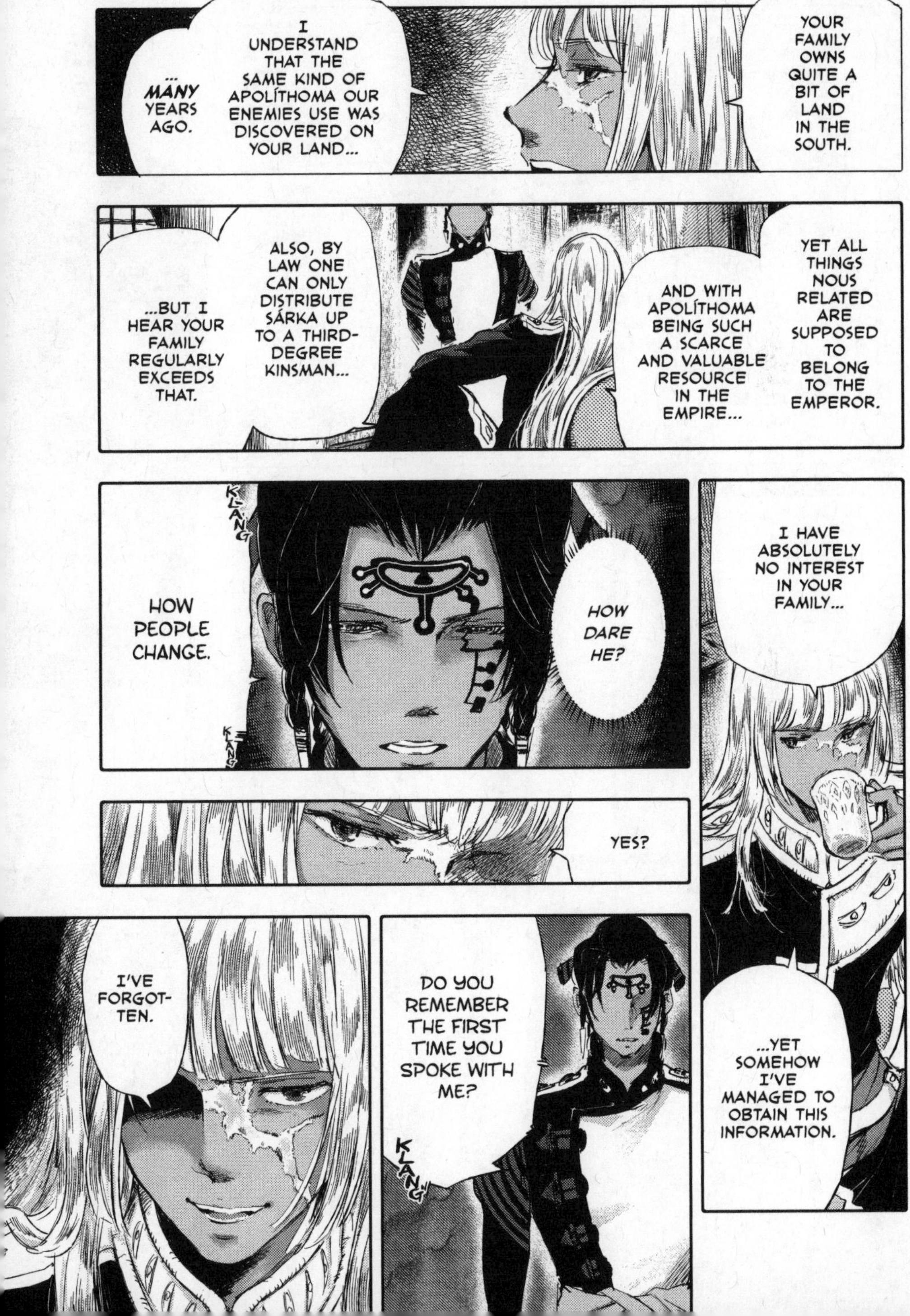
YOUR FAMILY OWNS QUITE A BIT OF LAND IN THE SOUTH.
I UNDERSTAND THAT THE SAME KIND OF APOLÍTHOMA OUR ENEMIES USE WAS DISCOVERED ON YOUR LAND...
...MANY YEARS AGO.
YET ALL THINGS NOUS RELATED ARE SUPPOSED TO BELONG TO THE EMPEROR.
AND WITH APOLÍTHOMA BEING SUCH A SCARCE AND VALUABLE RESOURCE IN THE EMPIRE...
ALSO, BY LAW ONE CAN ONLY DISTRIBUTE SÁRKA UP TO A THIRD-DEGREE KINSMAN...
...BUT I HEAR YOUR FAMILY REGULARLY EXCEEDS THAT.
I HAVE ABSOLUTELY NO INTEREST IN YOUR FAMILY...
...YET SOMEHOW I'VE MANAGED TO OBTAIN THIS INFORMATION.
KLANG
HOW DARE HE?
HOW PEOPLE CHANGE.
KLANG
YES?
DO YOU REMEMBER THE FIRST TIME YOU SPOKE WITH ME?
KLANG
I'VE FORGOT-TEN.

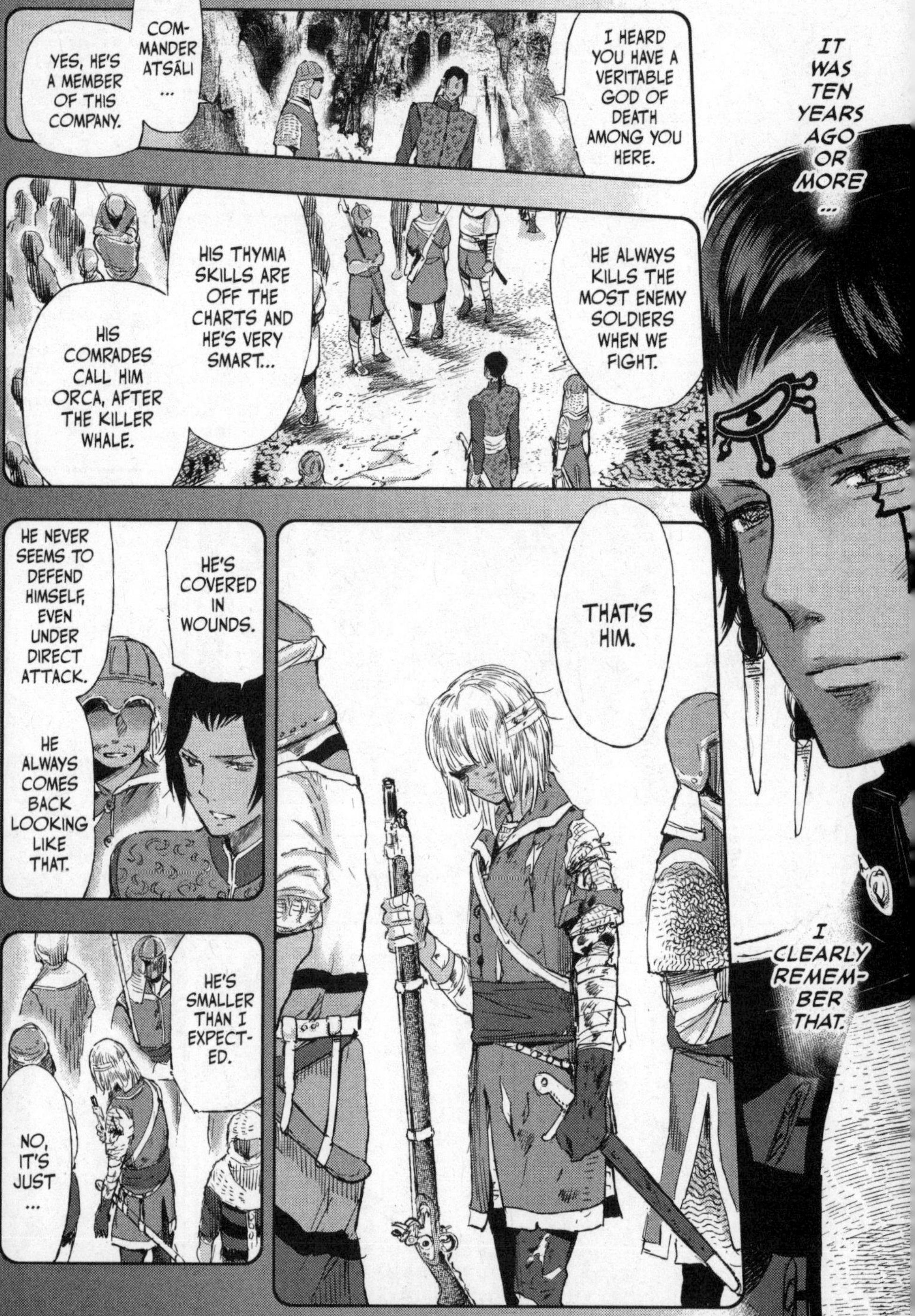
IT WAS TEN YEARS AGO OR MORE ...
I CLEARLY REMEMBER THAT.
I HEARD YOU HAVE A VERITABLE GOD OF DEATH AMONG YOU HERE.
COMMANDER ATSÁLI ...
YES, HE'S A MEMBER OF THIS COMPANY.
HE ALWAYS KILLS THE MOST ENEMY SOLDIERS WHEN WE FIGHT.
HIS THYMIA SKILLS ARE OFF THE CHARTS AND HE'S VERY SMART...
HIS COMRADES CALL HIM ORCA, AFTER THE KILLER WHALE.
THAT'S HIM.
HE'S COVERED IN WOUNDS.
HE NEVER SEEMS TO DEFEND HIMSELF, EVEN UNDER DIRECT ATTACK.
HE ALWAYS COMES BACK LOOKING LIKE THAT.
HE'S SMALLER THAN I EXPECTED.
NO, IT'S JUST ...

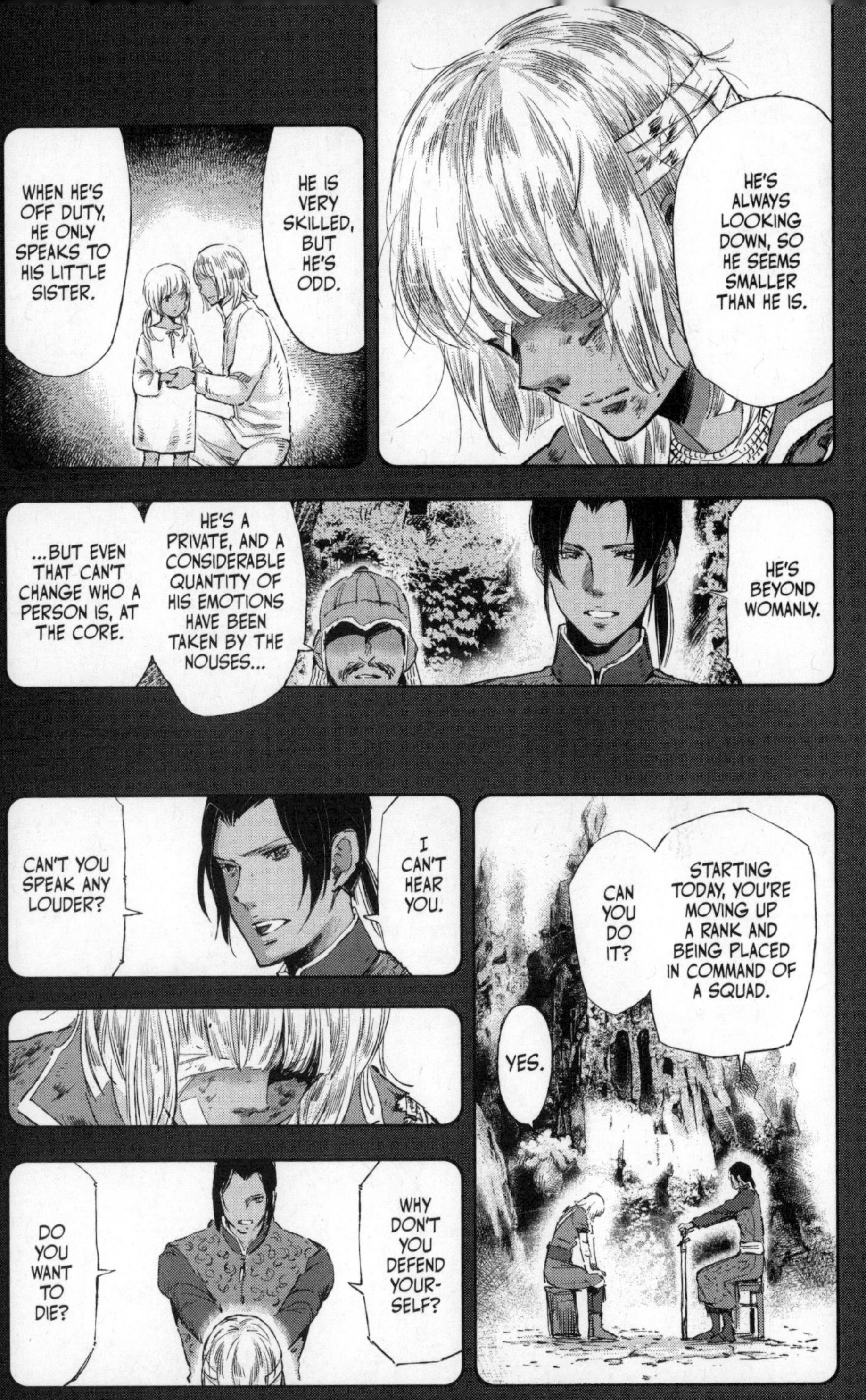
HE'S ALWAYS LOOKING DOWN, SO HE SEEMS SMALLER THAN HE IS.
HE IS VERY SKILLED, BUT HE'S ODD.
WHEN HE'S OFF DUTY, HE ONLY SPEAKS TO HIS LITTLE SISTER.
HE'S BEYOND WOMANLY.
HE'S A PRIVATE, AND A CONSIDERABLE QUANTITY OF HIS EMOTIONS HAVE BEEN TAKEN BY THE NOUSES...
...BUT EVEN THAT CAN'T CHANGE WHO A PERSON IS, AT THE CORE.
STARTING TODAY, YOU'RE MOVING UP A RANK AND BEING PLACED IN COMMAND OF A SQUAD.
CAN YOU DO IT?
YES.
I CAN'T HEAR YOU.
CAN'T YOU SPEAK ANY LOUDER?
WHY DON'T YOU DEFEND YOUR-SELF?
DO YOU WANT TO DIE?

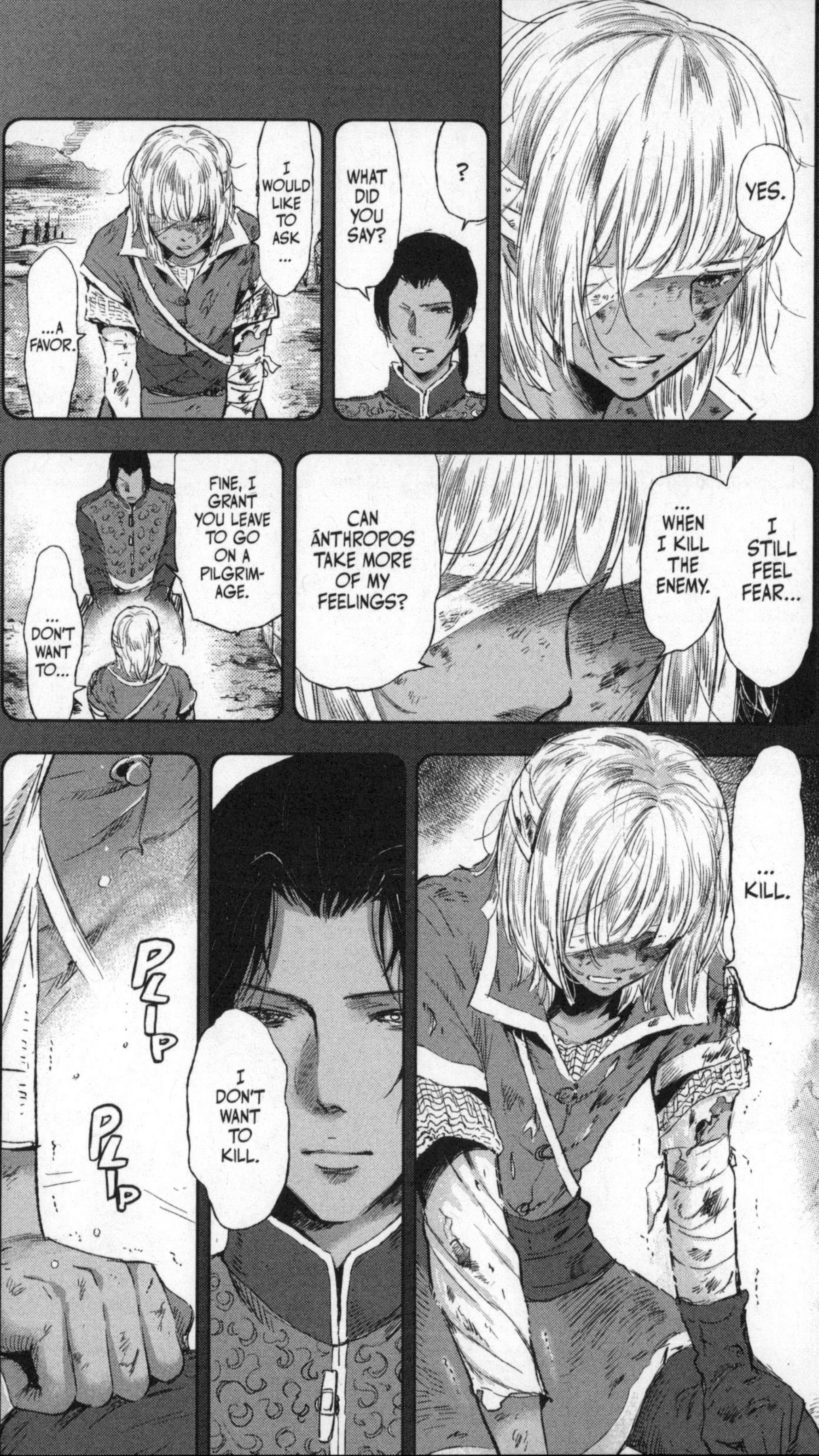
YES.
?
WHAT DID YOU SAY?
I WOULD LIKE TO ASK...
...A FAVOR.
I STILL FEEL FEAR...
...WHEN I KILL THE ENEMY.
CAN ĀNTHROPOS TAKE MORE OF MY FEELINGS?
FINE, I GRANT YOU LEAVE TO GO ON A PILGRIMAGE.
...DON'T WANT TO...
...KILL.
I DON'T WANT TO KILL.
PLIP
PLIP

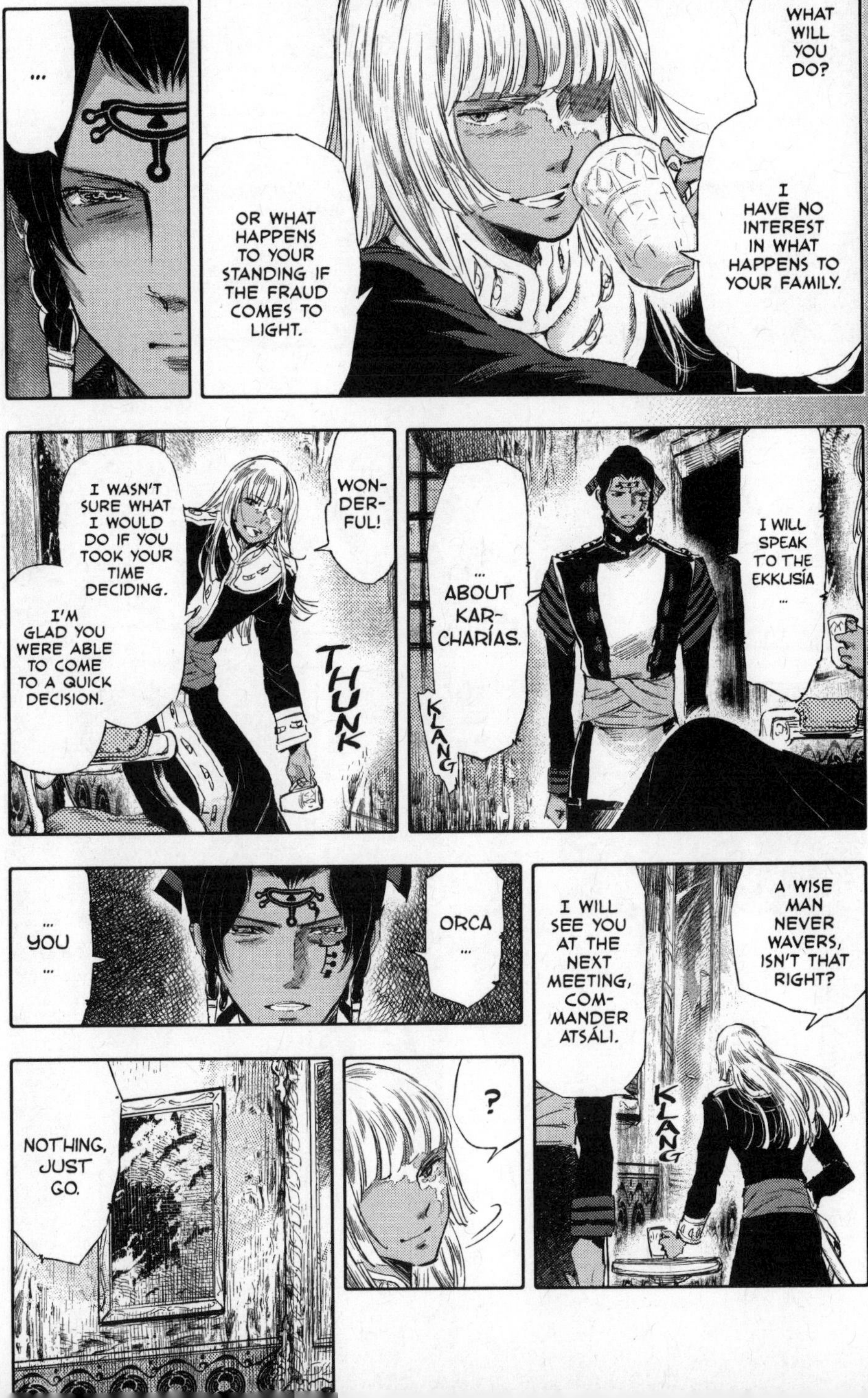
WHAT WILL YOU DO?
I HAVE NO INTEREST IN WHAT HAPPENS TO YOUR FAMILY.
OR WHAT HAPPENS TO YOUR STANDING IF THE FRAUD COMES TO LIGHT.
...
I WILL SPEAK TO THE EKKUSÍA ...
... ABOUT KARCHARÍAS.
KLANG
WONDERFUL!
I WASN'T SURE WHAT I WOULD DO IF YOU TOOK YOUR TIME DECIDING.
I'M GLAD YOU WERE ABLE TO COME TO A QUICK DECISION.
THUNK
A WISE MAN NEVER WAVERS, ISN'T THAT RIGHT?
I WILL SEE YOU AT THE NEXT MEETING, COMMANDER ATSÁLI.
KLANG
ORCA ...
... YOU ...
?
NOTHING, JUST GO.

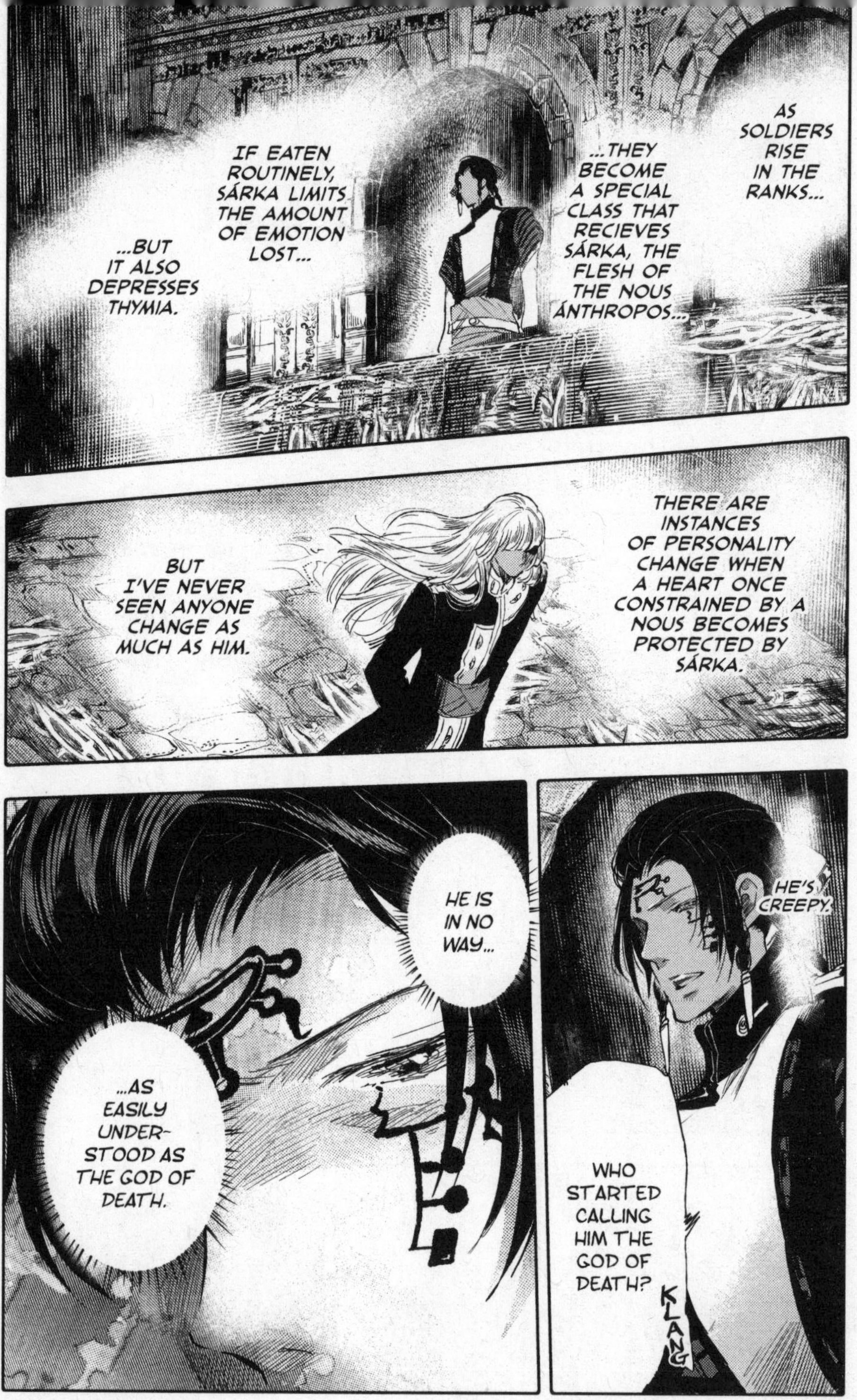
AS SOLDIERS RISE IN THE RANKS...
...THEY BECOME A SPECIAL CLASS THAT RECIEVES SÁRKA, THE FLESH OF THE NOUS ÁNTHROPOS...
IF EATEN ROUTINELY, SÁRKA LIMITS THE AMOUNT OF EMOTION LOST...
...BUT IT ALSO DEPRESSES THYMIA.
THERE ARE INSTANCES OF PERSONALITY CHANGE WHEN A HEART ONCE CONSTRAINED BY A NOUS BECOMES PROTECTED BY SÁRKA.
BUT I'VE NEVER SEEN ANYONE CHANGE AS MUCH AS HIM.
HE'S CREEPY.
WHO STARTED CALLING HIM THE GOD OF DEATH?
KLANG
HE IS IN NO WAY...
...AS EASILY UNDER-STOOD AS THE GOD OF DEATH.

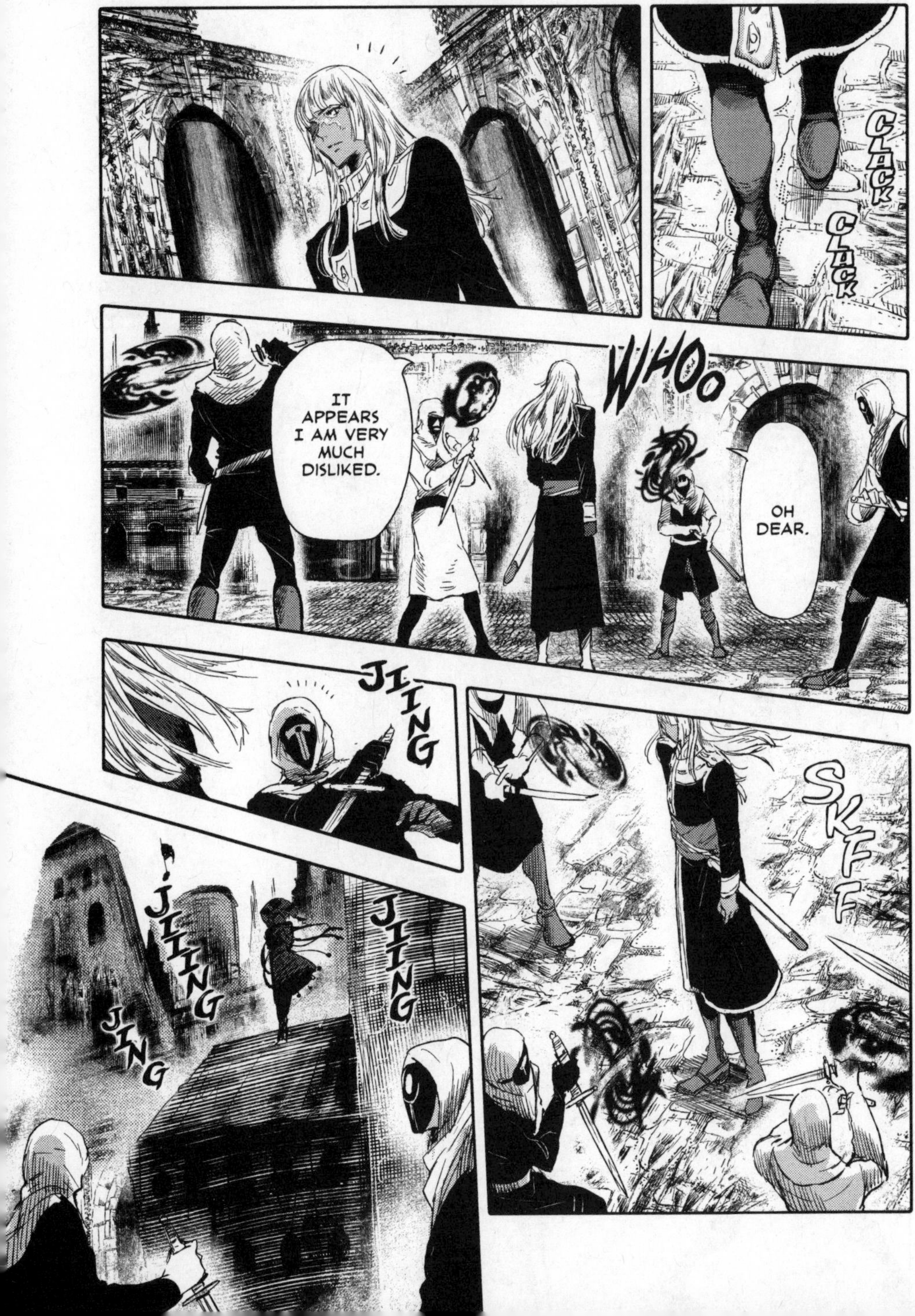
CLACK
CLACK
WHOOO
OH DEAR.
IT APPEARS I AM VERY MUCH DISLIKED.
SKFF
JIING
JIING
JIIING
JING

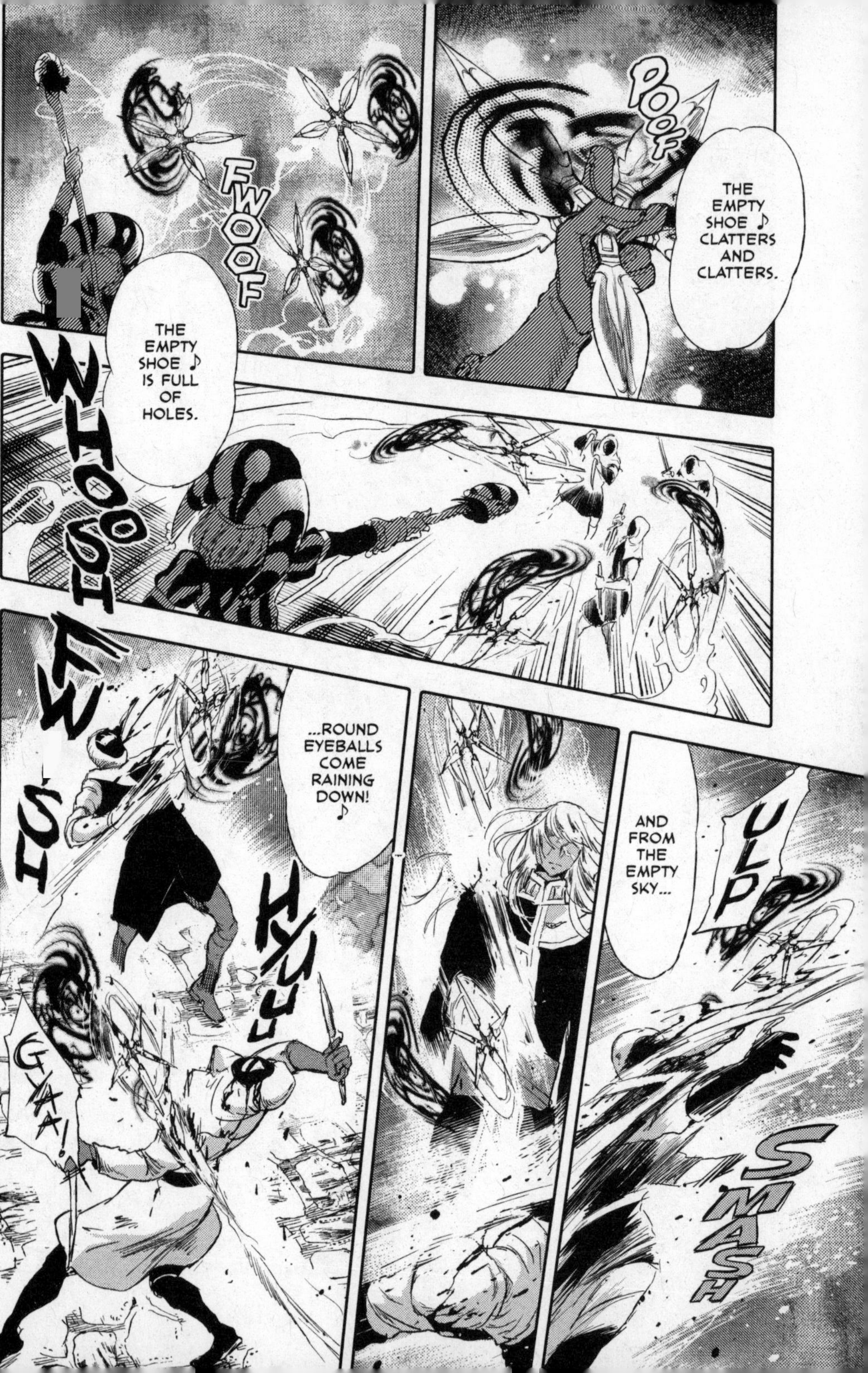
POOF
THE EMPTY SHOE ♪ CLATTERS AND CLATTERS.
FWOOF
THE EMPTY SHOE ♪ IS FULL OF HOLES.
WHOOSH
AND FROM THE EMPTY SKY...
ULP
SMASH
...ROUND EYEBALLS COME RAINING DOWN! ♪
HYUUU
GYAA!

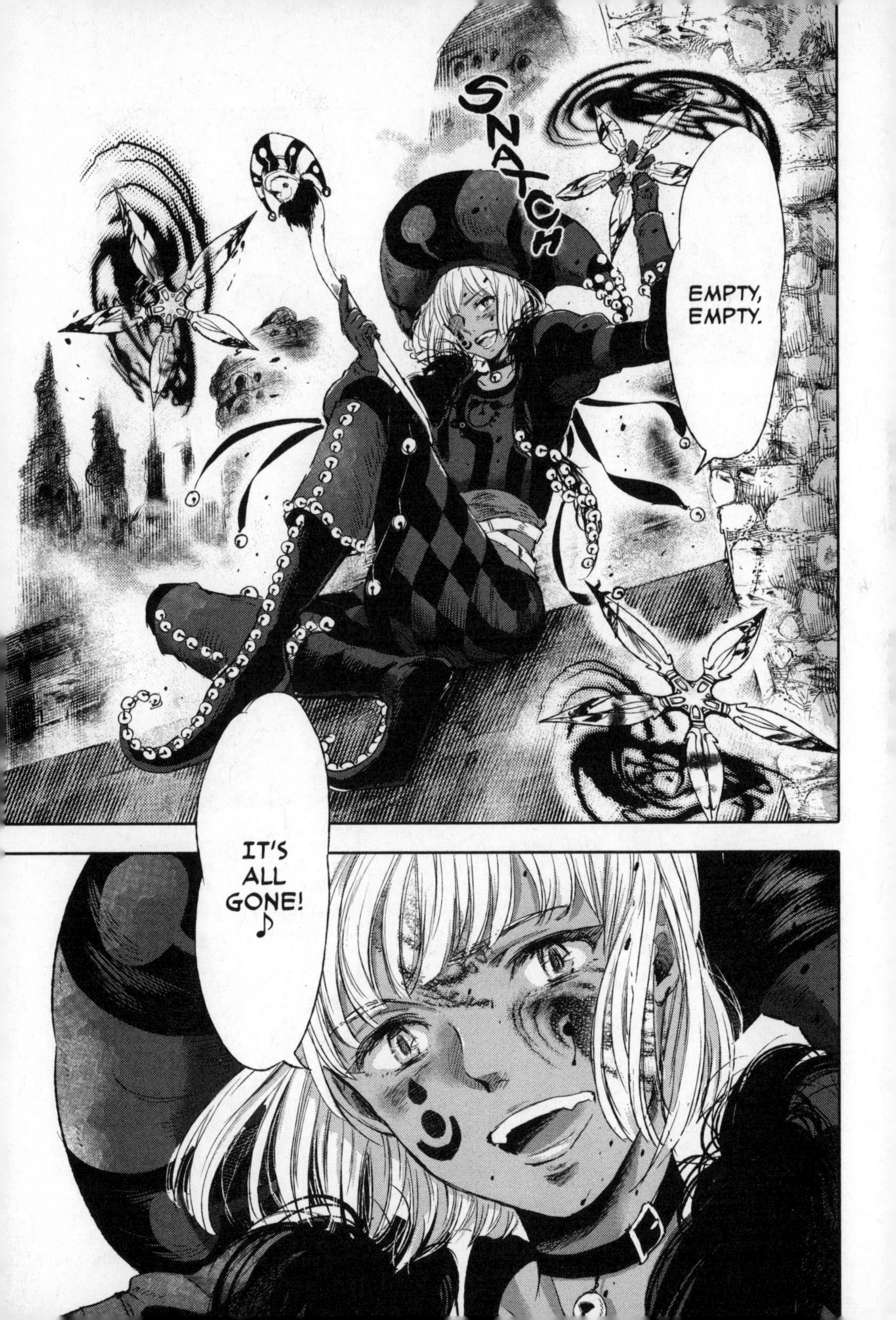
SNATCH
EMPTY, EMPTY.
IT'S ALL GONE! ♪

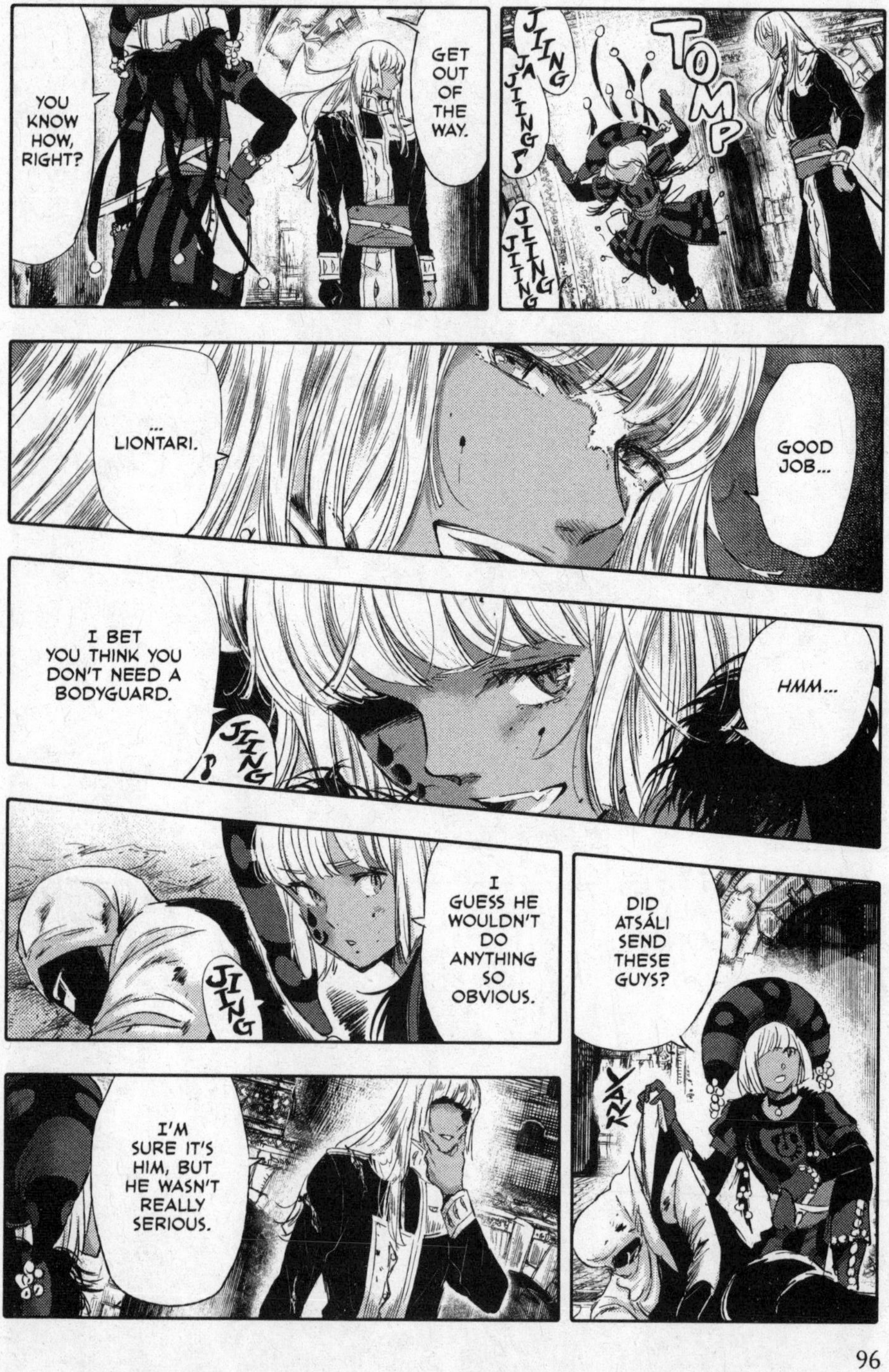
TOMP
JIING JA JIING JIING ♪
JIING JIING
GET OUT OF THE WAY.
YOU KNOW HOW, RIGHT?
GOOD JOB...
... LIONTARI.
HMM...
I BET YOU THINK YOU DON'T NEED A BODYGUARD.
JIING ♪
DID ATSÁLI SEND THESE GUYS?
YANK
I GUESS HE WOULDN'T DO ANYTHING SO OBVIOUS.
JIING
I'M SURE IT'S HIM, BUT HE WASN'T REALLY SERIOUS.

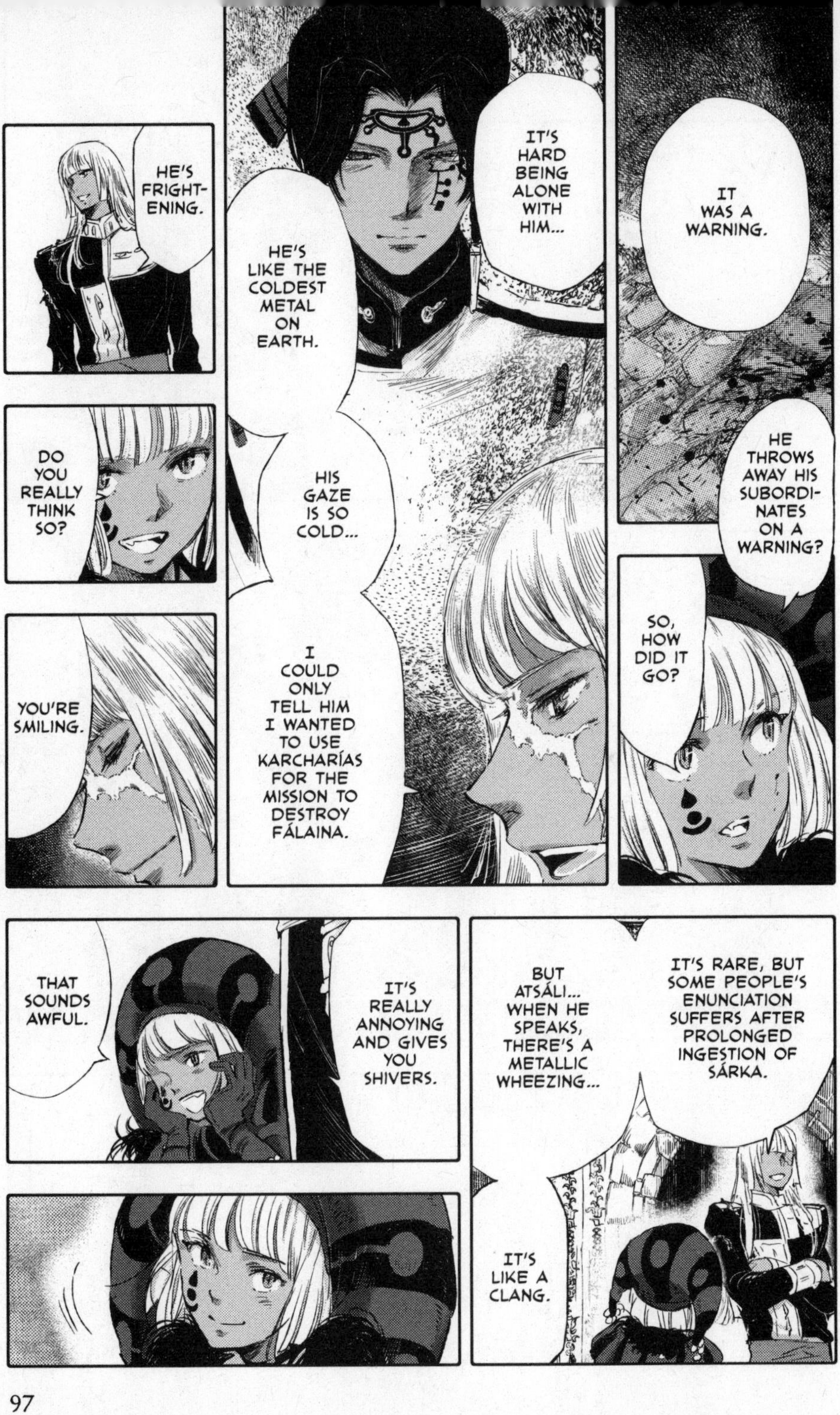
IT WAS A WARNING.
HE THROWS AWAY HIS SUBORDINATES ON A WARNING?
SO, HOW DID IT GO?
IT'S HARD BEING ALONE WITH HIM...
HE'S LIKE THE COLDEST METAL ON EARTH.
HIS GAZE IS SO COLD...
I COULD ONLY TELL HIM I WANTED TO USE KARCHARÍAS FOR THE MISSION TO DESTROY FÁLAINA.
HE'S FRIGHT-ENING.
DO YOU REALLY THINK SO?
YOU'RE SMILING.
IT'S RARE, BUT SOME PEOPLE'S ENUNCIATION SUFFERS AFTER PROLONGED INGESTION OF SÁRKA.
BUT ATSÁLI... WHEN HE SPEAKS, THERE'S A METALLIC WHEEZING...
IT'S LIKE A CLANG.
IT'S REALLY ANNOYING AND GIVES YOU SHIVERS.
THAT SOUNDS AWFUL.

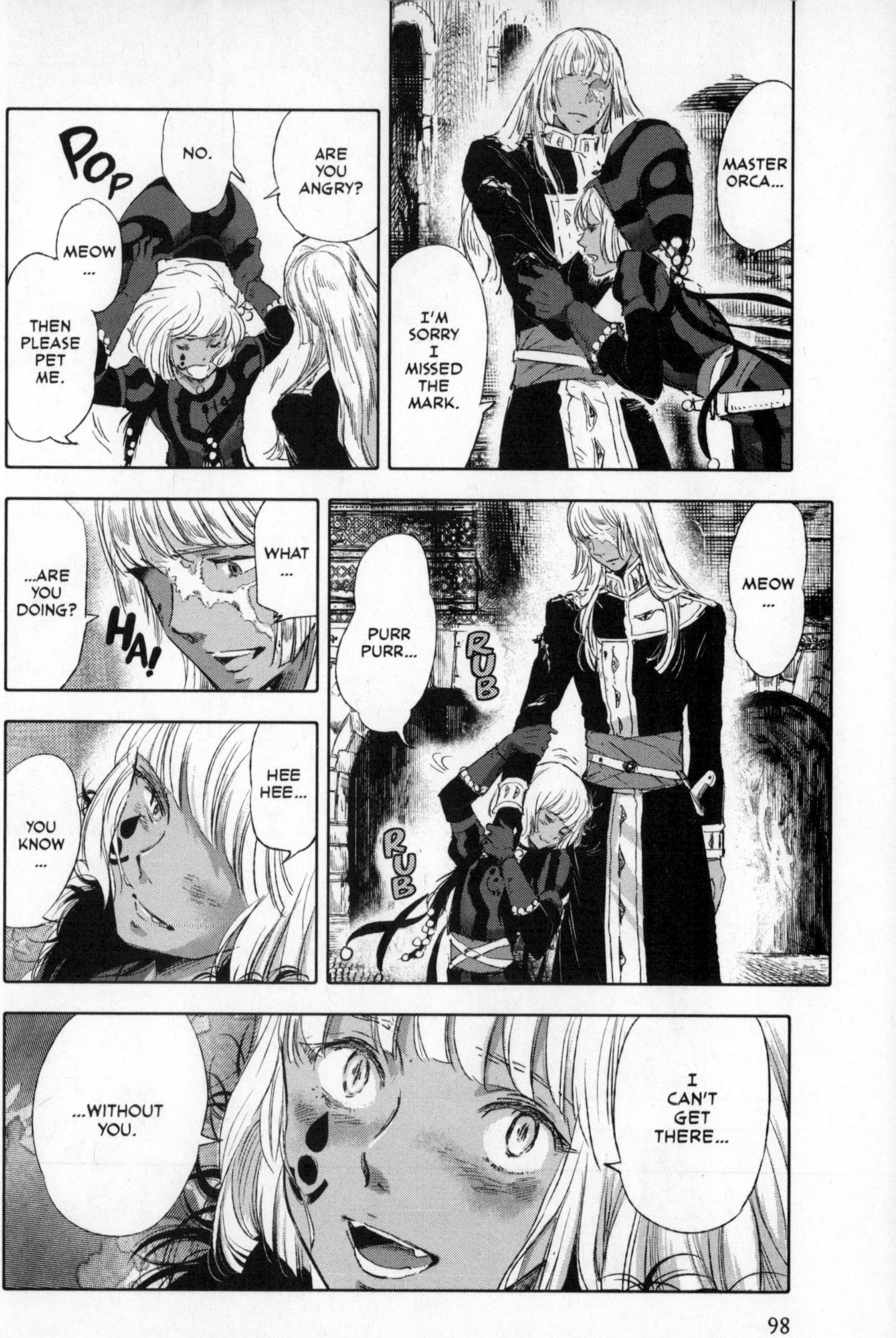
MASTER ORCA...
I'M SORRY I MISSED THE MARK.
ARE YOU ANGRY?
NO.
POP
MEOW...
THEN PLEASE PET ME.
MEOW...
PURR PURR...
RUB
RUB
WHAT...
...ARE YOU DOING?
HA!
HEE HEE...
YOU KNOW...
I CAN'T GET THERE...
...WITHOUT YOU.

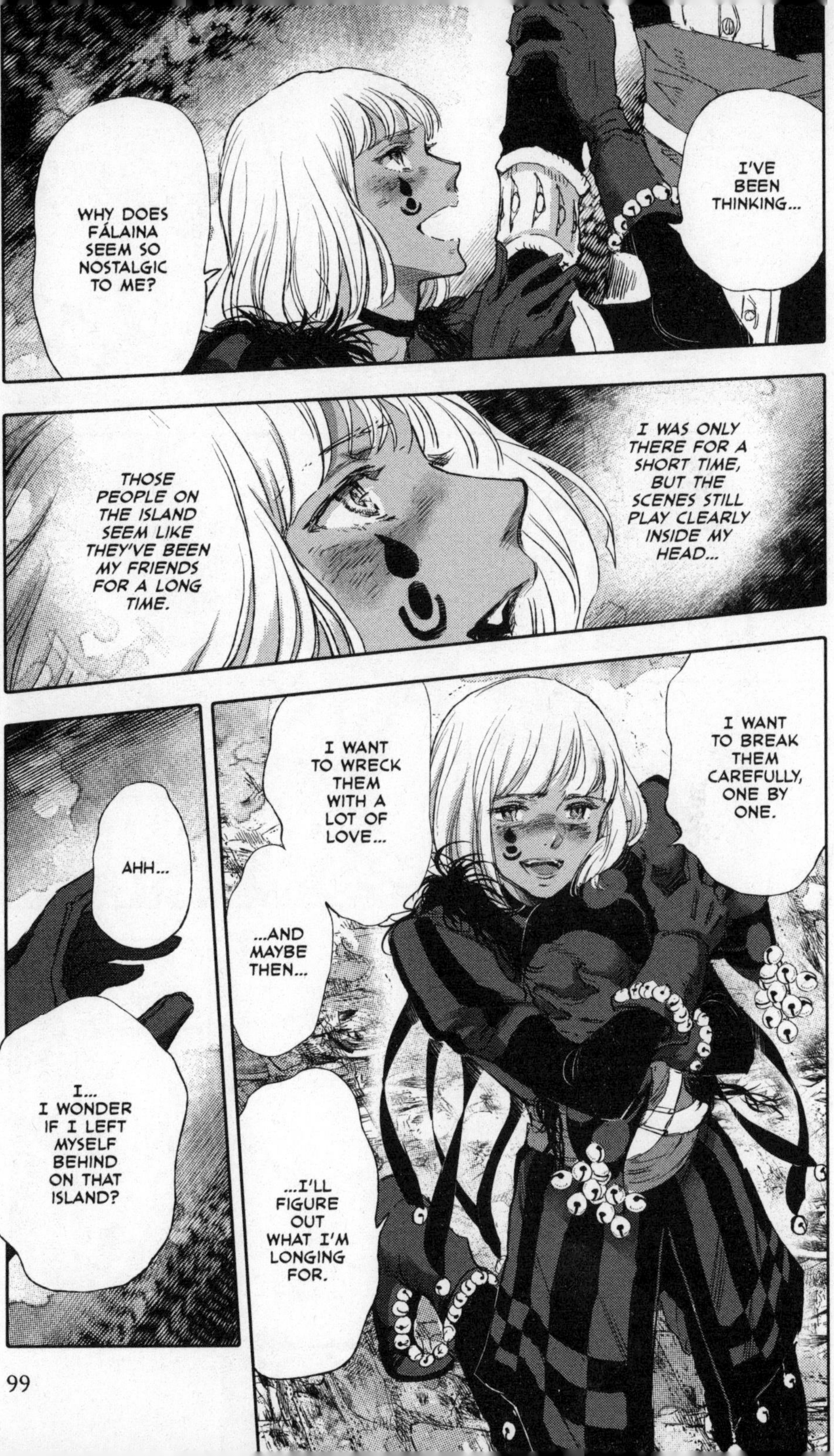
I'VE BEEN THINKING...
WHY DOES FÁLAINA SEEM SO NOSTALGIC TO ME?
I WAS ONLY THERE FOR A SHORT TIME, BUT THE SCENES STILL PLAY CLEARLY INSIDE MY HEAD...
THOSE PEOPLE ON THE ISLAND SEEM LIKE THEY'VE BEEN MY FRIENDS FOR A LONG TIME.
I WANT TO BREAK THEM CAREFULLY, ONE BY ONE.
I WANT TO WRECK THEM WITH A LOT OF LOVE...
...AND MAYBE THEN...
...I'LL FIGURE OUT WHAT I'M LONGING FOR.
AHH...
I... I WONDER IF I LEFT MYSELF BEHIND ON THAT ISLAND?

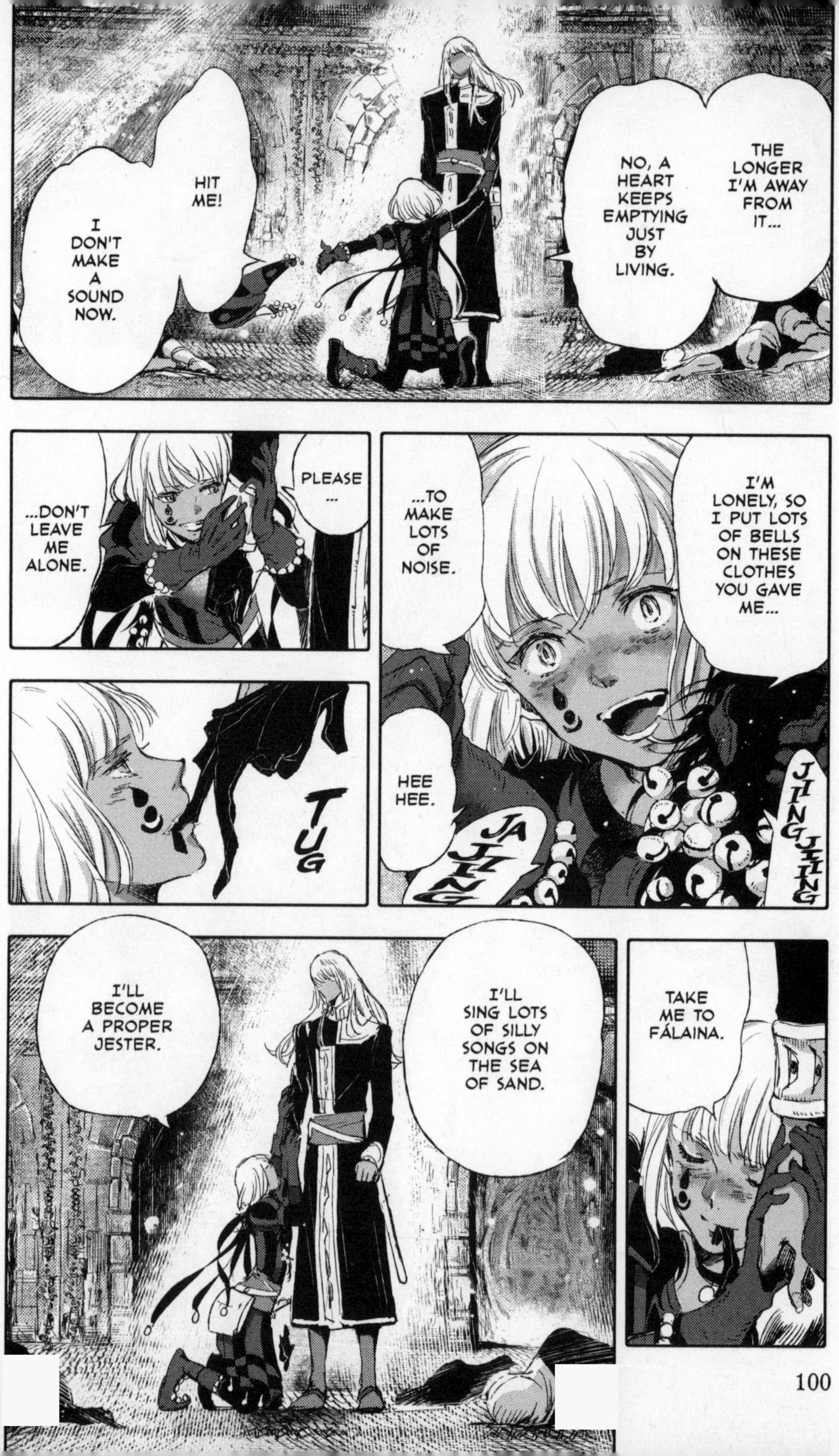
THE LONGER I'M AWAY FROM IT...
NO, A HEART KEEPS EMPTYING JUST BY LIVING.
HIT ME!
I DON'T MAKE A SOUND NOW.
I'M LONELY, SO I PUT LOTS OF BELLS ON THESE CLOTHES YOU GAVE ME...
...TO MAKE LOTS OF NOISE.
HEE HEE.
JINGJING
JAJING
PLEASE...
...DON'T LEAVE ME ALONE.
TUG
TAKE ME TO FÁLAINA.
I'LL SING LOTS OF SILLY SONGS ON THE SEA OF SAND.
I'LL BECOME A PROPER JESTER.

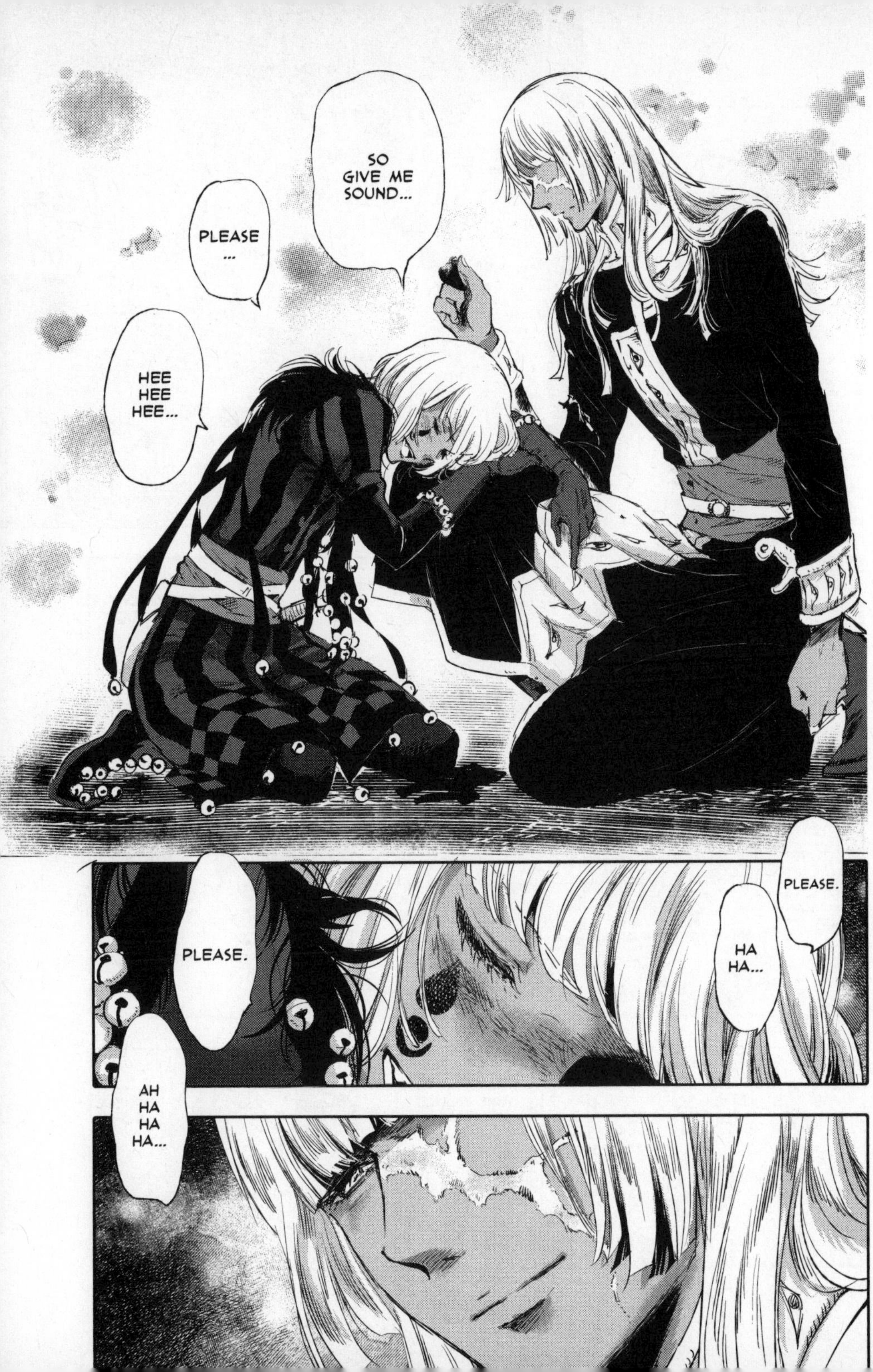
SO GIVE ME SOUND...
PLEASE ...
HEE HEE HEE...
PLEASE.
HA HA...
PLEASE.
AH HA HA HA...

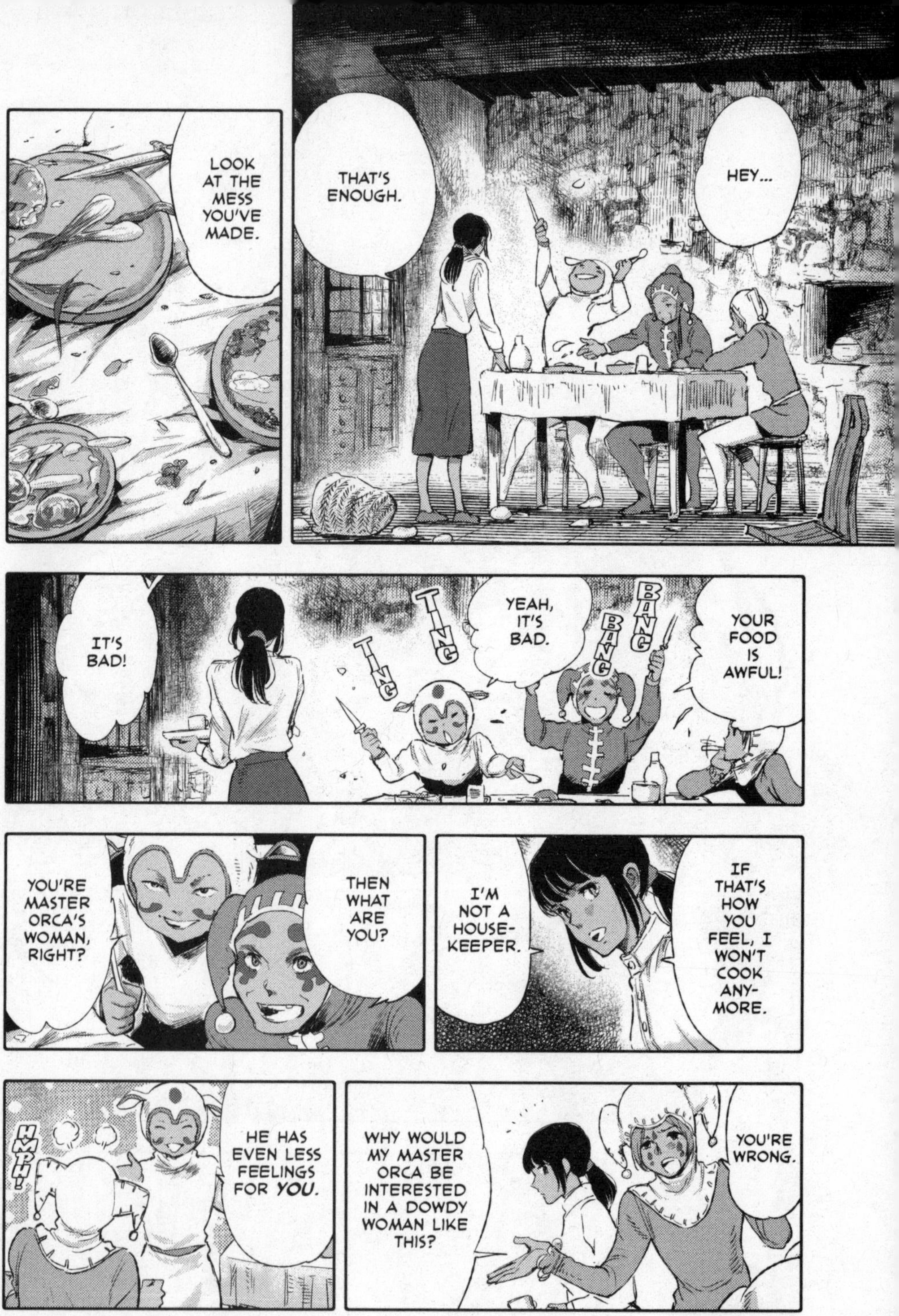

HEY...
THAT'S ENOUGH.
LOOK AT THE MESS YOU'VE MADE.
YOUR FOOD IS AWFUL!
BING
BING
YEAH, IT'S BAD.
TING
TING
IT'S BAD!
IF THAT'S HOW YOU FEEL, I WON'T COOK ANYMORE.
I'M NOT A HOUSEKEEPER.
THEN WHAT ARE YOU?
YOU'RE MASTER ORCA'S WOMAN, RIGHT?
YOU'RE WRONG.
WHY WOULD MY MASTER ORCA BE INTERESTED IN A DOWDY WOMAN LIKE THIS?
HE HAS EVEN LESS FEELINGS FOR *YOU*.
HMPH!

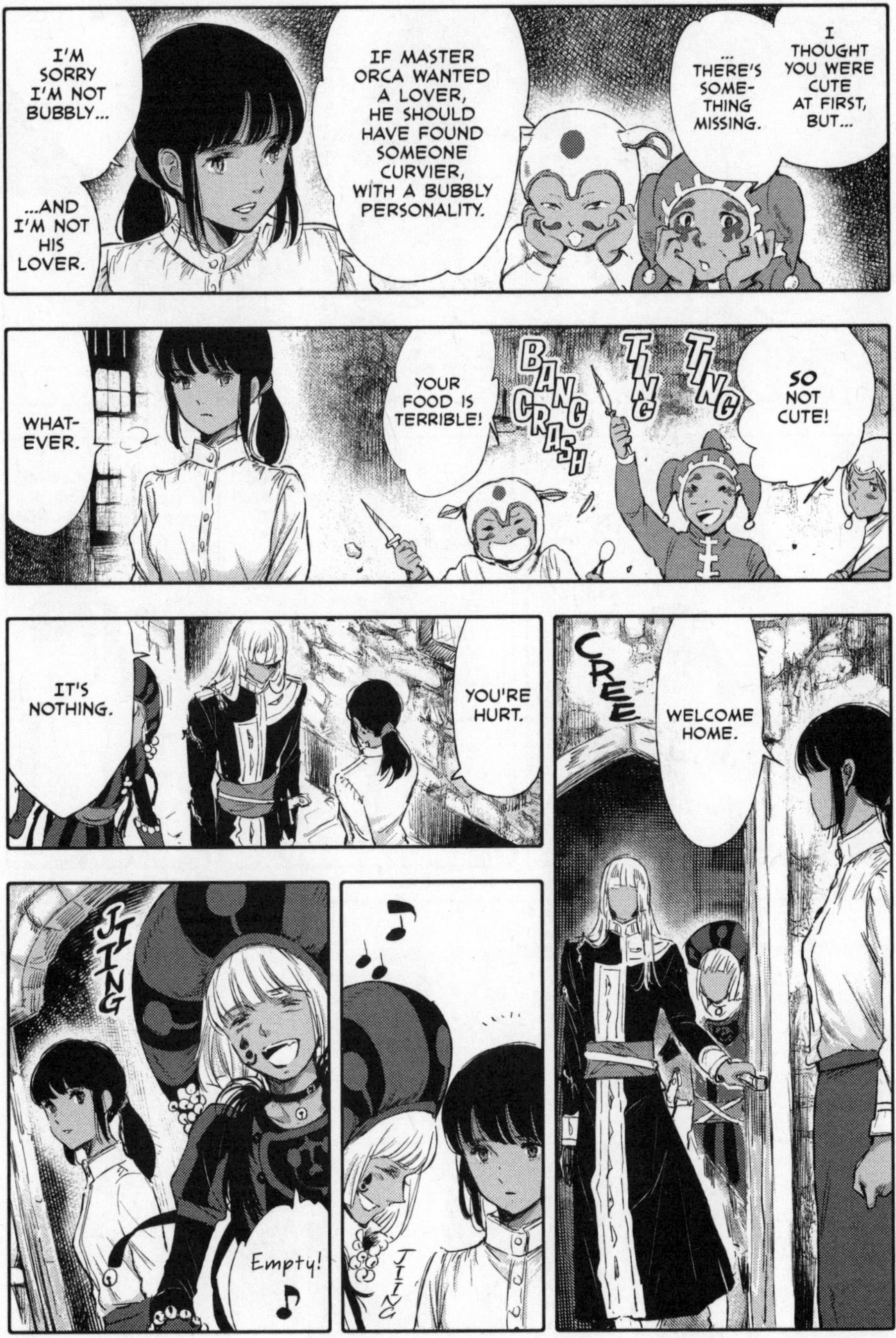
I THOUGHT YOU WERE CUTE AT FIRST, BUT...
...THERE'S SOME-THING MISSING.
IF MASTER ORCA WANTED A LOVER, HE SHOULD HAVE FOUND SOMEONE CURVIER, WITH A BUBBLY PERSONALITY.
I'M SORRY I'M NOT BUBBLY...
...AND I'M NOT HIS LOVER.
SO NOT CUTE!
TING
TING
BANG
CRASH
YOUR FOOD IS TERRIBLE!
WHAT-EVER.
CREE
WELCOME HOME.
YOU'RE HURT.
IT'S NOTHING.
JIING
JIING
Empty!

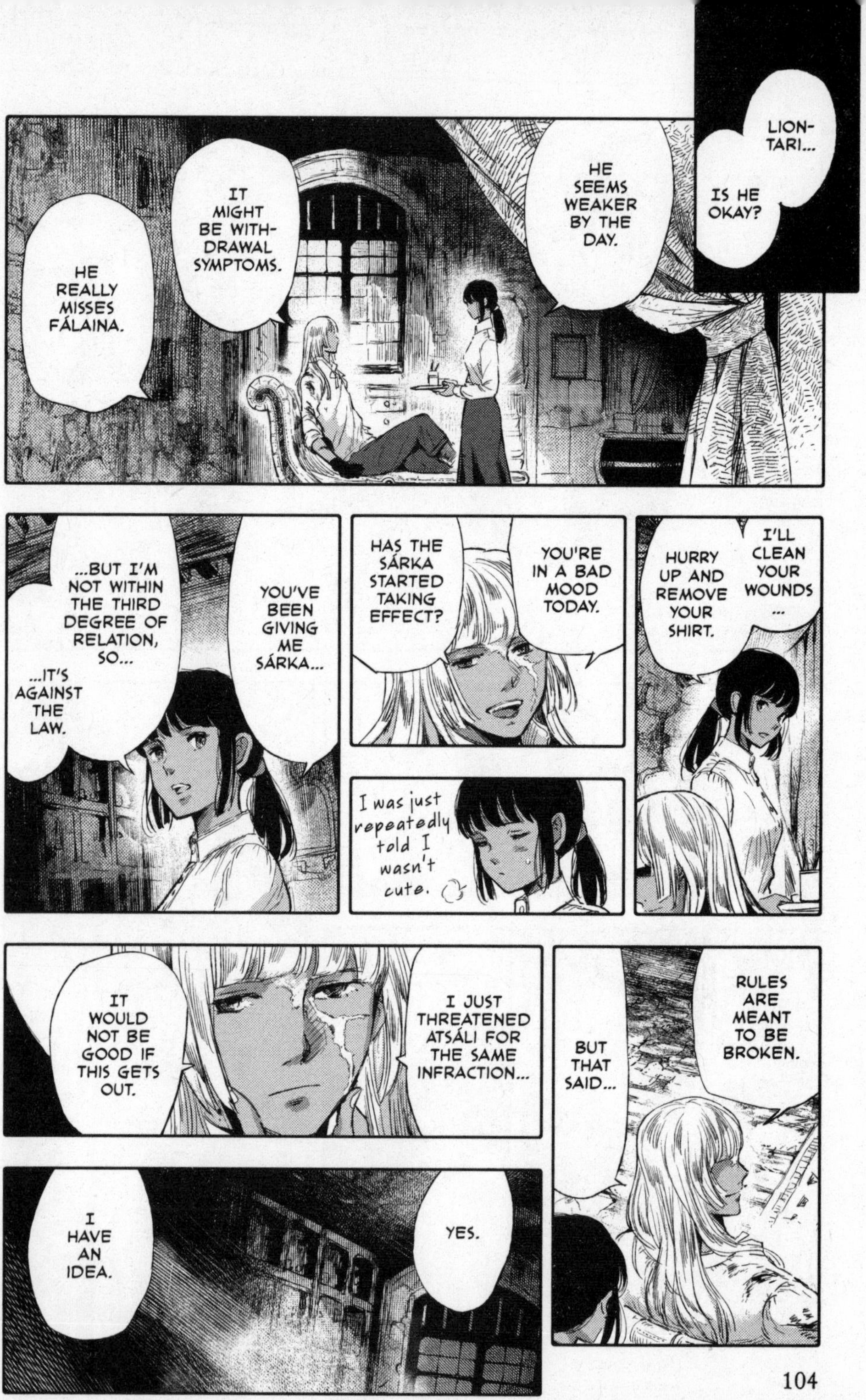
LION-TARI...
IS HE OKAY?
HE SEEMS WEAKER BY THE DAY.
IT MIGHT BE WITH-DRAWAL SYMPTOMS.
HE REALLY MISSES FÁLAINA.
I'LL CLEAN YOUR WOUNDS...
HURRY UP AND REMOVE YOUR SHIRT.
YOU'RE IN A BAD MOOD TODAY.
HAS THE SÁRKA STARTED TAKING EFFECT?
I was just repeatedly told I wasn't cute.
YOU'VE BEEN GIVING ME SÁRKA...
...BUT I'M NOT WITHIN THE THIRD DEGREE OF RELATION, SO...
...IT'S AGAINST THE LAW.
RULES ARE MEANT TO BE BROKEN.
BUT THAT SAID...
I JUST THREATENED ATSÁLI FOR THE SAME INFRACTION...
IT WOULD NOT BE GOOD IF THIS GETS OUT.
YES.
I HAVE AN IDEA.

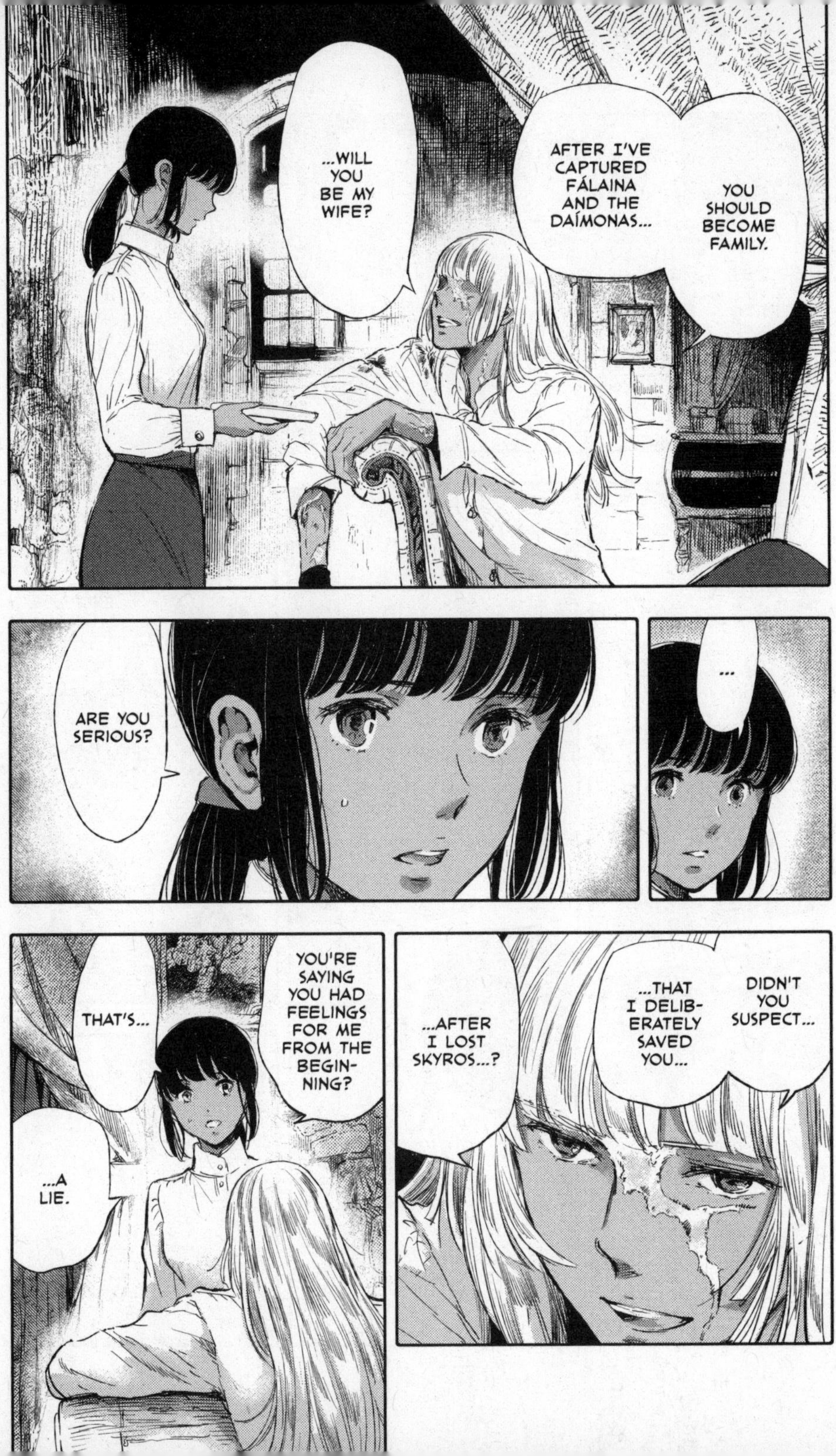
AFTER I'VE CAPTURED FÁLAINA AND THE DAÍMONAS...
YOU SHOULD BECOME FAMILY.
...WILL YOU BE MY WIFE?
...
ARE YOU SERIOUS?
DIDN'T YOU SUSPECT...
...THAT I DELIB-ERATELY SAVED YOU...
...AFTER I LOST SKYROS...?
YOU'RE SAYING YOU HAD FEELINGS FOR ME FROM THE BEGIN-NING?
THAT'S...
...A LIE.

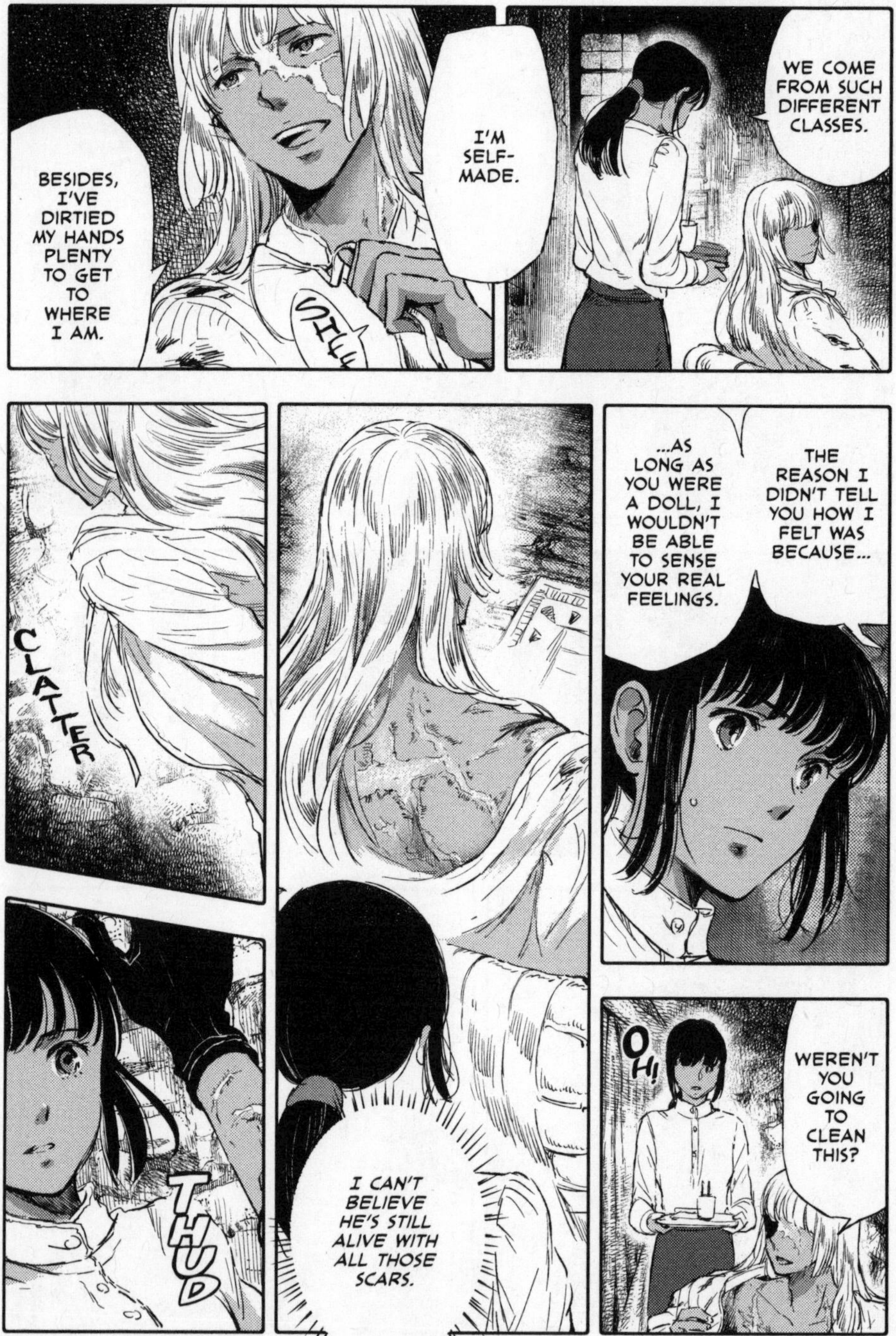
WE COME FROM SUCH DIFFERENT CLASSES.
I'M SELF-MADE.
BESIDES, I'VE DIRTIED MY HANDS PLENTY TO GET TO WHERE I AM.
THE REASON I DIDN'T TELL YOU HOW I FELT WAS BECAUSE...
...AS LONG AS YOU WERE A DOLL, I WOULDN'T BE ABLE TO SENSE YOUR REAL FEELINGS.
OH!
WEREN'T YOU GOING TO CLEAN THIS?
I CAN'T BELIEVE HE'S STILL ALIVE WITH ALL THOSE SCARS.
CLATTER
THUD

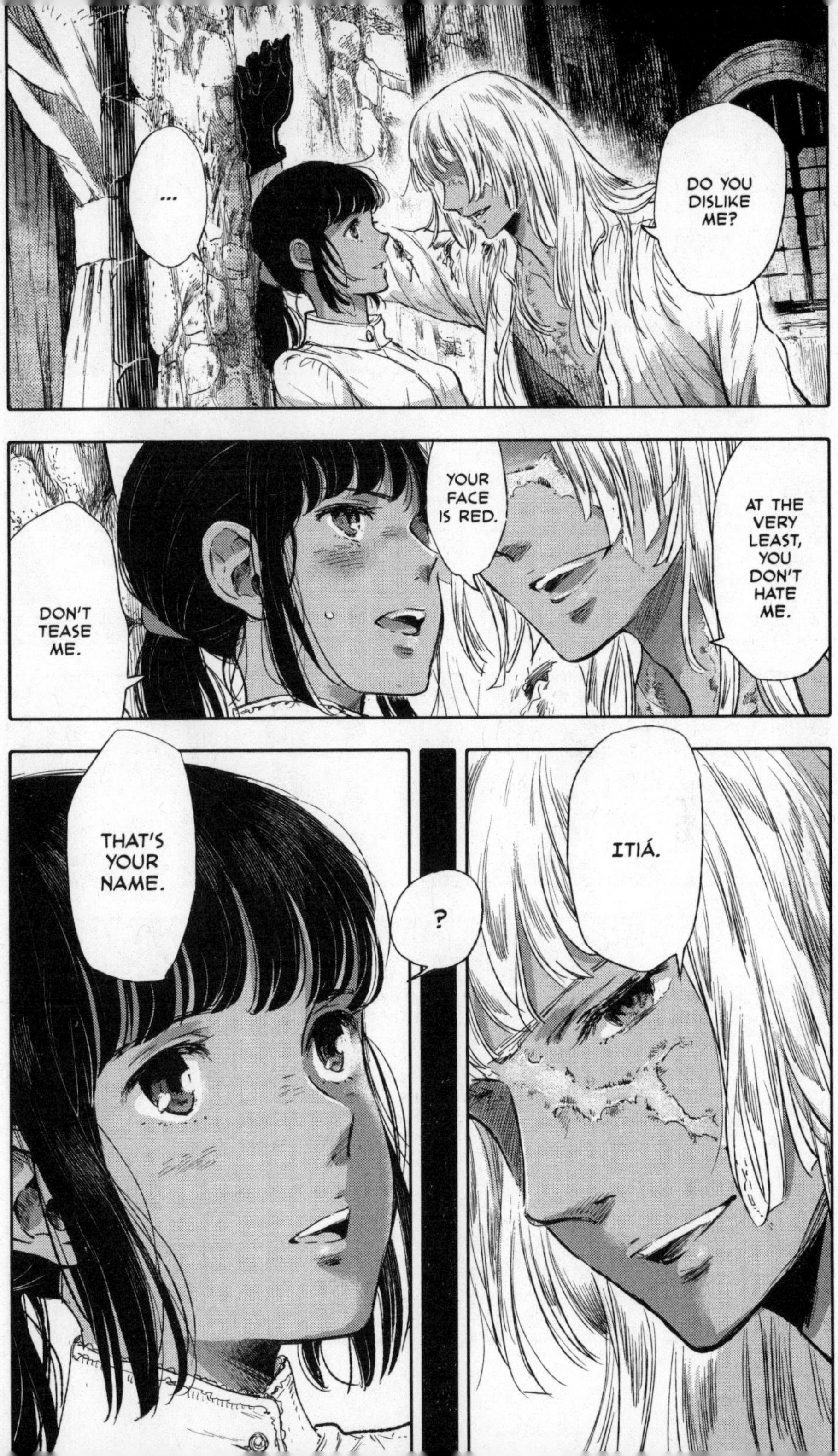
DO YOU DISLIKE ME?
...
AT THE VERY LEAST, YOU DON'T HATE ME.
YOUR FACE IS RED.
DON'T TEASE ME.
ITIÁ.
?
THAT'S YOUR NAME.

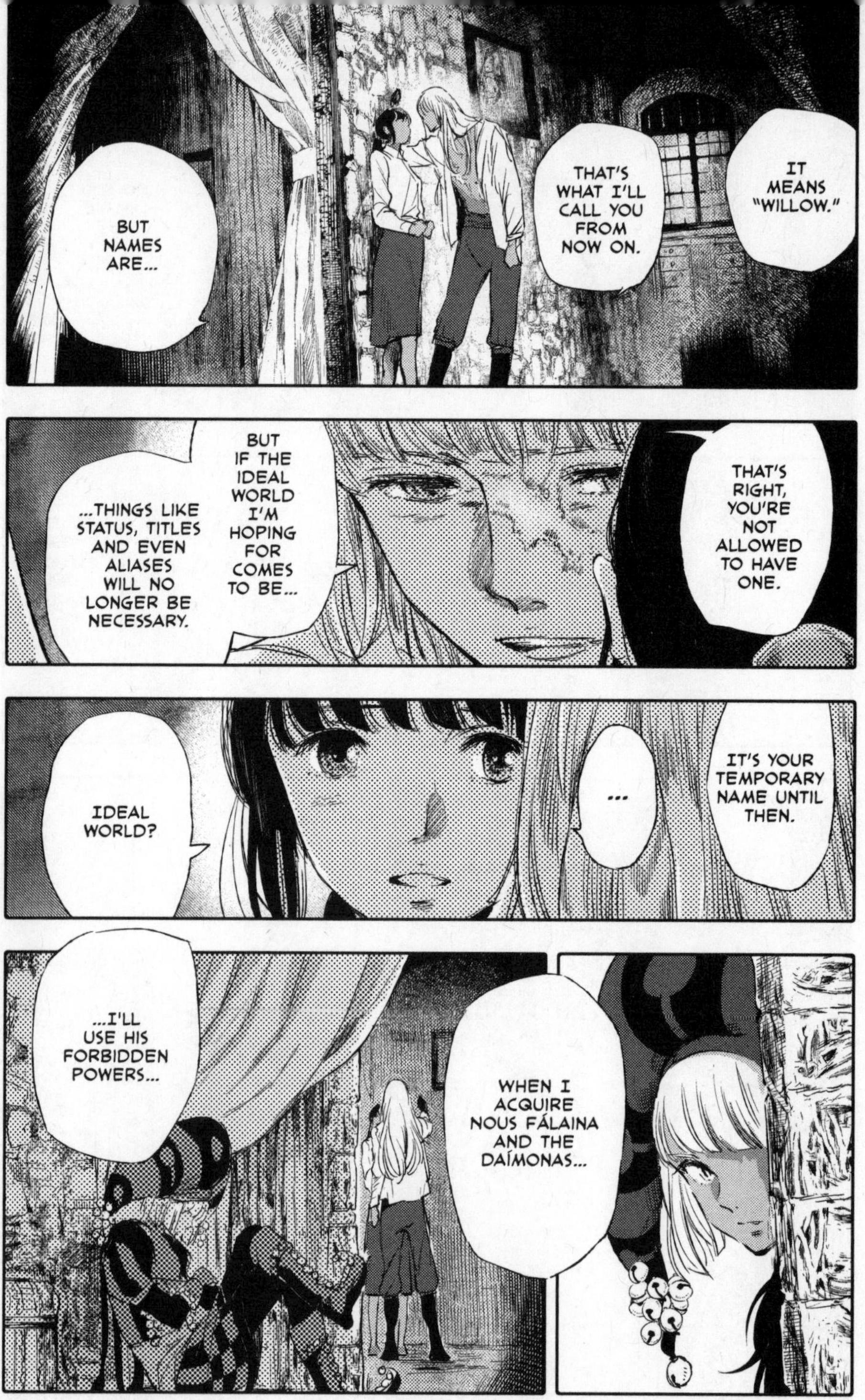
IT MEANS "WILLOW."
THAT'S WHAT I'LL CALL YOU FROM NOW ON.
BUT NAMES ARE...
THAT'S RIGHT, YOU'RE NOT ALLOWED TO HAVE ONE.
BUT IF THE IDEAL WORLD I'M HOPING FOR COMES TO BE...
...THINGS LIKE STATUS, TITLES AND EVEN ALIASES WILL NO LONGER BE NECESSARY.
IT'S YOUR TEMPORARY NAME UNTIL THEN.
...
IDEAL WORLD?
WHEN I ACQUIRE NOUS FÁLAINA AND THE DAÍMONAS...
...I'LL USE HIS FORBIDDEN POWERS...

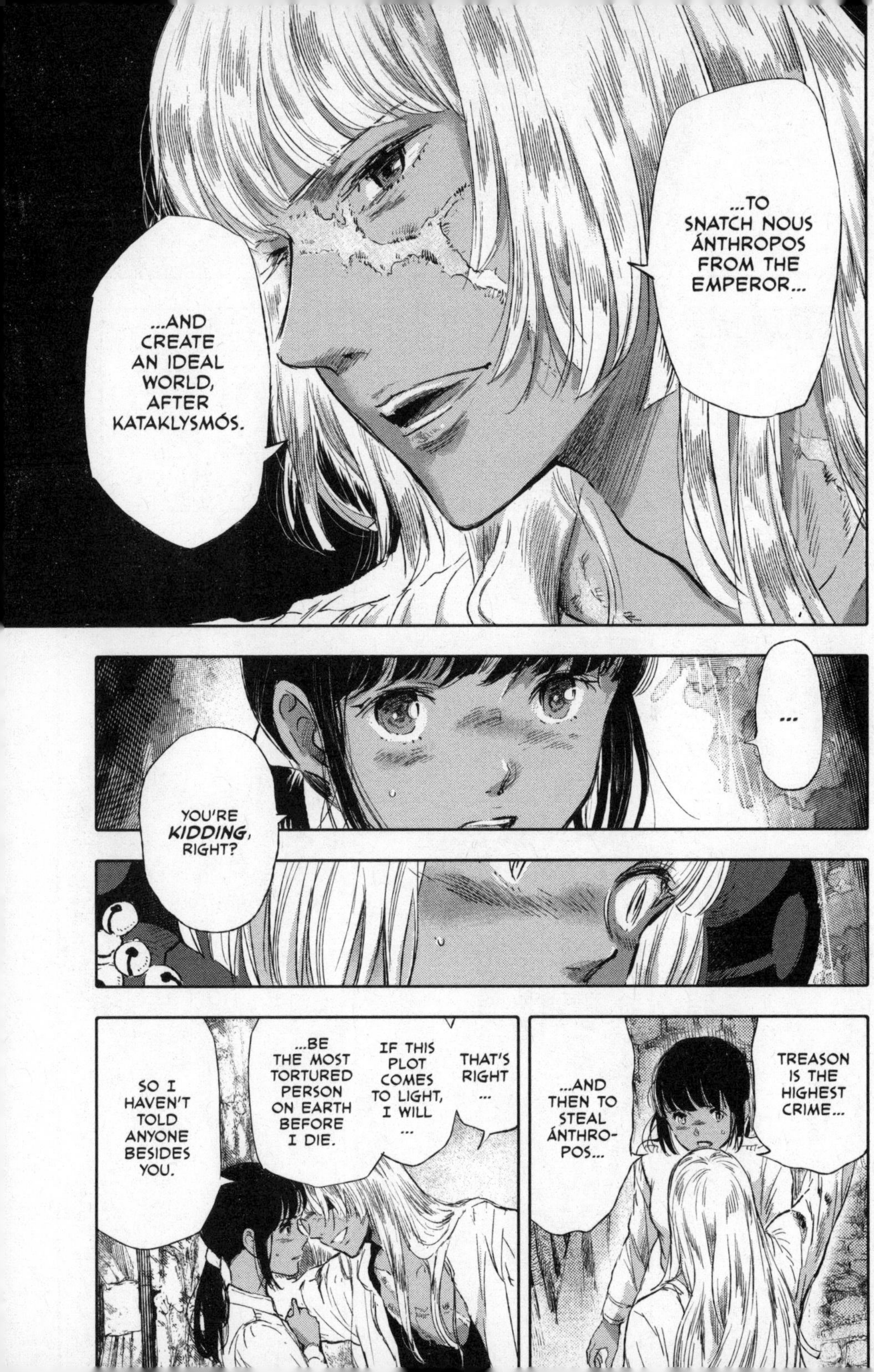
...TO SNATCH NOUS ÁNTHROPOS FROM THE EMPEROR...
...AND CREATE AN IDEAL WORLD, AFTER KATAKLYSMÓS.
...
YOU'RE **KIDDING**, RIGHT?
TREASON IS THE HIGHEST CRIME...
...AND THEN TO STEAL ÁNTHROPOS...
THAT'S RIGHT ...
IF THIS PLOT COMES TO LIGHT, I WILL ...
...BE THE MOST TORTURED PERSON ON EARTH BEFORE I DIE.
SO I HAVEN'T TOLD ANYONE BESIDES YOU.

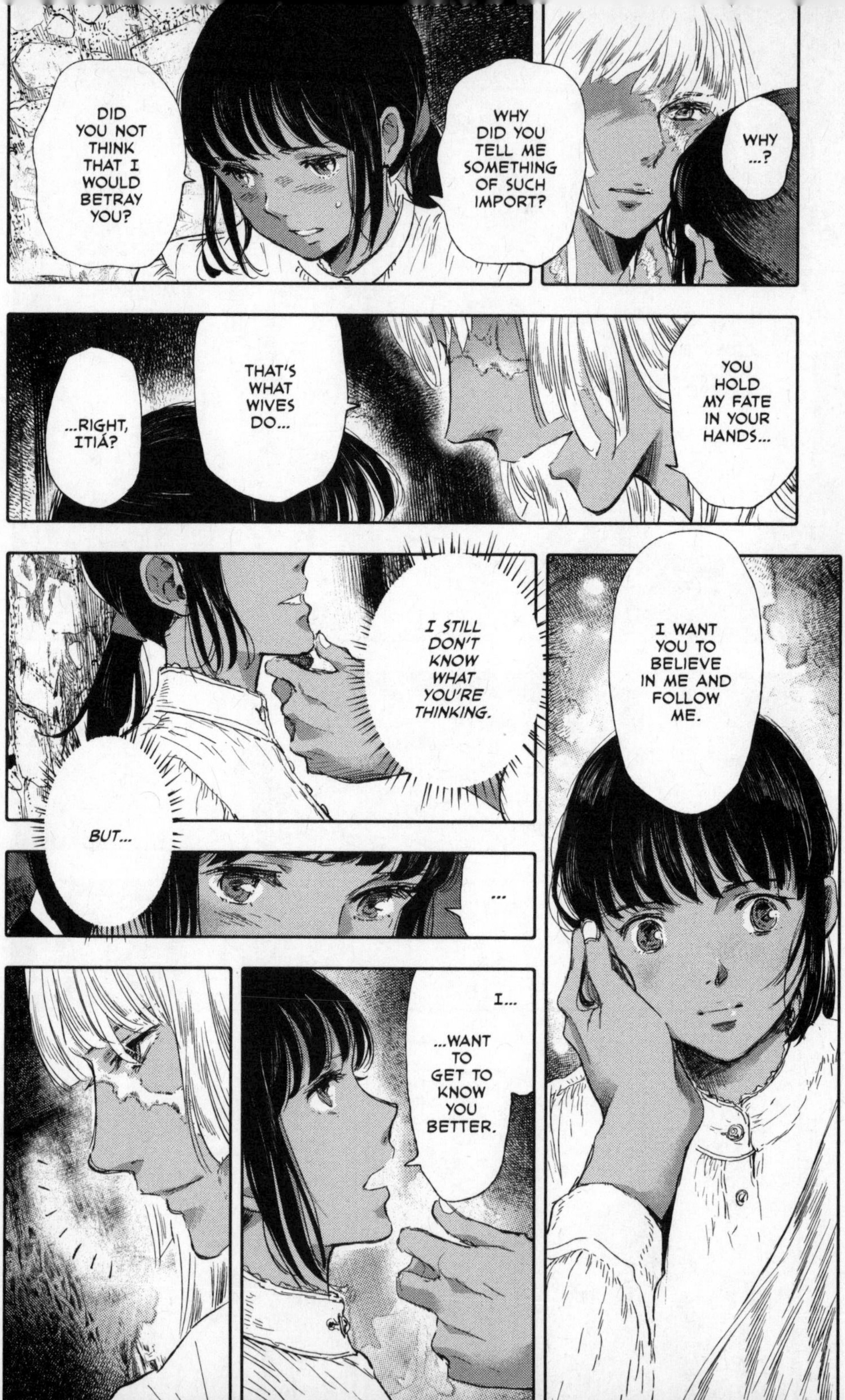
WHY ...?
WHY DID YOU TELL ME SOMETHING OF SUCH IMPORT?
DID YOU NOT THINK THAT I WOULD BETRAY YOU?
YOU HOLD MY FATE IN YOUR HANDS...
THAT'S WHAT WIVES DO...
...RIGHT, ITIÁ?
I WANT YOU TO BELIEVE IN ME AND FOLLOW ME.
I STILL DON'T KNOW WHAT YOU'RE THINKING.
BUT...
...
I...
...WANT TO GET TO KNOW YOU BETTER.

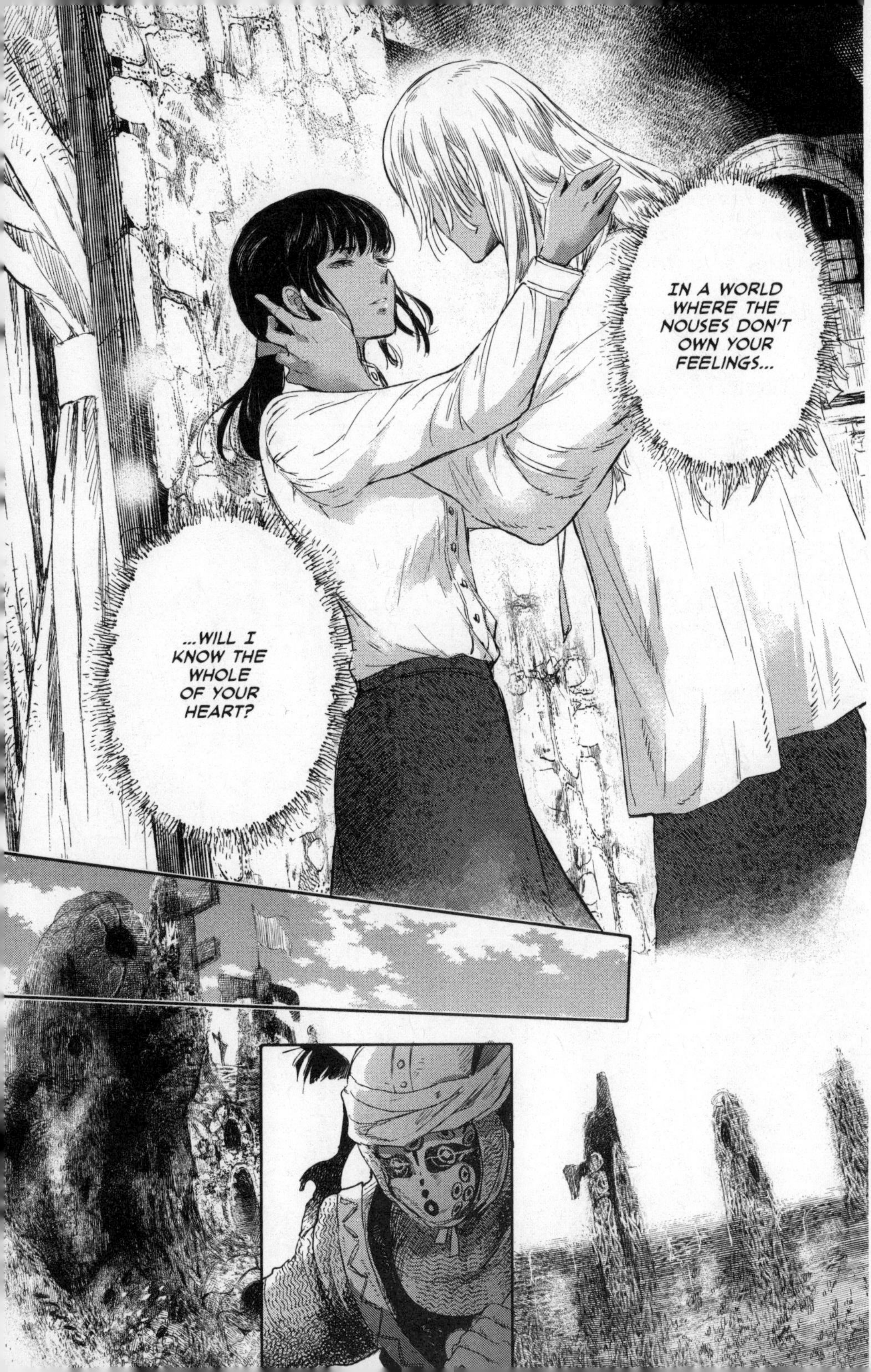
IN A WORLD WHERE THE NOUSES DON'T OWN YOUR FEELINGS...
...WILL I KNOW THE WHOLE OF YOUR HEART?

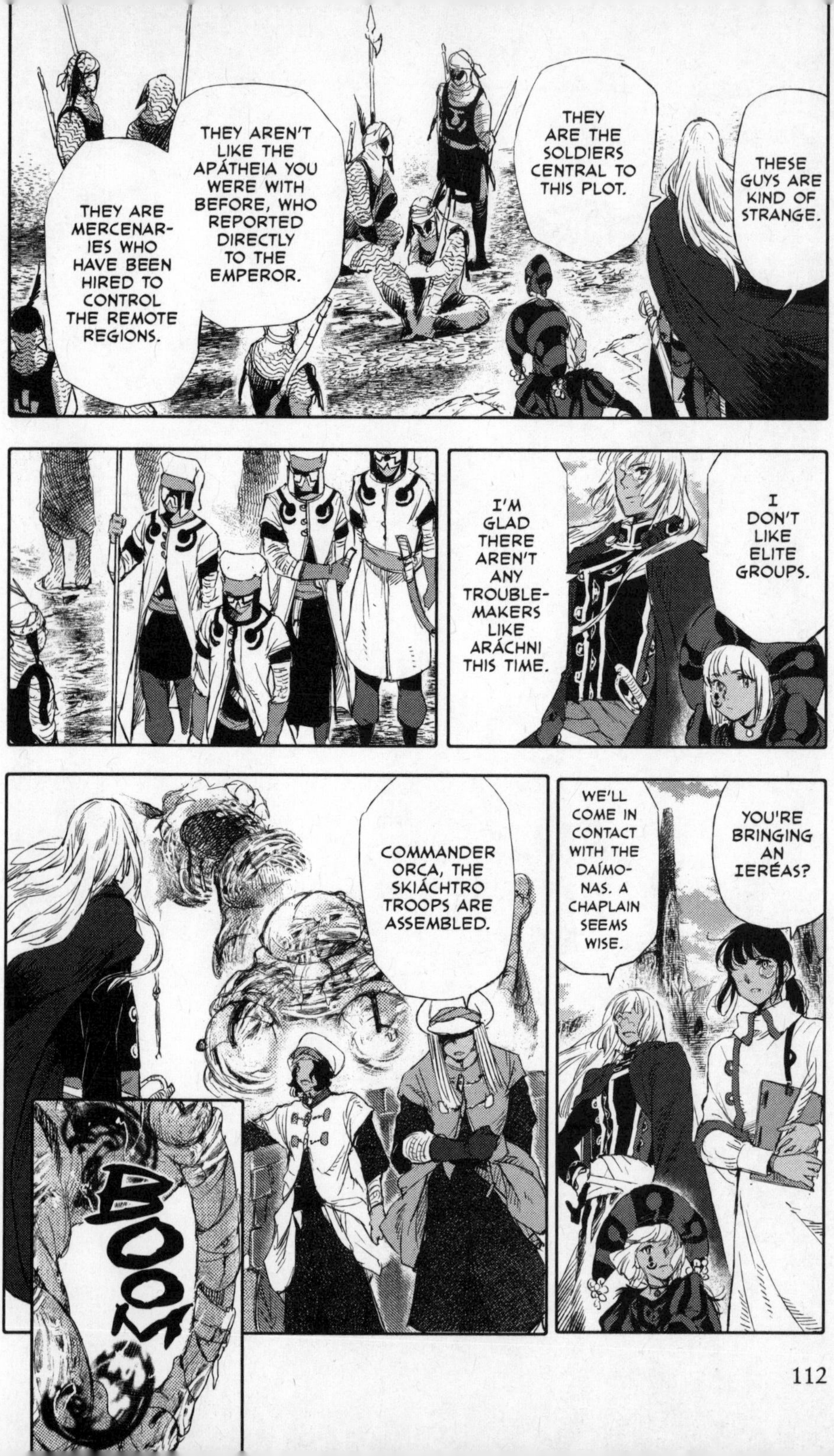
THESE GUYS ARE KIND OF STRANGE.
THEY ARE THE SOLDIERS CENTRAL TO THIS PLOT.
THEY AREN'T LIKE THE APÁTHEIA YOU WERE WITH BEFORE, WHO REPORTED DIRECTLY TO THE EMPEROR.
THEY ARE MERCENARIES WHO HAVE BEEN HIRED TO CONTROL THE REMOTE REGIONS.
I DON'T LIKE ELITE GROUPS.
I'M GLAD THERE AREN'T ANY TROUBLEMAKERS LIKE ARÁCHNI THIS TIME.
YOU'RE BRINGING AN IERÉAS?
WE'LL COME IN CONTACT WITH THE DAÍMONAS. A CHAPLAIN SEEMS WISE.
COMMANDER ORCA, THE SKIÁCHTRO TROOPS ARE ASSEMBLED.
BOOM

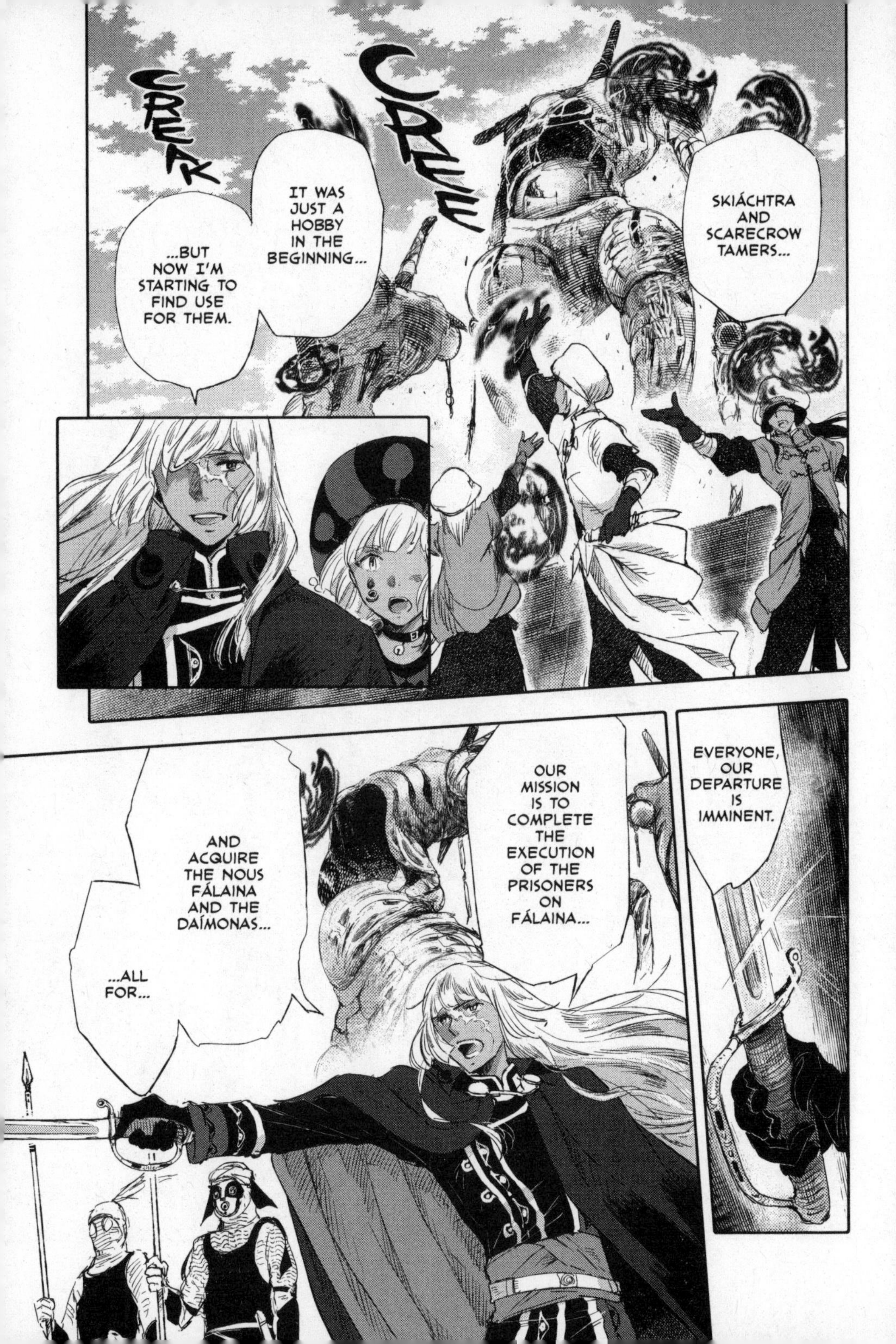
SKIÁCHTRA AND SCARECROW TAMERS...
CREE
CREAK
IT WAS JUST A HOBBY IN THE BEGINNING...
...BUT NOW I'M STARTING TO FIND USE FOR THEM.
EVERYONE, OUR DEPARTURE IS IMMINENT.
OUR MISSION IS TO COMPLETE THE EXECUTION OF THE PRISONERS ON FÁLAINA...
AND ACQUIRE THE NOUS FÁLAINA AND THE DAÍMONAS...
...ALL FOR...

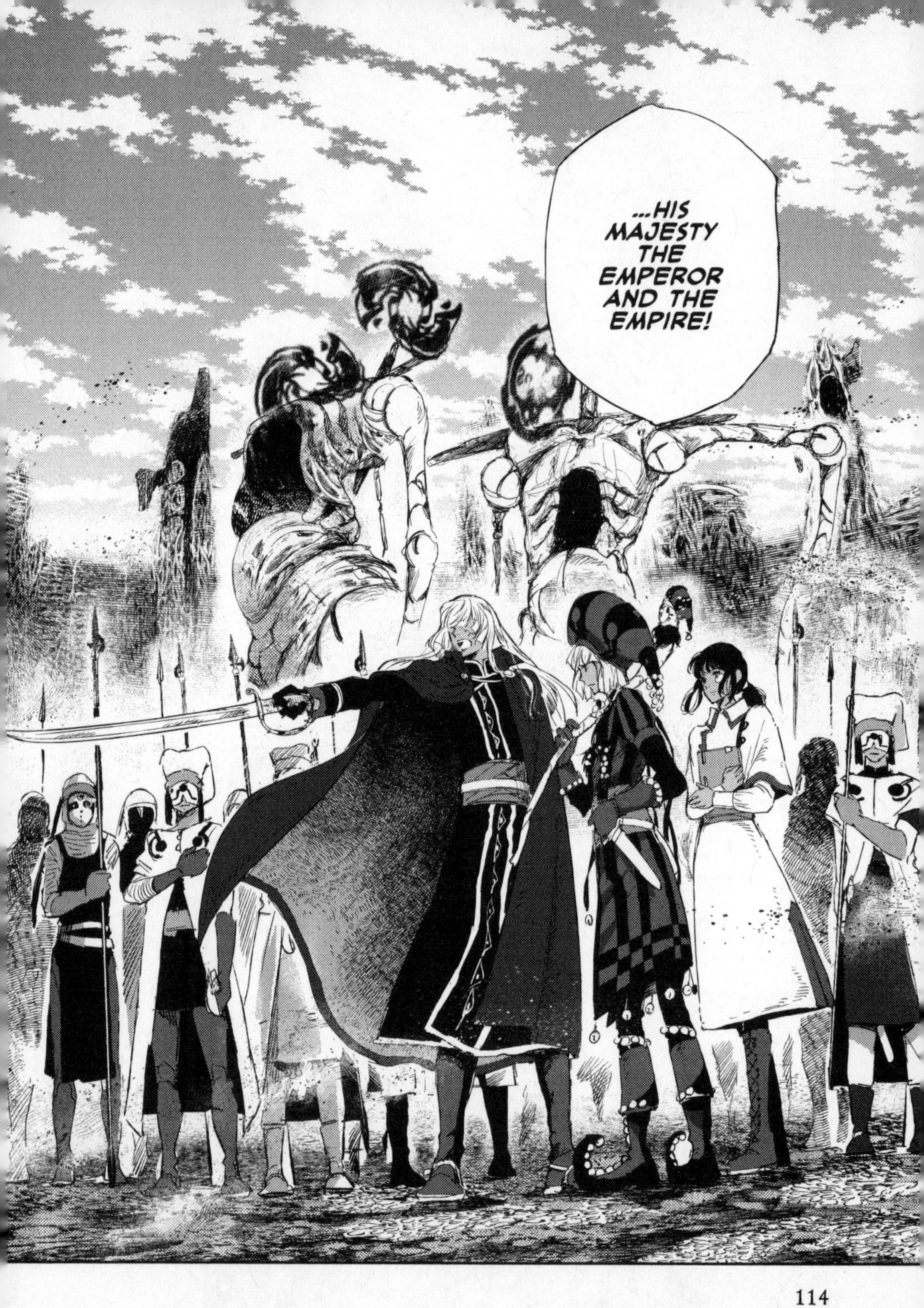
...HIS MAJESTY THE EMPEROR AND THE EMPIRE!

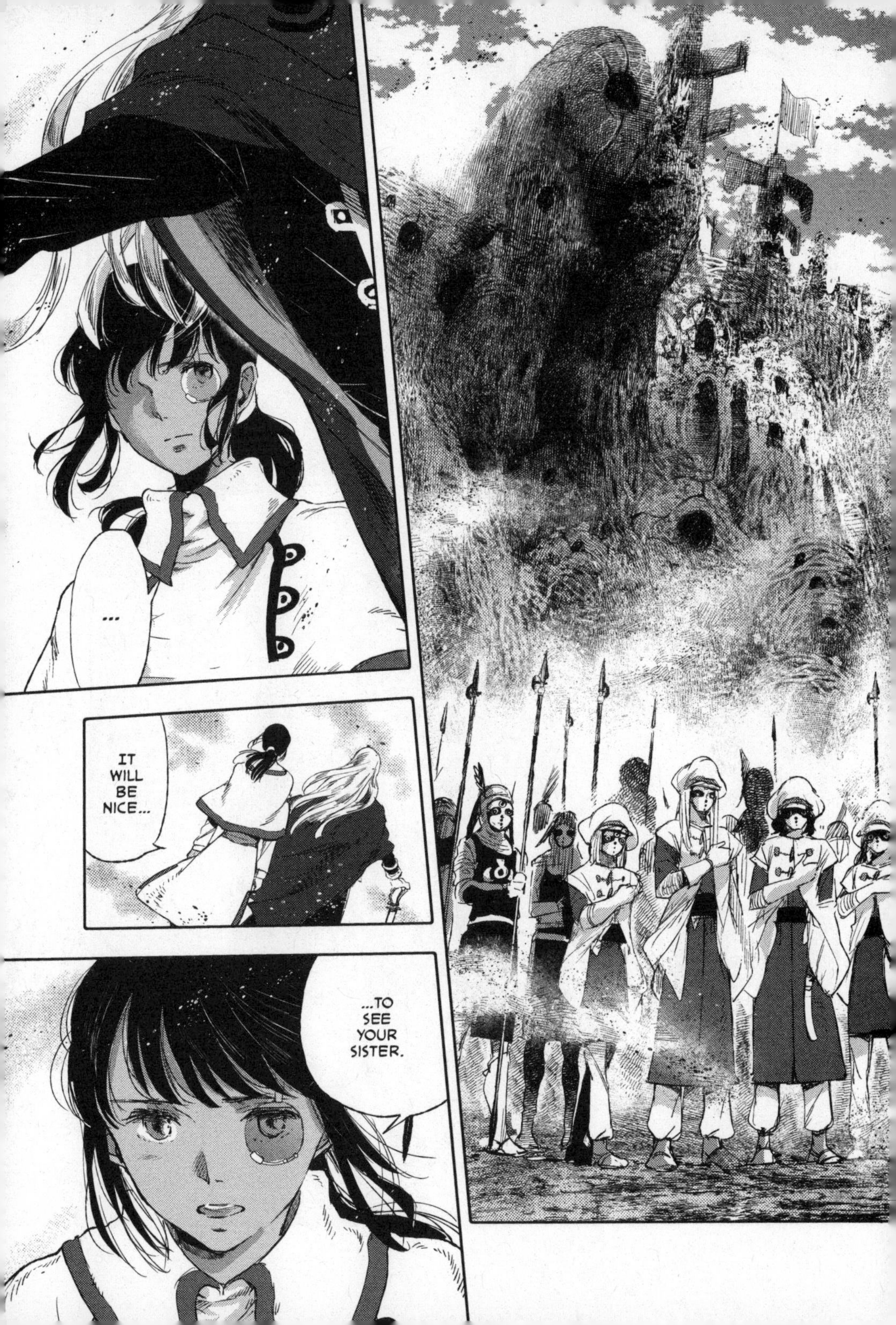
...
IT WILL BE NICE...
...TO SEE YOUR SISTER.

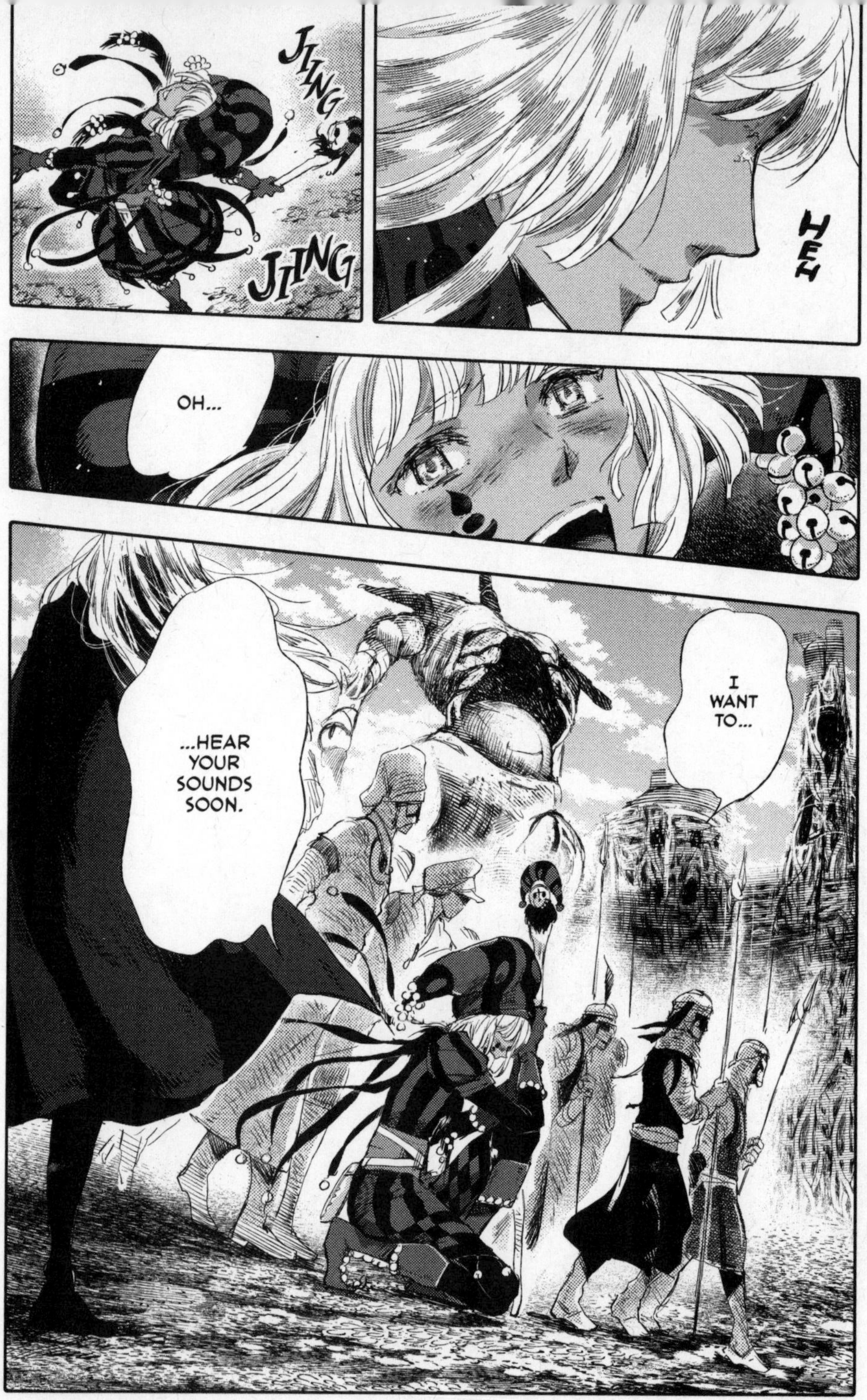
HEH
JIING
JIING
OH...
I WANT TO...
...HEAR YOUR SOUNDS SOON.

The Hollow Sound of Bells -The End-

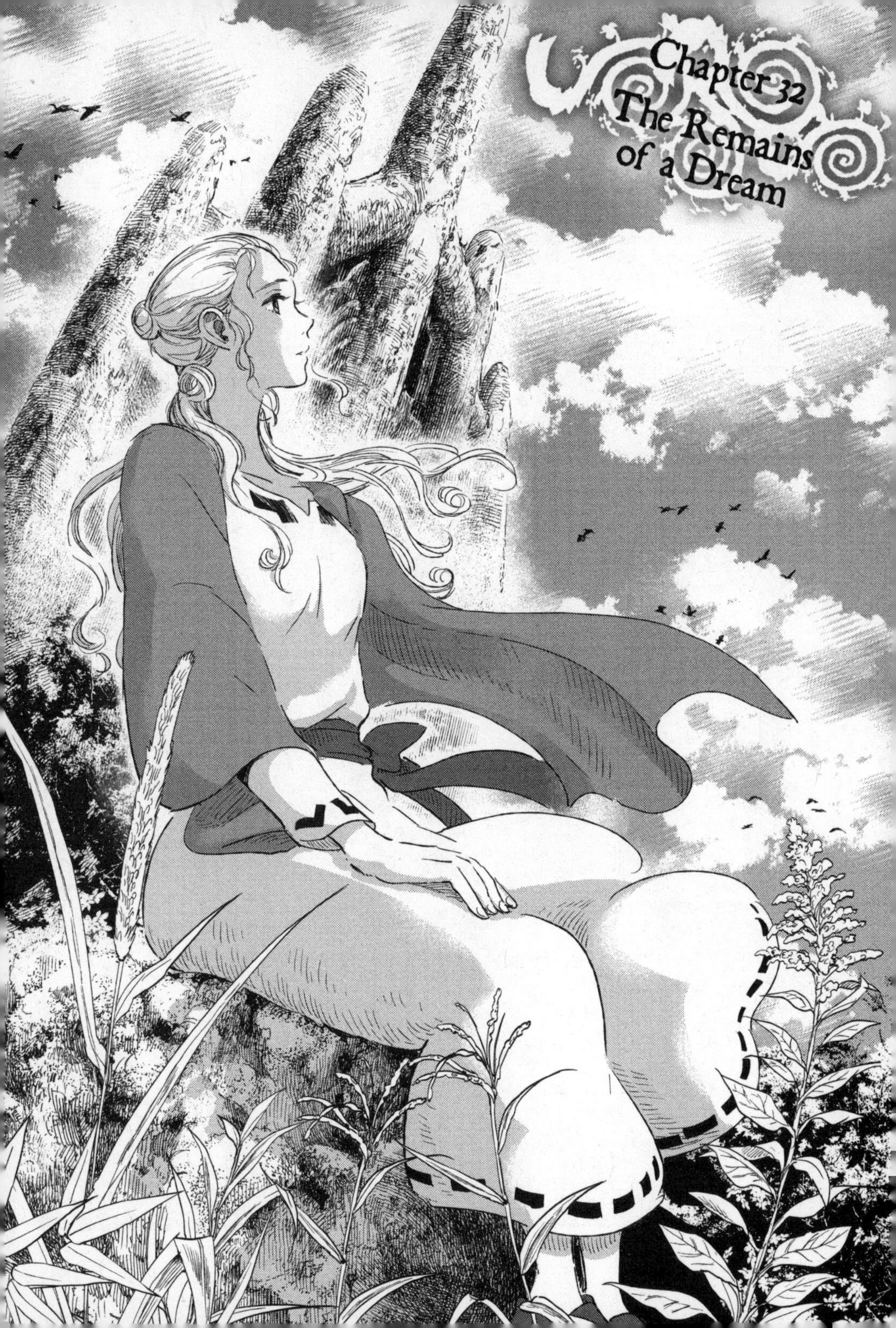
Chapter 32
The Remains of a Dream

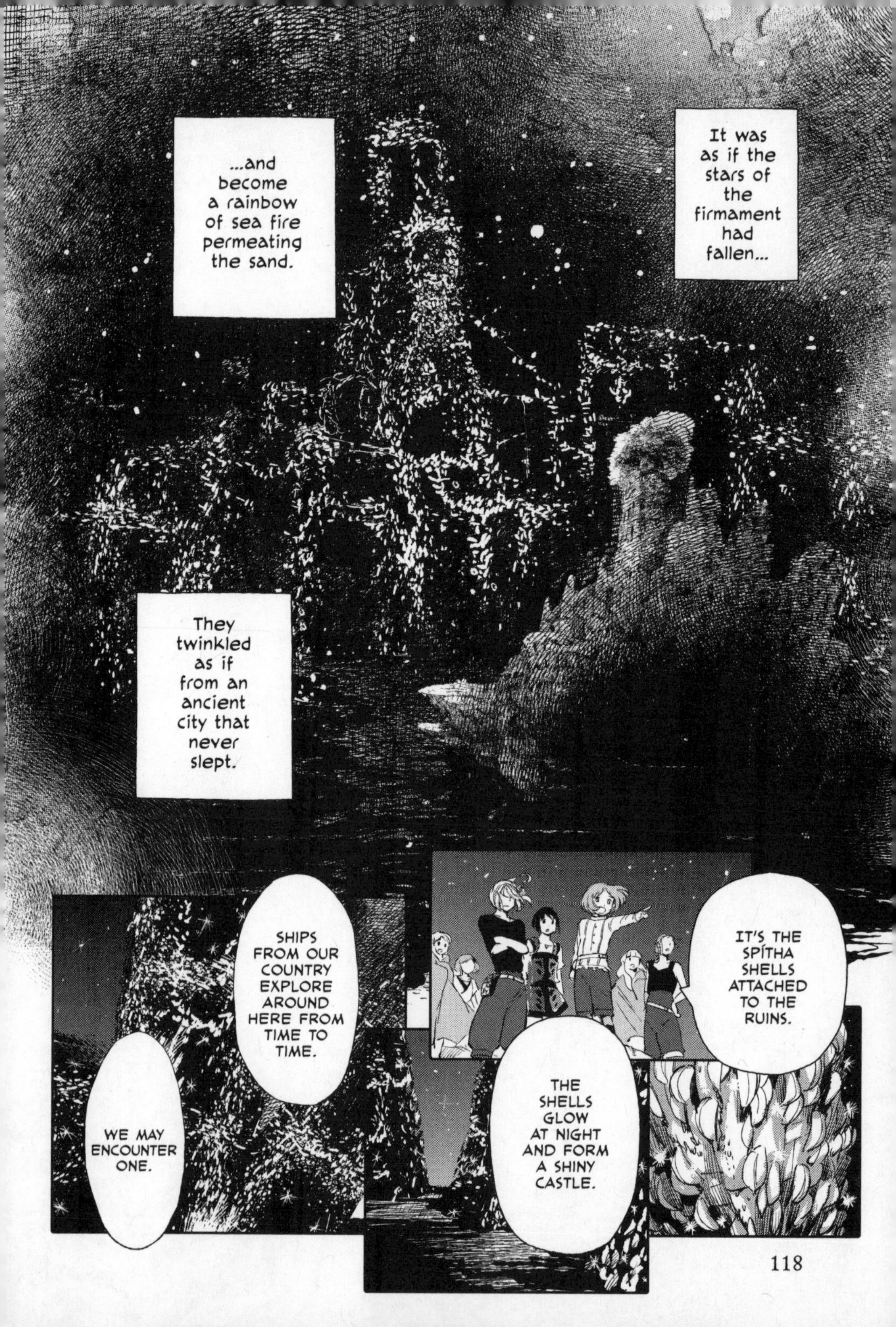
It was as if the stars of the firmament had fallen...
...and become a rainbow of sea fire permeating the sand.
They twinkled as if from an ancient city that never slept.
IT'S THE SPÍTHA SHELLS ATTACHED TO THE RUINS.
THE SHELLS GLOW AT NIGHT AND FORM A SHINY CASTLE.
SHIPS FROM OUR COUNTRY EXPLORE AROUND HERE FROM TIME TO TIME.
WE MAY ENCOUNTER ONE.

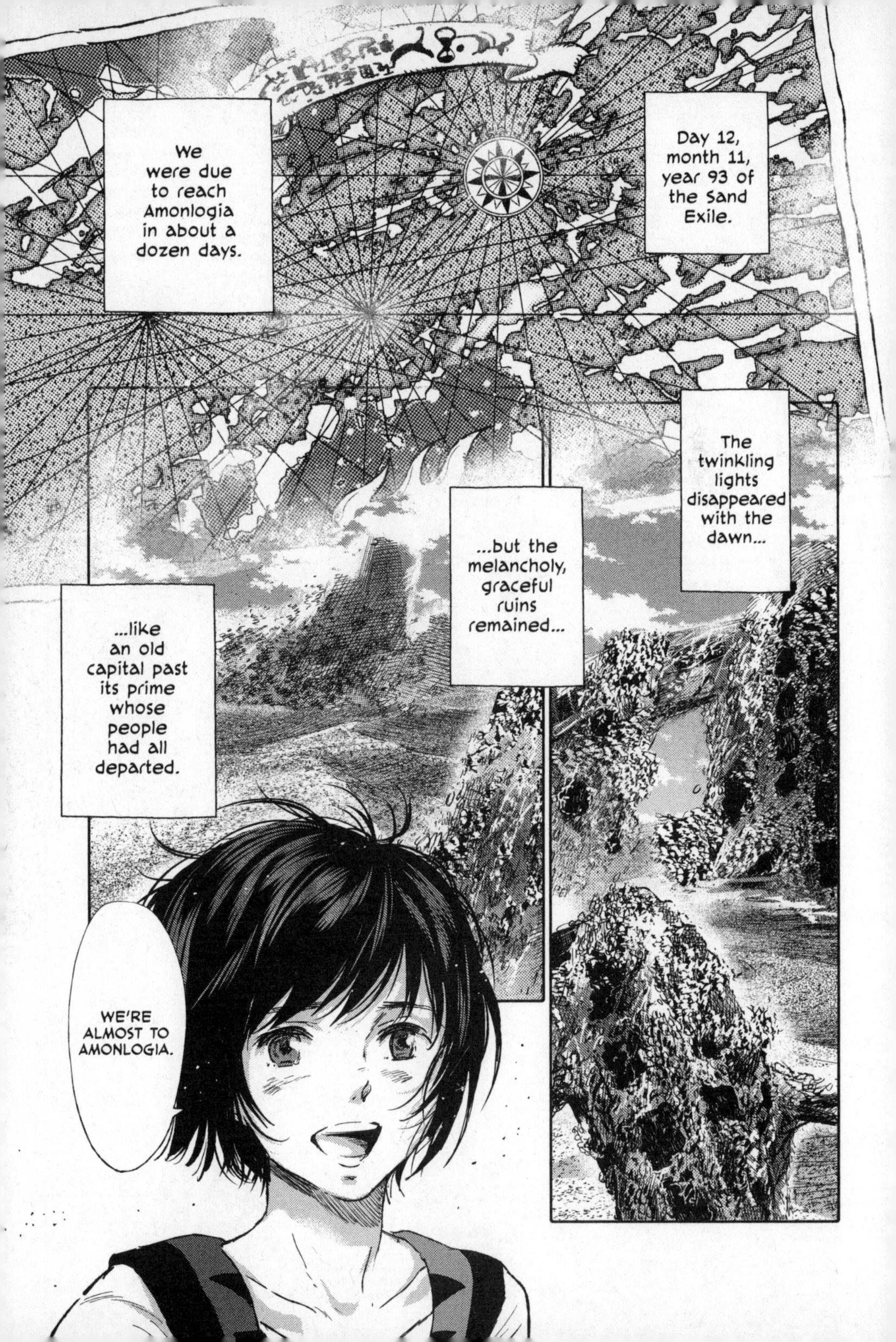
Day 12, month 11, year 93 of the Sand Exile.
We were due to reach Amonlogia in about a dozen days.
The twinkling lights disappeared with the dawn...
...but the melancholy, graceful ruins remained...
...like an old capital past its prime whose people had all departed.
WE'RE ALMOST TO AMONLOGIA.

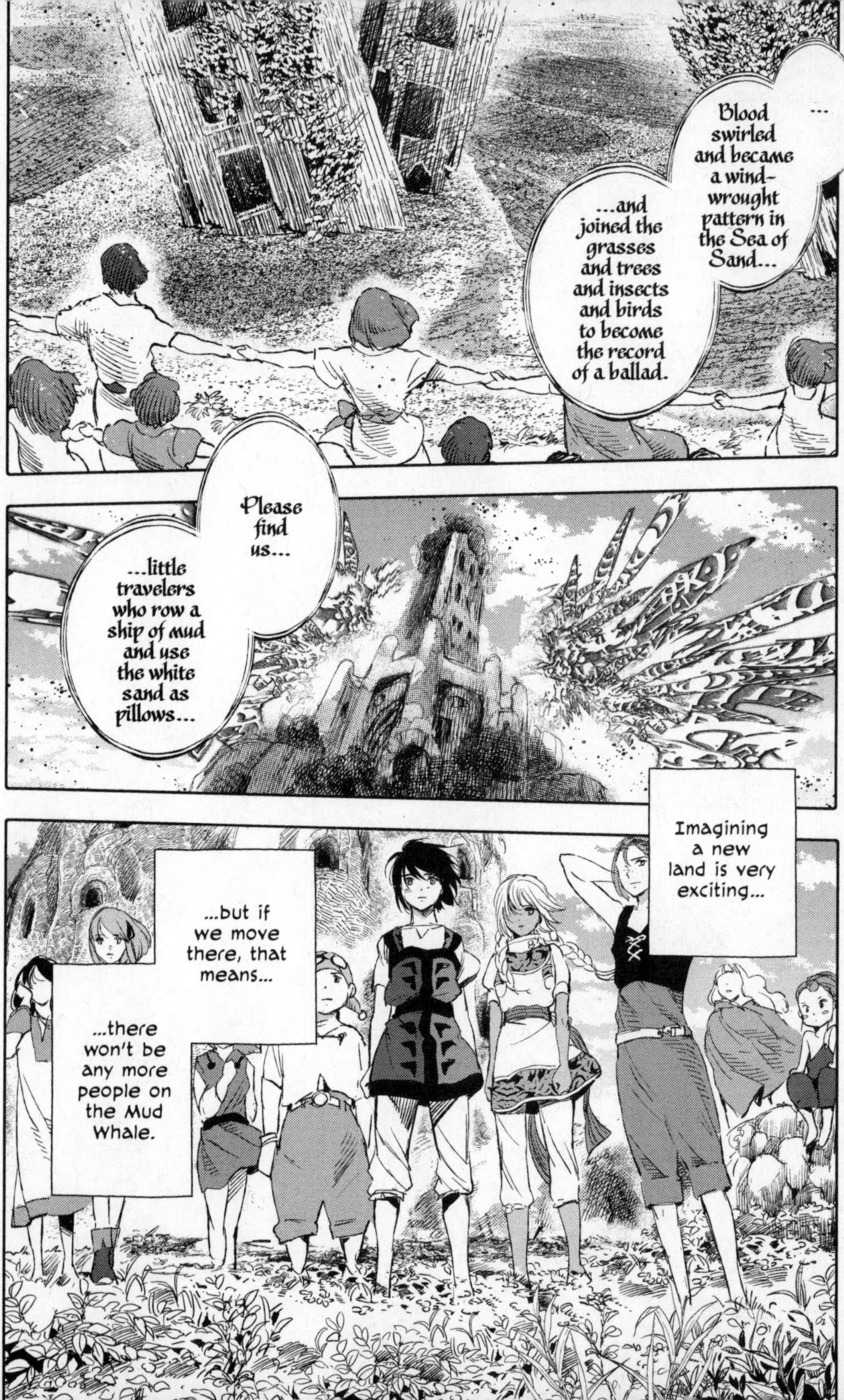

...Blood swirled and became a wind-wrought pattern in the Sea of Sand...
...and joined the grasses and trees and insects and birds to become the record of a ballad.
Please find us...
...little travelers who row a ship of mud and use the white sand as pillows...
Imagining a new land is very exciting...
...but if we move there, that means...
...there won't be any more people on the Mud Whale.

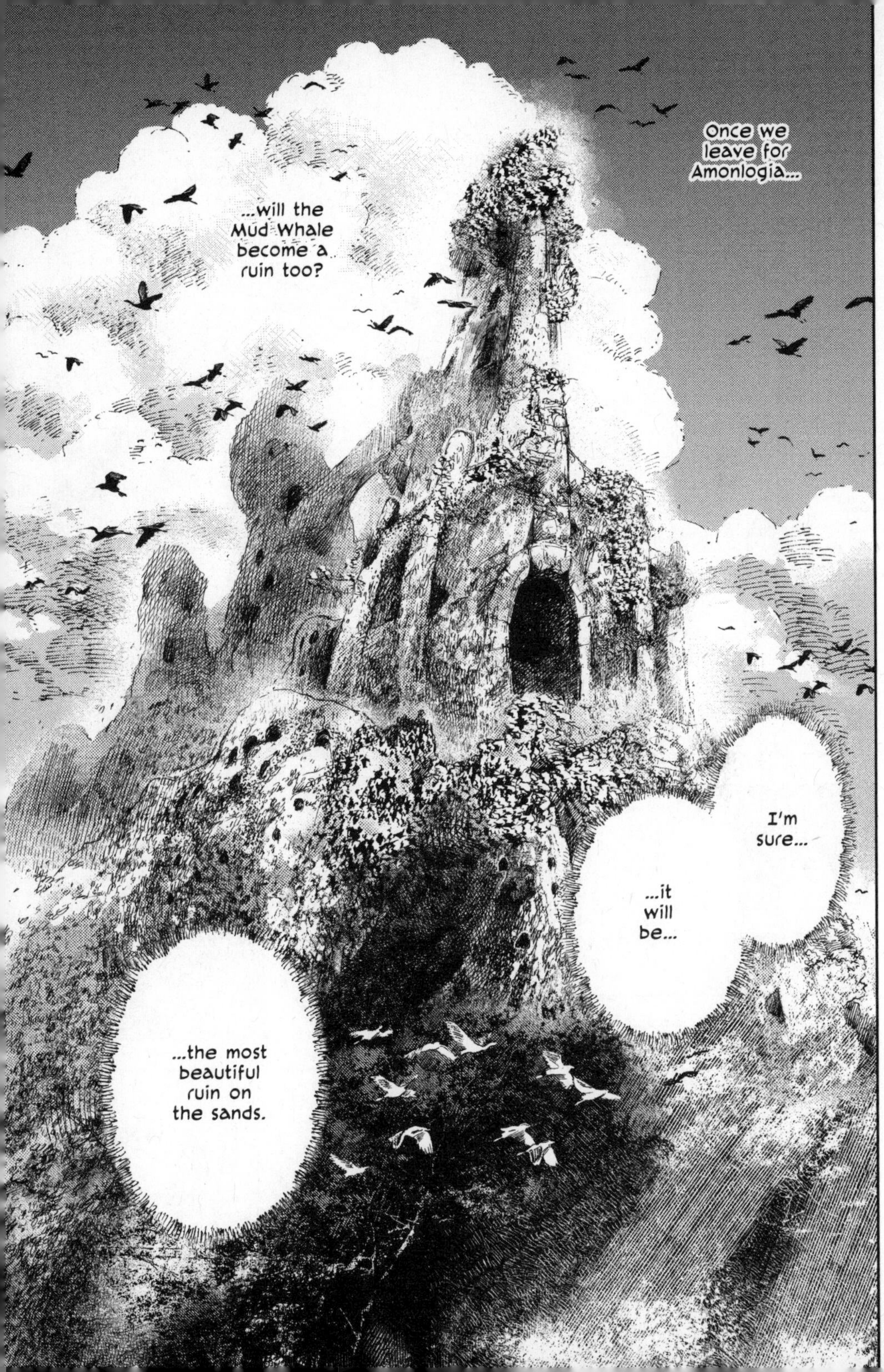
Once we leave for Amonlogia...
...will the Mud Whale become a ruin too?
I'm sure...
...it will be...
...the most beautiful ruin on the sands.

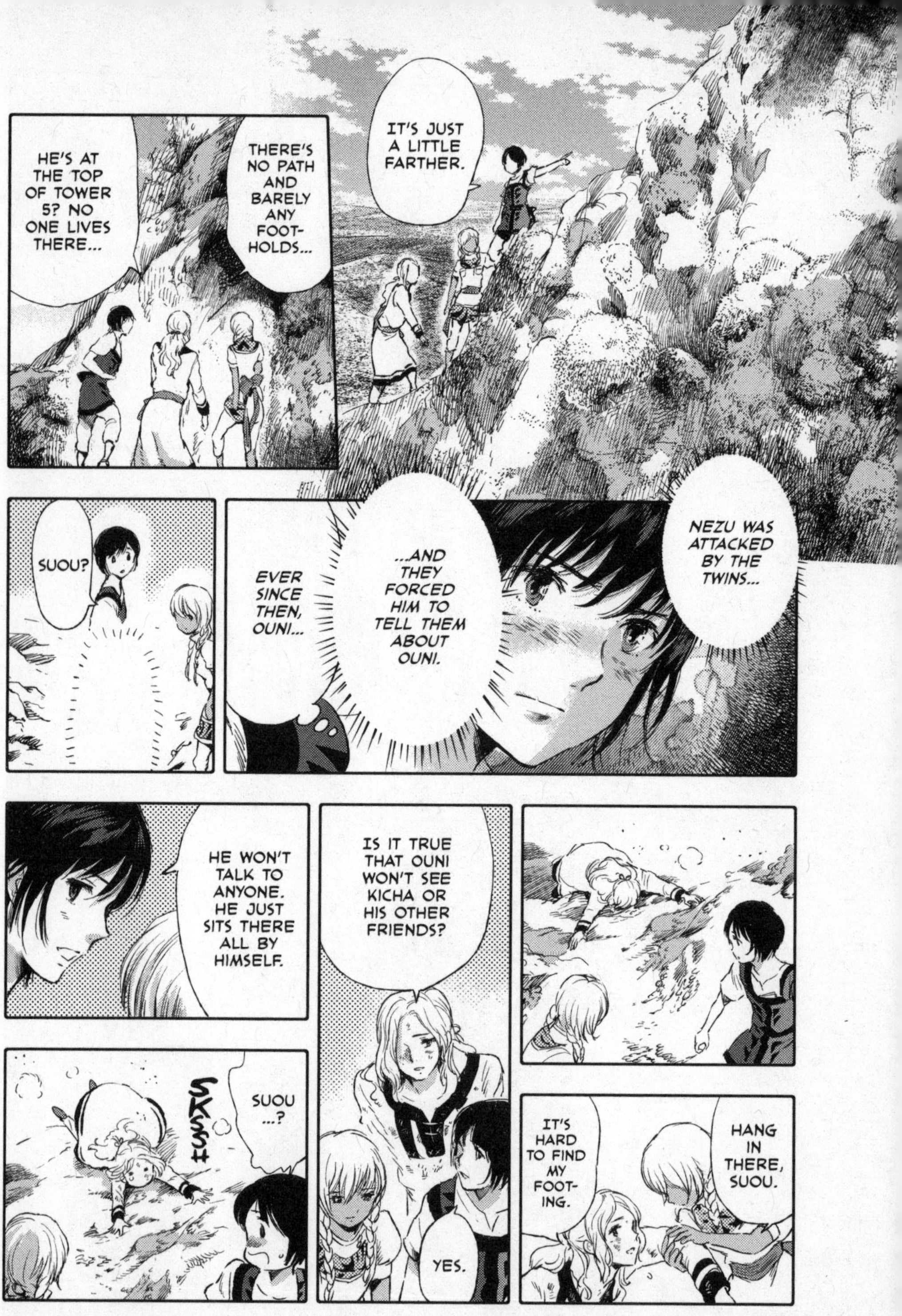
IT'S JUST A LITTLE FARTHER.
THERE'S NO PATH AND BARELY ANY FOOT-HOLDS...
HE'S AT THE TOP OF TOWER 5? NO ONE LIVES THERE...
NEZU WAS ATTACKED BY THE TWINS...
...AND THEY FORCED HIM TO TELL THEM ABOUT OUNI.
EVER SINCE THEN, OUNI...
SUOU?
HANG IN THERE, SUOU.
IT'S HARD TO FIND MY FOOT-ING.
IS IT TRUE THAT OUNI WON'T SEE KICHA OR HIS OTHER FRIENDS?
YES.
HE WON'T TALK TO ANYONE. HE JUST SITS THERE ALL BY HIMSELF.
SUOU ...?
SKSSH

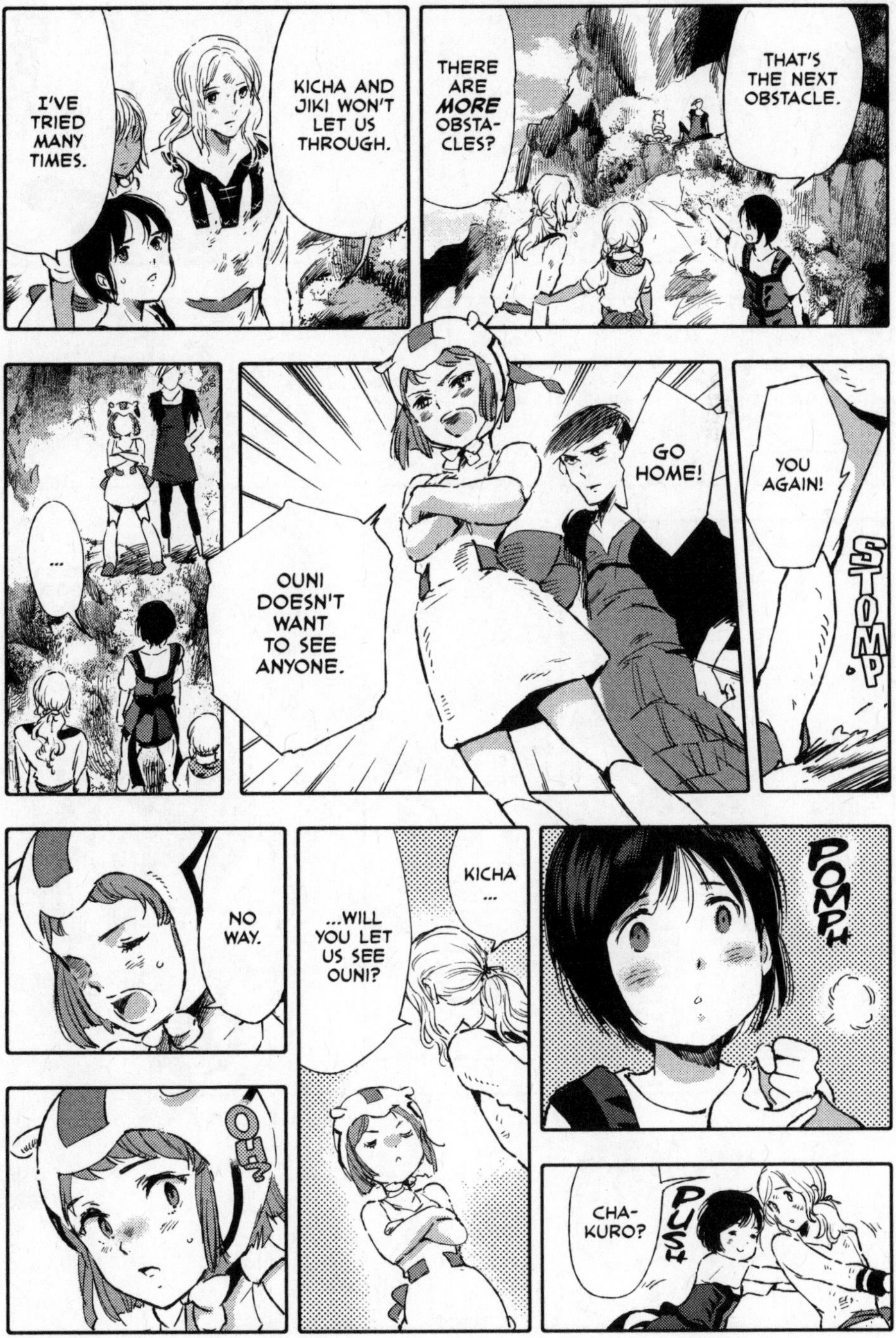
THAT'S THE NEXT OBSTACLE.
THERE ARE *MORE* OBSTACLES?
KICHA AND JIKI WON'T LET US THROUGH.
I'VE TRIED MANY TIMES.
YOU AGAIN!
STOMP
GO HOME!
OUNI DOESN'T WANT TO SEE ANYONE.
...
POMPH
KICHA ...
...WILL YOU LET US SEE OUNI?
NO WAY.
PUSH
CHA-KURO?
OH?

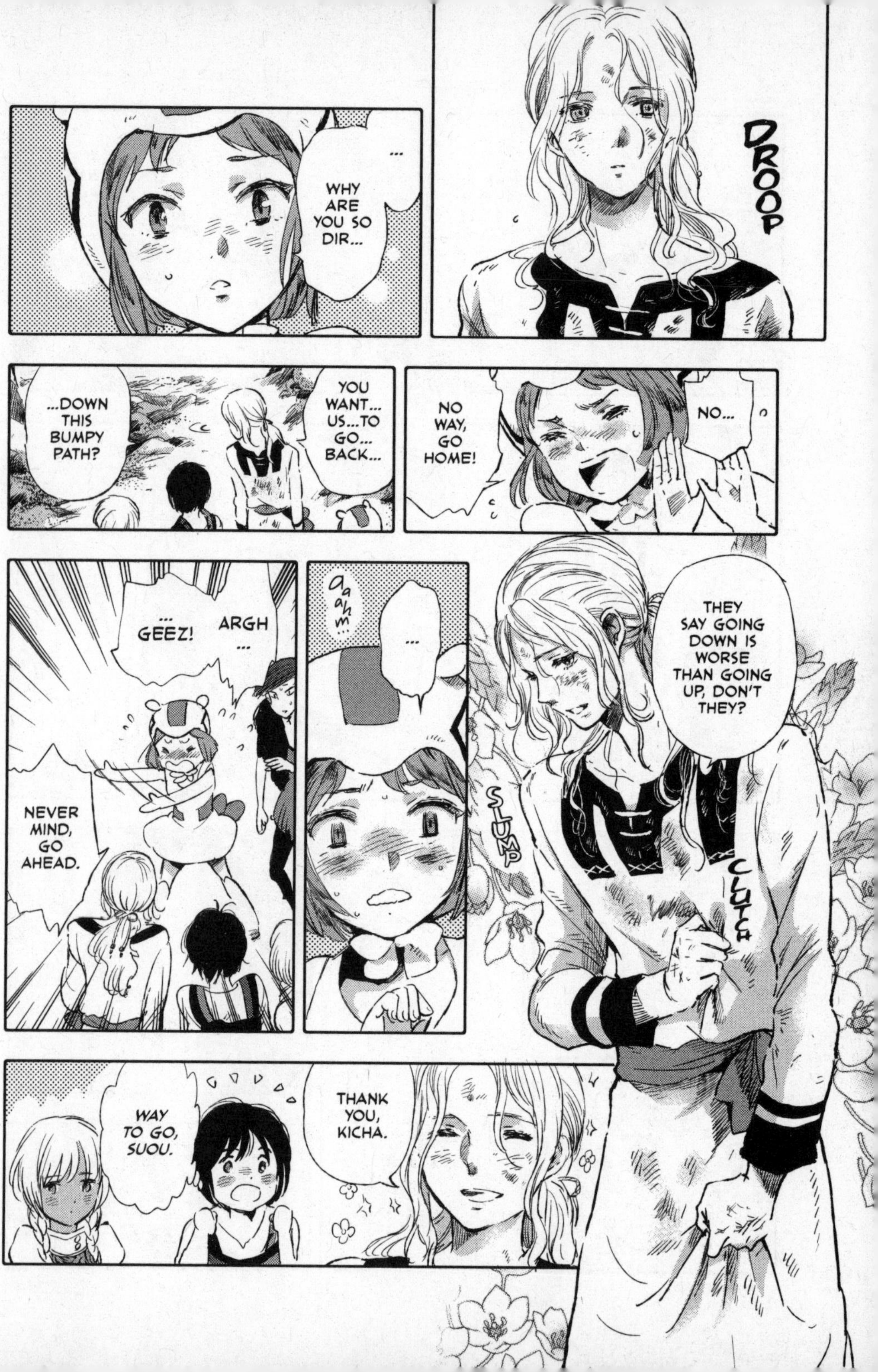
DROOP
...
WHY ARE YOU SO DIR...
NO...
NO WAY, GO HOME!
YOU WANT... US...TO GO... BACK...
...DOWN THIS BUMPY PATH?
THEY SAY GOING DOWN IS WORSE THAN GOING UP, DON'T THEY?
CLUTCH
SLUMP
aaahm...
...
ARGH...
...GEEZ!
NEVER MIND, GO AHEAD.
THANK YOU, KICHA.
WAY TO GO, SUOU.

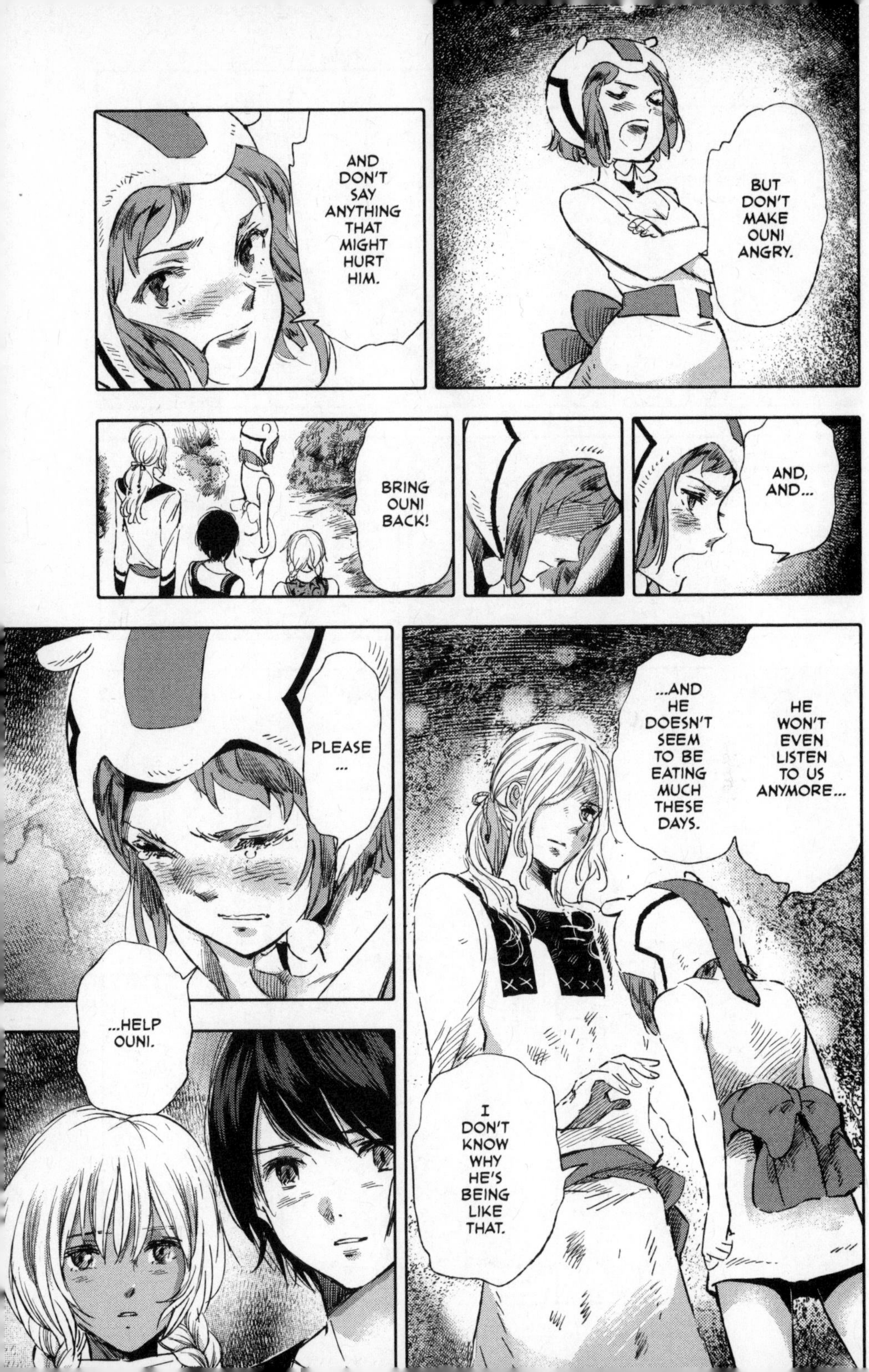
BUT DON'T MAKE OUNI ANGRY.
AND DON'T SAY ANYTHING THAT MIGHT HURT HIM.
AND, AND...
BRING OUNI BACK!
HE WON'T EVEN LISTEN TO US ANYMORE...
...AND HE DOESN'T SEEM TO BE EATING MUCH THESE DAYS.
I DON'T KNOW WHY HE'S BEING LIKE THAT.
PLEASE ...
...HELP OUNI.

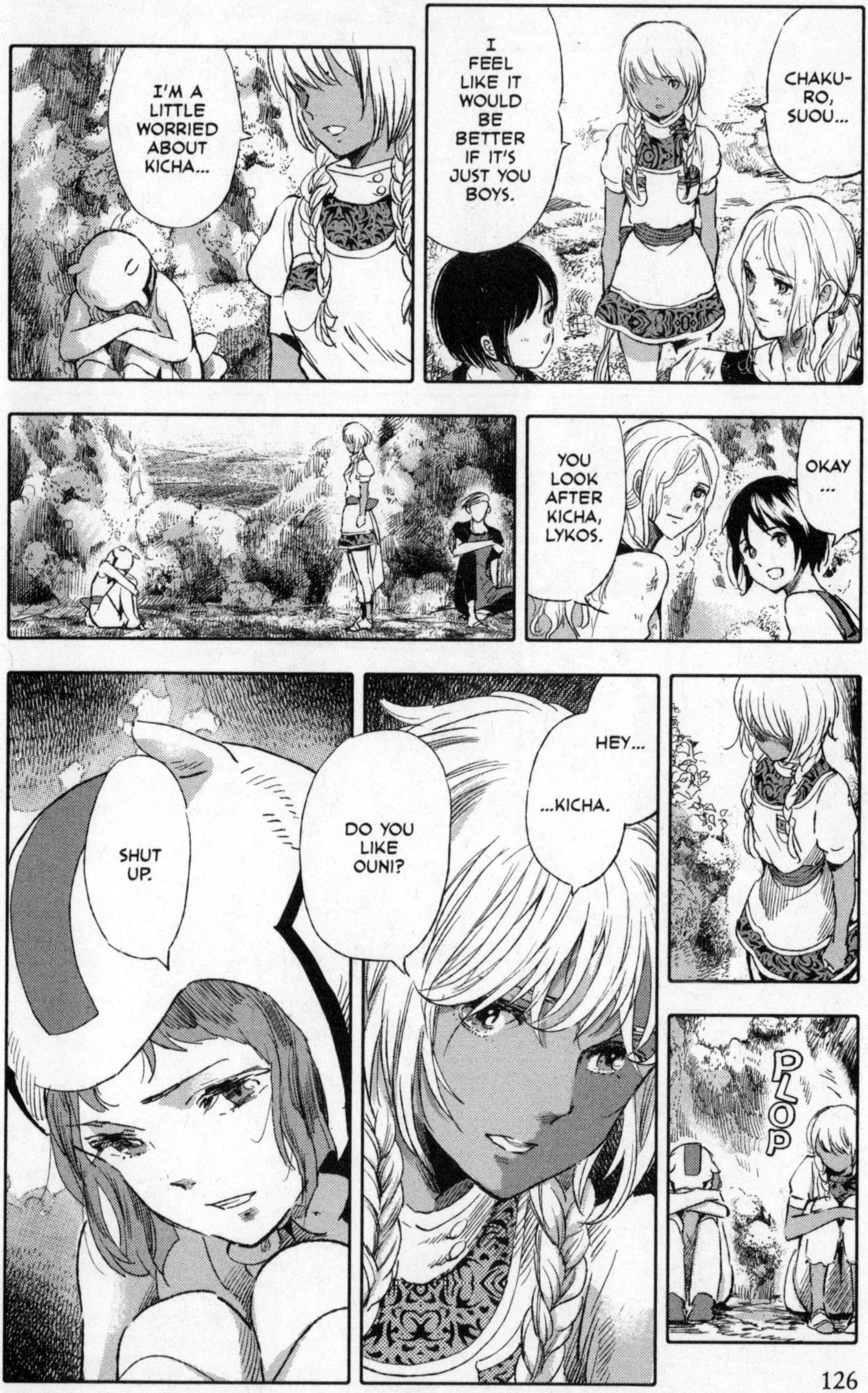
CHAKU-RO, SUOU...
I FEEL LIKE IT WOULD BE BETTER IF IT'S JUST YOU BOYS.
I'M A LITTLE WORRIED ABOUT KICHA...
OKAY ...
YOU LOOK AFTER KICHA, LYKOS.
PLOP
HEY...
...KICHA.
DO YOU LIKE OUNI?
SHUT UP.

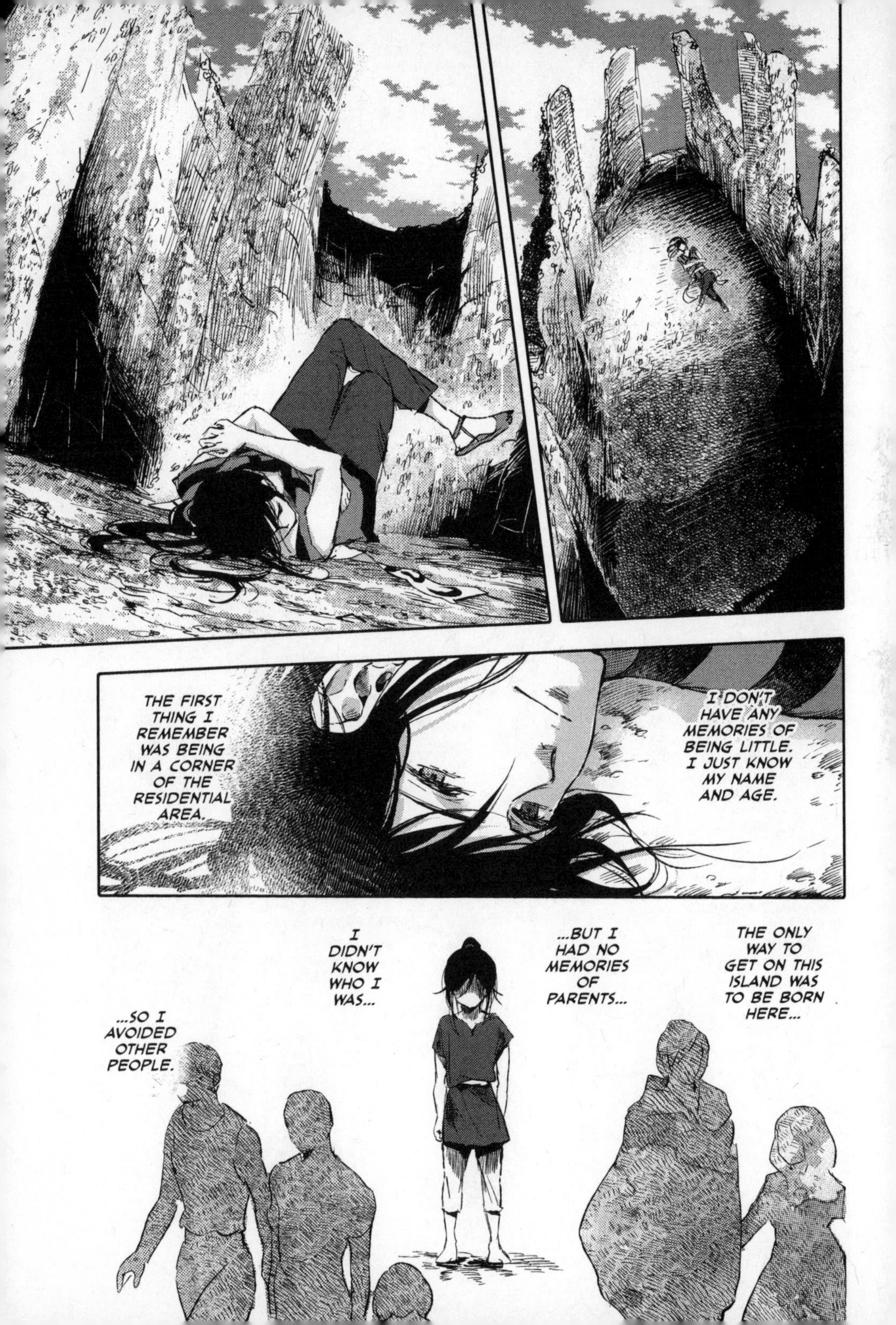
I DON'T HAVE ANY MEMORIES OF BEING LITTLE. I JUST KNOW MY NAME AND AGE.
THE FIRST THING I REMEMBER WAS BEING IN A CORNER OF THE RESIDENTIAL AREA.
THE ONLY WAY TO GET ON THIS ISLAND WAS TO BE BORN HERE...
...BUT I HAD NO MEMORIES OF PARENTS...
I DIDN'T KNOW WHO I WAS...
...SO I AVOIDED OTHER PEOPLE.

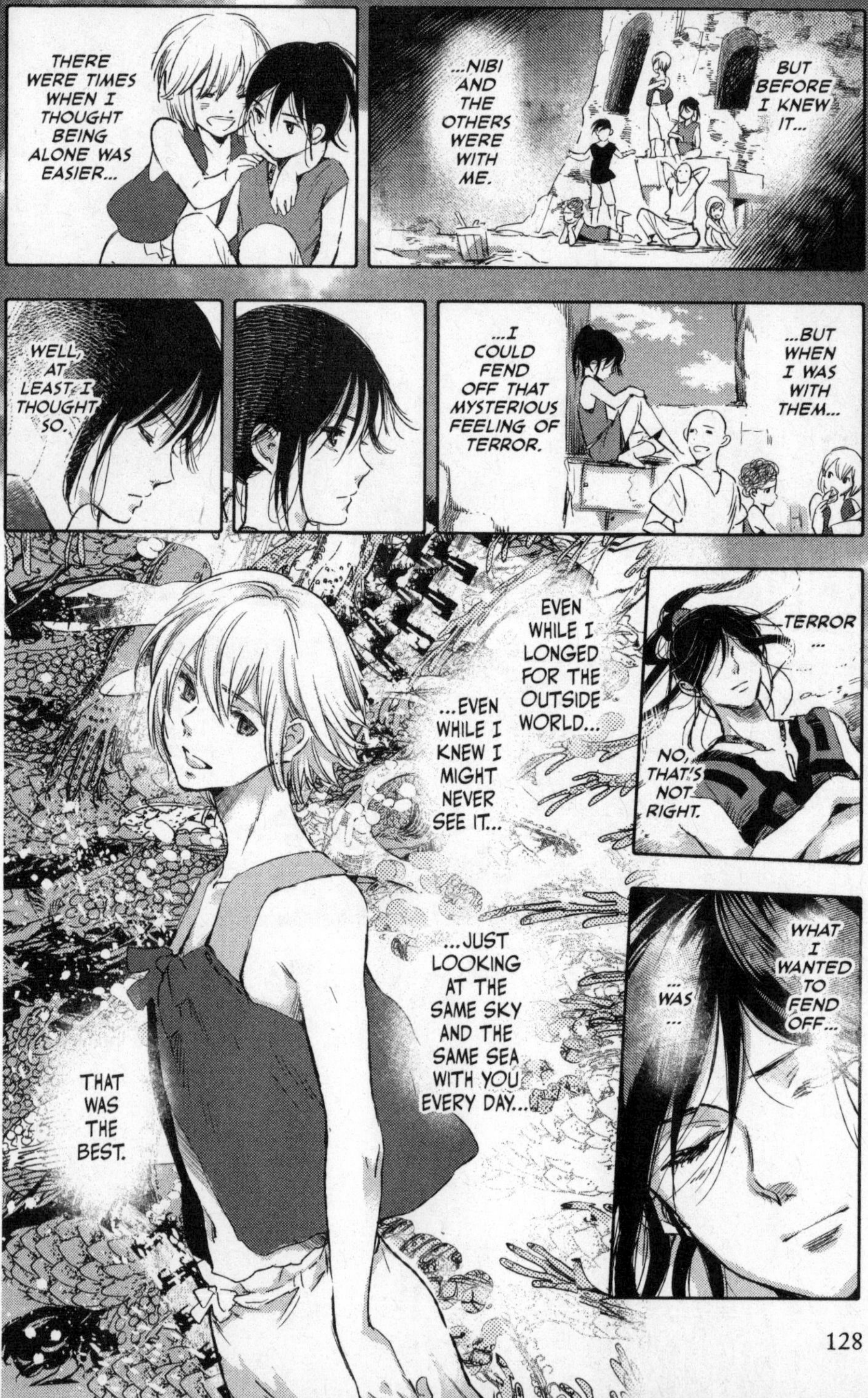
BUT BEFORE I KNEW IT...
...NIBI AND THE OTHERS WERE WITH ME.
THERE WERE TIMES WHEN I THOUGHT BEING ALONE WAS EASIER...
...BUT WHEN I WAS WITH THEM...
...I COULD FEND OFF THAT MYSTERIOUS FEELING OF TERROR.
WELL, AT LEAST I THOUGHT SO.
TERROR...
NO, THAT'S NOT RIGHT.
WHAT I WANTED TO FEND OFF...
...WAS...
EVEN WHILE I LONGED FOR THE OUTSIDE WORLD...
...EVEN WHILE I KNEW I MIGHT NEVER SEE IT...
...JUST LOOKING AT THE SAME SKY AND THE SAME SEA WITH YOU EVERY DAY...
THAT WAS THE BEST.

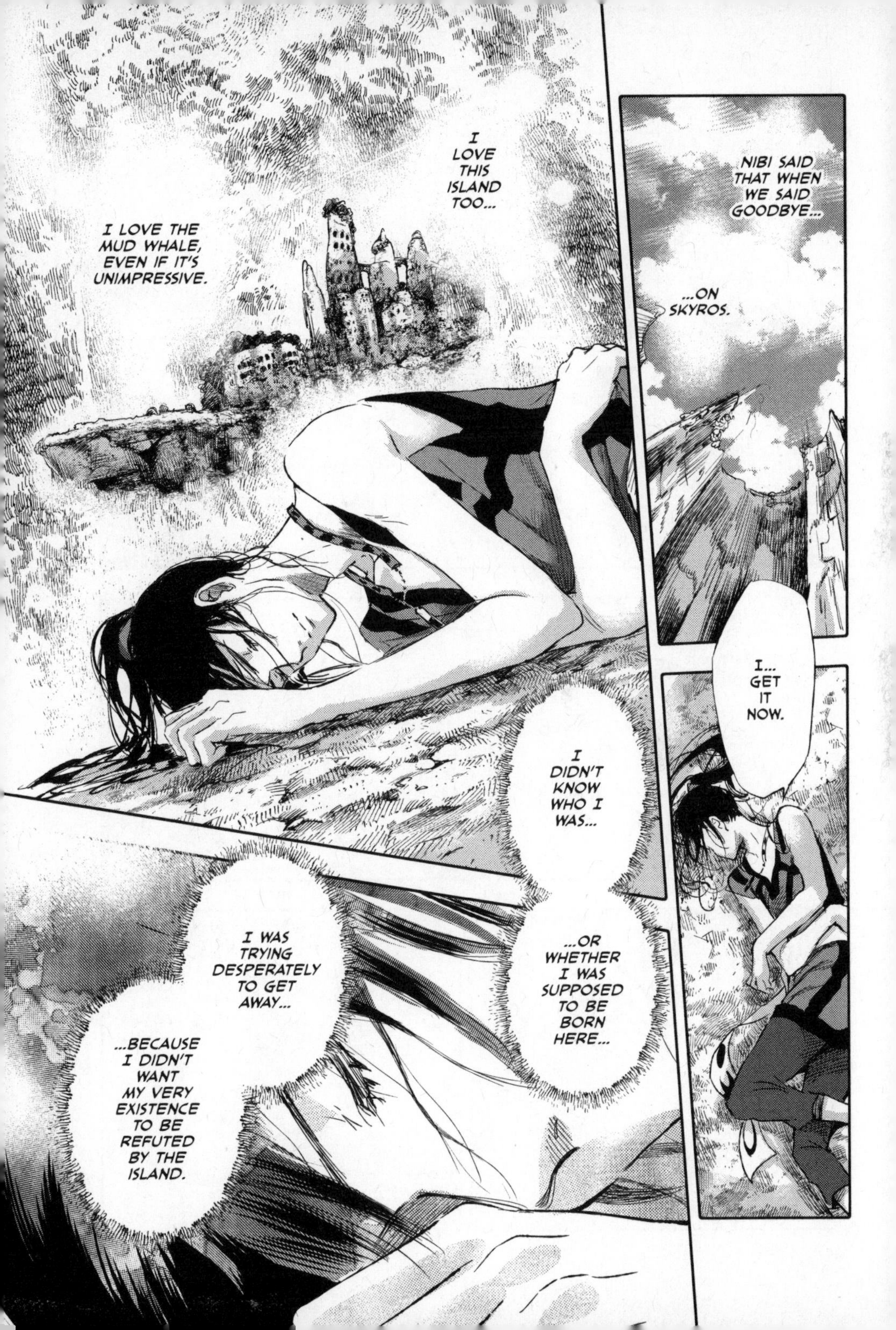
NIBI SAID THAT WHEN WE SAID GOODBYE...
...ON SKYROS.
I LOVE THIS ISLAND TOO...
I LOVE THE MUD WHALE, EVEN IF IT'S UNIMPRESSIVE.
I... GET IT NOW.
I DIDN'T KNOW WHO I WAS...
...OR WHETHER I WAS SUPPOSED TO BE BORN HERE...
I WAS TRYING DESPERATELY TO GET AWAY...
...BECAUSE I DIDN'T WANT MY VERY EXISTENCE TO BE REFUTED BY THE ISLAND.

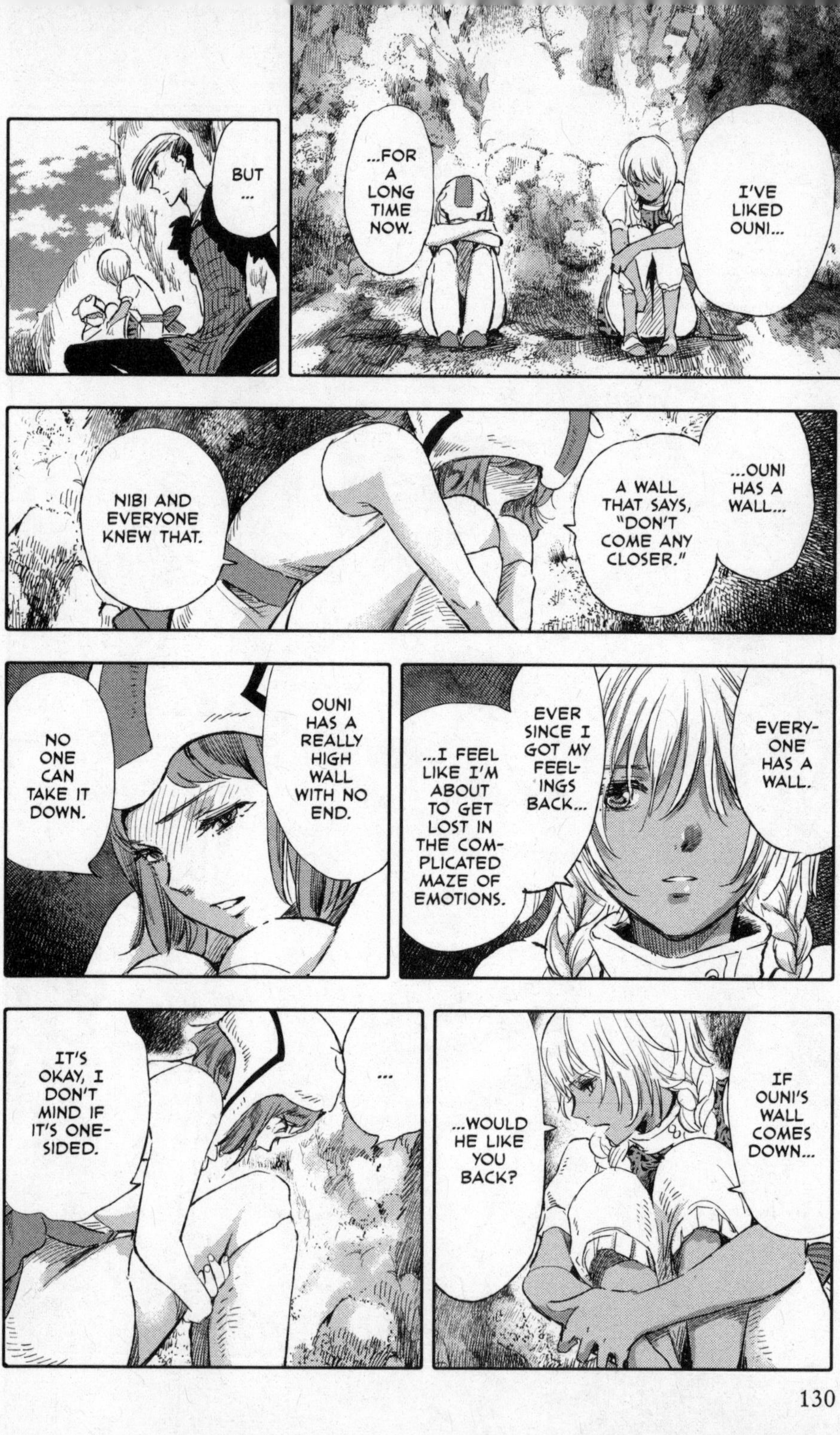
I'VE LIKED OUNI...
...FOR A LONG TIME NOW.
BUT ...
...OUNI HAS A WALL...
A WALL THAT SAYS, "DON'T COME ANY CLOSER."
NIBI AND EVERYONE KNEW THAT.
EVERYONE HAS A WALL.
EVER SINCE I GOT MY FEELINGS BACK...
...I FEEL LIKE I'M ABOUT TO GET LOST IN THE COMPLICATED MAZE OF EMOTIONS.
OUNI HAS A REALLY HIGH WALL WITH NO END.
NO ONE CAN TAKE IT DOWN.
IF OUNI'S WALL COMES DOWN...
...WOULD HE LIKE YOU BACK?
...
IT'S OKAY, I DON'T MIND IF IT'S ONE-SIDED.

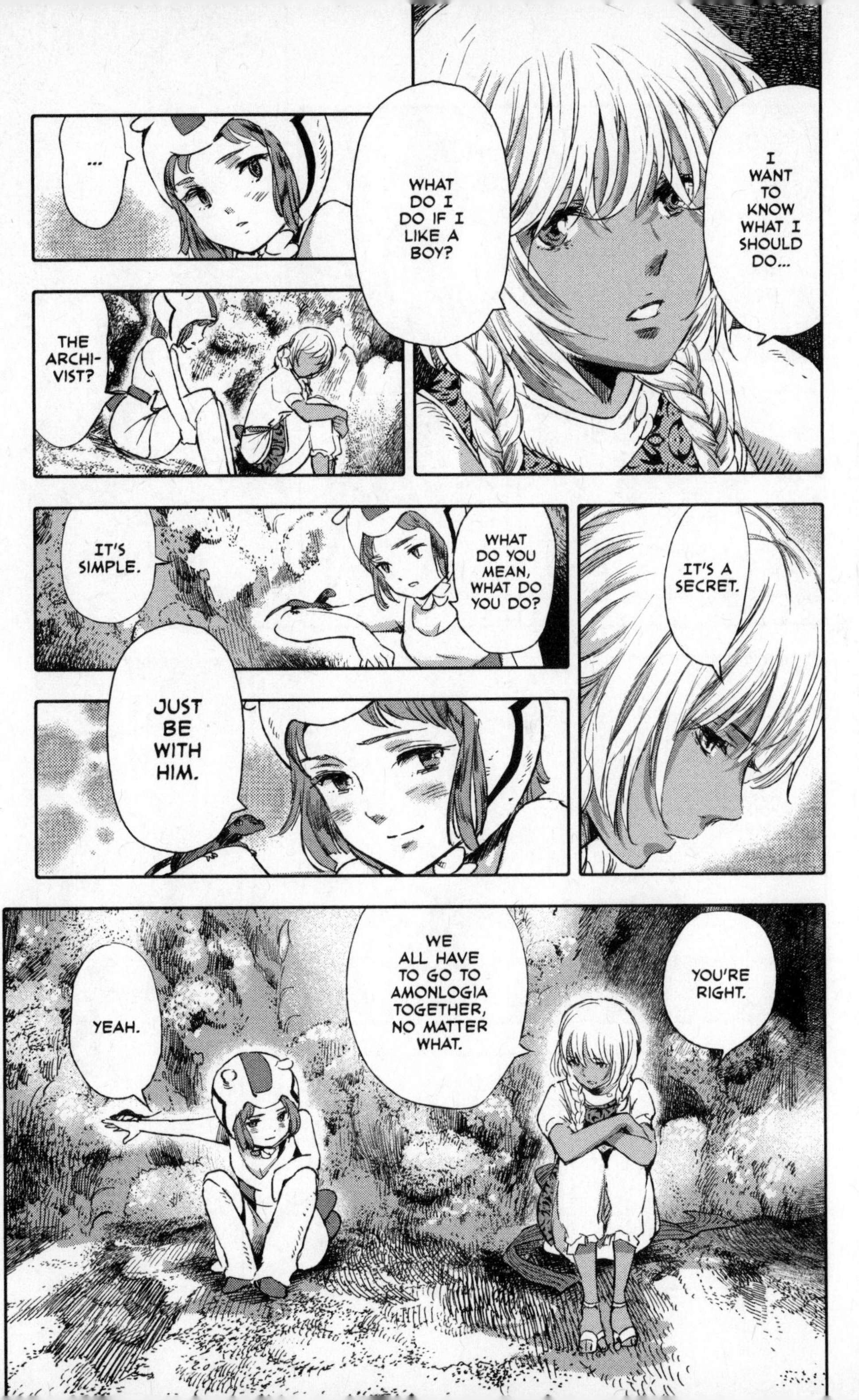
I WANT TO KNOW WHAT I SHOULD DO...
WHAT DO I DO IF I LIKE A BOY?
...
THE ARCHI- VIST?
IT'S A SECRET.
WHAT DO YOU MEAN, WHAT DO YOU DO?
IT'S SIMPLE.
JUST BE WITH HIM.
YOU'RE RIGHT.
WE ALL HAVE TO GO TO AMONLOGIA TOGETHER, NO MATTER WHAT.
YEAH.

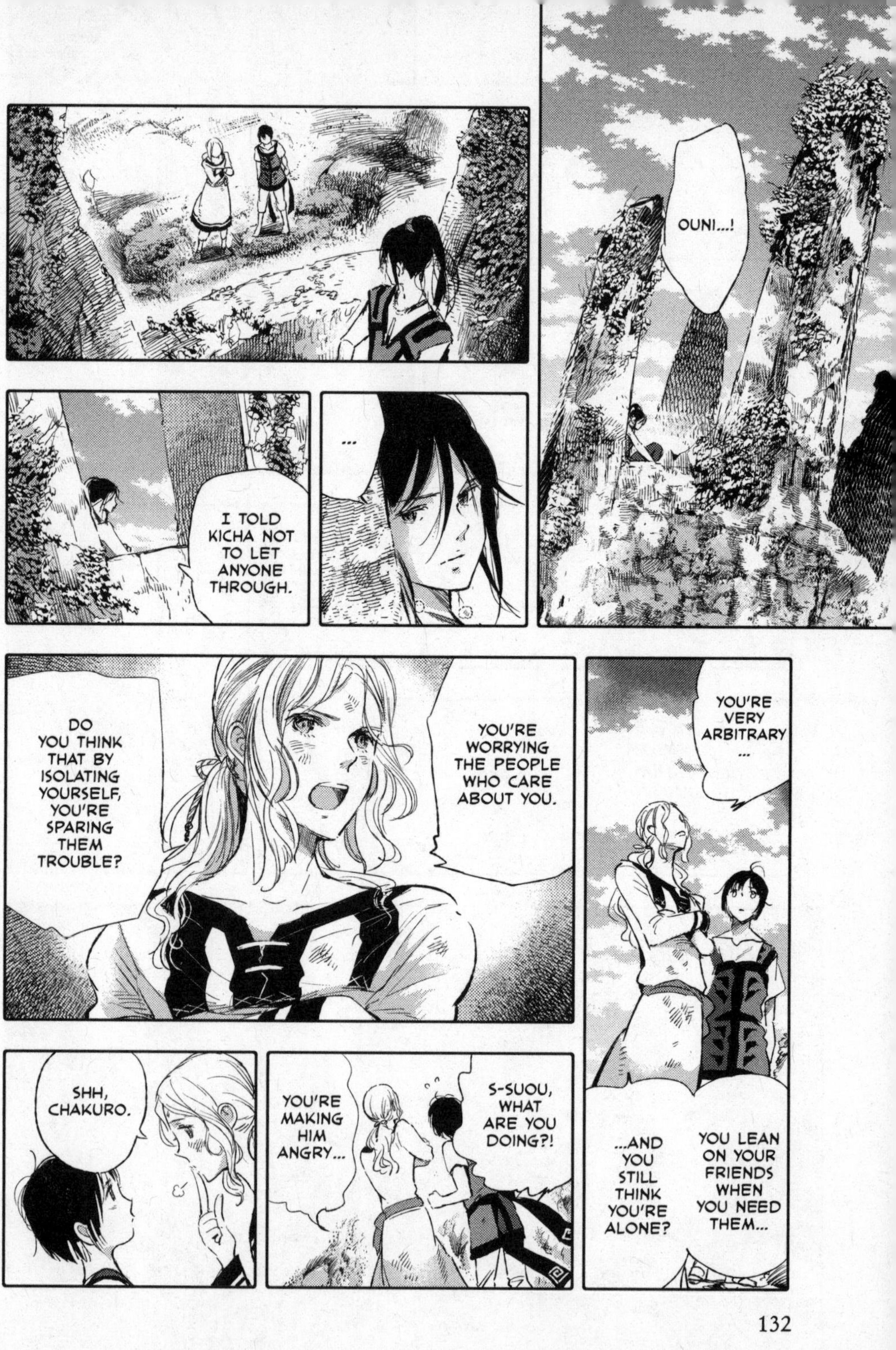
OUNI...!
...
I TOLD KICHA NOT TO LET ANYONE THROUGH.
YOU'RE VERY ARBITRARY ...
YOU LEAN ON YOUR FRIENDS WHEN YOU NEED THEM...
...AND YOU STILL THINK YOU'RE ALONE?
YOU'RE WORRYING THE PEOPLE WHO CARE ABOUT YOU.
DO YOU THINK THAT BY ISOLATING YOURSELF, YOU'RE SPARING THEM TROUBLE?
S-SUOU, WHAT ARE YOU DOING?!
YOU'RE MAKING HIM ANGRY...
SHH, CHAKURO.

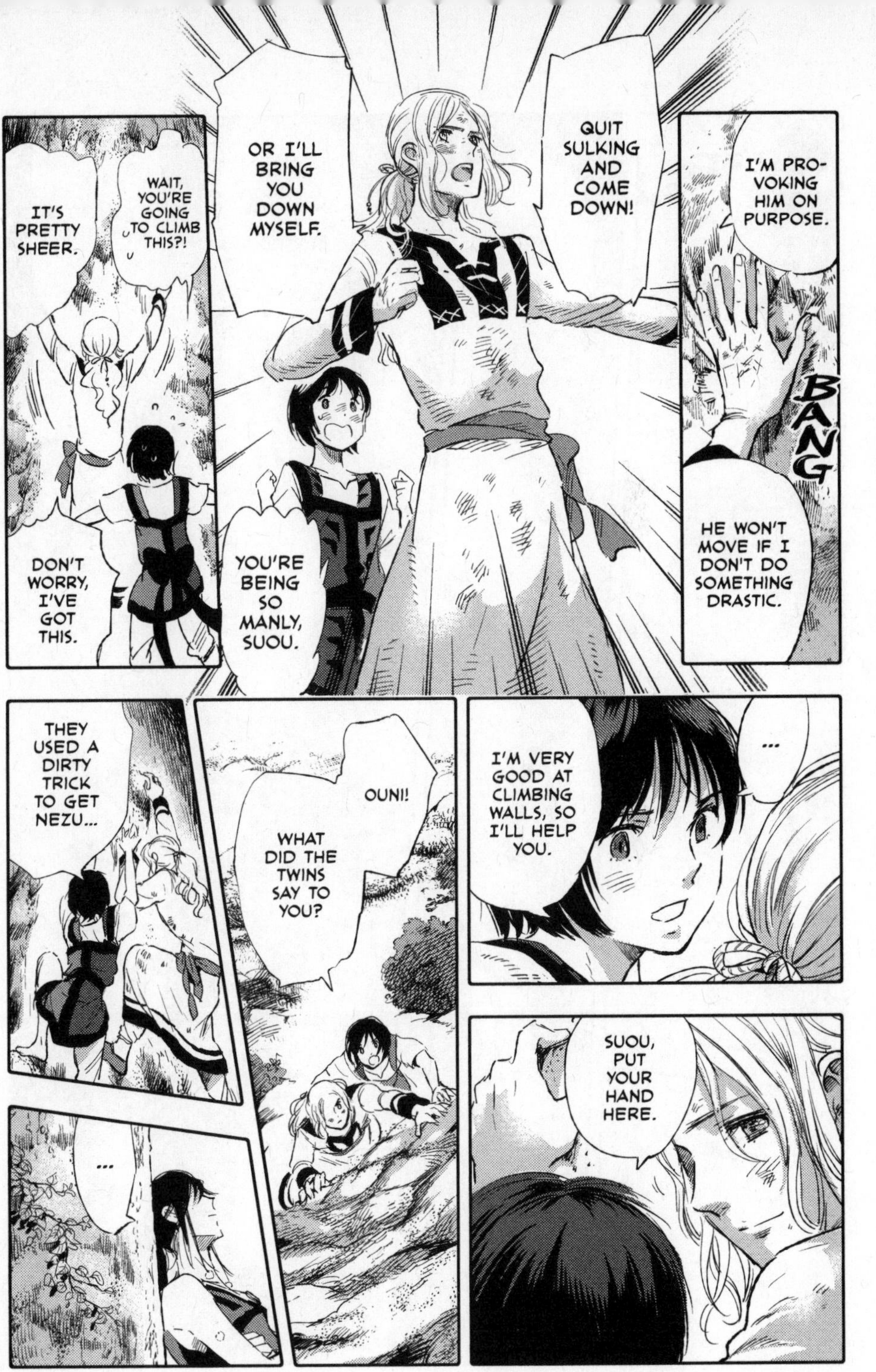
I'M PRO-VOKING HIM ON PURPOSE.
BANG
HE WON'T MOVE IF I DON'T DO SOMETHING DRASTIC.
QUIT SULKING AND COME DOWN!
OR I'LL BRING YOU DOWN MYSELF.
YOU'RE BEING SO MANLY, SUOU.
WAIT, YOU'RE GOING TO CLIMB THIS?!
IT'S PRETTY SHEER.
DON'T WORRY, I'VE GOT THIS.
...
I'M VERY GOOD AT CLIMBING WALLS, SO I'LL HELP YOU.
SUOU, PUT YOUR HAND HERE.
OUNI!
WHAT DID THE TWINS SAY TO YOU?
THEY USED A DIRTY TRICK TO GET NEZU...
...

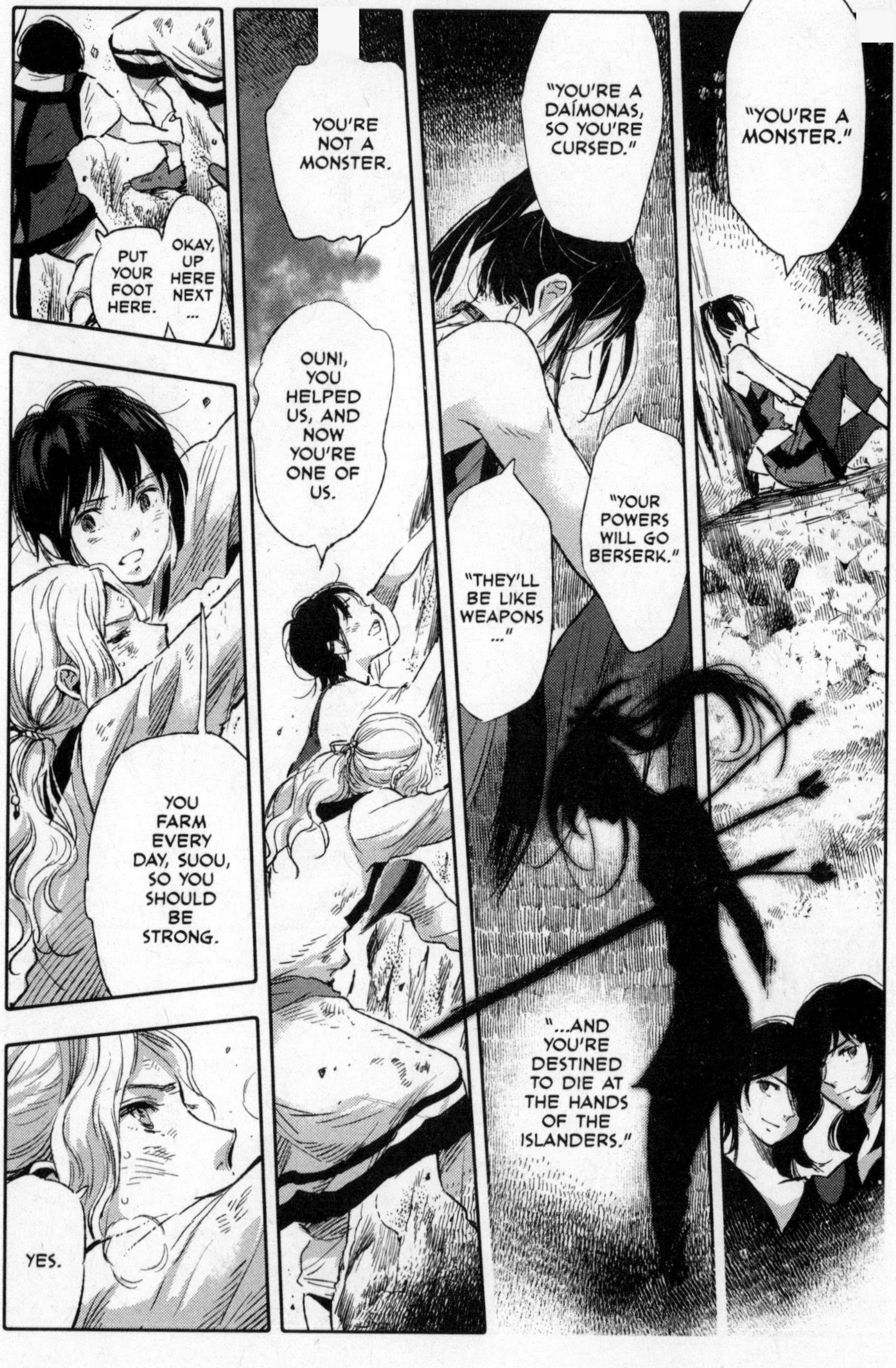
"YOU'RE A MONSTER."
"YOU'RE A DAÍMONAS, SO YOU'RE CURSED."
"YOUR POWERS WILL GO BERSERK."
"THEY'LL BE LIKE WEAPONS..."
"...AND YOU'RE DESTINED TO DIE AT THE HANDS OF THE ISLANDERS."
YOU'RE NOT A MONSTER.
OUNI, YOU HELPED US, AND NOW YOU'RE ONE OF US.
OKAY, UP HERE NEXT...
PUT YOUR FOOT HERE.
YOU FARM EVERY DAY, SUOU, SO YOU SHOULD BE STRONG.
YES.

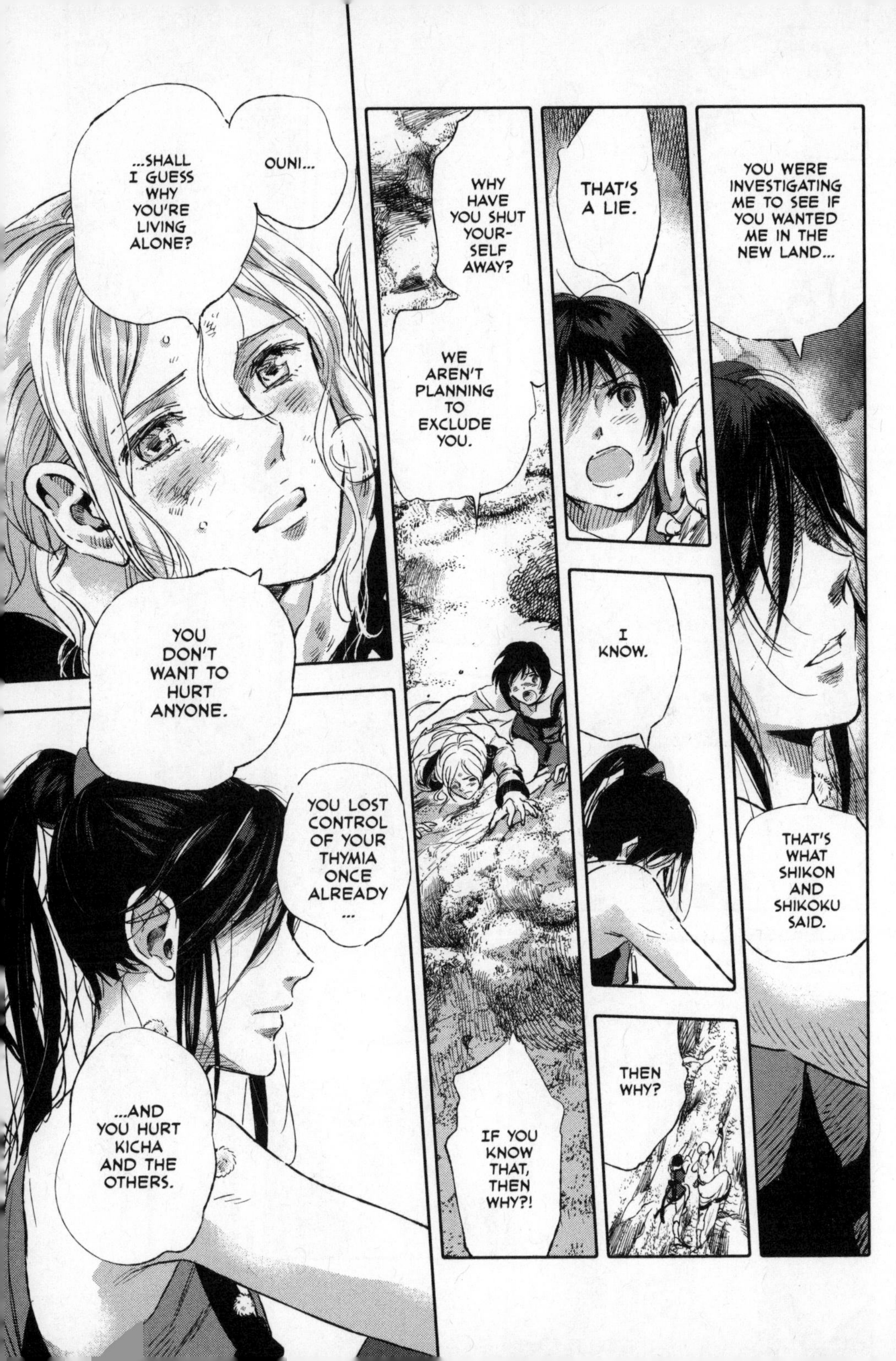
YOU WERE INVESTIGATING ME TO SEE IF YOU WANTED ME IN THE NEW LAND...
THAT'S WHAT SHIKON AND SHIKOKU SAID.
THAT'S A LIE.
I KNOW.
THEN WHY?
WHY HAVE YOU SHUT YOUR-SELF AWAY?
WE AREN'T PLANNING TO EXCLUDE YOU.
IF YOU KNOW THAT, THEN WHY?!
OUNI...
...SHALL I GUESS WHY YOU'RE LIVING ALONE?
YOU DON'T WANT TO HURT ANYONE.
YOU LOST CONTROL OF YOUR THYMIA ONCE ALREADY...
...AND YOU HURT KICHA AND THE OTHERS.

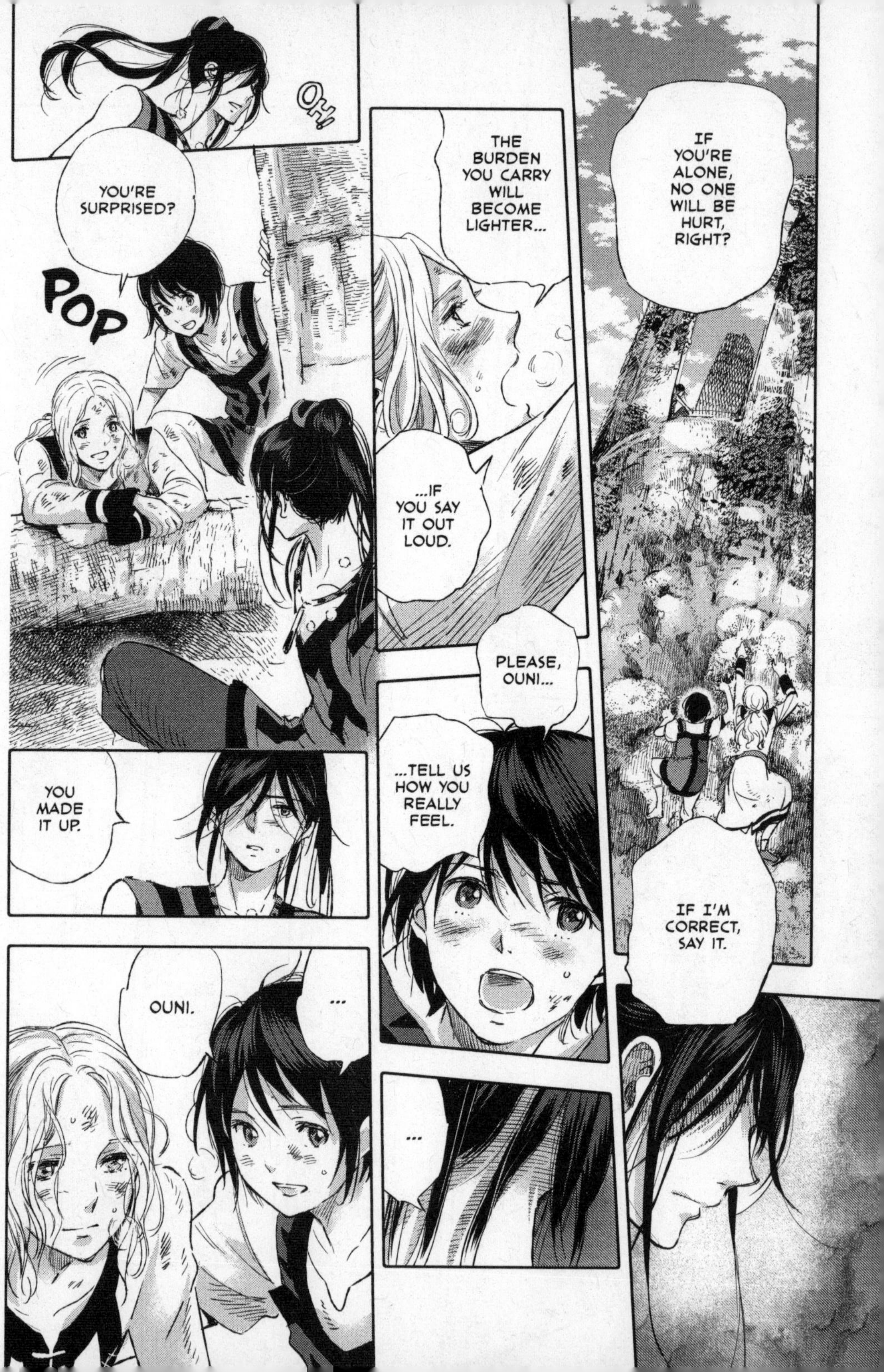
IF YOU'RE ALONE, NO ONE WILL BE HURT, RIGHT?
IF I'M CORRECT, SAY IT.
THE BURDEN YOU CARRY WILL BECOME LIGHTER...
...IF YOU SAY IT OUT LOUD.
PLEASE, OUNI...
...TELL US HOW YOU REALLY FEEL.
...
OH!
YOU'RE SURPRISED?
POP
YOU MADE IT UP.
...
OUNI.

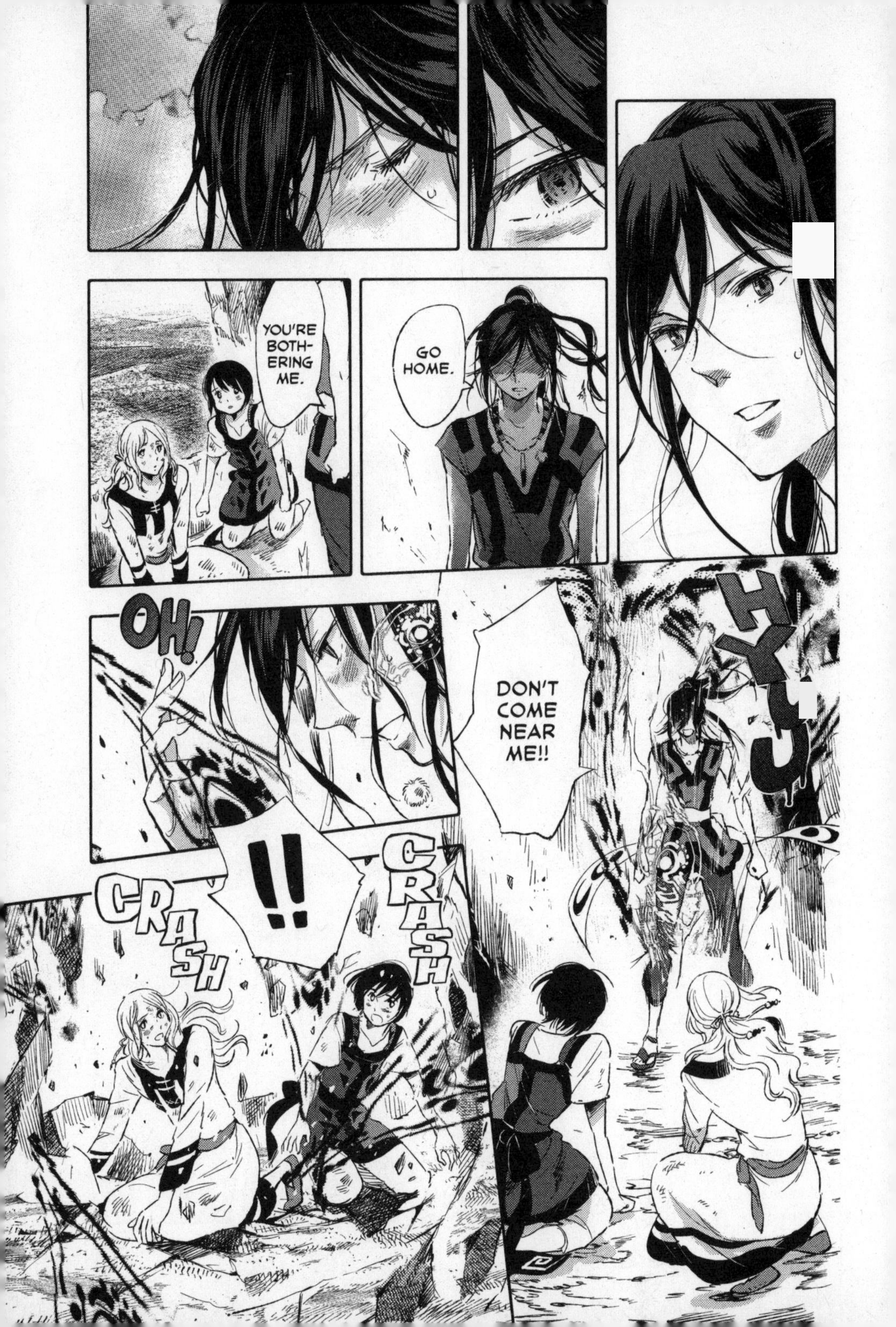
GO HOME.
YOU'RE BOTH-ERING ME.
HYU
DON'T COME NEAR ME!!
OH!
CRASH
!!
CRASH

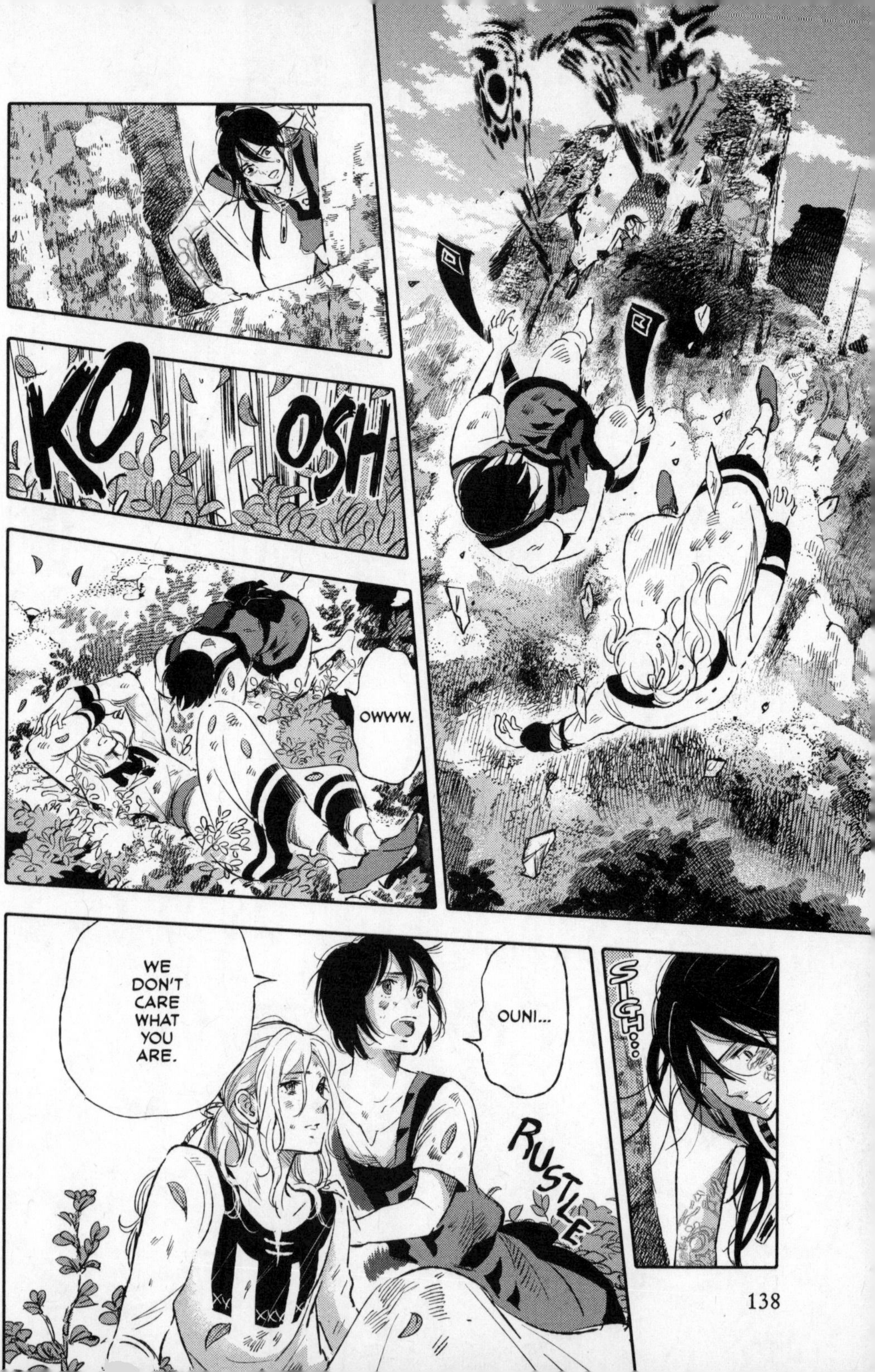
KO OSH
OWWW.
SIGH...
OUNI...
WE DON'T CARE WHAT YOU ARE.
RUSTLE

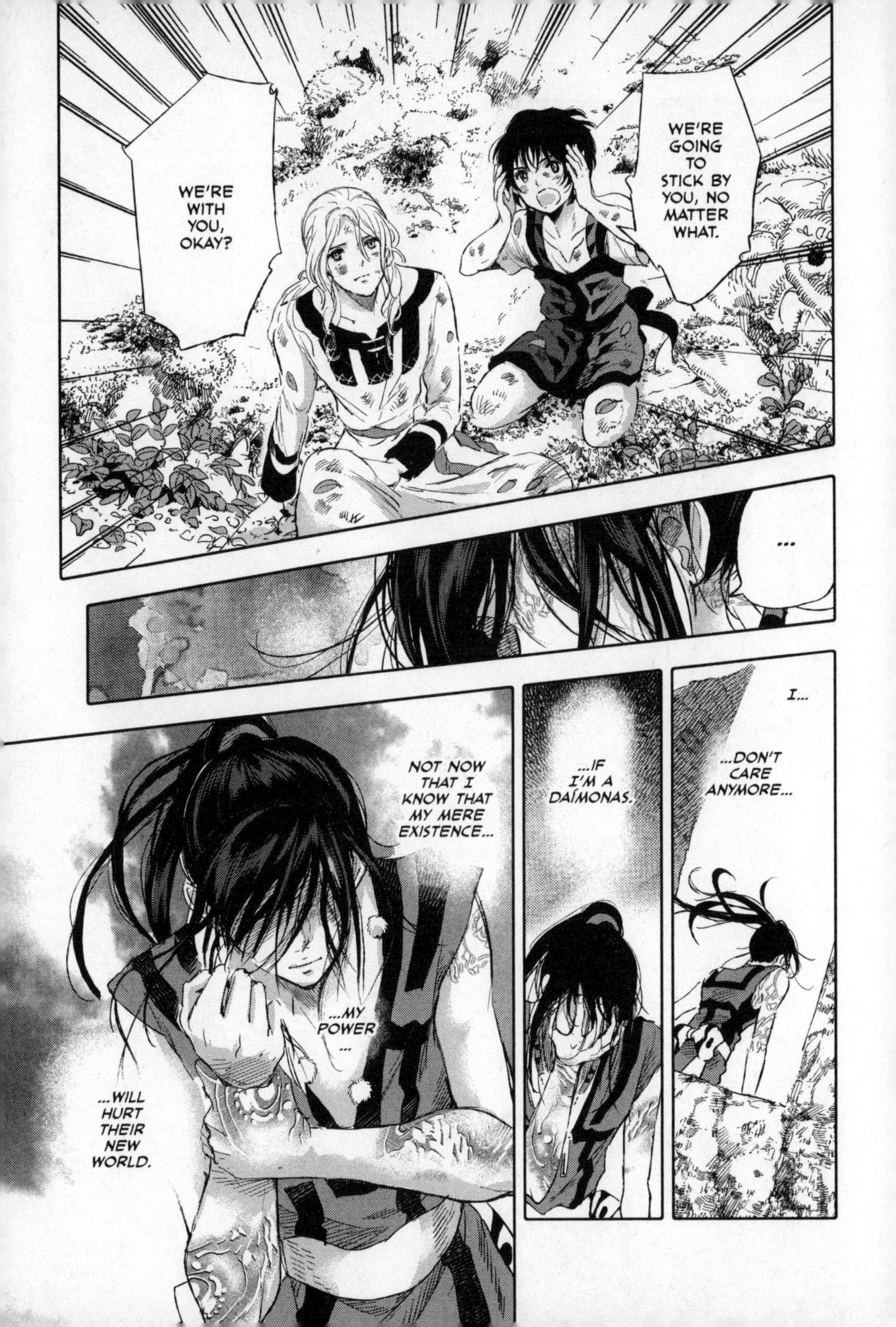
WE'RE GOING TO STICK BY YOU, NO MATTER WHAT.
WE'RE WITH YOU, OKAY?
...
I...
...DON'T CARE ANYMORE...
...IF I'M A DAÏMONAS.
NOT NOW THAT I KNOW THAT MY MERE EXISTENCE...
...MY POWER ...
...WILL HURT THEIR NEW WORLD.

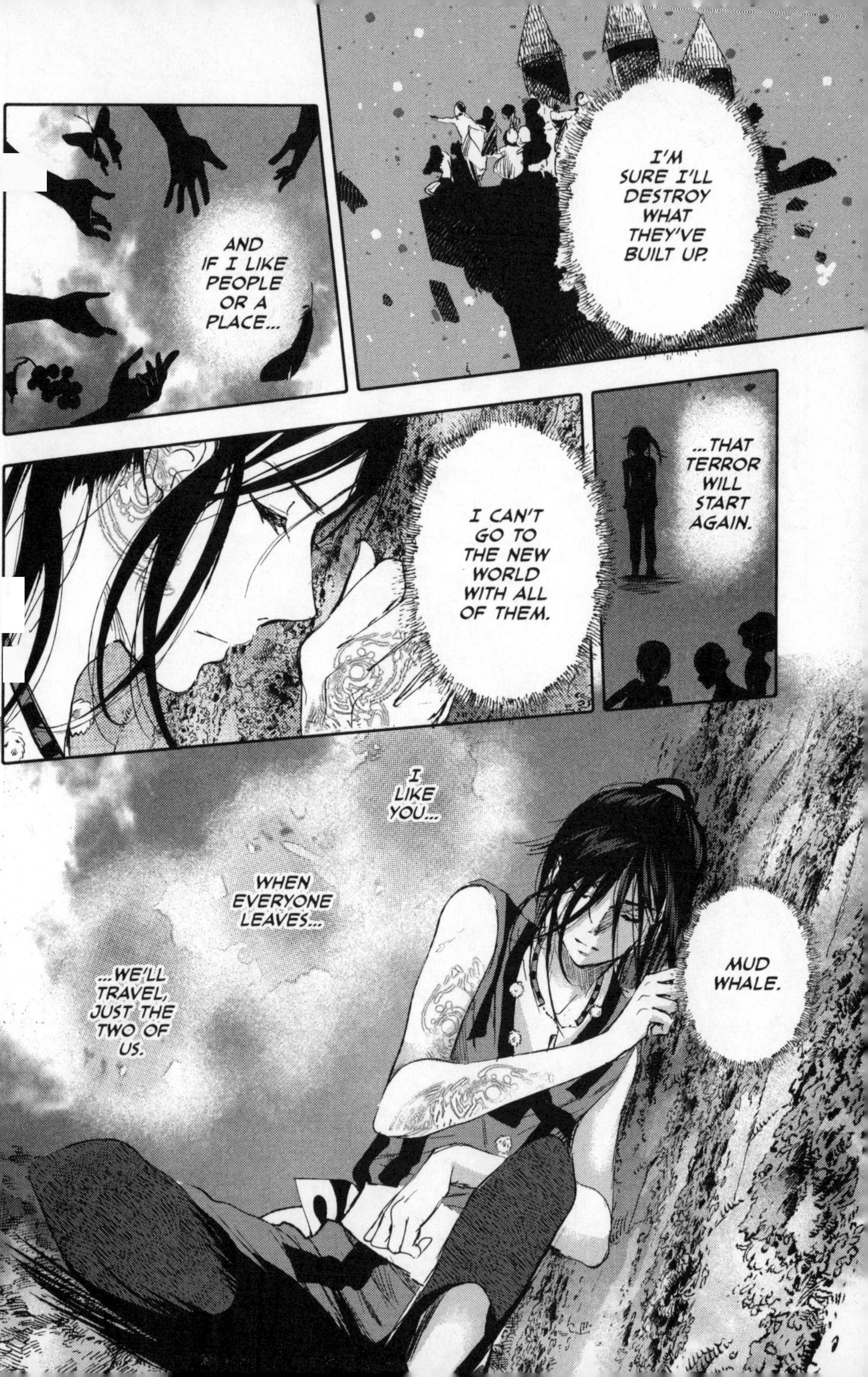
I'M SURE I'LL DESTROY WHAT THEY'VE BUILT UP.
AND IF I LIKE PEOPLE OR A PLACE...
...THAT TERROR WILL START AGAIN.
I CAN'T GO TO THE NEW WORLD WITH ALL OF THEM.
MUD WHALE.
I LIKE YOU...
WHEN EVERYONE LEAVES...
...WE'LL TRAVEL, JUST THE TWO OF US.

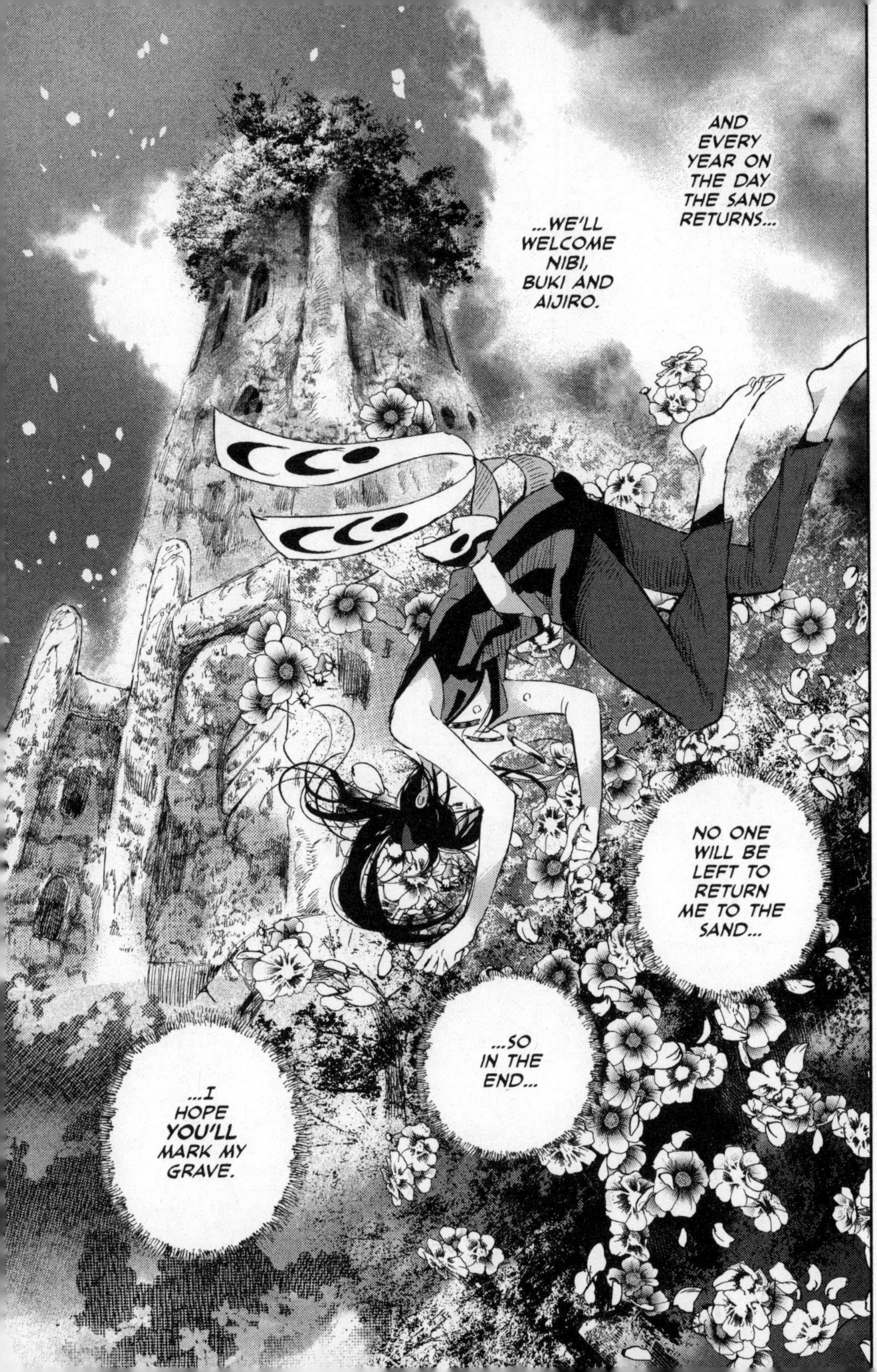
AND EVERY YEAR ON THE DAY THE SAND RETURNS...
...WE'LL WELCOME NIBI, BUKI AND AIJIRO.
NO ONE WILL BE LEFT TO RETURN ME TO THE SAND...
...SO IN THE END...
...I HOPE YOU'LL MARK MY GRAVE.

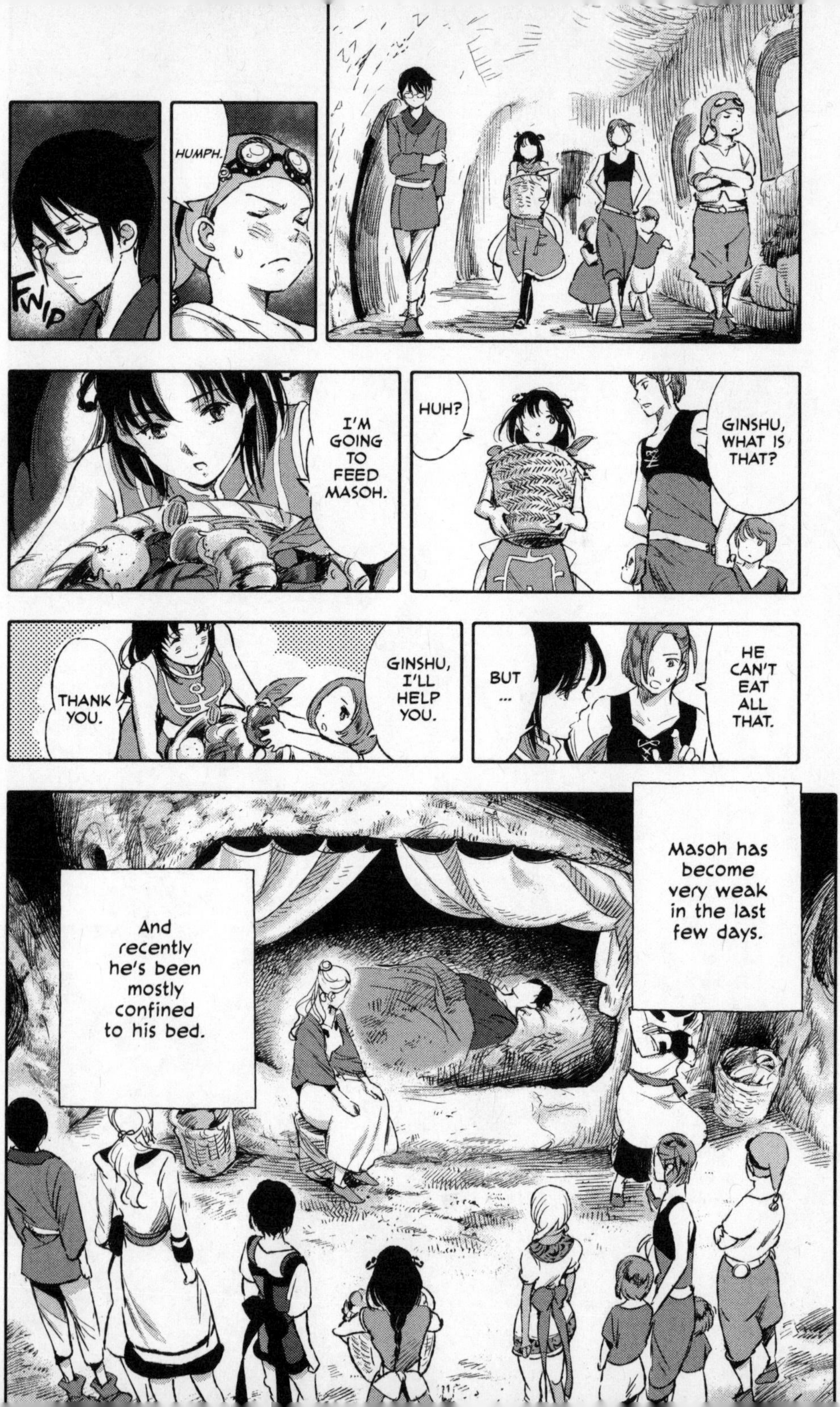
HUMPH.
FWIP
GINSHU, WHAT IS THAT?
HUH?
I'M GOING TO FEED MASOH.
HE CAN'T EAT ALL THAT.
BUT...
GINSHU, I'LL HELP YOU.
THANK YOU.
Masoh has become very weak in the last few days.
And recently he's been mostly confined to his bed.

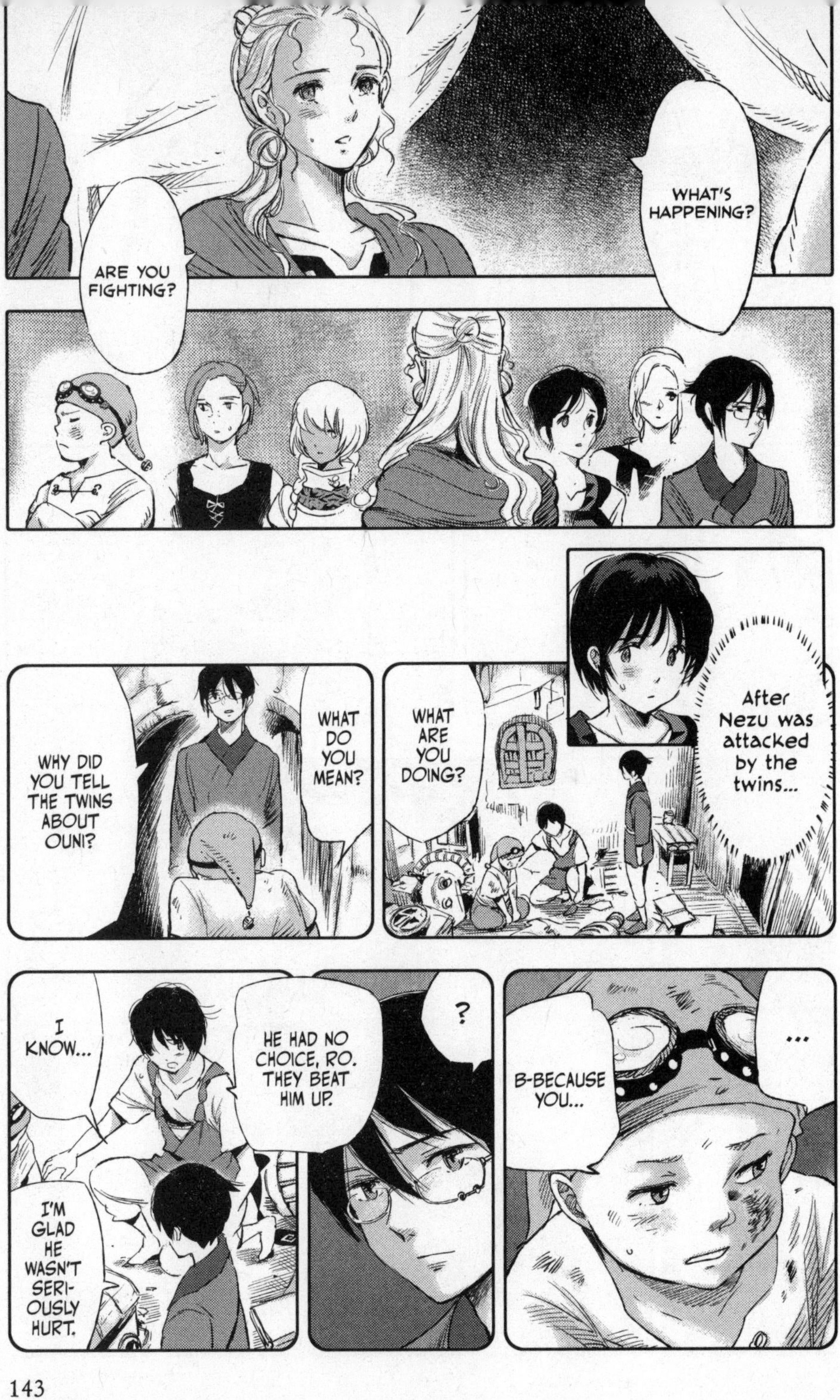
WHAT'S HAPPENING?
ARE YOU FIGHTING?
After Nezu was attacked by the twins...
WHAT ARE YOU DOING?
WHAT DO YOU MEAN?
WHY DID YOU TELL THE TWINS ABOUT OUNI?
...
B-BECAUSE YOU...
?
HE HAD NO CHOICE, RO. THEY BEAT HIM UP.
I KNOW...
I'M GLAD HE WASN'T SERIOUSLY HURT.

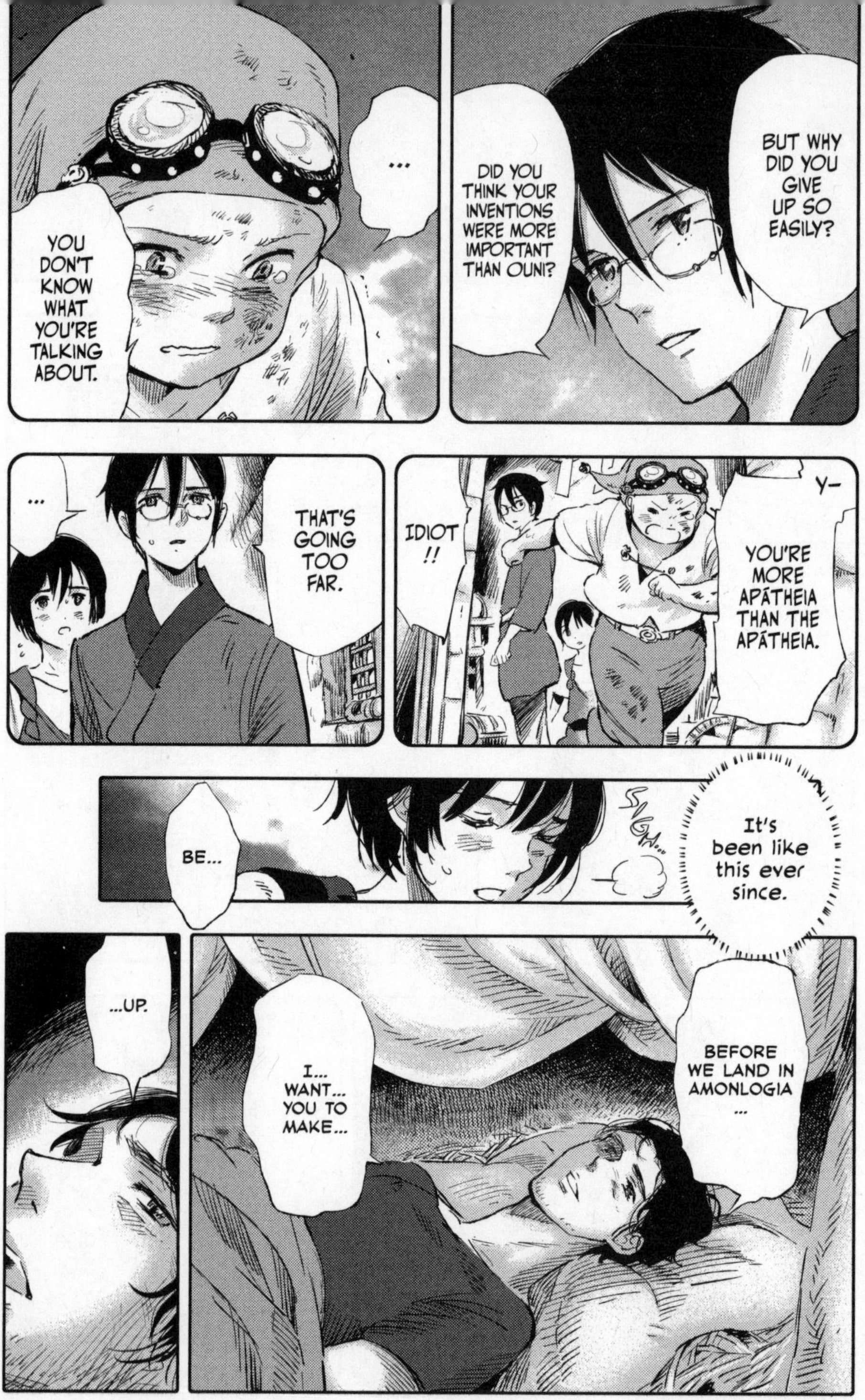
BUT WHY DID YOU GIVE UP SO EASILY?
DID YOU THINK YOUR INVENTIONS WERE MORE IMPORTANT THAN OUNI?
...
YOU DON'T KNOW WHAT YOU'RE TALKING ABOUT.
Y-
YOU'RE MORE APÁTHEIA THAN THE APÁTHEIA.
IDIOT !!
THAT'S GOING TOO FAR.
...
It's been like this ever since.
SIGH...
BE...
BEFORE WE LAND IN AMONLOGIA ...
I... WANT... YOU TO MAKE...
...UP.

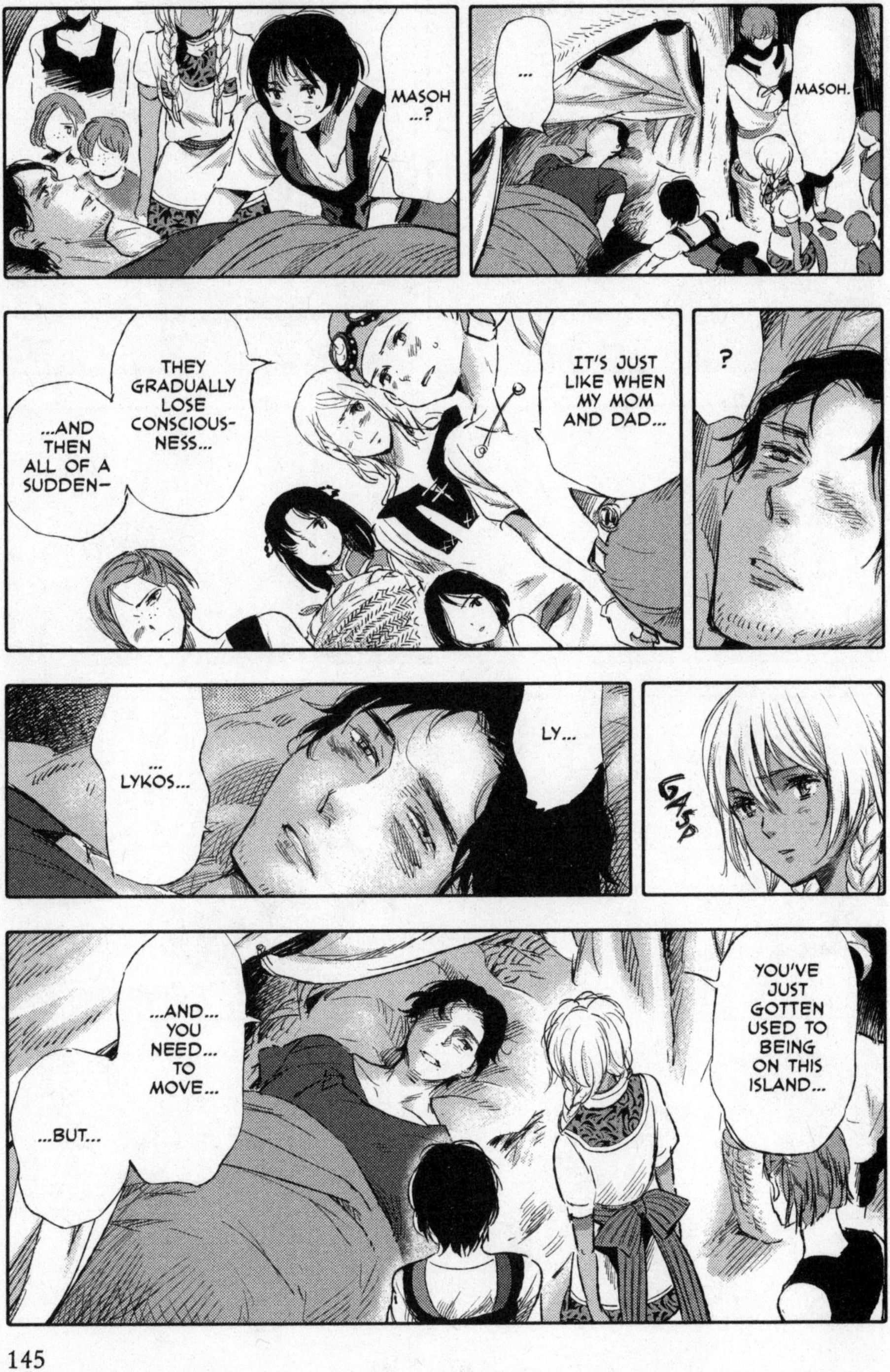
MASOH.
...
MASOH ...?
?
IT'S JUST LIKE WHEN MY MOM AND DAD...
THEY GRADUALLY LOSE CONSCIOUS-NESS...
...AND THEN ALL OF A SUDDEN—
GASA
LY...
... LYKOS...
YOU'VE JUST GOTTEN USED TO BEING ON THIS ISLAND...
...AND... YOU NEED... TO MOVE...
...BUT...

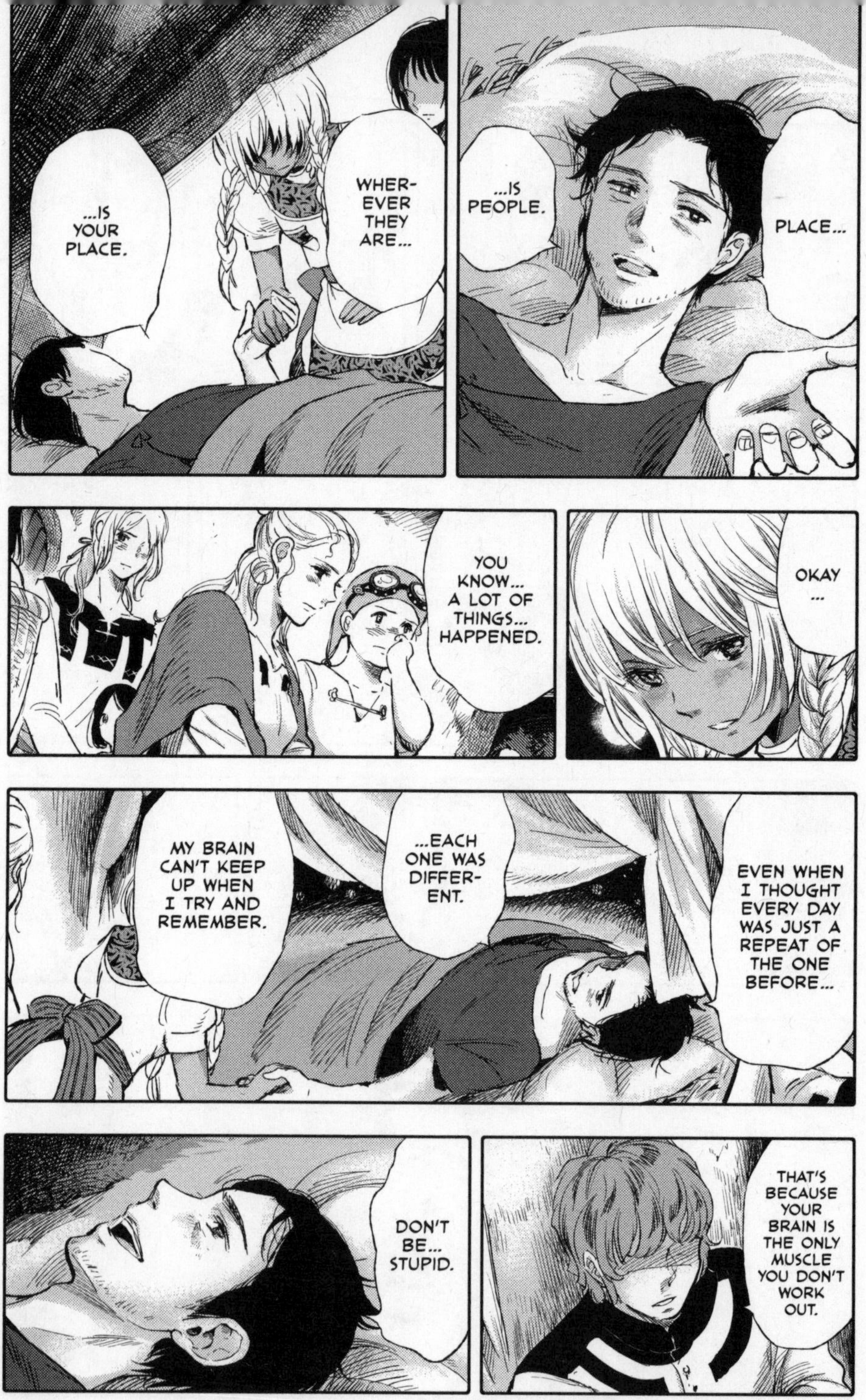
PLACE...
...IS PEOPLE.
WHER-EVER THEY ARE...
...IS YOUR PLACE.
OKAY ...
YOU KNOW... A LOT OF THINGS... HAPPENED.
EVEN WHEN I THOUGHT EVERY DAY WAS JUST A REPEAT OF THE ONE BEFORE...
...EACH ONE WAS DIFFER-ENT.
MY BRAIN CAN'T KEEP UP WHEN I TRY AND REMEMBER.
THAT'S BECAUSE YOUR BRAIN IS THE ONLY MUSCLE YOU DON'T WORK OUT.
DON'T BE... STUPID.

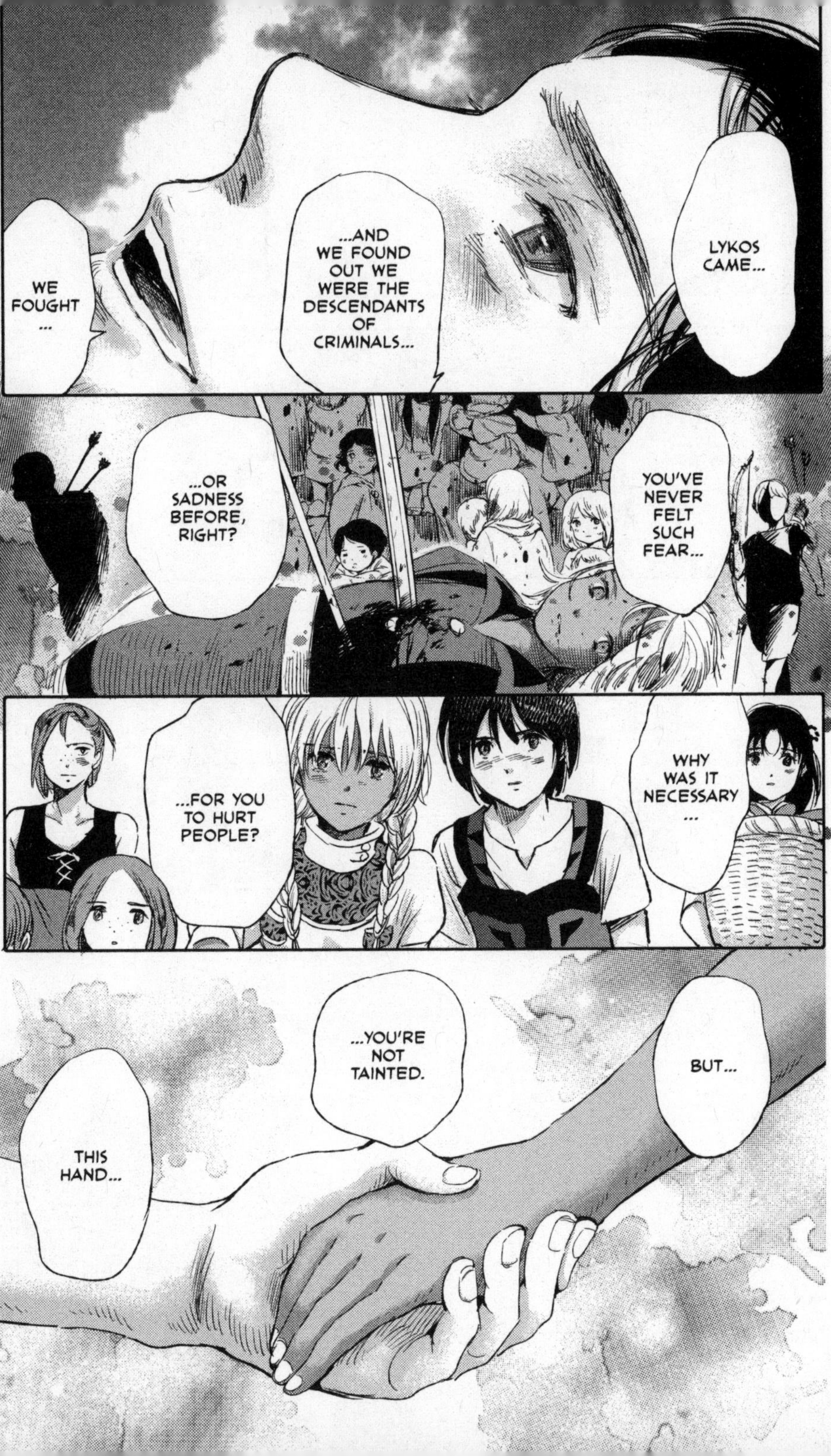
LYKOS CAME...
...AND WE FOUND OUT WE WERE THE DESCENDANTS OF CRIMINALS...
WE FOUGHT ...
YOU'VE NEVER FELT SUCH FEAR...
...OR SADNESS BEFORE, RIGHT?
WHY WAS IT NECESSARY ...
...FOR YOU TO HURT PEOPLE?
BUT...
...YOU'RE NOT TAINTED.
THIS HAND...

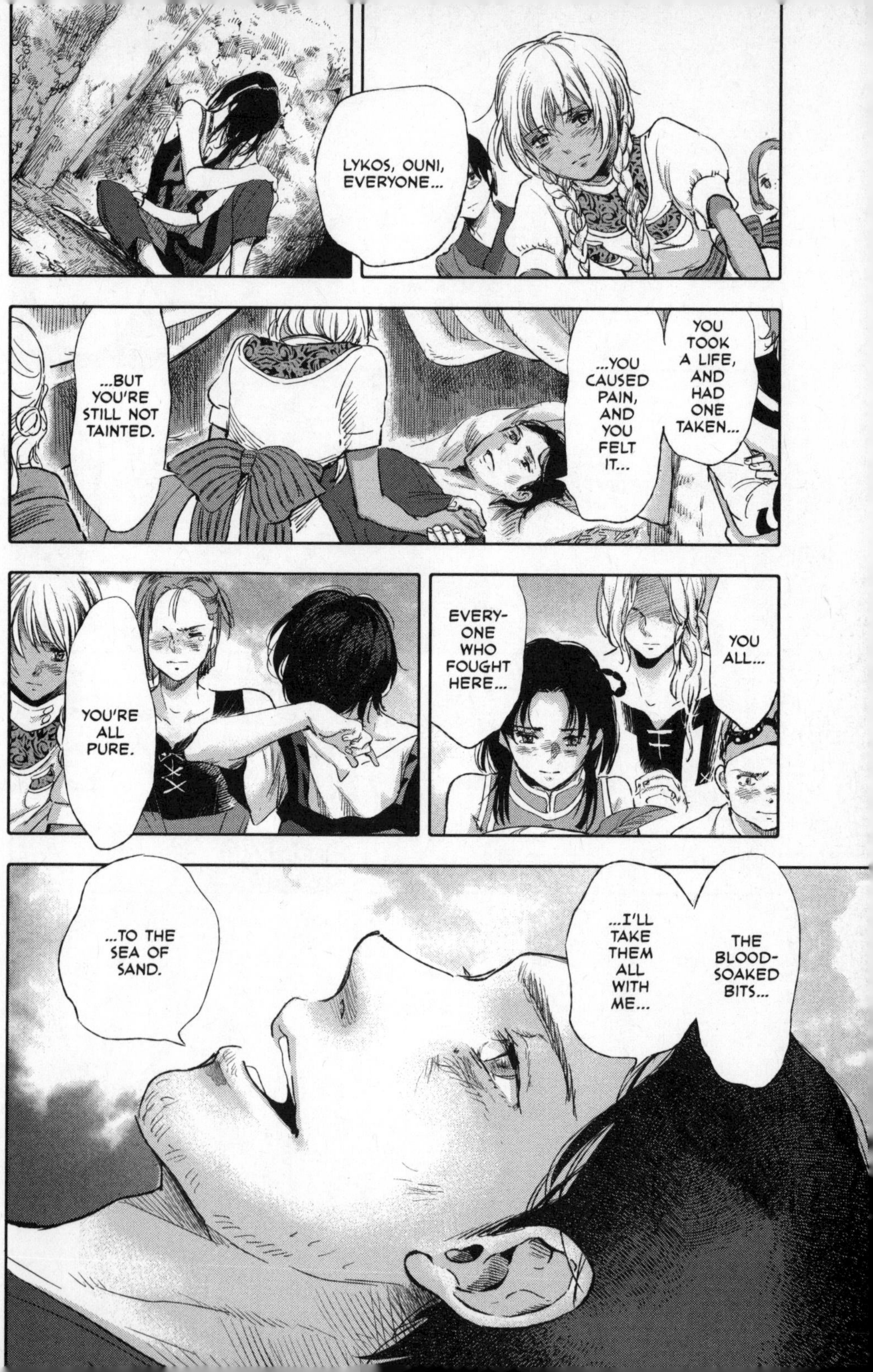
LYKOS, OUNI, EVERYONE...
YOU TOOK A LIFE, AND HAD ONE TAKEN...
...YOU CAUSED PAIN, AND YOU FELT IT...
...BUT YOU'RE STILL NOT TAINTED.
YOU ALL...
EVERY-ONE WHO FOUGHT HERE...
YOU'RE ALL PURE.
THE BLOOD-SOAKED BITS...
...I'LL TAKE THEM ALL WITH ME...
...TO THE SEA OF SAND.

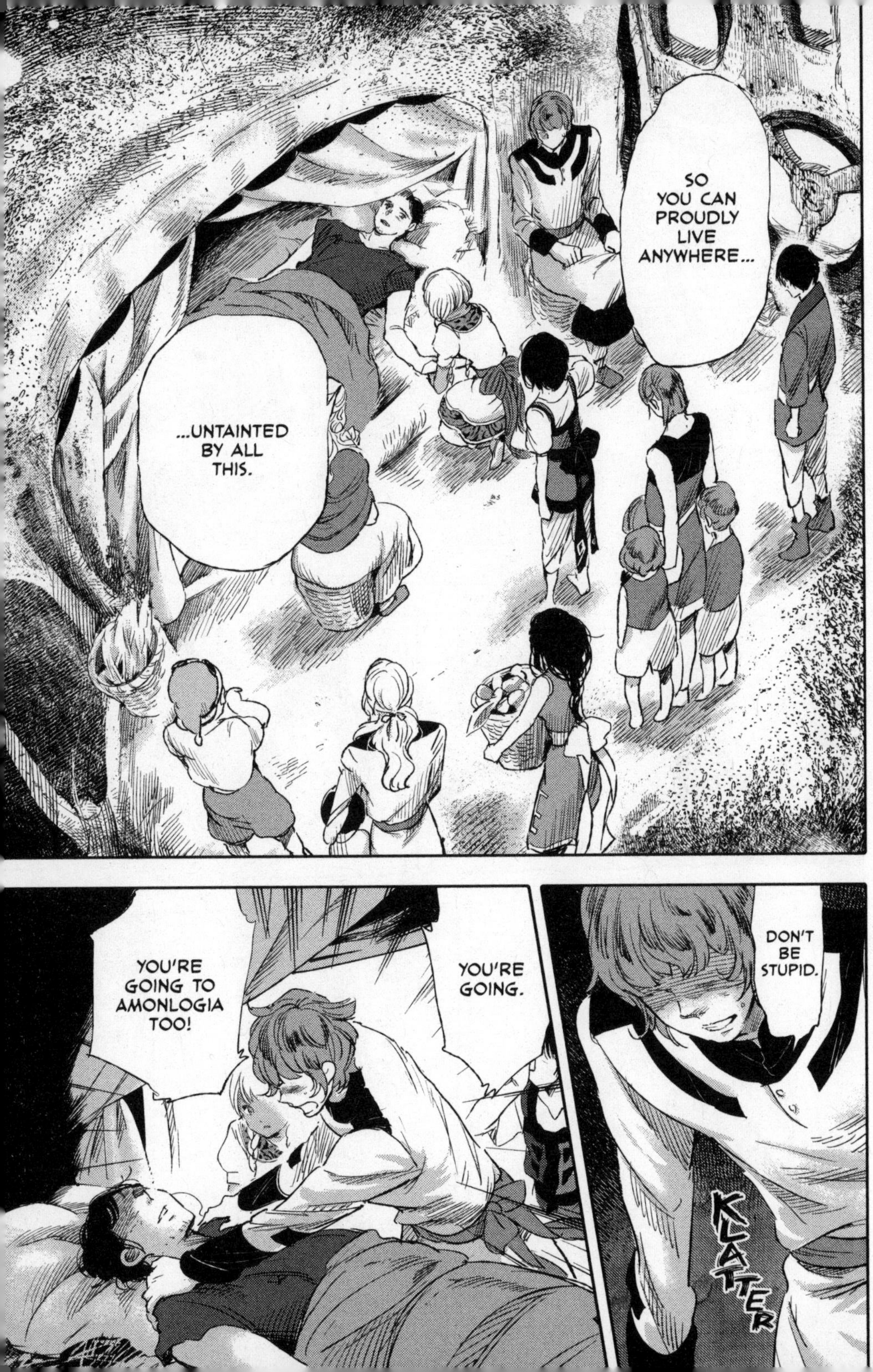
SO YOU CAN PROUDLY LIVE ANYWHERE...
...UNTAINTED BY ALL THIS.
DON'T BE STUPID.
KLATTER
YOU'RE GOING.
YOU'RE GOING TO AMONLOGIA TOO!

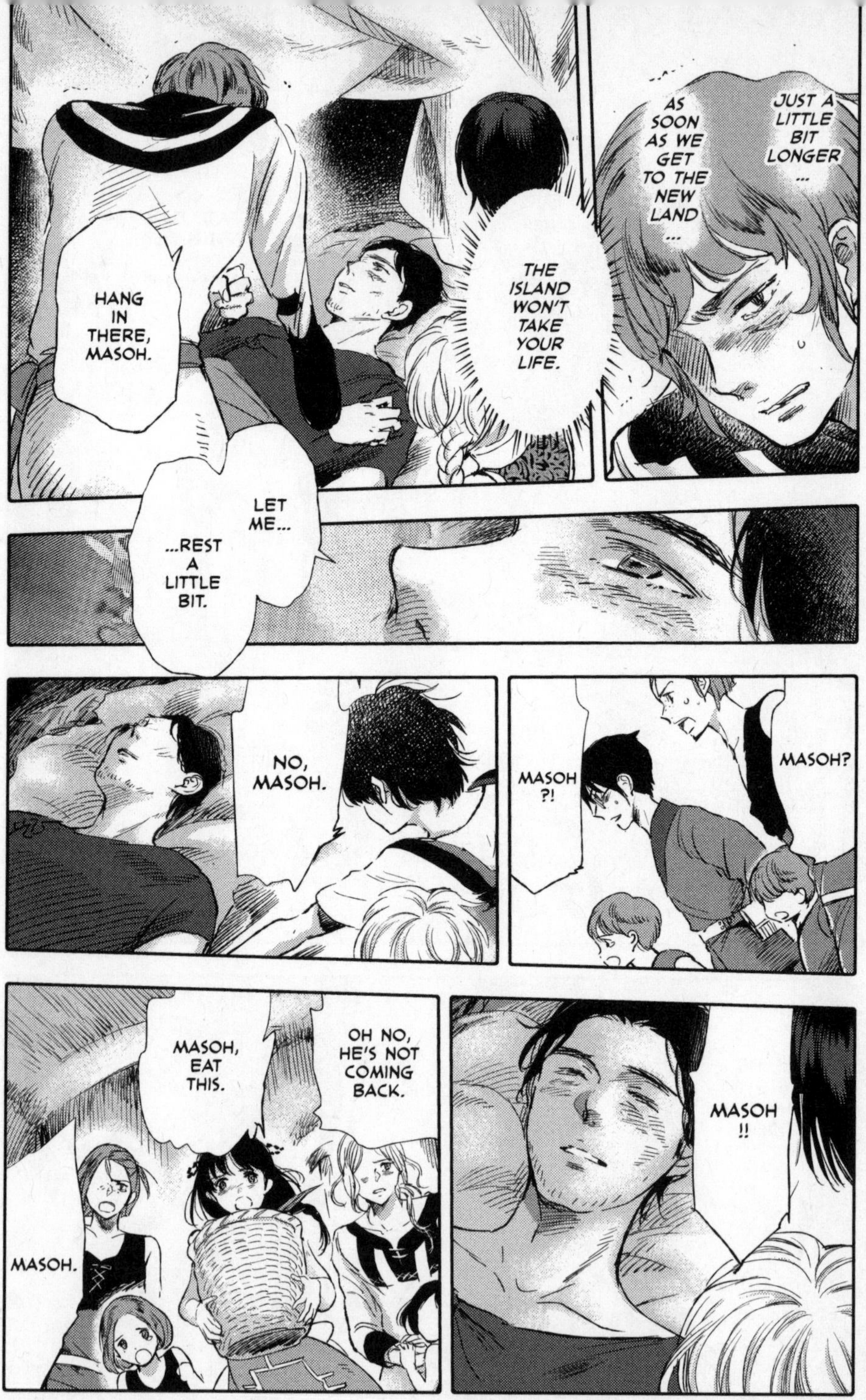
JUST A LITTLE BIT LONGER ...
AS SOON AS WE GET TO THE NEW LAND ...
THE ISLAND WON'T TAKE YOUR LIFE.
HANG IN THERE, MASOH.
LET ME...
...REST A LITTLE BIT.
MASOH?
MASOH ?!
NO, MASOH.
MASOH !!
OH NO, HE'S NOT COMING BACK.
MASOH, EAT THIS.
MASOH.

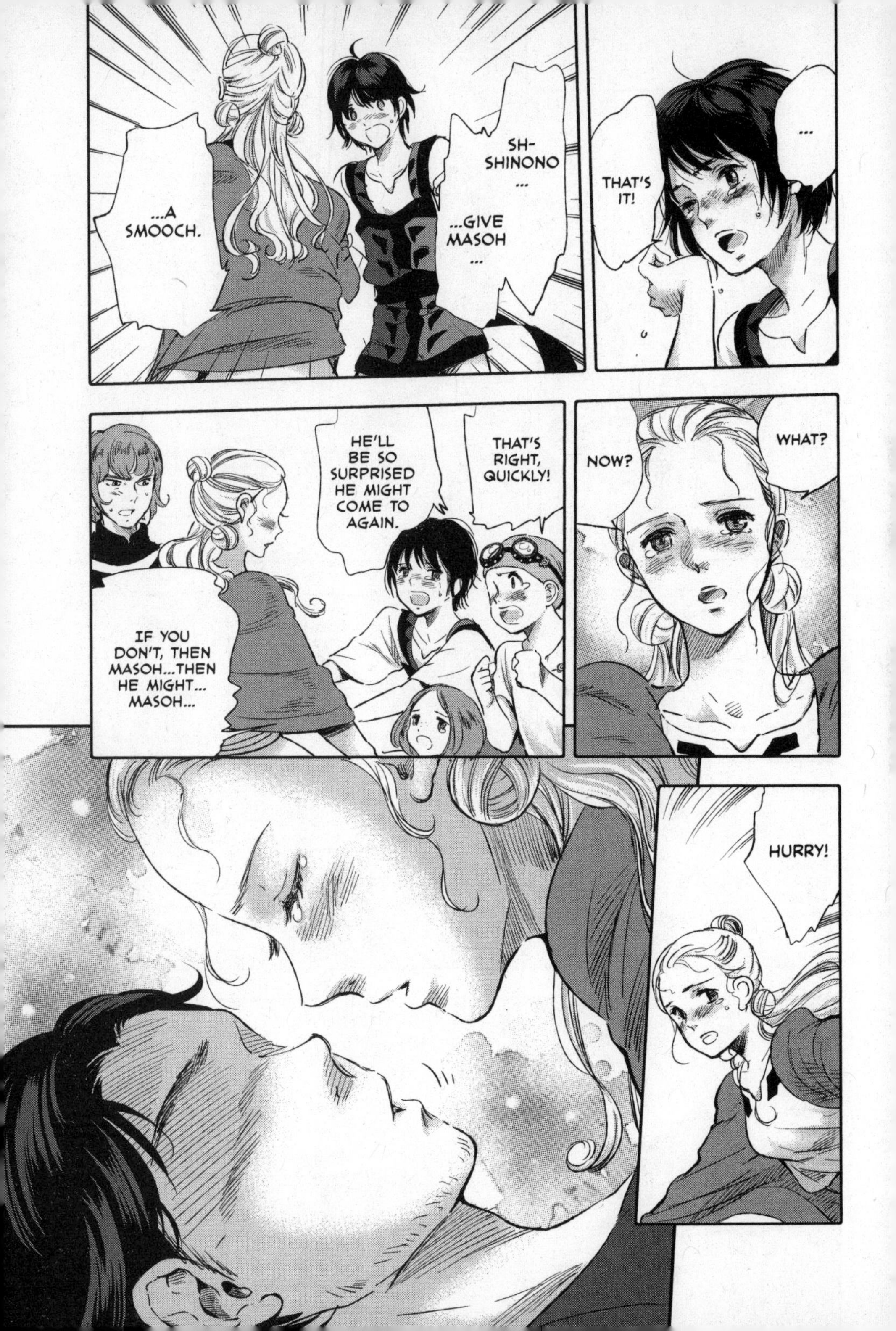
...
THAT'S IT!
SH-SHINONO ...
...GIVE MASOH ...
...A SMOOCH.
WHAT?
NOW?
THAT'S RIGHT, QUICKLY!
HE'LL BE SO SURPRISED HE MIGHT COME TO AGAIN.
IF YOU DON'T, THEN MASOH...THEN HE MIGHT... MASOH...
HURRY!

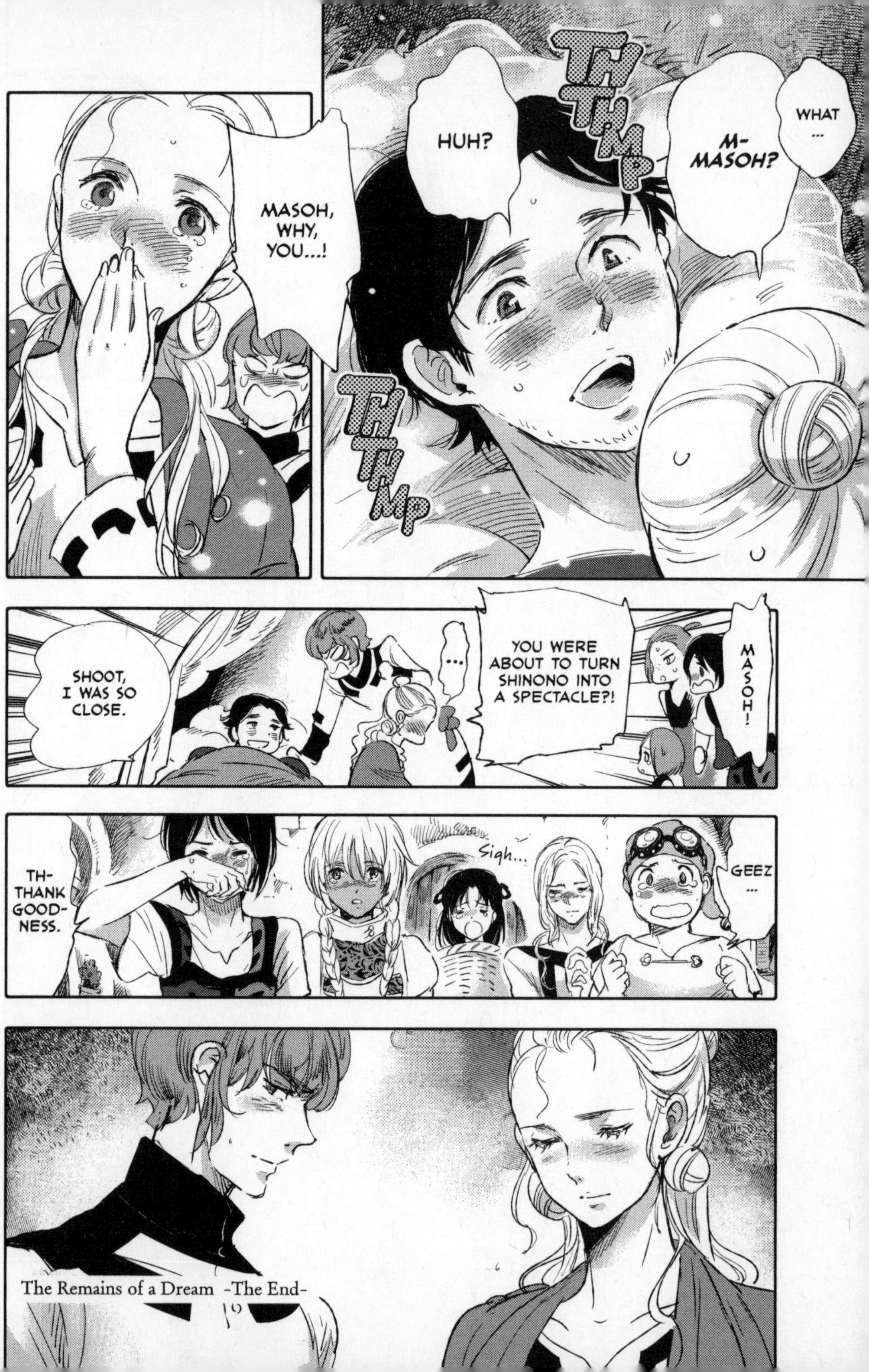
WHAT ...
M-MASOH?
HUH?
THTHMP
THTHMP
MASOH, WHY, YOU...!
MASOH!
YOU WERE ABOUT TO TURN SHINONO INTO A SPECTACLE?!
...
SHOOT, I WAS SO CLOSE.
GEEZ ...
Sigh...
TH-THANK GOODNESS.
The Remains of a Dream -The End-

The Archivist's Notes

Sailing on the Sea of Sand

On the Sea of Sand, people and things get swallowed up by the sand swells and sink, so you need some way to traverse it.

On the Mud Whale, the small boats are propelled by the thymia of the Marked. The Mud Whale gained the ability to move freely when the rudder kókalo was added to the power of the Nous Fálaina.

The United Kingdom of Suidelasia, where the Mud Whale is headed, successfully harnessed the buoyant energy of the rare fossils, apolithomata, found in the Sea of Sand.

Apolithomata have properties that make them float on the sea, so some people have even constructed ships of the material.

There is some evidence that certain people train fish and sea monsters that are suited to life in the Sea of Sand to pull their ships.

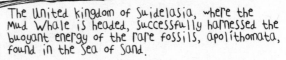

These methods are still a mystery to the citizens of the Mud Whale, who have just begun their journey on the Sea of Sand.

Sketch 10
Dangerous sectors of the Mud Whale

The mud buildings on the island are fragile. In particular, Tower 4 and Tower 5 towards the stern have begun to lean with the passage of time.

For this reason, no one lives in these two towers or visits very often.

The dorms around Tower 4 are also starting to lean, so there are many empty chambers.

The Moles, however, have made this danger zone their home base. The Purple-Winged Rudder led by Shikon and Shikoku met near Tower 5.

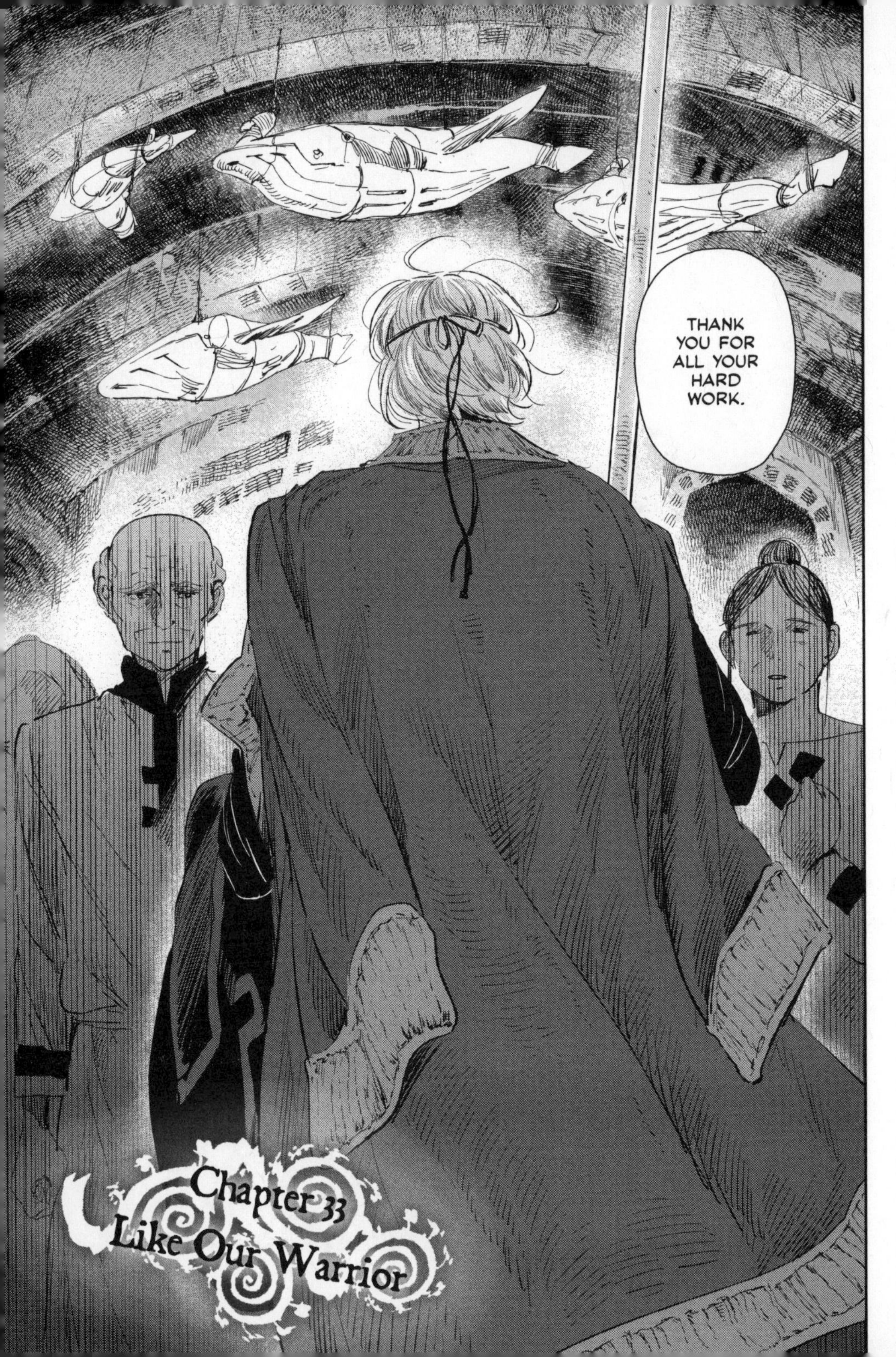
THANK YOU FOR ALL YOUR HARD WORK.
Chapter 33
Like Our Warrior

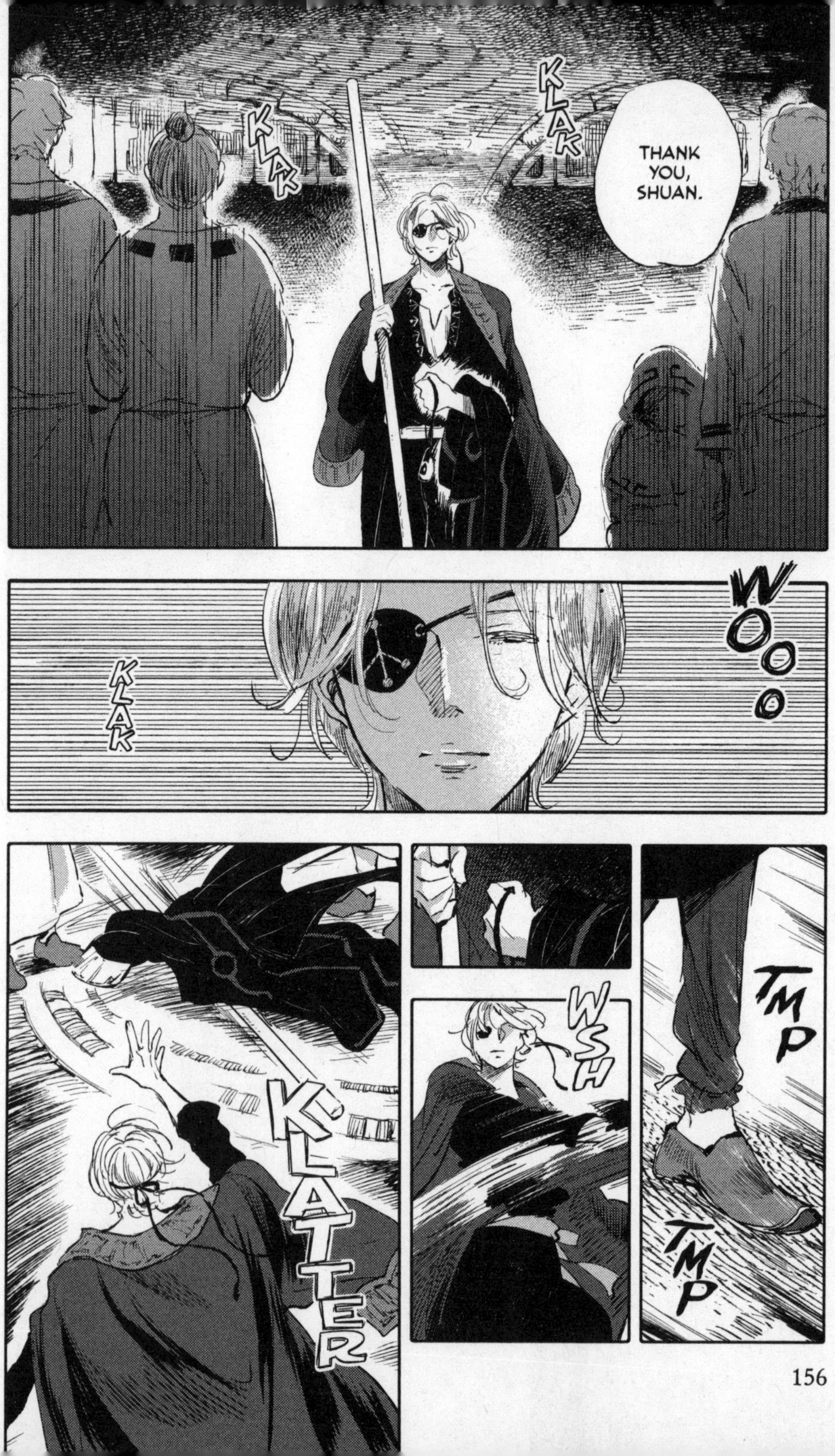
THANK YOU, SHUAN.
KLAK
KLAK
WOOOO
KLAK
TMP
TMP
WSH
KLATTER

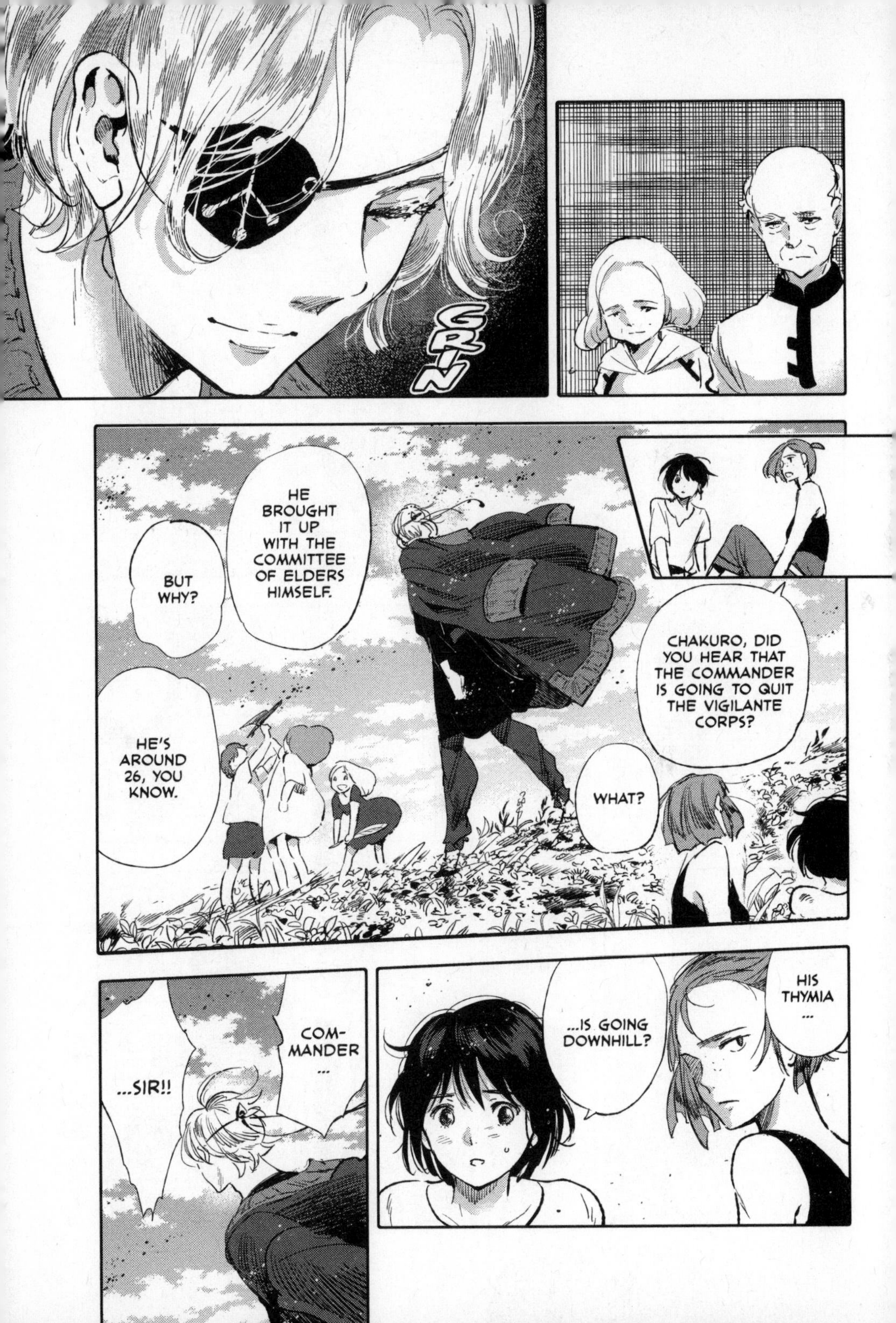
GRIN
CHAKURO, DID YOU HEAR THAT THE COMMANDER IS GOING TO QUIT THE VIGILANTE CORPS?
WHAT?
HE BROUGHT IT UP WITH THE COMMITTEE OF ELDERS HIMSELF.
BUT WHY?
HE'S AROUND 26, YOU KNOW.
HIS THYMIA ...
...IS GOING DOWNHILL?
COM-MANDER ...
...SIR!!

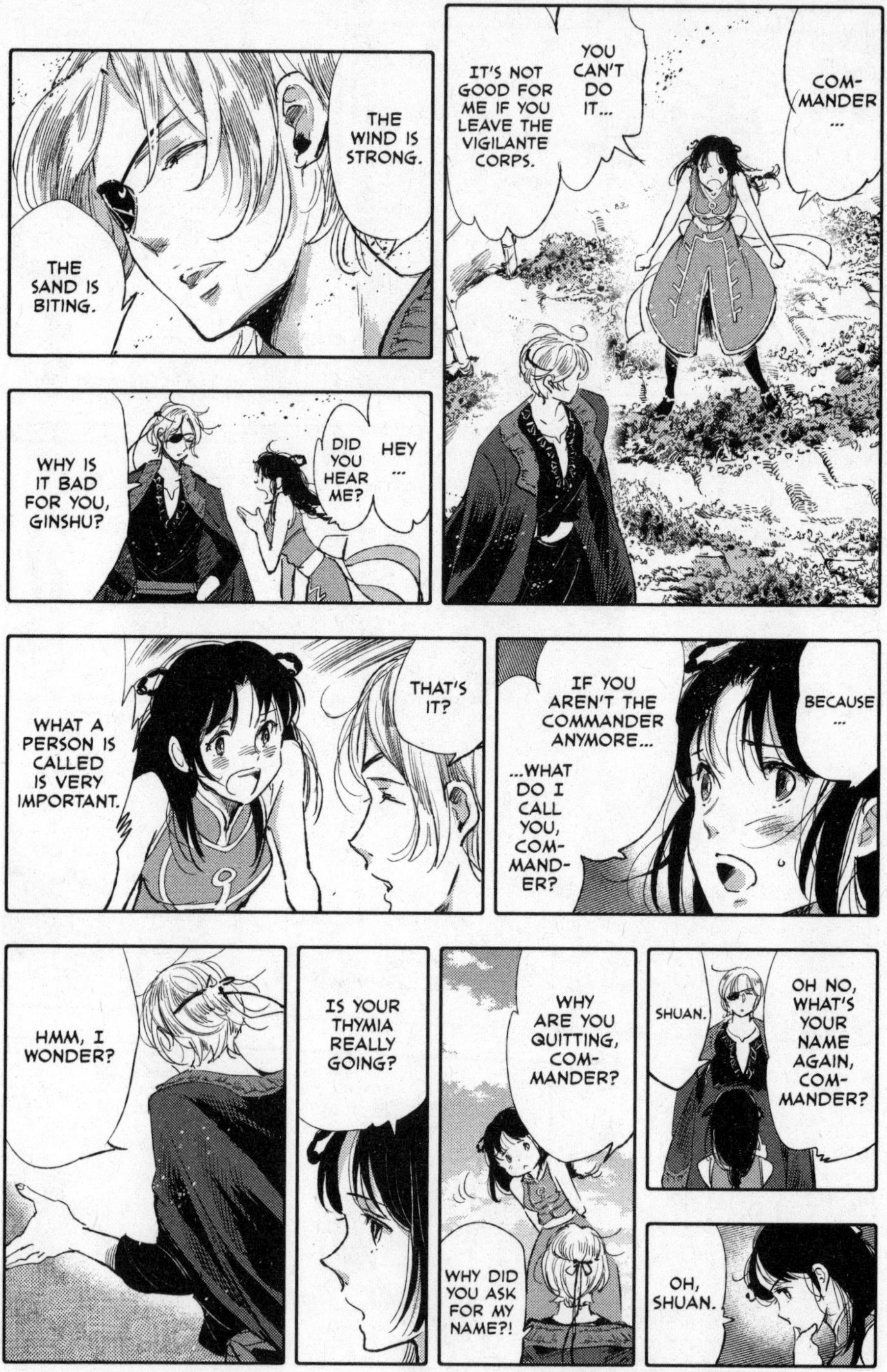
COM-MANDER ...
YOU CAN'T DO IT...
IT'S NOT GOOD FOR ME IF YOU LEAVE THE VIGILANTE CORPS.
THE WIND IS STRONG.
THE SAND IS BITING.
HEY ...
DID YOU HEAR ME?
WHY IS IT BAD FOR YOU, GINSHU?
BECAUSE ...
IF YOU AREN'T THE COMMANDER ANYMORE...
...WHAT DO I CALL YOU, COM-MAND-ER?
THAT'S IT?
WHAT A PERSON IS CALLED IS VERY IMPORTANT.
OH NO, WHAT'S YOUR NAME AGAIN, COM-MANDER?
SHUAN.
OH, SHUAN.
WHY ARE YOU QUITTING, COM-MANDER?
WHY DID YOU ASK FOR MY NAME?!
IS YOUR THYMIA REALLY GOING?
HMM, I WONDER?

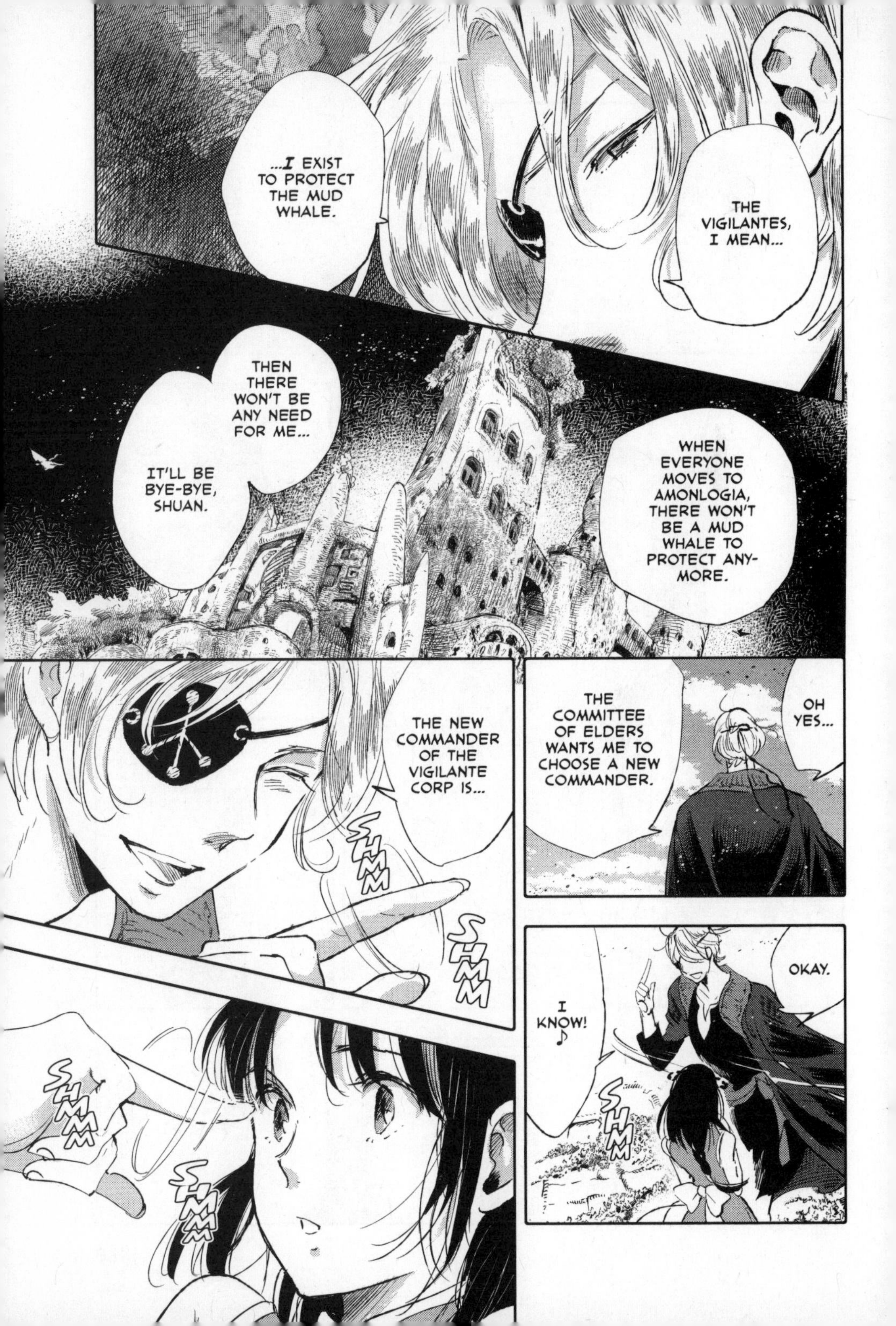
THE VIGILANTES, I MEAN...
...I EXIST TO PROTECT THE MUD WHALE.
WHEN EVERYONE MOVES TO AMONLOGIA, THERE WON'T BE A MUD WHALE TO PROTECT ANY-MORE.
THEN THERE WON'T BE ANY NEED FOR ME...
IT'LL BE BYE-BYE, SHUAN.
OH YES...
THE COMMITTEE OF ELDERS WANTS ME TO CHOOSE A NEW COMMANDER.
OKAY.
I KNOW! ♪
SHMM
THE NEW COMMANDER OF THE VIGILANTE CORP IS...
SHMM
SHMM
SHMM
SHMM

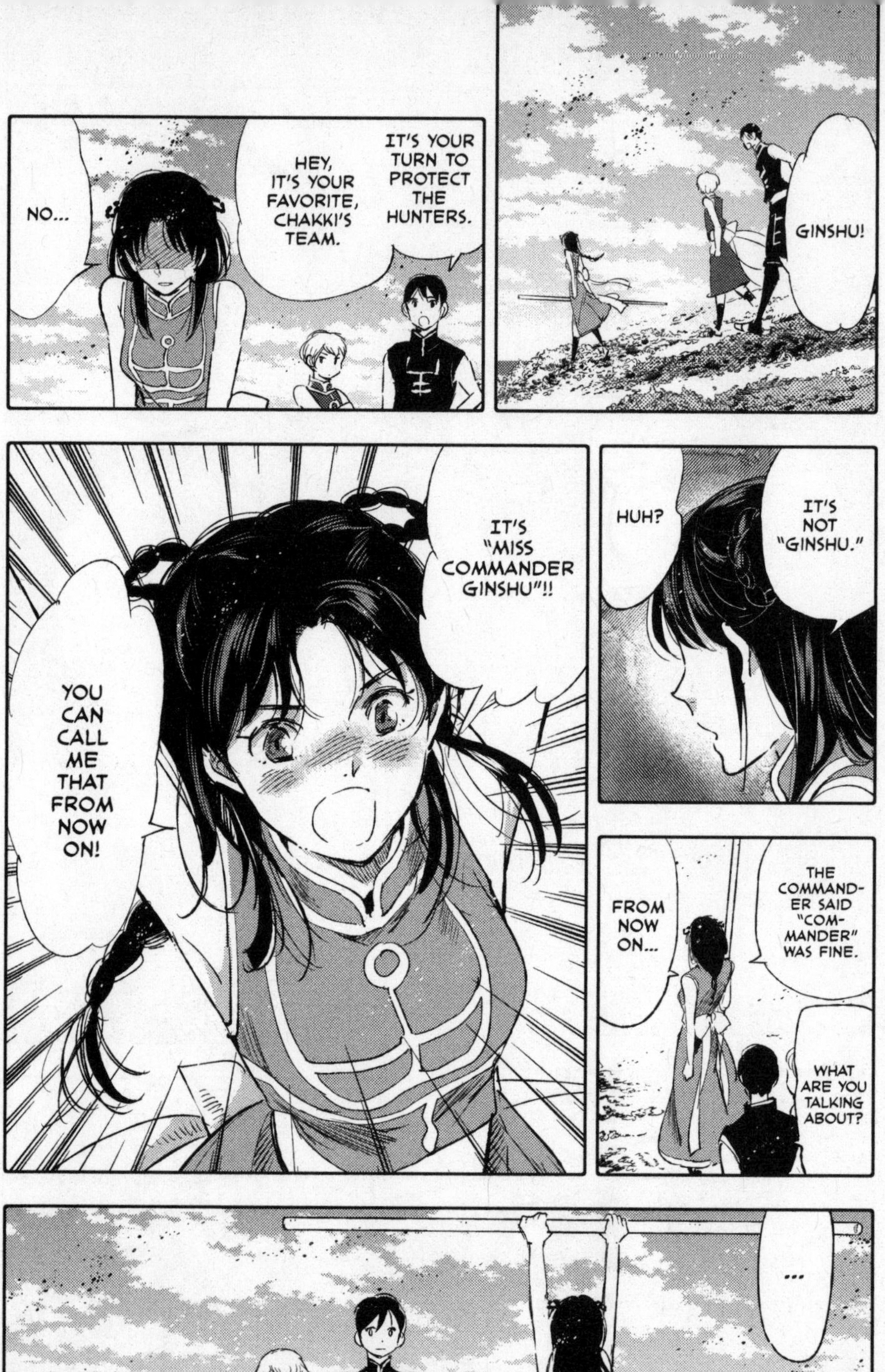
GINSHU!
IT'S YOUR TURN TO PROTECT THE HUNTERS.
HEY, IT'S YOUR FAVORITE, CHAKKI'S TEAM.
NO...
IT'S NOT "GINSHU."
HUH?
THE COMMANDER SAID "COMMANDER" WAS FINE.
FROM NOW ON...
WHAT ARE YOU TALKING ABOUT?
IT'S "MISS COMMANDER GINSHU"!!
YOU CAN CALL ME THAT FROM NOW ON!
...

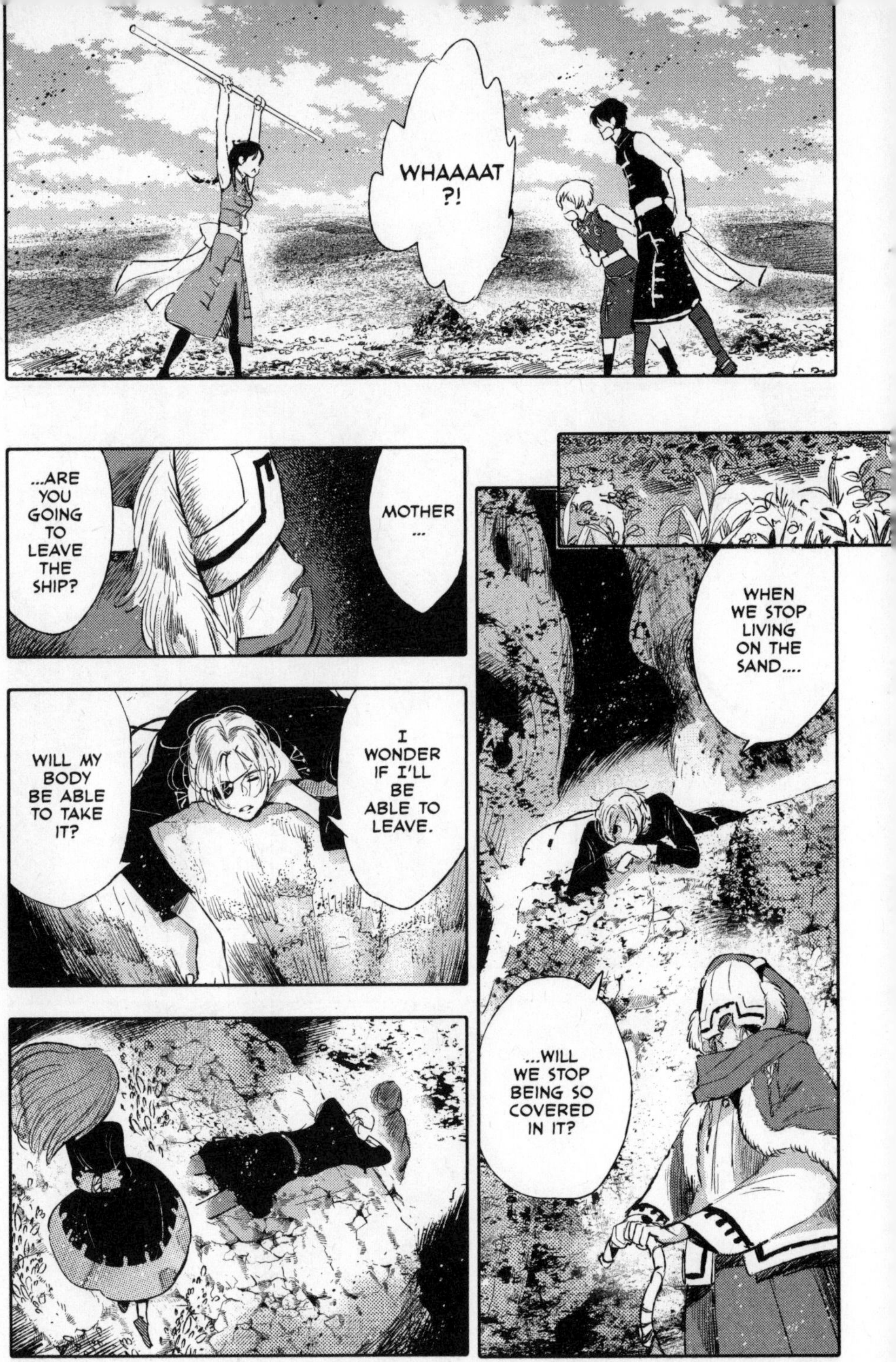
WHAAAAT ?!
WHEN WE STOP LIVING ON THE SAND....
...WILL WE STOP BEING SO COVERED IN IT?
MOTHER ...
...ARE YOU GOING TO LEAVE THE SHIP?
I WONDER IF I'LL BE ABLE TO LEAVE.
WILL MY BODY BE ABLE TO TAKE IT?

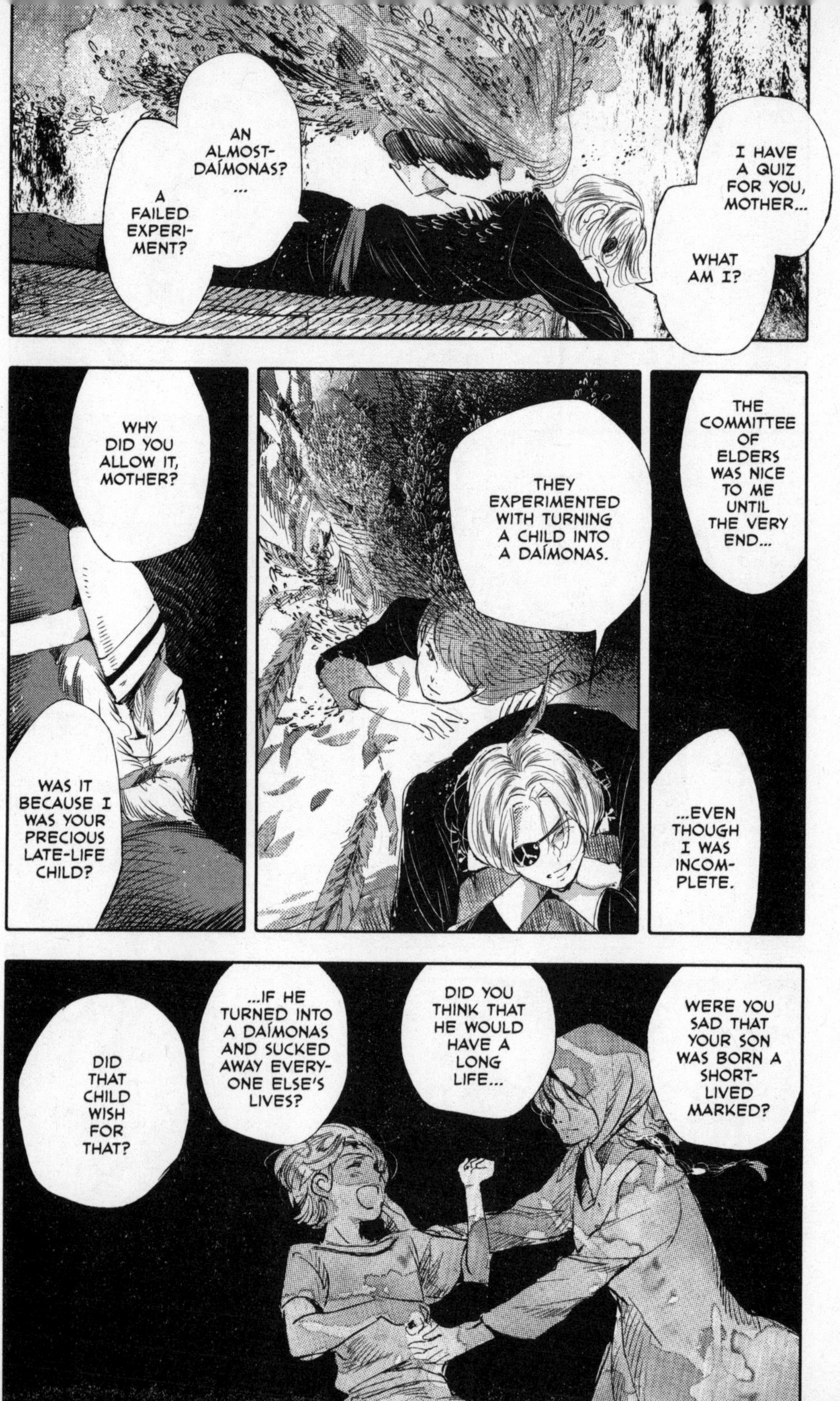
I HAVE A QUIZ FOR YOU, MOTHER...
WHAT AM I?
AN ALMOST-DAÍMONAS?
...
A FAILED EXPERIMENT?
THE COMMITTEE OF ELDERS WAS NICE TO ME UNTIL THE VERY END...
...EVEN THOUGH I WAS INCOMPLETE.
THEY EXPERIMENTED WITH TURNING A CHILD INTO A DAÍMONAS.
WHY DID YOU ALLOW IT, MOTHER?
WAS IT BECAUSE I WAS YOUR PRECIOUS LATE-LIFE CHILD?
WERE YOU SAD THAT YOUR SON WAS BORN A SHORT-LIVED MARKED?
DID YOU THINK THAT HE WOULD HAVE A LONG LIFE...
...IF HE TURNED INTO A DAÍMONAS AND SUCKED AWAY EVERYONE ELSE'S LIVES?
DID THAT CHILD WISH FOR THAT?

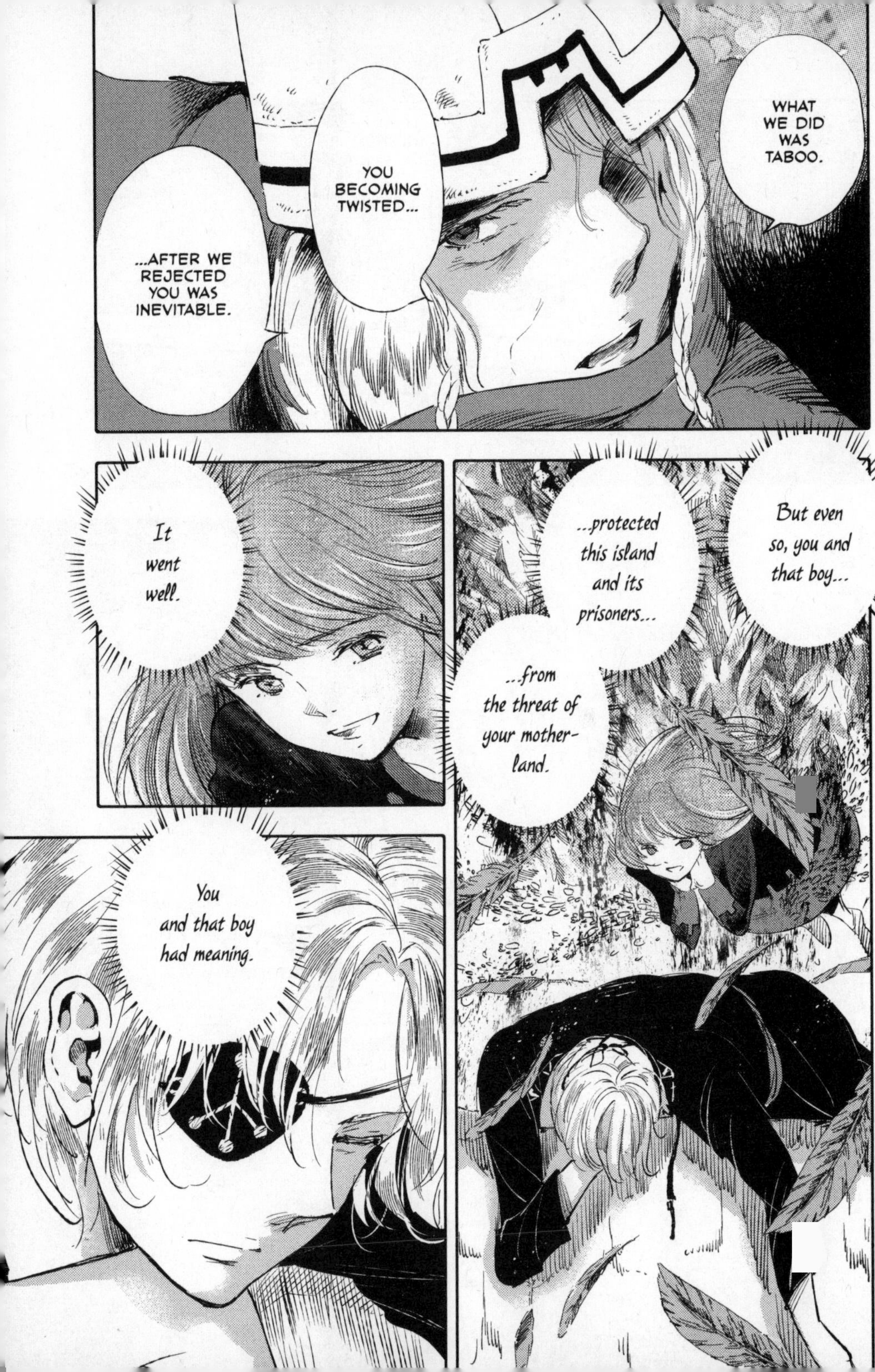
WHAT WE DID WAS TABOO.
YOU BECOMING TWISTED...
...AFTER WE REJECTED YOU WAS INEVITABLE.
But even so, you and that boy...
...protected this island and its prisoners...
...from the threat of your mother-land.
It went well.
You and that boy had meaning.

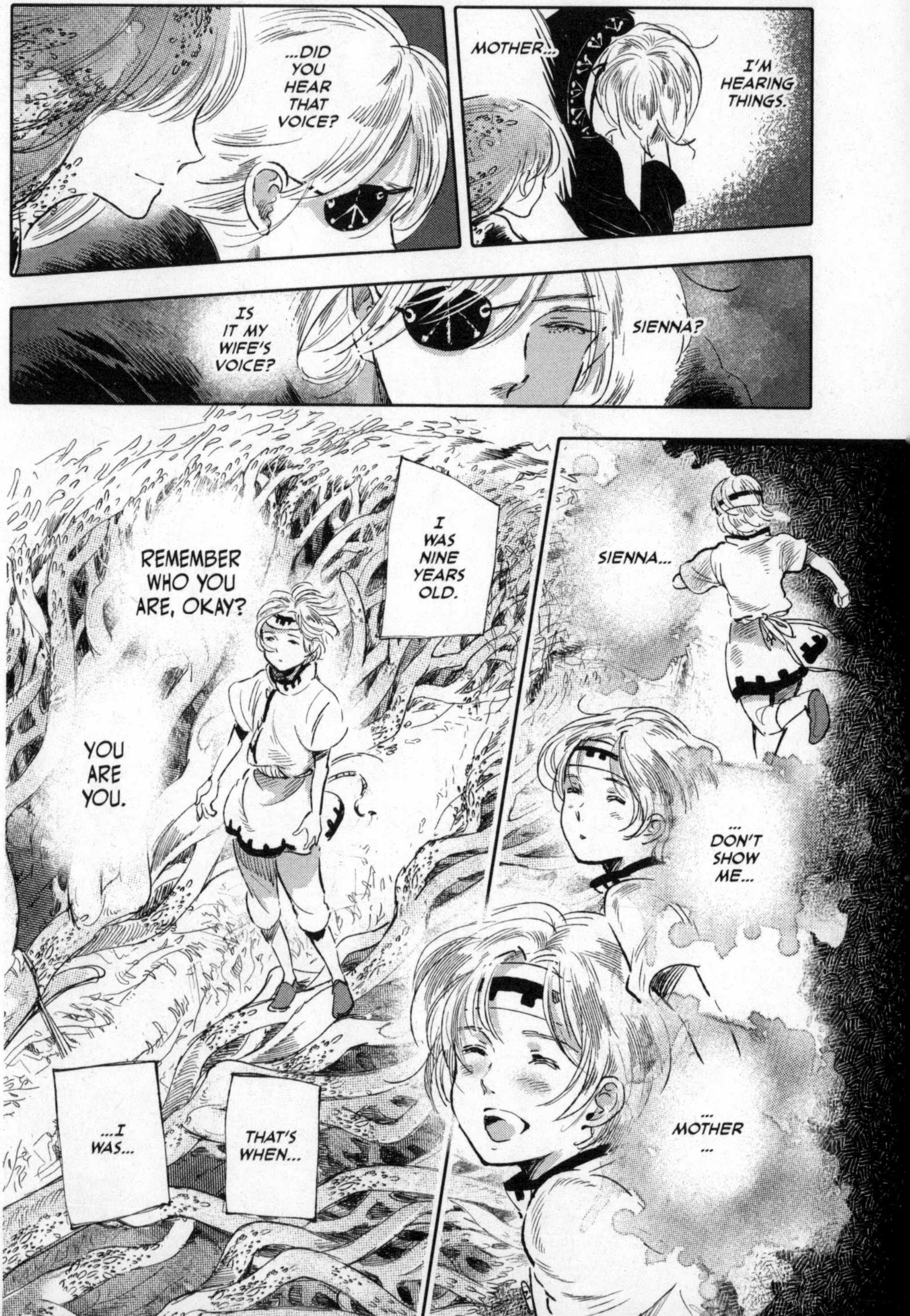
I'M HEARING THINGS.
MOTHER...
...DID YOU HEAR THAT VOICE?
SIENNA?
IS IT MY WIFE'S VOICE?
SIENNA...
...DON'T SHOW ME...
...MOTHER...
I WAS NINE YEARS OLD.
REMEMBER WHO YOU ARE, OKAY?
YOU ARE YOU.
THAT'S WHEN...
...I WAS...

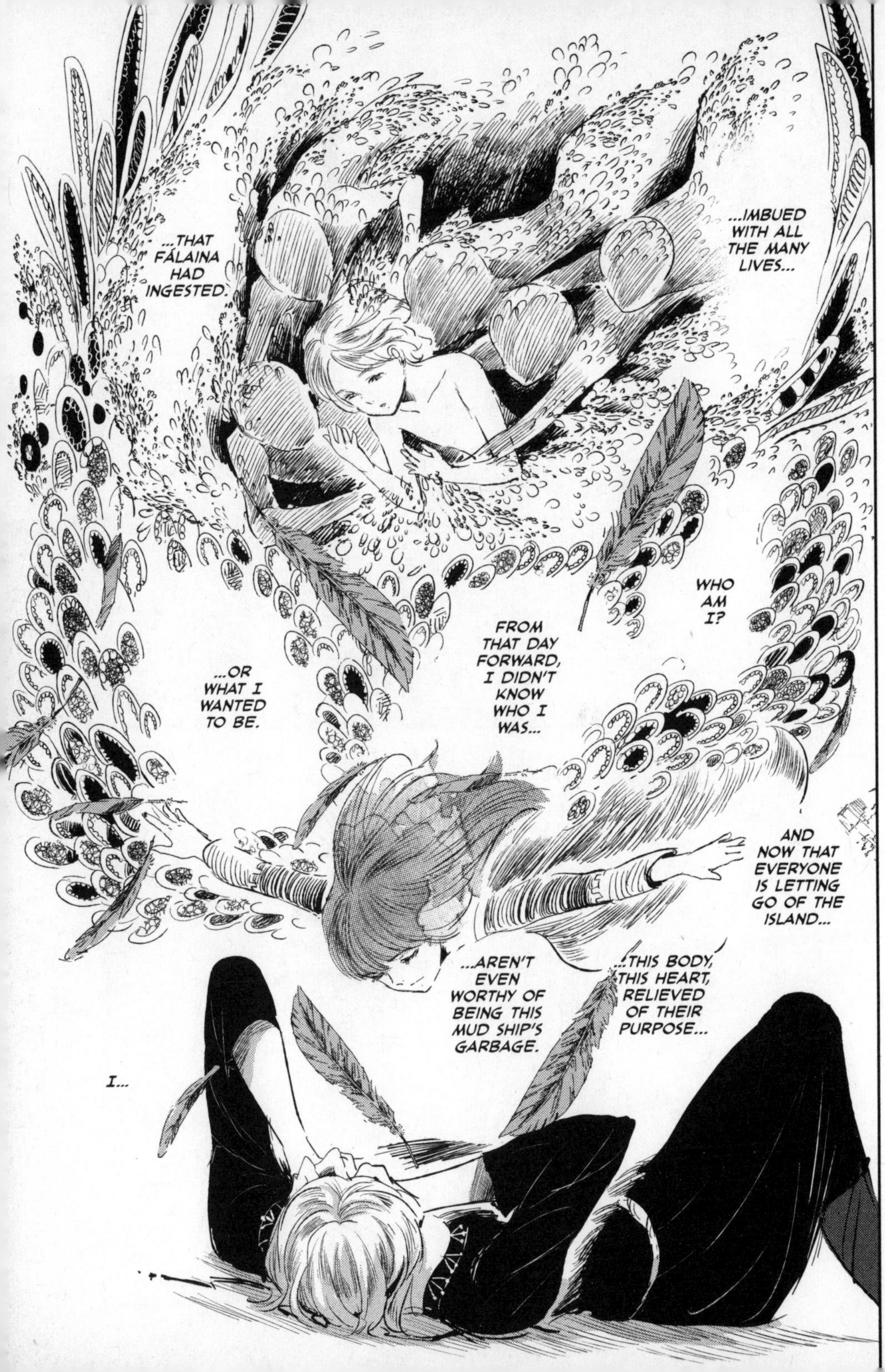
...IMBUED WITH ALL THE MANY LIVES...
...THAT FÁLAINA HAD INGESTED.
WHO AM I?
FROM THAT DAY FORWARD, I DIDN'T KNOW WHO I WAS...
...OR WHAT I WANTED TO BE.
AND NOW THAT EVERYONE IS LETTING GO OF THE ISLAND...
...THIS BODY, THIS HEART, RELIEVED OF THEIR PURPOSE...
...AREN'T EVEN WORTHY OF BEING THIS MUD SHIP'S GARBAGE.
I...

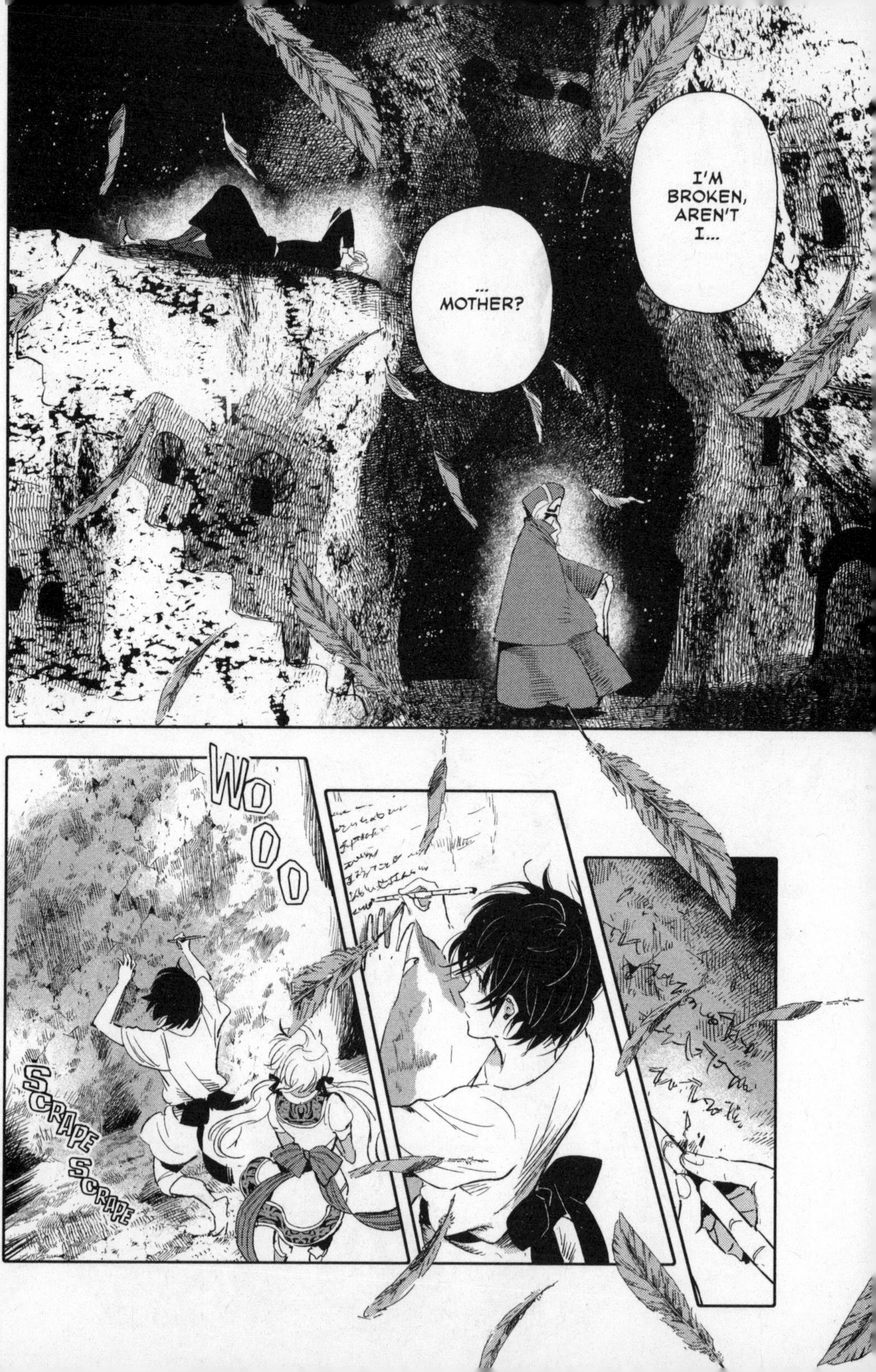
I'M BROKEN, AREN'T I...
...MOTHER?
WOOOO
SCRAPE SCRAPE

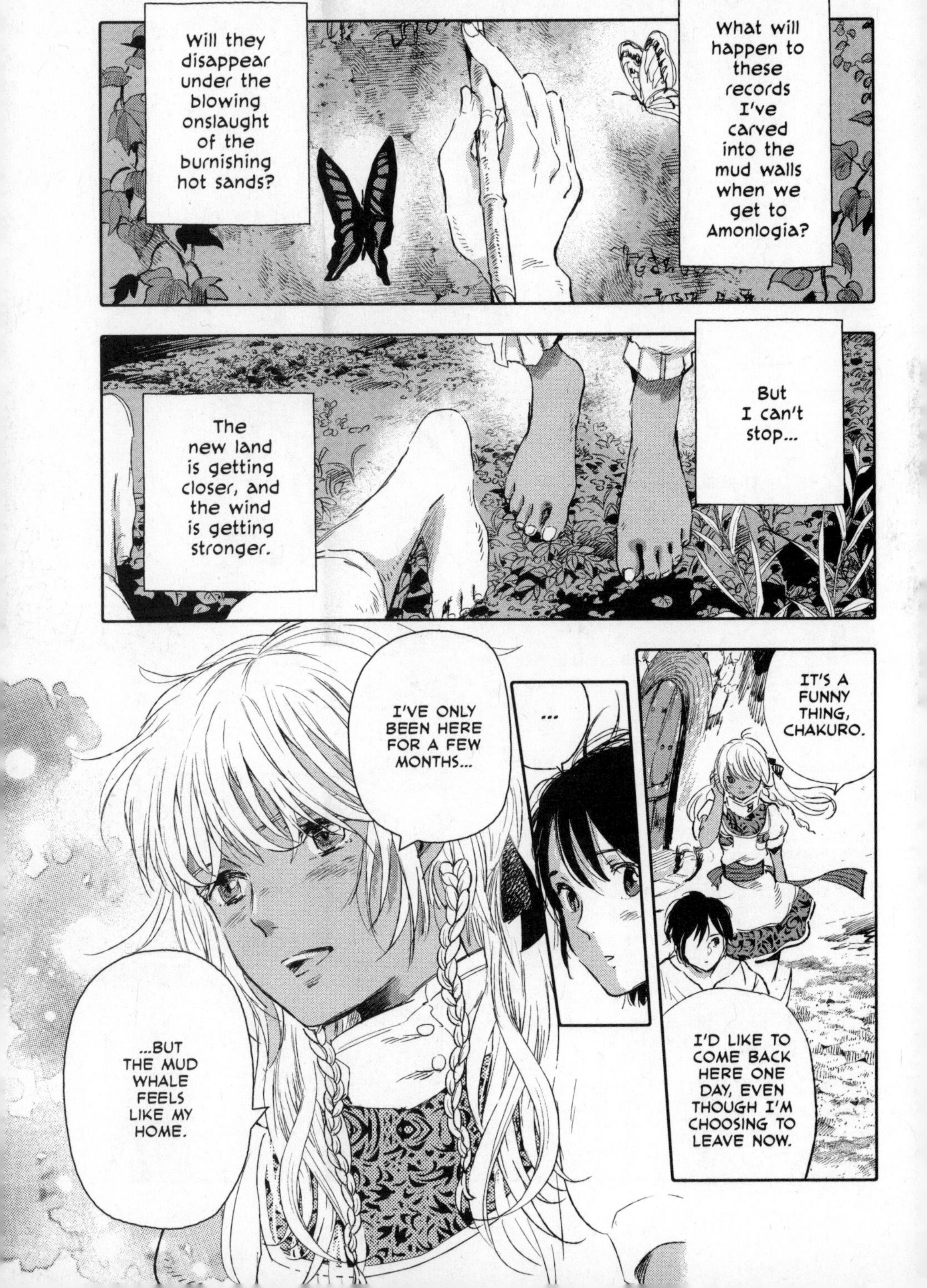
What will happen to these records I've carved into the mud walls when we get to Amonlogia?
Will they disappear under the blowing onslaught of the burnishing hot sands?
But I can't stop...
The new land is getting closer, and the wind is getting stronger.
IT'S A FUNNY THING, CHAKURO.
...
I'VE ONLY BEEN HERE FOR A FEW MONTHS...
...BUT THE MUD WHALE FEELS LIKE MY HOME.
I'D LIKE TO COME BACK HERE ONE DAY, EVEN THOUGH I'M CHOOSING TO LEAVE NOW.

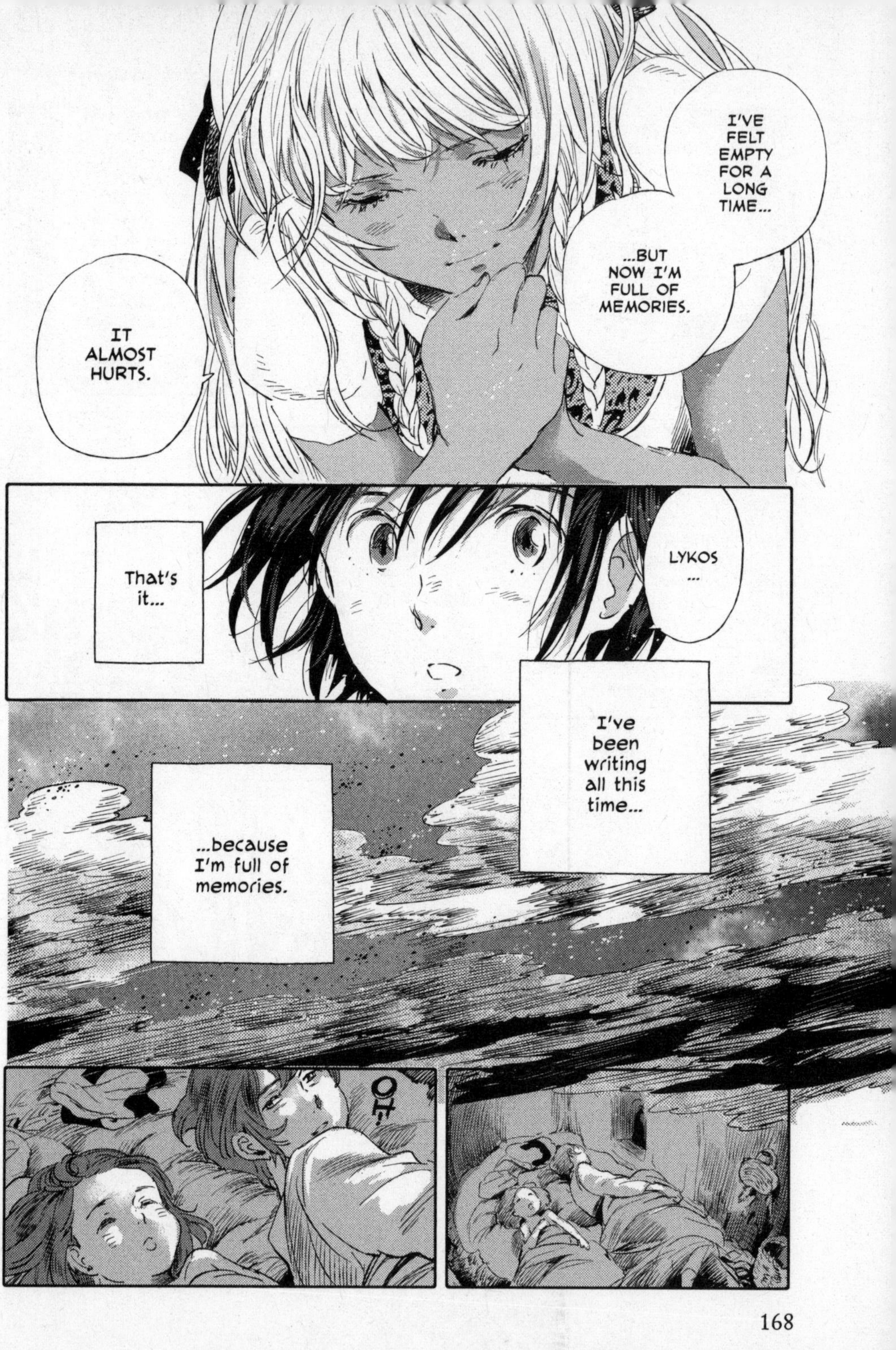
I'VE FELT EMPTY FOR A LONG TIME...
...BUT NOW I'M FULL OF MEMORIES.
IT ALMOST HURTS.
LYKOS ...
That's it...
I've been writing all this time...
...because I'm full of memories.

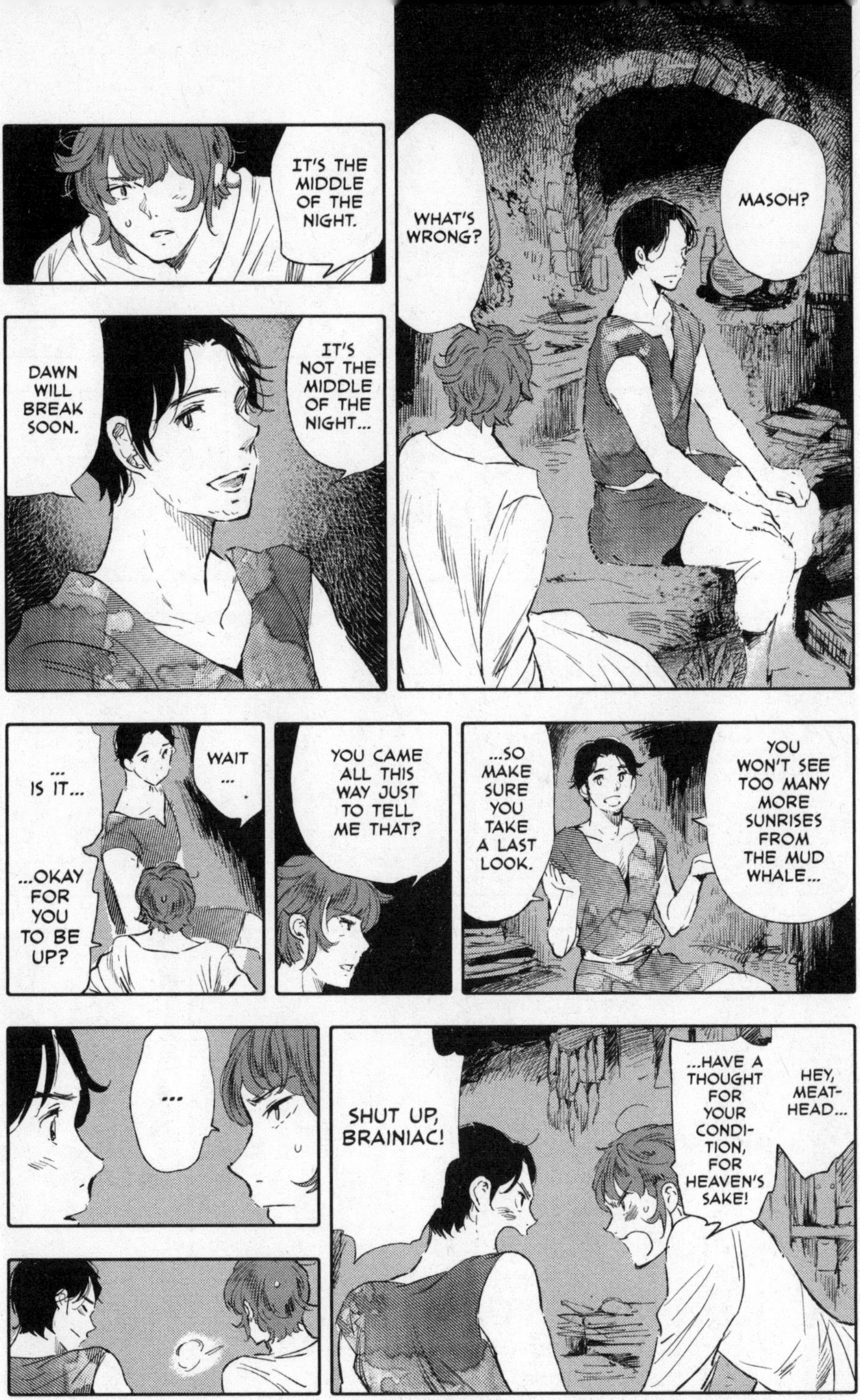
MASOH?
WHAT'S WRONG?
IT'S THE MIDDLE OF THE NIGHT.
IT'S NOT THE MIDDLE OF THE NIGHT...
DAWN WILL BREAK SOON.
YOU WON'T SEE TOO MANY MORE SUNRISES FROM THE MUD WHALE...
...SO MAKE SURE YOU TAKE A LAST LOOK.
YOU CAME ALL THIS WAY JUST TO TELL ME THAT?
WAIT...
...IS IT...
...OKAY FOR YOU TO BE UP?
HEY, MEATHEAD...
...HAVE A THOUGHT FOR YOUR CONDITION, FOR HEAVEN'S SAKE!
SHUT UP, BRAINIAC!
...

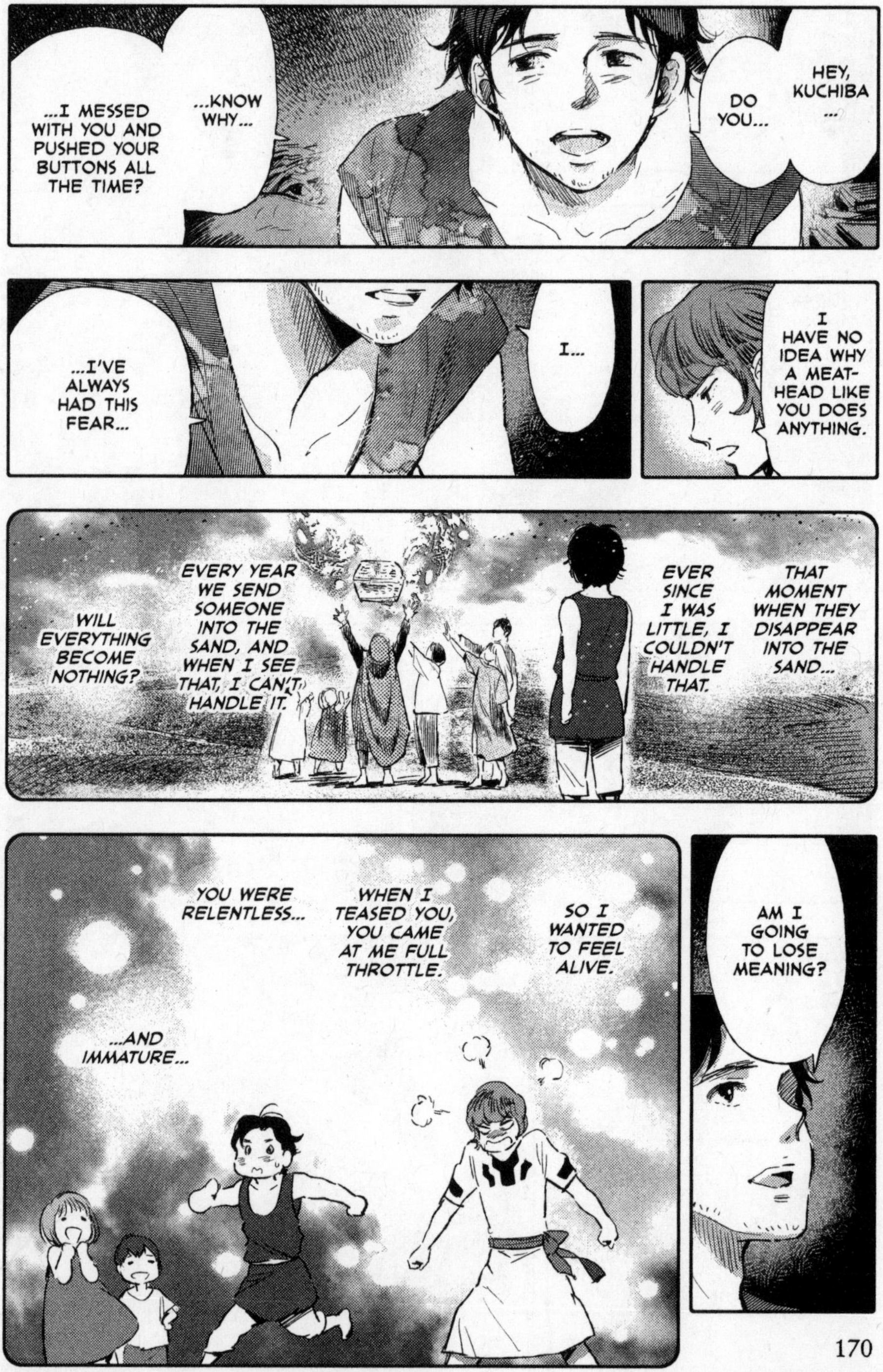
HEY, KUCHIBA...
DO YOU...
...KNOW WHY...
...I MESSED WITH YOU AND PUSHED YOUR BUTTONS ALL THE TIME?
I HAVE NO IDEA WHY A MEAT-HEAD LIKE YOU DOES ANYTHING.
I...
...I'VE ALWAYS HAD THIS FEAR...
THAT MOMENT WHEN THEY DISAPPEAR INTO THE SAND...
EVER SINCE I WAS LITTLE, I COULDN'T HANDLE THAT.
EVERY YEAR WE SEND SOMEONE INTO THE SAND, AND WHEN I SEE THAT, I CAN'T HANDLE IT.
WILL EVERYTHING BECOME NOTHING?
AM I GOING TO LOSE MEANING?
SO I WANTED TO FEEL ALIVE.
WHEN I TEASED YOU, YOU CAME AT ME FULL THROTTLE.
YOU WERE RELENTLESS...
...AND IMMATURE...

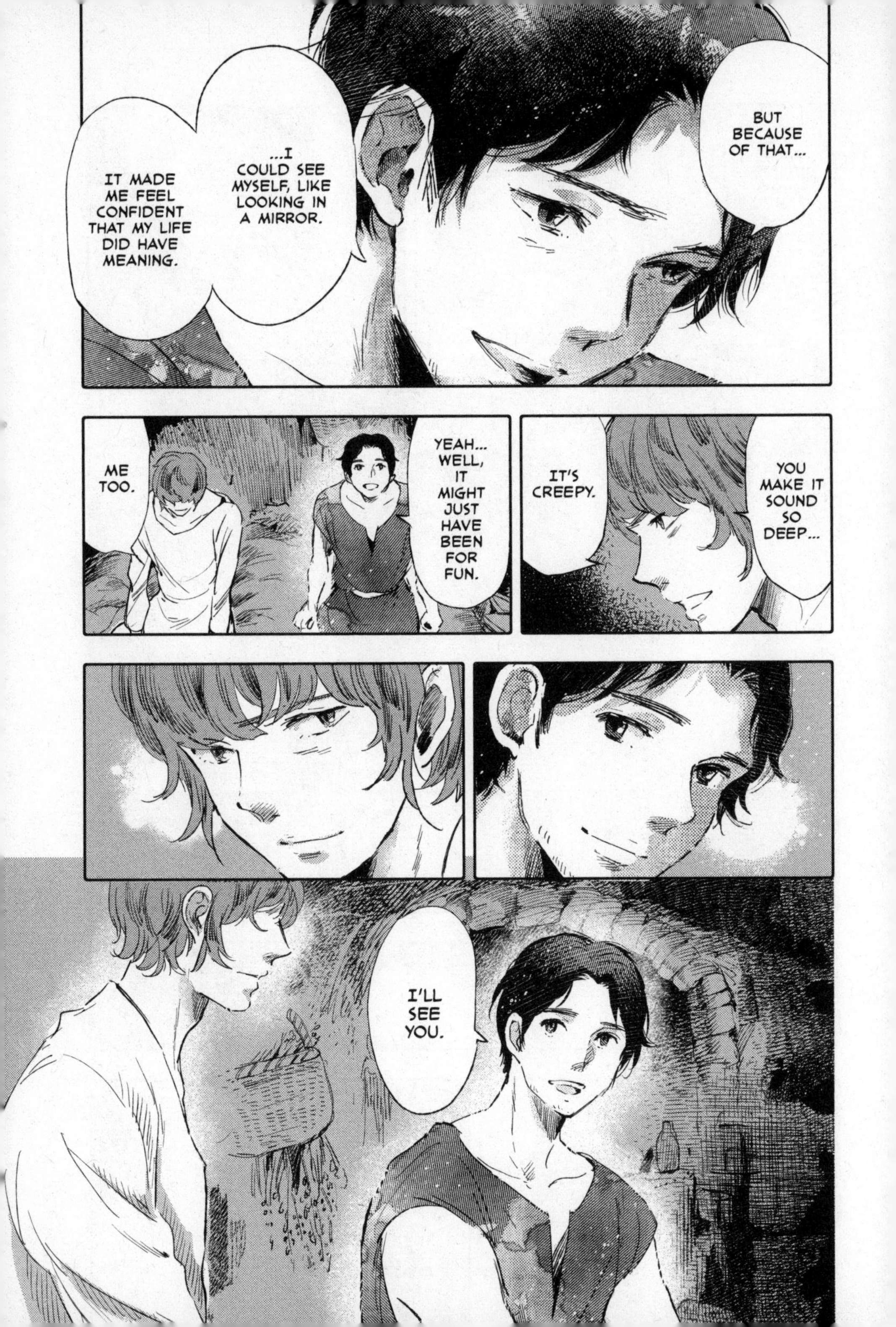
BUT BECAUSE OF THAT...
...I COULD SEE MYSELF, LIKE LOOKING IN A MIRROR.
IT MADE ME FEEL CONFIDENT THAT MY LIFE DID HAVE MEANING.
YOU MAKE IT SOUND SO DEEP...
IT'S CREEPY.
YEAH... WELL, IT MIGHT JUST HAVE BEEN FOR FUN.
ME TOO.
I'LL SEE YOU.

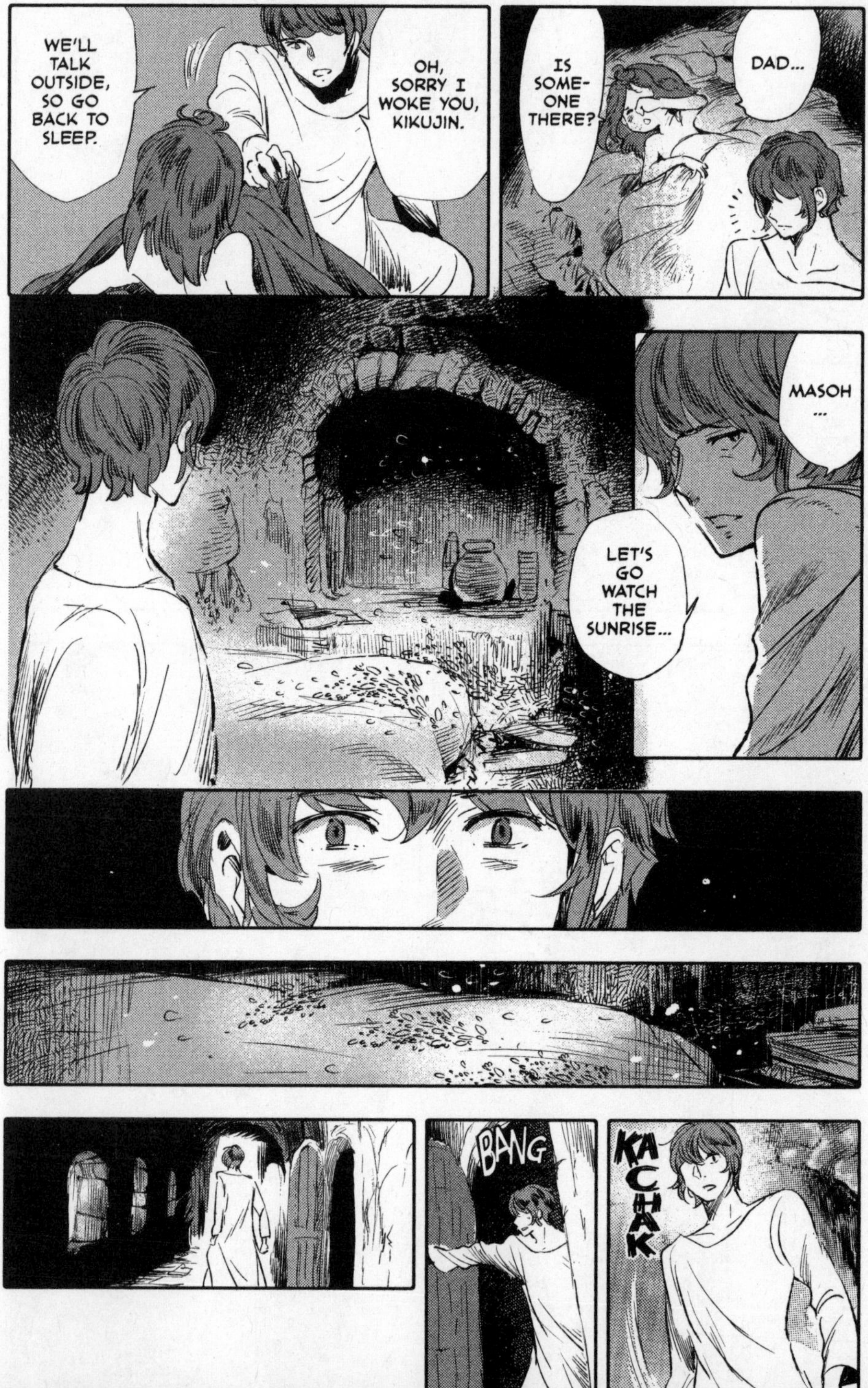
DAD...
IS SOME-ONE THERE?
OH, SORRY I WOKE YOU, KIKUJIN.
WE'LL TALK OUTSIDE, SO GO BACK TO SLEEP.
MASOH ...
LET'S GO WATCH THE SUNRISE...
KACHAK
BANG

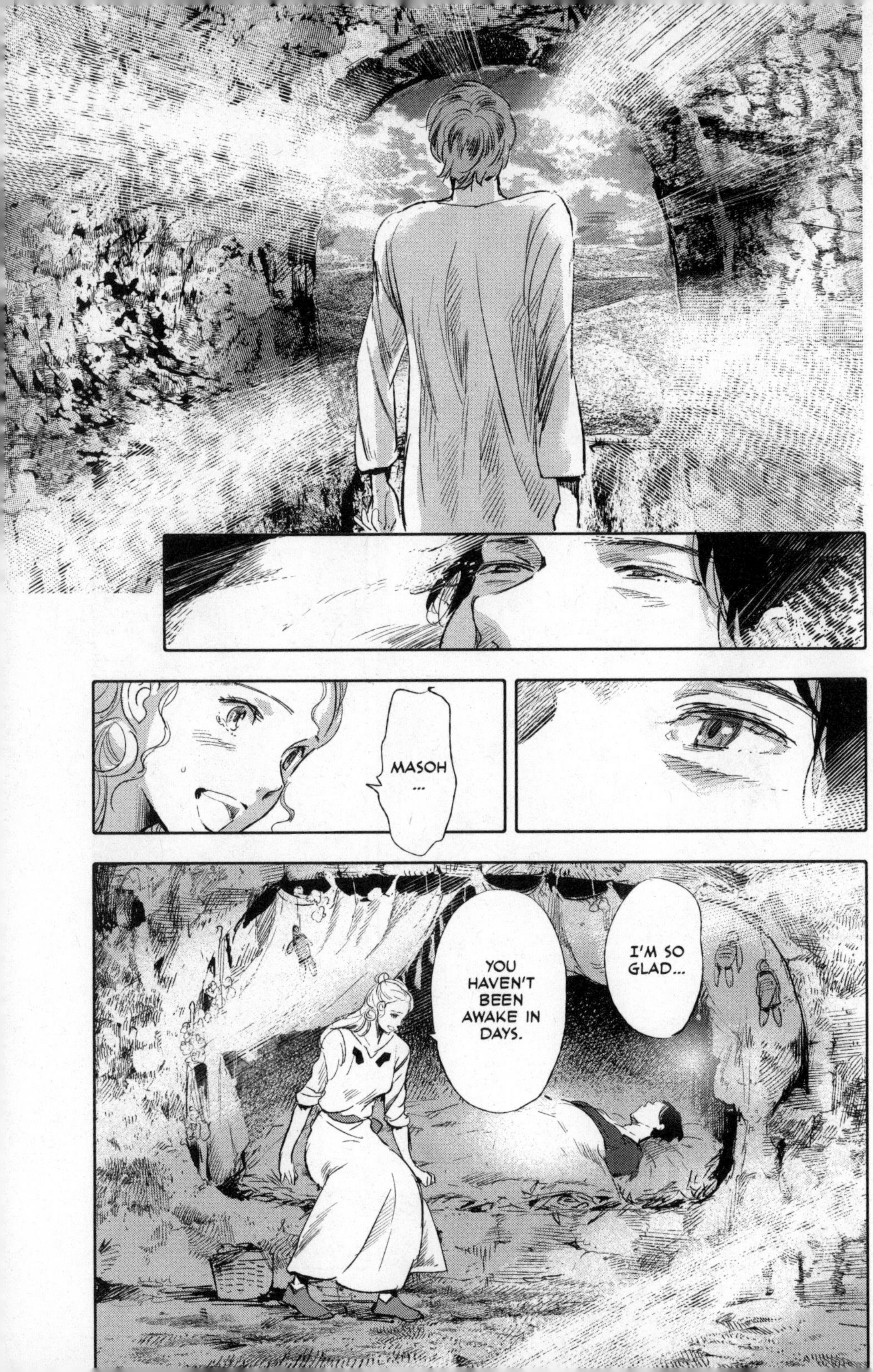
MASOH ...
I'M SO GLAD...
YOU HAVEN'T BEEN AWAKE IN DAYS.

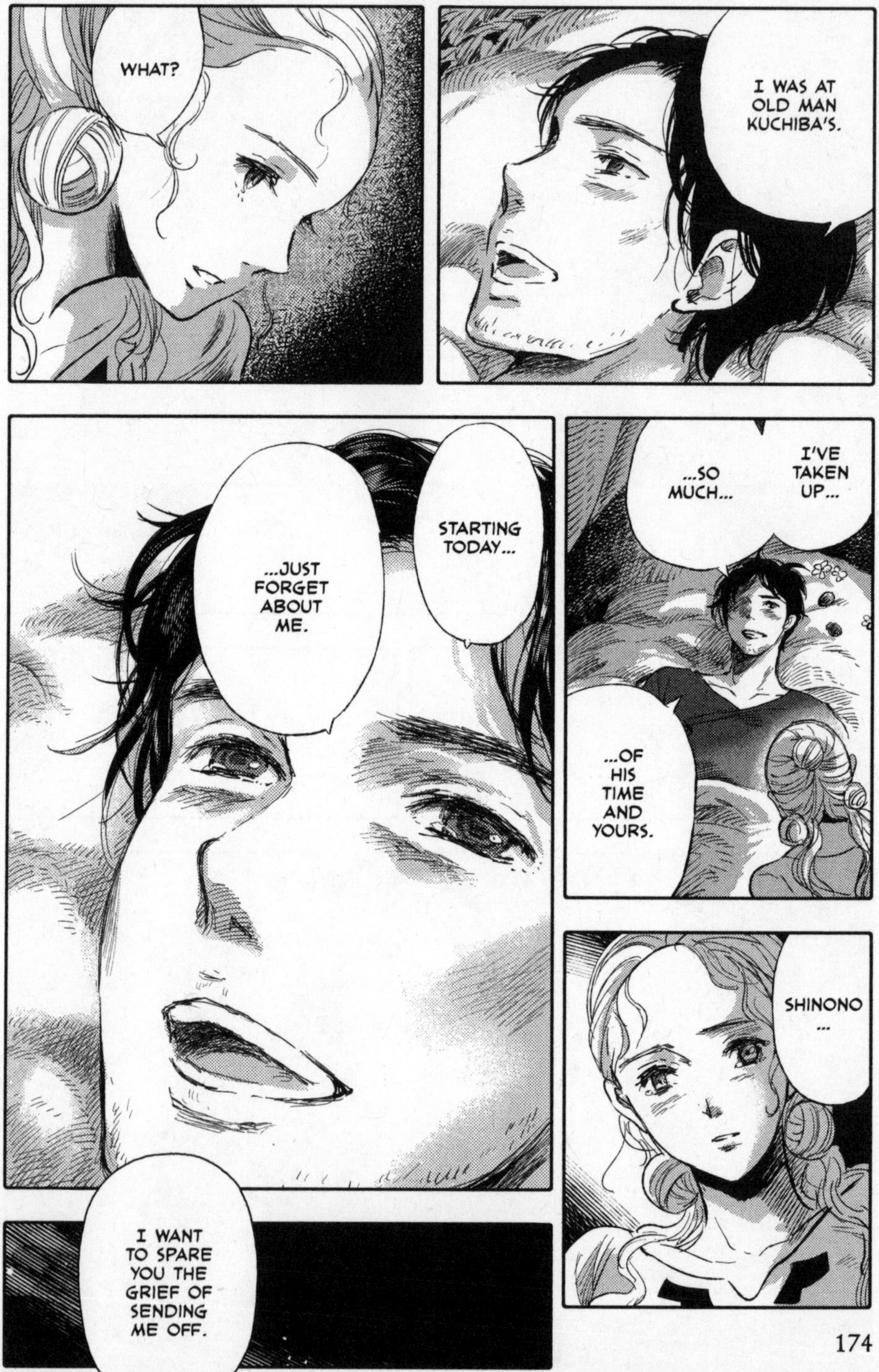
I WAS AT OLD MAN KUCHIBA'S.
WHAT?
I'VE TAKEN UP...
...SO MUCH...
...OF HIS TIME AND YOURS.
SHINONO...
STARTING TODAY...
...JUST FORGET ABOUT ME.
I WANT TO SPARE YOU THE GRIEF OF SENDING ME OFF.

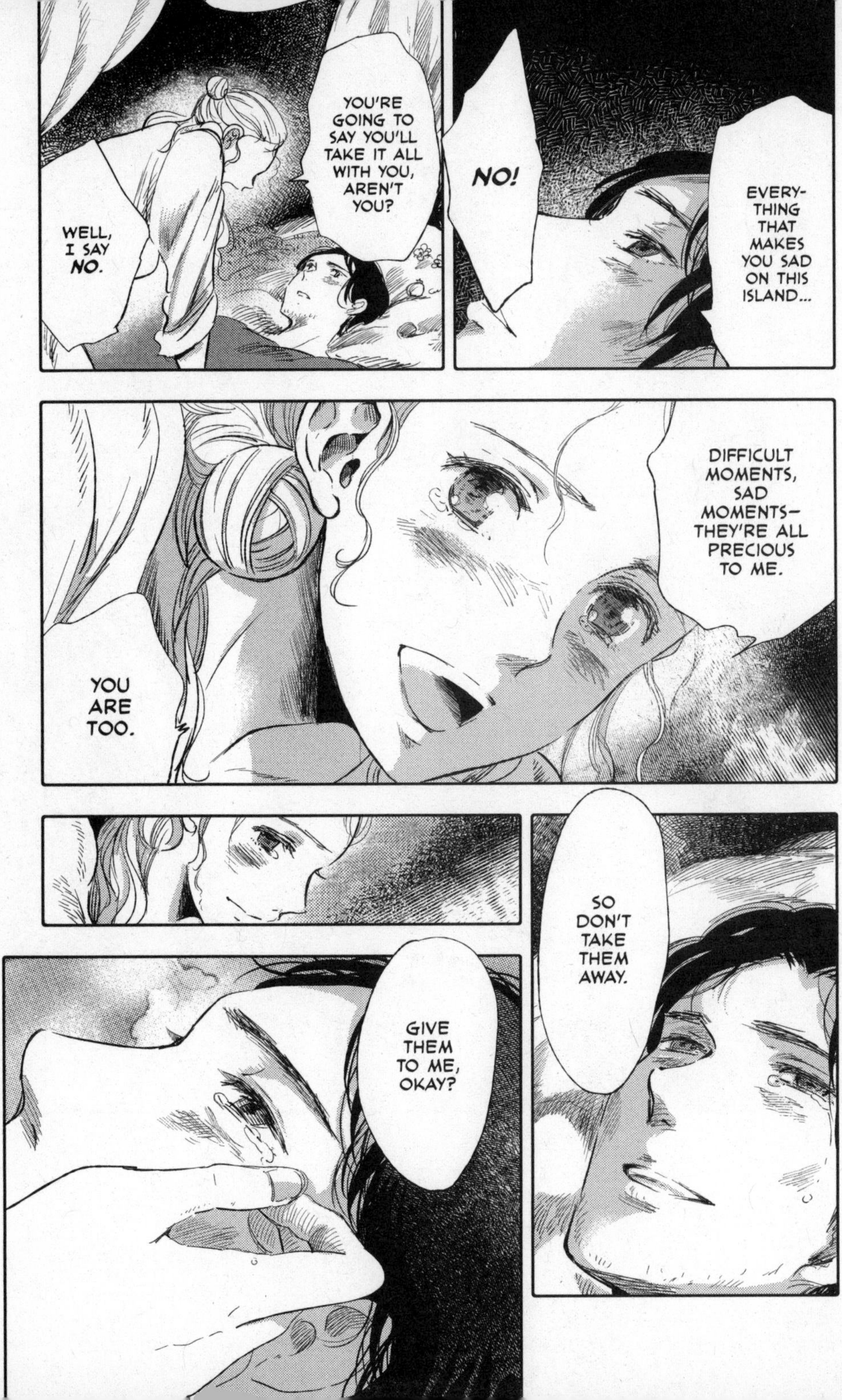
EVERY-THING THAT MAKES YOU SAD ON THIS ISLAND...
NO!
YOU'RE GOING TO SAY YOU'LL TAKE IT ALL WITH YOU, AREN'T YOU?
WELL, I SAY NO.
DIFFICULT MOMENTS, SAD MOMENTS— THEY'RE ALL PRECIOUS TO ME.
YOU ARE TOO.
SO DON'T TAKE THEM AWAY.
GIVE THEM TO ME, OKAY?

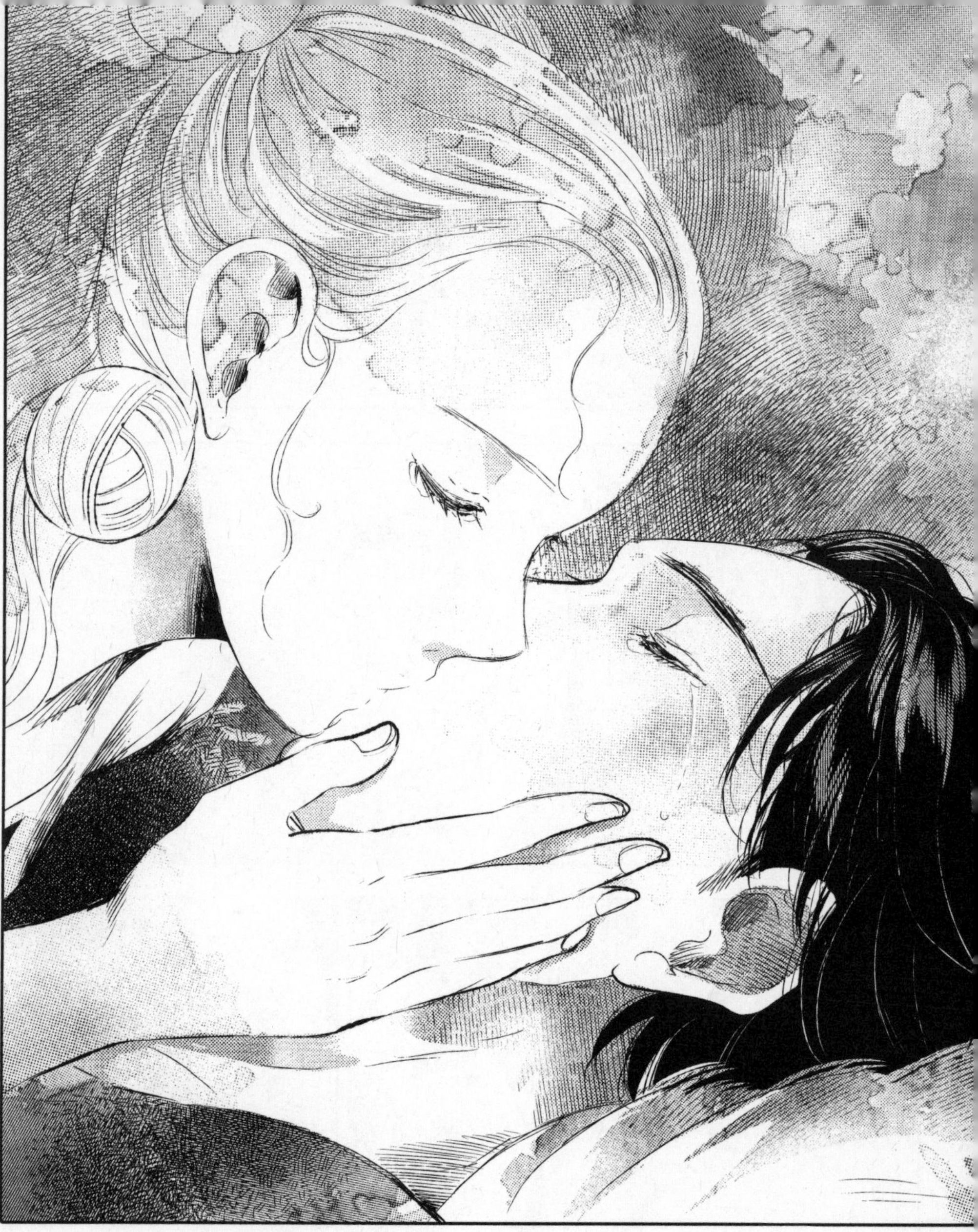

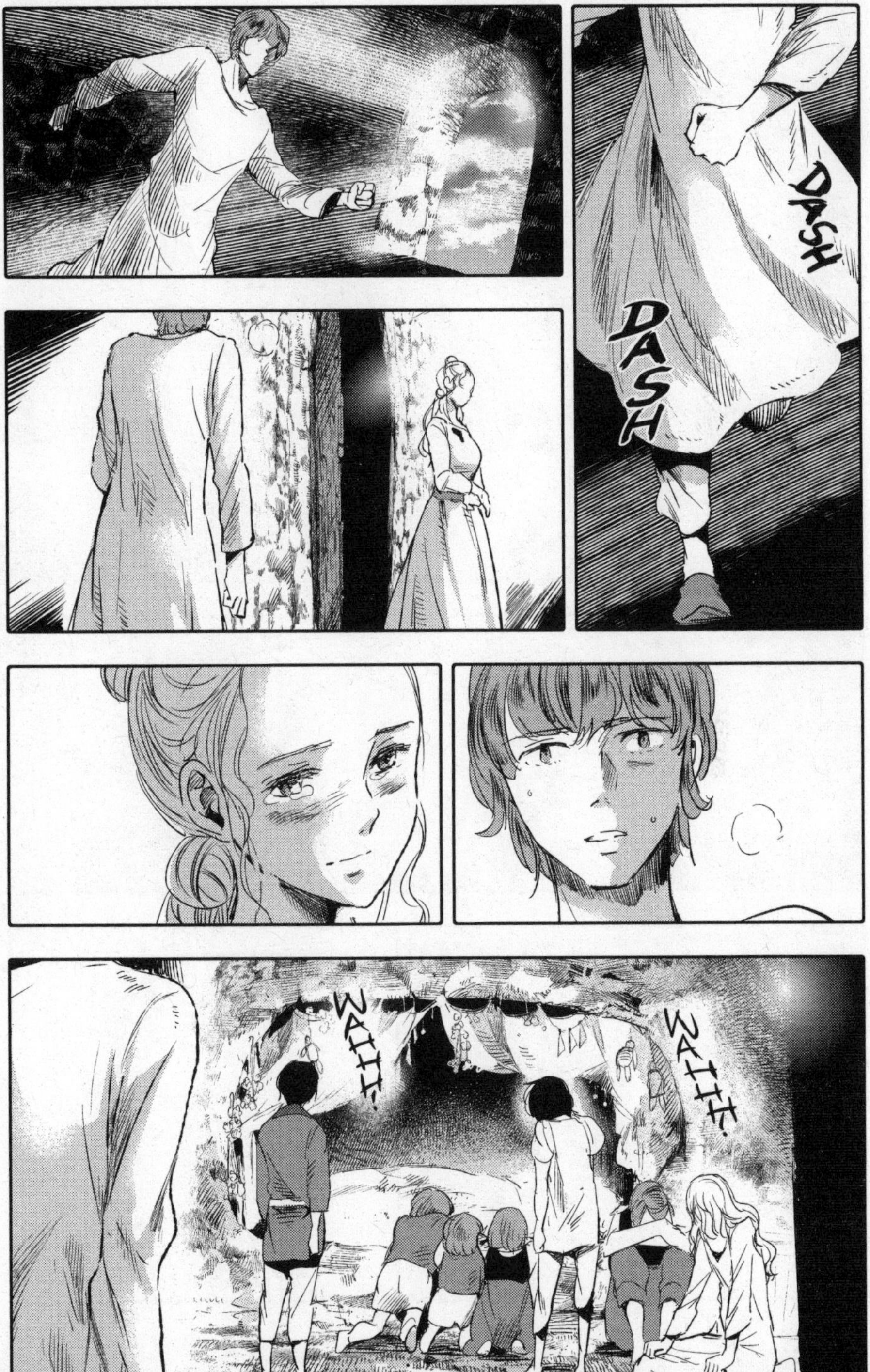
DASH
DASH
WAHH!
WAHH!

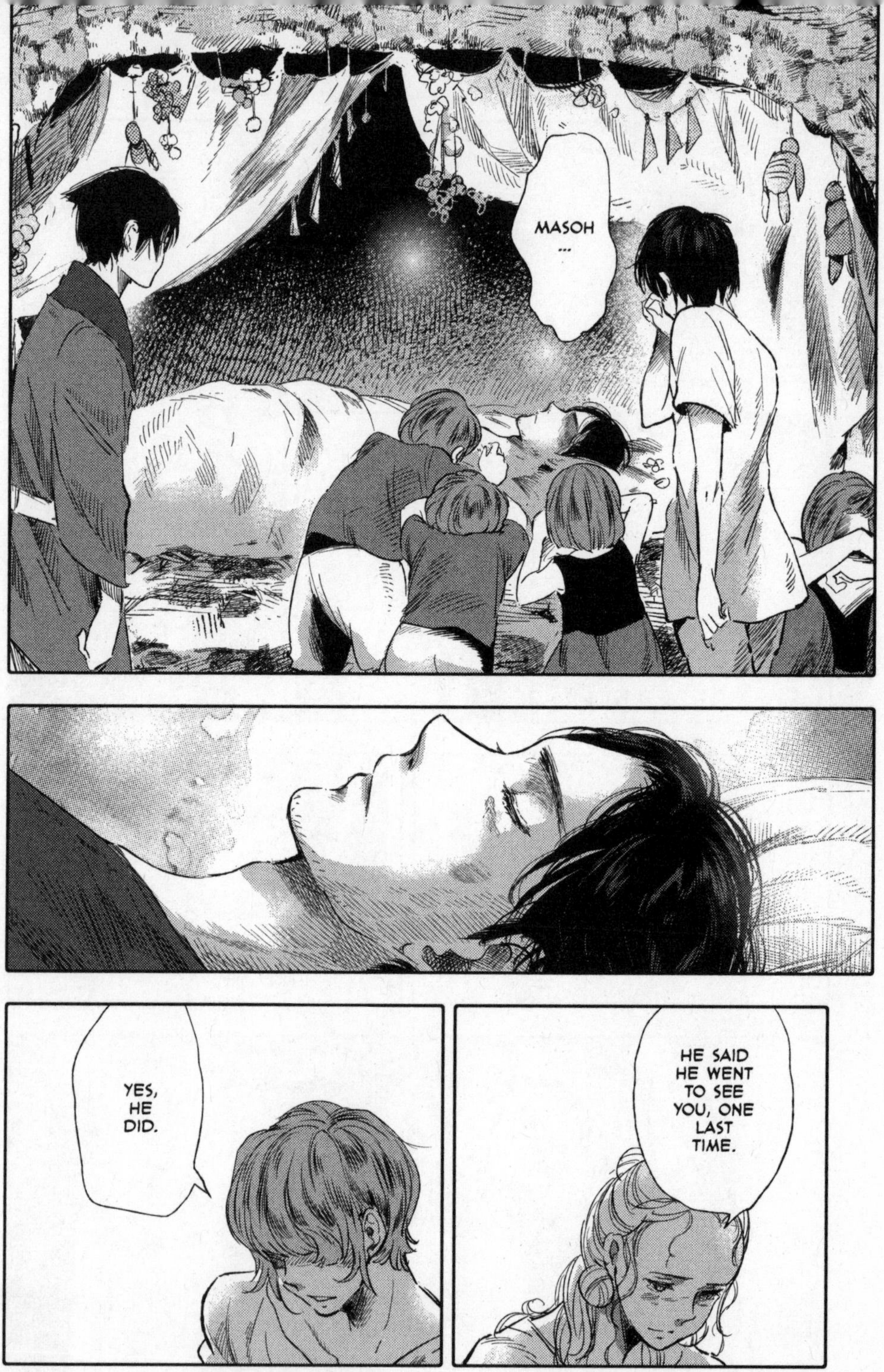
MASOH ...
HE SAID HE WENT TO SEE YOU, ONE LAST TIME.
YES, HE DID.

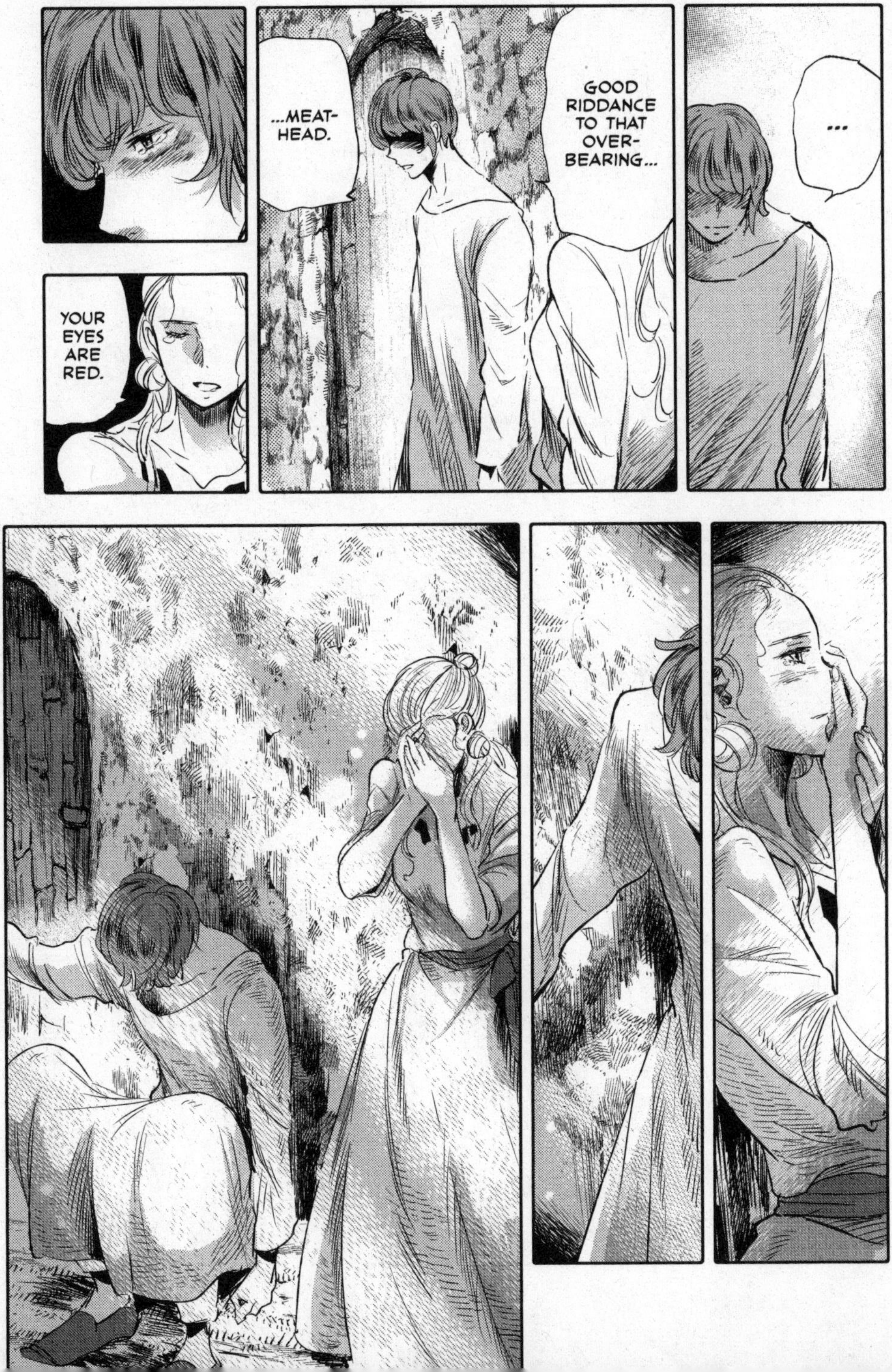
...
GOOD RIDDANCE TO THAT OVER-BEARING...
...MEAT-HEAD.
YOUR EYES ARE RED.

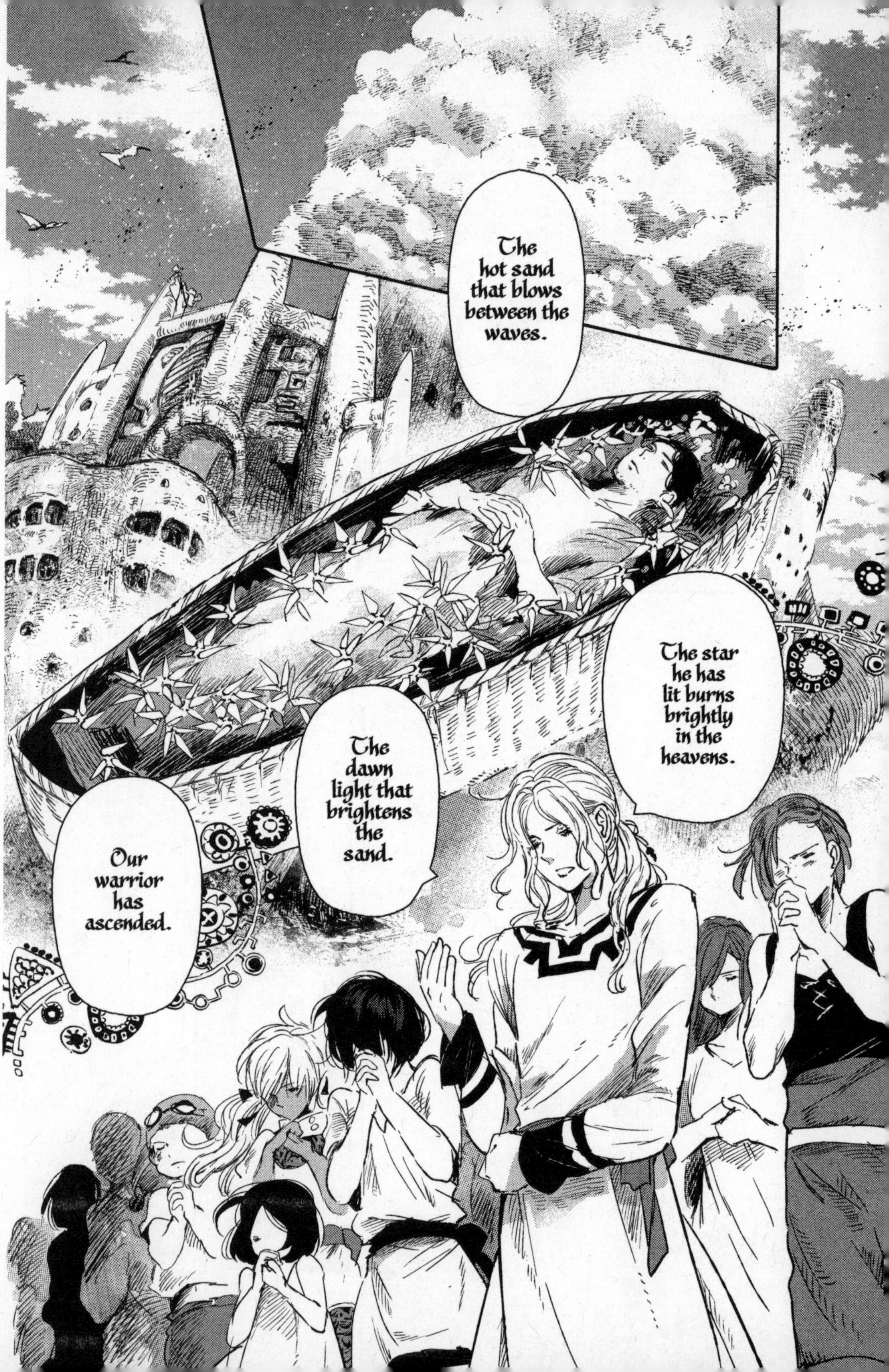
The hot sand that blows between the waves.
The star he has lit burns brightly in the heavens.
The dawn light that brightens the sand.
Our warrior has ascended.

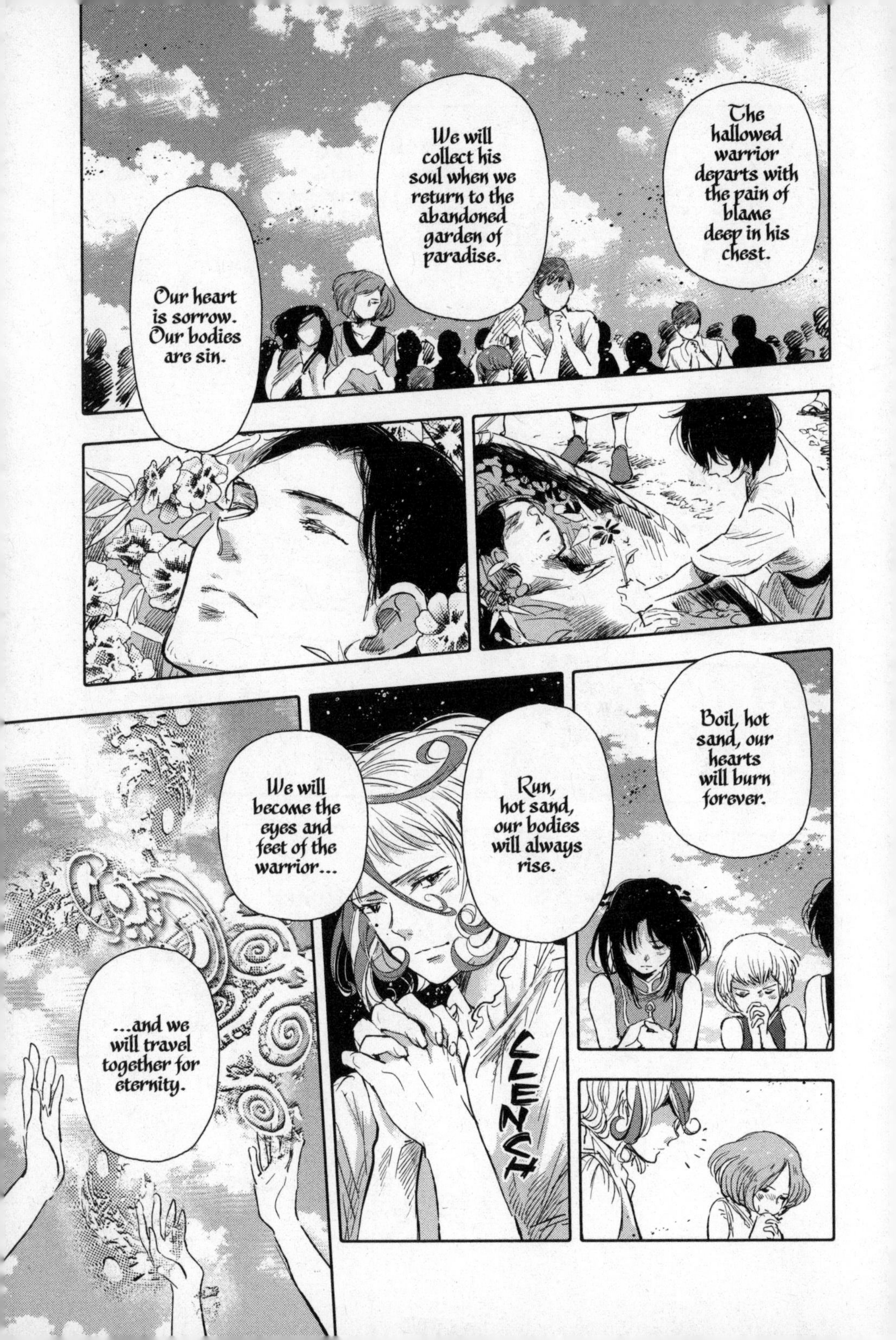
The hallowed warrior departs with the pain of blame deep in his chest.
We will collect his soul when we return to the abandoned garden of paradise.
Our heart is sorrow. Our bodies are sin.
Boil, hot sand, our hearts will burn forever.
Run, hot sand, our bodies will always rise.
We will become the eyes and feet of the warrior...
CLENCH
...and we will travel together for eternity.

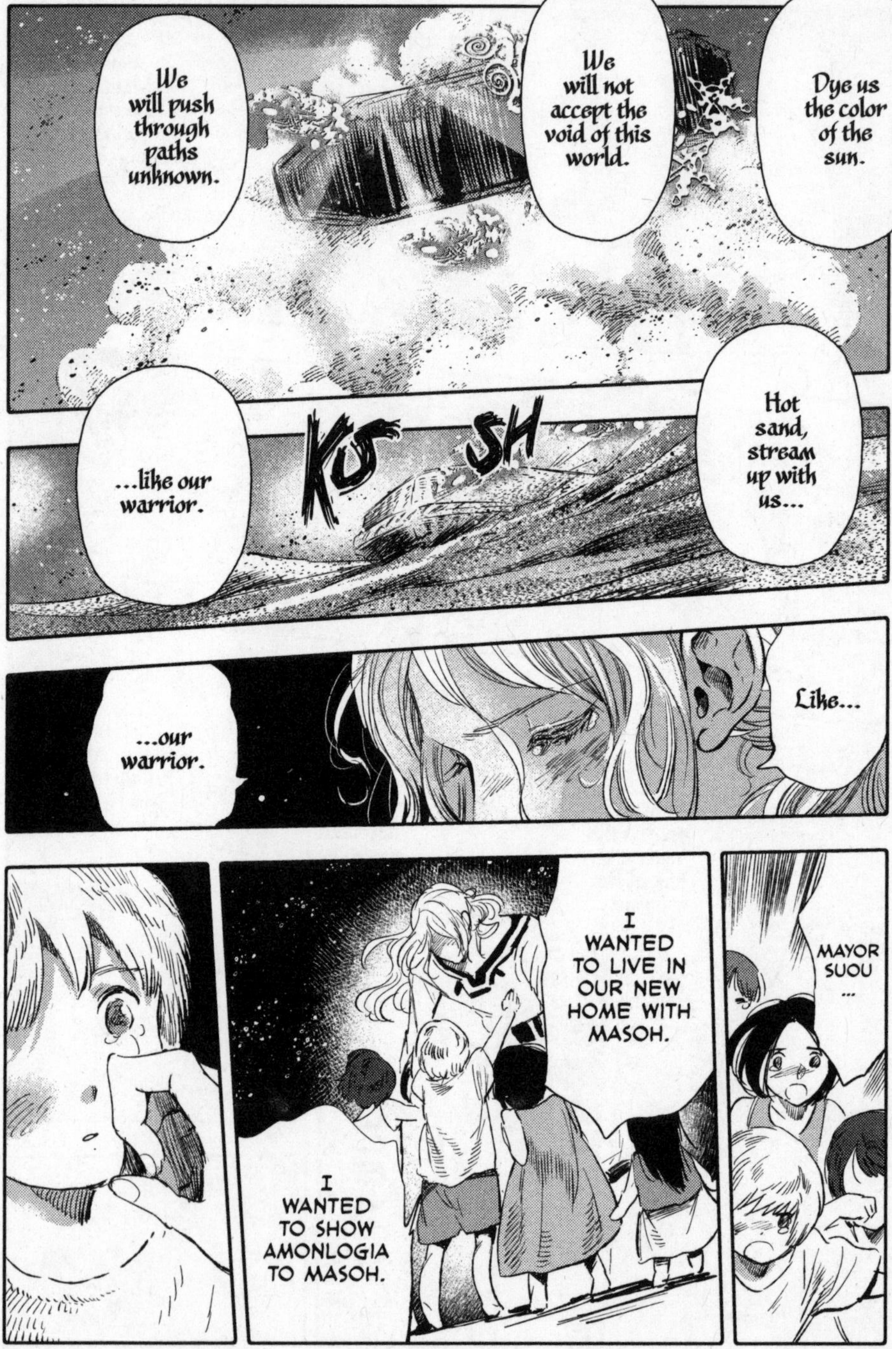
Dye us the color of the sun.
We will not accept the void of this world.
We will push through paths unknown.
Hot sand, stream up with us...
KUSH
...like our warrior.
Like...
...our warrior.
MAYOR SUOU ...
I WANTED TO LIVE IN OUR NEW HOME WITH MASOH.
I WANTED TO SHOW AMONLOGIA TO MASOH.

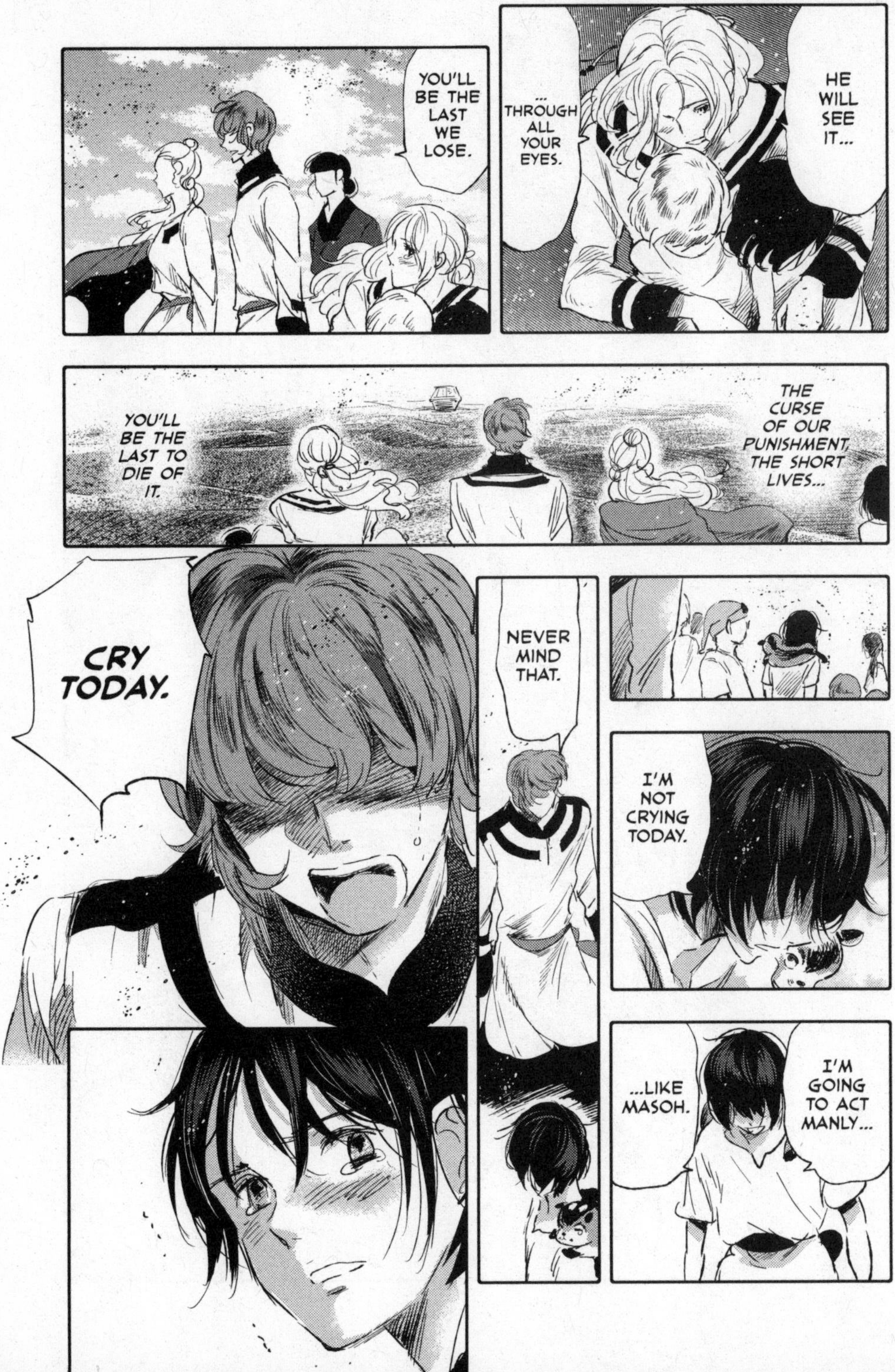
HE WILL SEE IT...
...THROUGH ALL YOUR EYES.
YOU'LL BE THE LAST WE LOSE.
THE CURSE OF OUR PUNISHMENT, THE SHORT LIVES...
YOU'LL BE THE LAST TO DIE OF IT.
I'M NOT CRYING TODAY.
I'M GOING TO ACT MANLY...
...LIKE MASOH.
NEVER MIND THAT.
CRY TODAY.

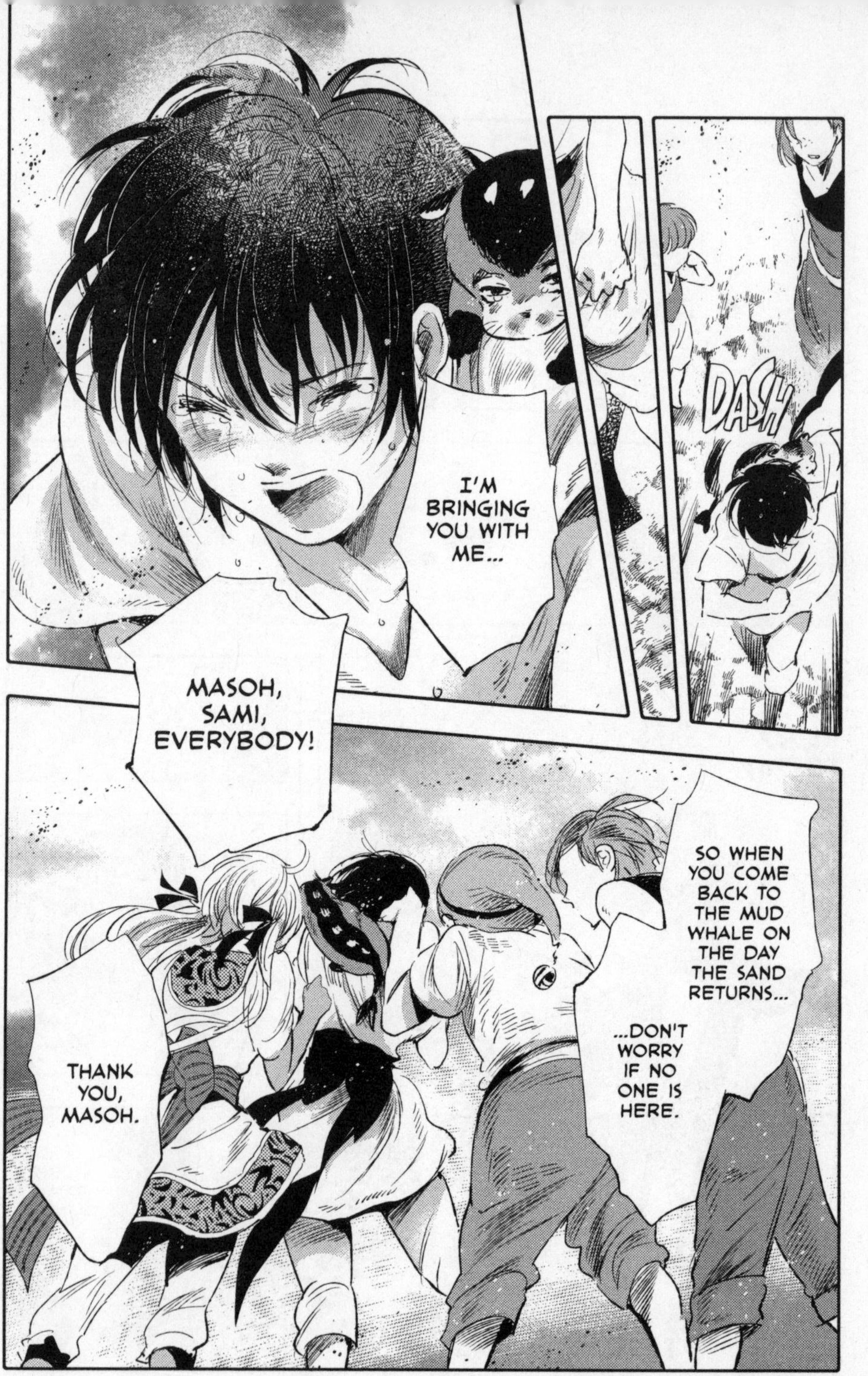
DASH
I'M BRINGING YOU WITH ME...
MASOH, SAMI, EVERYBODY!
SO WHEN YOU COME BACK TO THE MUD WHALE ON THE DAY THE SAND RETURNS...
...DON'T WORRY IF NO ONE IS HERE.
THANK YOU, MASOH.

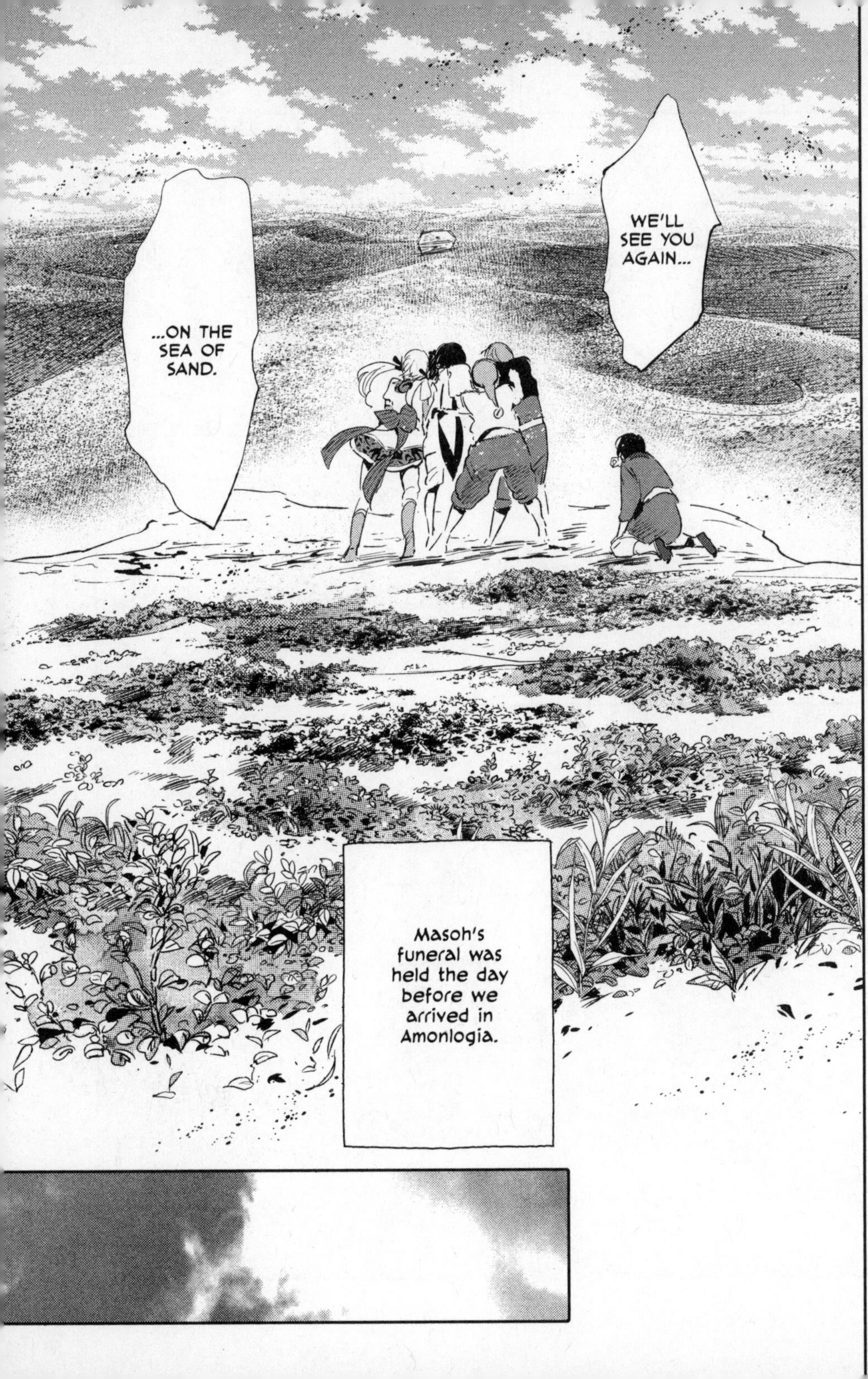
WE'LL SEE YOU AGAIN...
...ON THE SEA OF SAND.
Masoh's funeral was held the day before we arrived in Amonlogia.

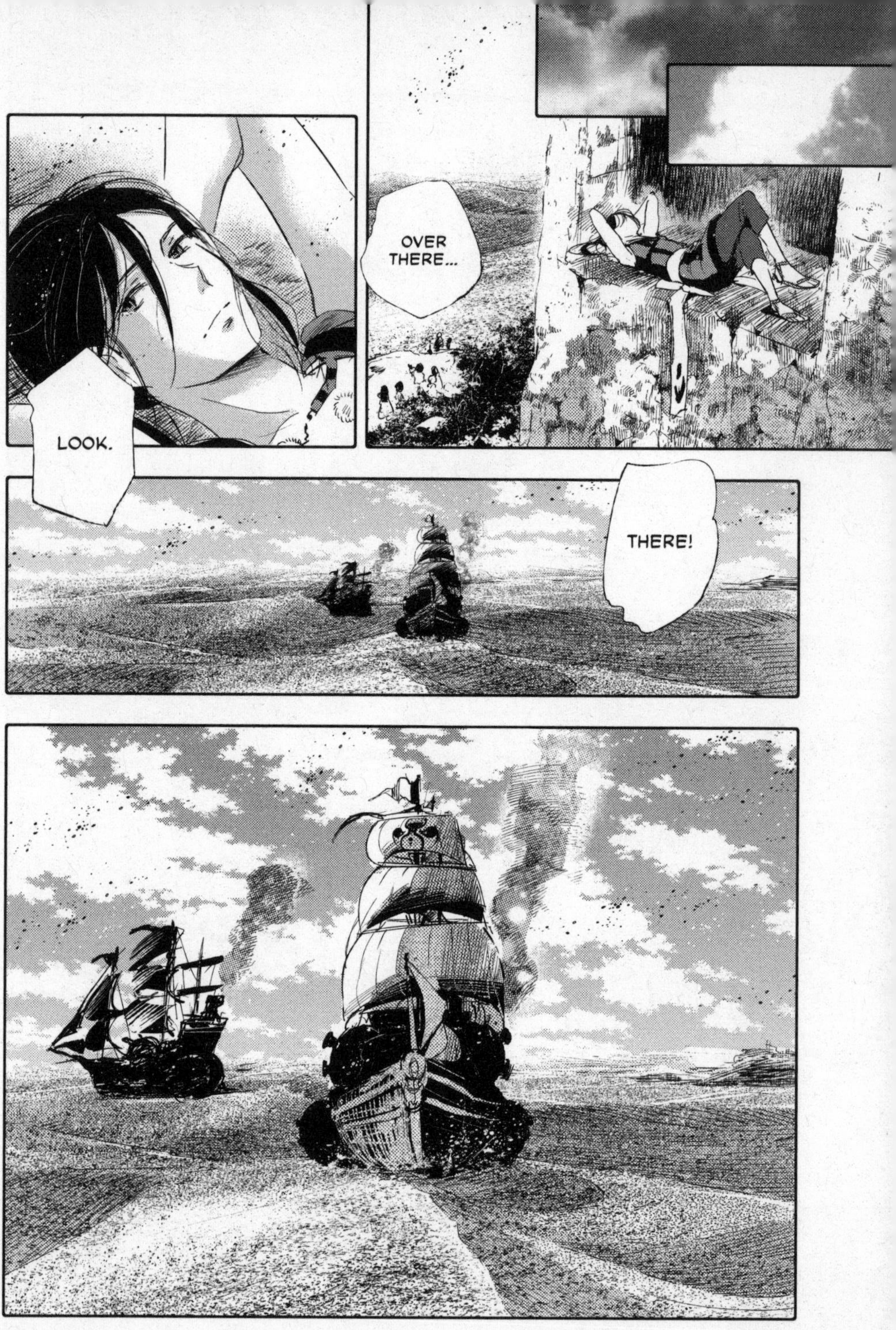
OVER THERE...
LOOK.
THERE!

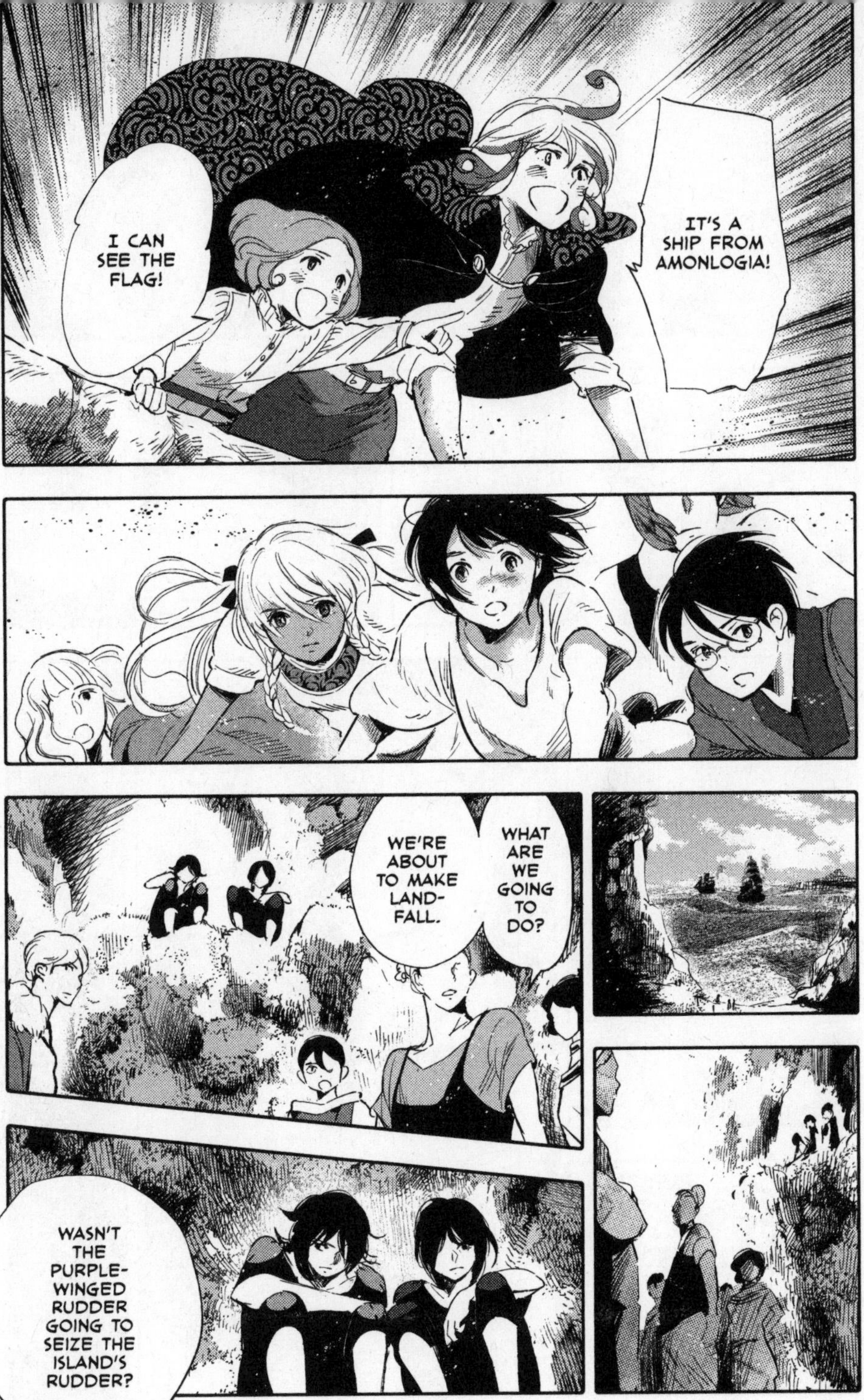
IT'S A SHIP FROM AMONLOGIA!
I CAN SEE THE FLAG!
WHAT ARE WE GOING TO DO?
WE'RE ABOUT TO MAKE LAND-FALL.
WASN'T THE PURPLE-WINGED RUDDER GOING TO SEIZE THE ISLAND'S RUDDER?

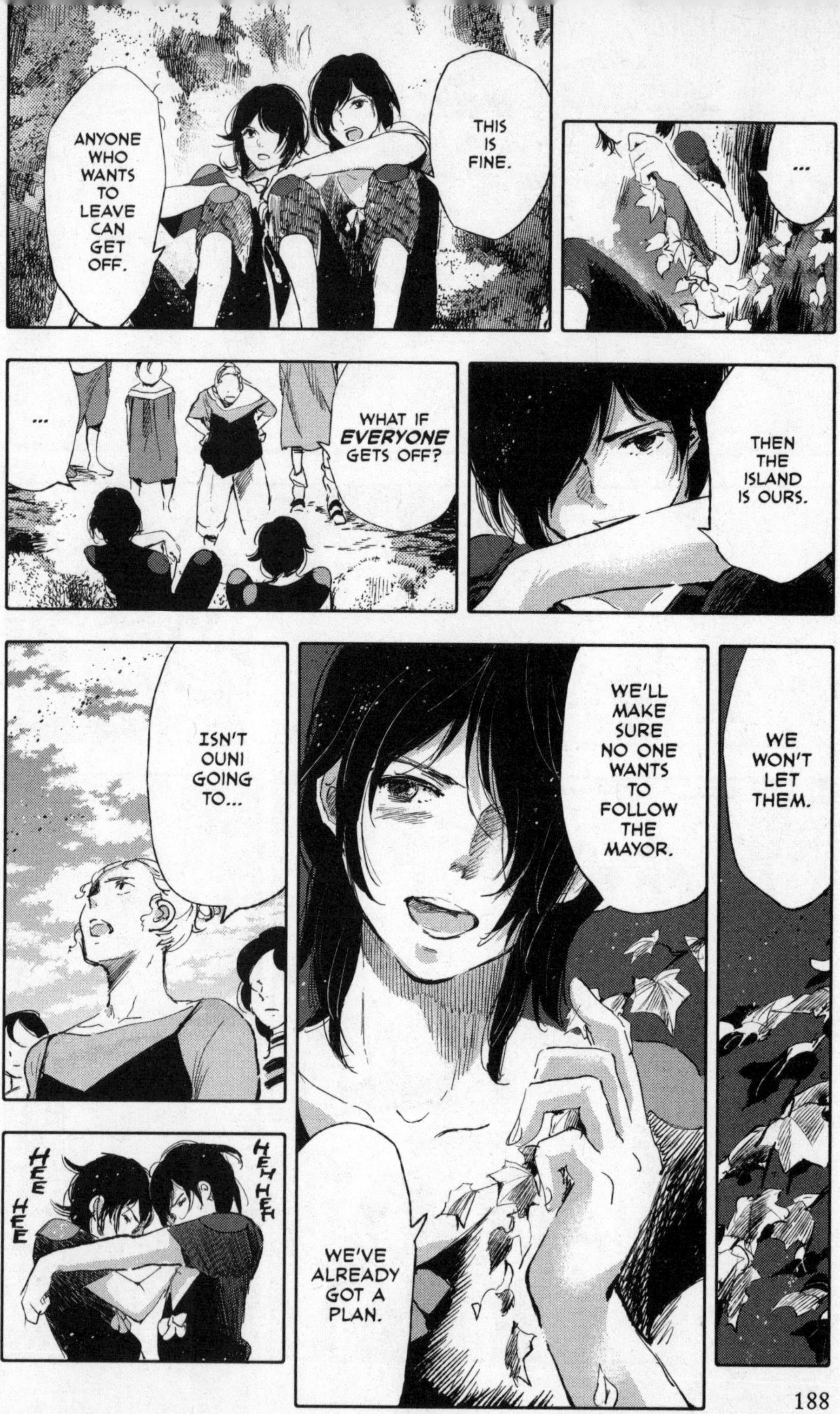
...
THIS IS FINE.
ANYONE WHO WANTS TO LEAVE CAN GET OFF.
THEN THE ISLAND IS OURS.
WHAT IF *EVERYONE* GETS OFF?
...
WE WON'T LET THEM.
WE'LL MAKE SURE NO ONE WANTS TO FOLLOW THE MAYOR.
WE'VE ALREADY GOT A PLAN.
ISN'T OUNI GOING TO...
HEH HEH
HEE HEE

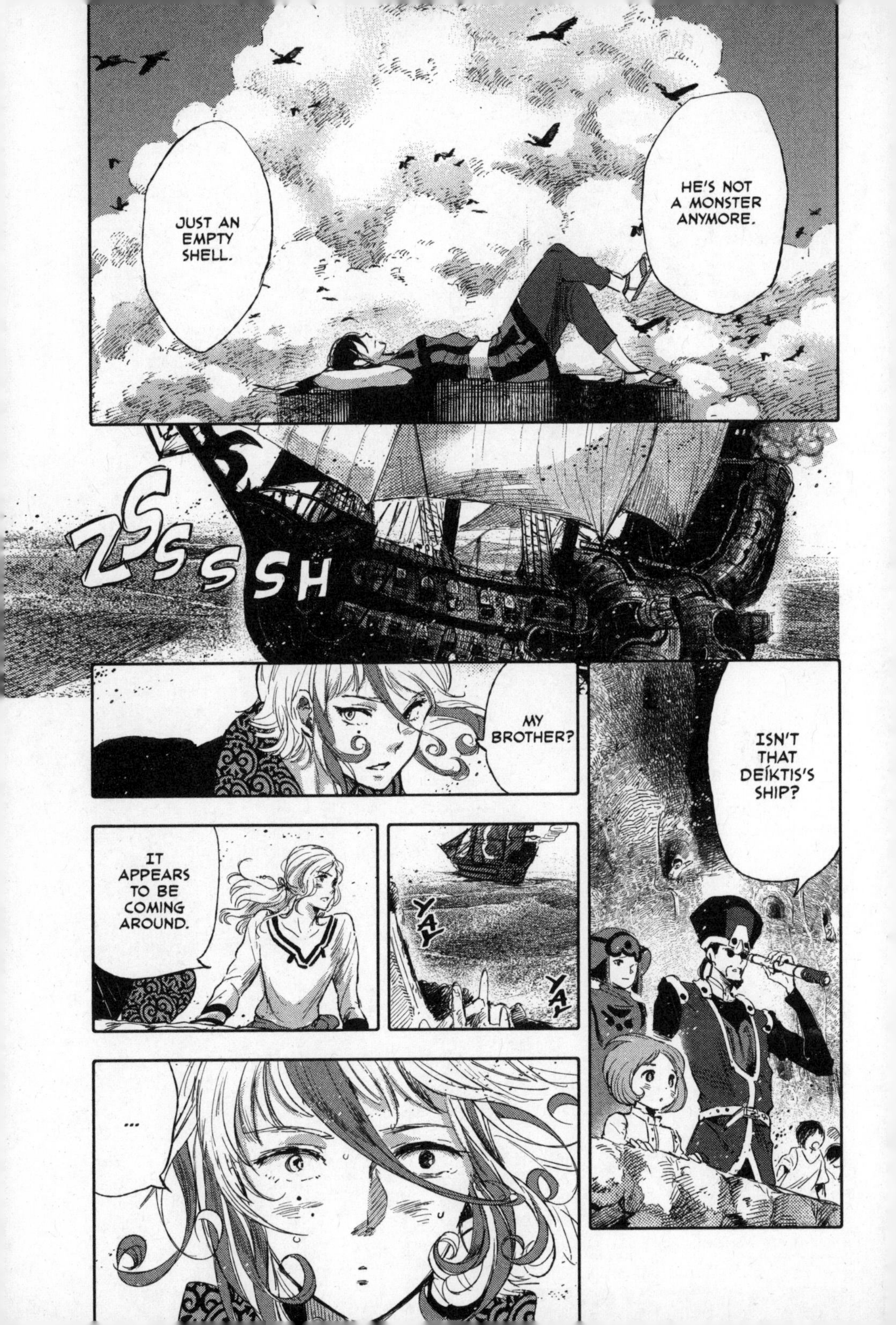
HE'S NOT A MONSTER ANYMORE.
JUST AN EMPTY SHELL.
ZSSSSH
ISN'T THAT DEIKTIS'S SHIP?
MY BROTHER?
YAY
YAY
IT APPEARS TO BE COMING AROUND.
...

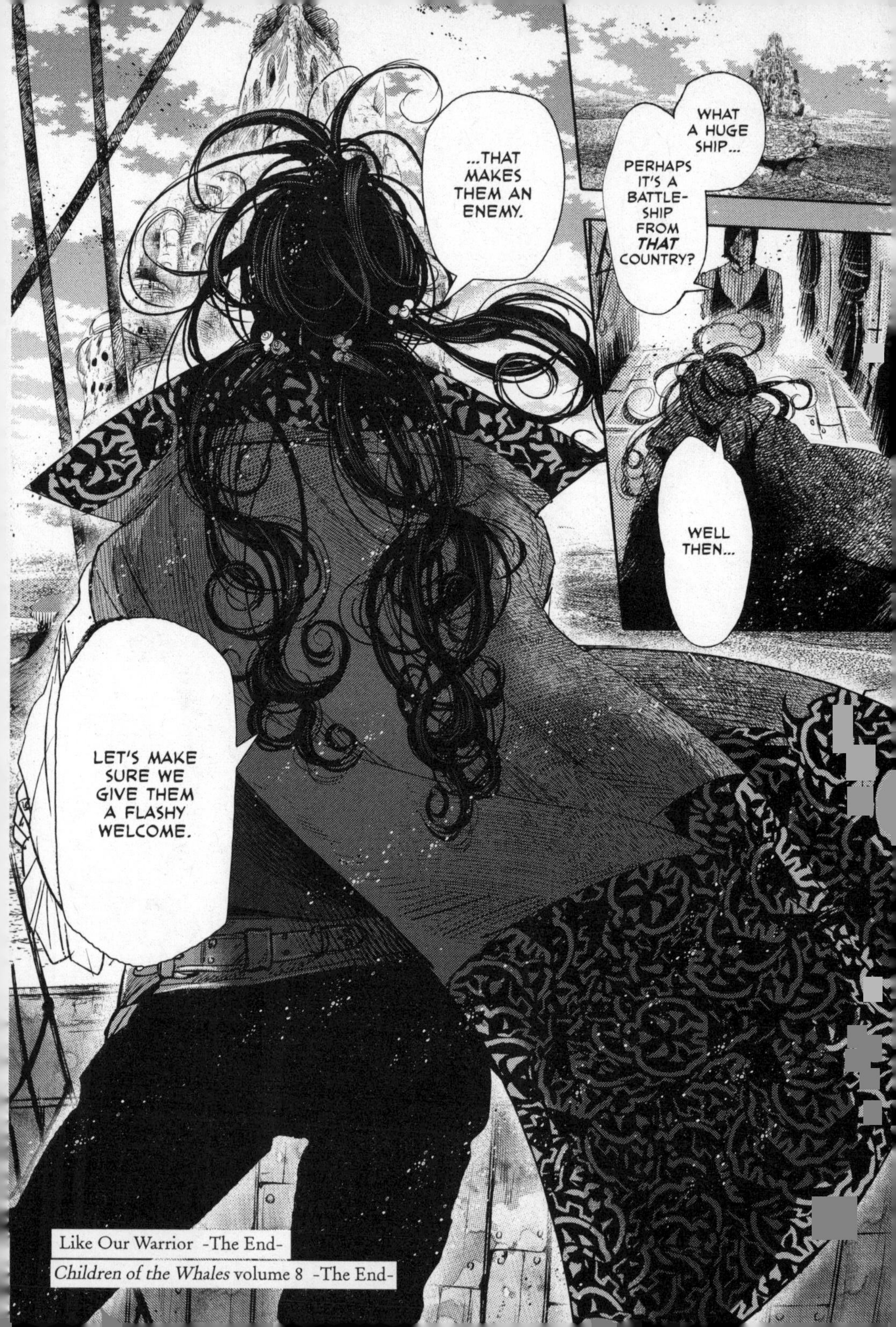
WHAT A HUGE SHIP... PERHAPS IT'S A BATTLE-SHIP FROM *THAT* COUNTRY?
...THAT MAKES THEM AN ENEMY.
WELL THEN...
LET'S MAKE SURE WE GIVE THEM A FLASHY WELCOME.

Like Our Warrior -The End-

Children of the Whales volume 8 -The End-

A Note on Names

Those who live on the Mud Whale are named after colors in a language unknown. Abi Umeda uses Japanese translations of the names, which we have maintained. Here is a list of the English equivalents for the curious.

Aijiro	pale blue
Benihi	scarlet
Buki	kerria flower (*yamabuki*)
Byakuroku	malachite mineral pigments, pale green tinged with white
Chakuro	blackish brown (*cha* = brown, *kuro* = black)
Ginshu	vermillion
Hakuji	porcelain white
Jiki	golden
Kicha	yellowish brown
Kikujin	koji mold, yellowish green
Kogare	burnt muskwood, dark reddish brown
Kuchiba	decayed-leaf brown
Masoh	cinnabar
Miru	seaweed green
Neri	silk white
Nezu	mouse gray
Nibi	dark gray
Ouni	safflower red
Rasha	darkest blue, nearly black
Ro	lacquer black
Sami	light green (*asa* = light, *midori* = green)
Shikoku	purple-tinged black
Shikon	purple-tinged navy

Shinono	the color of dawn (*shinonome*)
Shuan	dark bloodred
Sienna	reddish brown
Sumi	ink black
Suou	raspberry red
Taisha	red ocher
Tobi	reddish brown like a kite's feather
Tokusa	scouring rush green
Urumi	muddy gray

Children of the Whales is now a live-action stage play. The characters have become more alive with the performance of each actor.

—Abi Umeda

ABI UMEDA debuted as a manga creator with the one-shot "Yukokugendan" in *Weekly Shonen Champion*. *Children of the Whales* is her eighth manga work.

CHILDREN OF THE WHALES

VOLUME 8
VIZ Signature Edition

Story and Art by **Abi Umeda**

Translation / JN Productions
Touch-Up Art & Lettering / Annaliese Christman
Design / Julian (JR) Robinson
Editor / Pancha Diaz

KUJIRANOKORAHA SAJOUNIUTAU Volume 8
© 2016 ABI UMEDA
First published in Japan in 2016 by AKITA PUBLISHING CO., LTD., Tokyo
English translation rights arranged with AKITA PUBLISHING CO., LTD. through
Tuttle-Mori Agency, Inc., Tokyo

Printed in the U.S.A.

Published by VIZ Media, LLC
P.O. Box 77010
San Francisco, CA 94107

10 9 8 7 6 5 4 3 2 1
First printing, January 2019

viz.com

PARENTAL ADVISORY
CHILDREN OF THE WHALES is rated T+ for
Older Teen and is recommended for ages
16 and up. Contains violence and death.

vizsignature.com

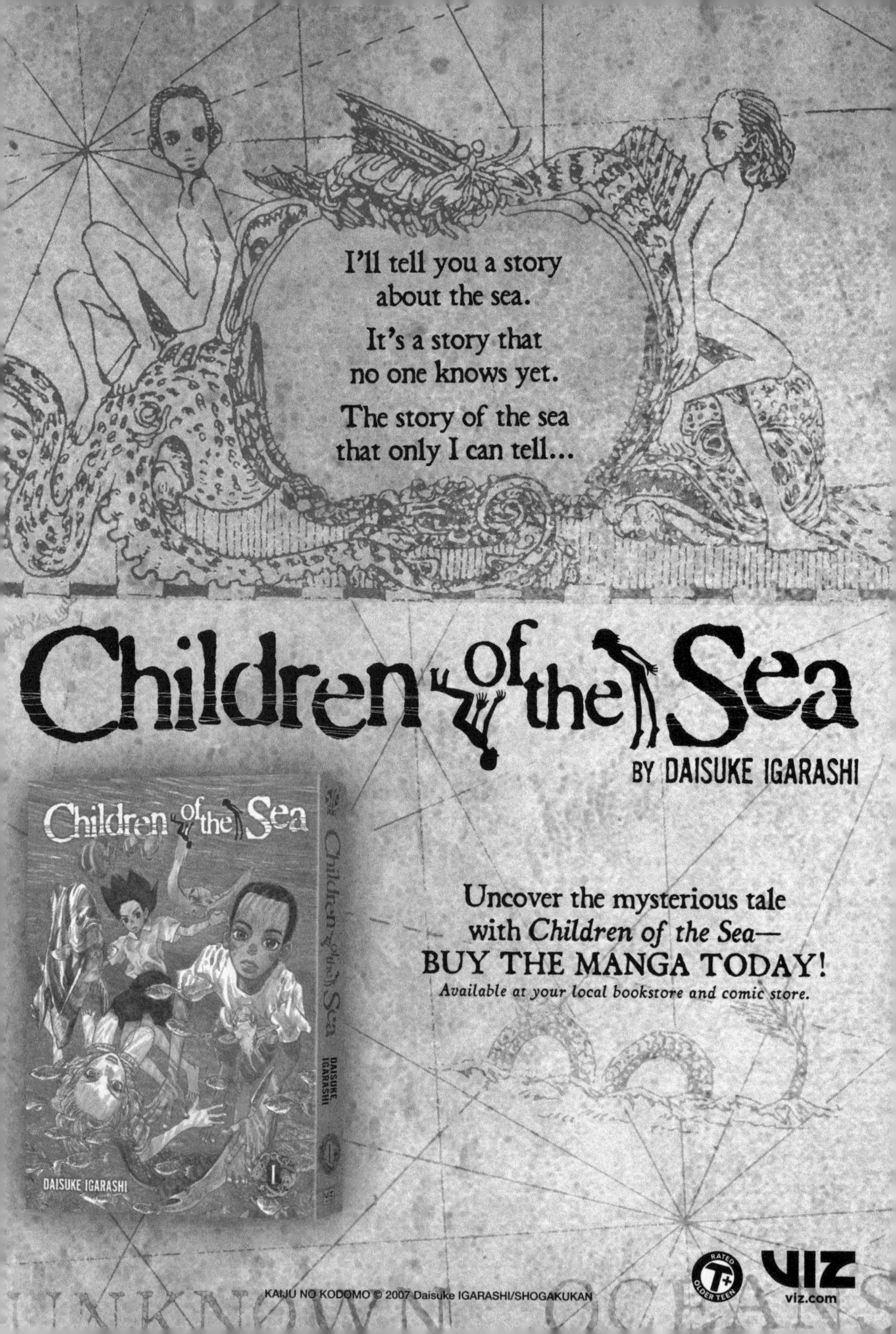
I'll tell you a story
about the sea.
It's a story that
no one knows yet.
The story of the sea
that only I can tell...
Children of the Sea
BY DAISUKE IGARASHI
Children of the Sea
DAISUKE IGARASHI
1
Uncover the mysterious tale
with Children of the Sea—
BUY THE MANGA TODAY!
Available at your local bookstore and comic store.
UNKNOWN OCEANS
KAIJU NO KODOMO © 2007 Daisuke IGARASHI/SHOGAKUKAN
RATED T+ OLDER TEEN
VIZ
viz.com

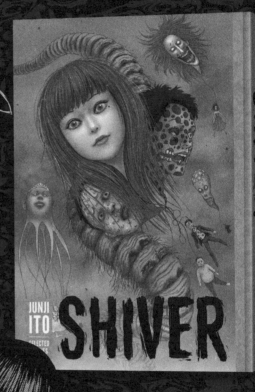

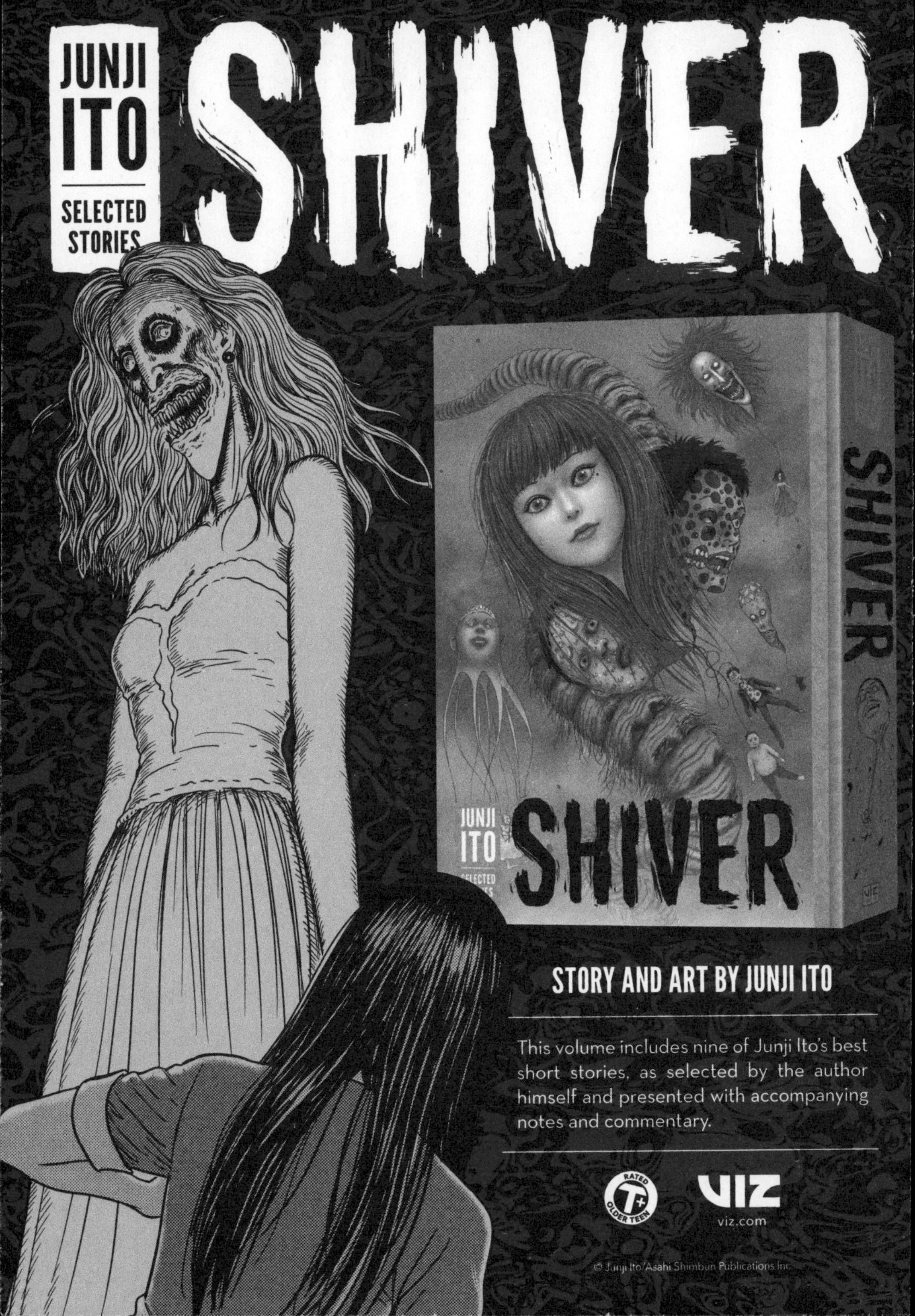

JUNJI ITO
SELECTED STORIES

SHIVER

STORY AND ART BY JUNJI ITO

This volume includes nine of Junji Ito's best short stories, as selected by the author himself and presented with accompanying notes and commentary.

viz.com

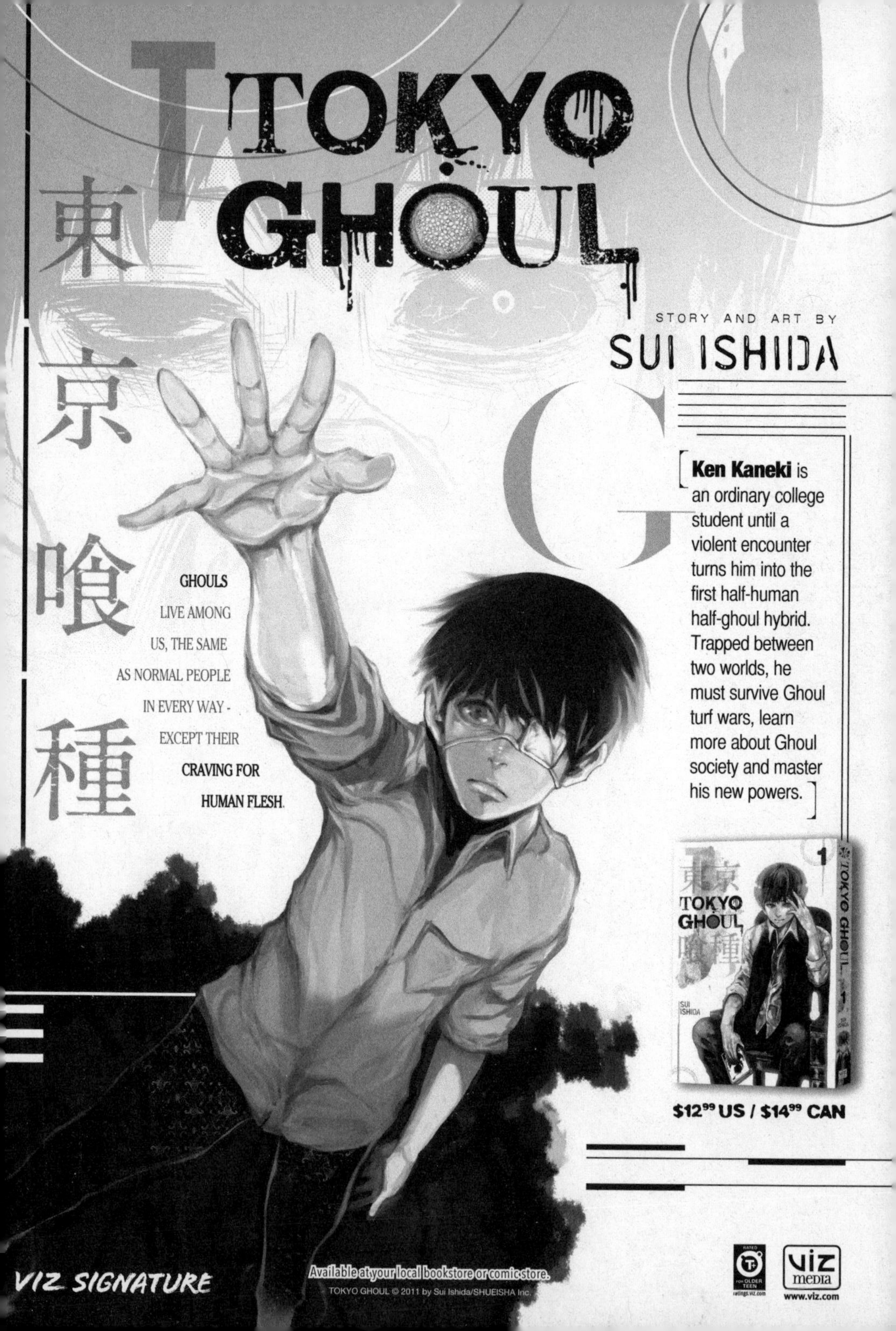
TOKYO GHOUL
東京喰種
STORY AND ART BY
SUI ISHIDA
GHOULS LIVE AMONG US, THE SAME AS NORMAL PEOPLE IN EVERY WAY - EXCEPT THEIR CRAVING FOR HUMAN FLESH.
[Ken Kaneki is an ordinary college student until a violent encounter turns him into the first half-human half-ghoul hybrid. Trapped between two worlds, he must survive Ghoul turf wars, learn more about Ghoul society and master his new powers.]
TOKYO GHOUL 1
SUI ISHIDA
$12.99 US / $14.99 CAN
VIZ SIGNATURE
Available at your local bookstore or comic store.
TOKYO GHOUL © 2011 by Sui Ishida/SHUEISHA Inc.
RATED T+ FOR OLDER TEEN ratings.viz.com
VIZ media
www.viz.com